READINGS IN THE PSYCHOLOGY OF PARENT-CHILD RELATIONS

READINGS IN THE
PSYCHOLOGY OF
PARENT-CHILD RELATIONS

Gene R. Medinnus

San Jose State College

John Wiley & Sons, Inc.   New York · London · Sydney

10 9 8 7 6 5 4

Library of Congress Catalog Card Number: 67-12565

Printed in the United States of America

ISBN 471 59010 X

Preface

A tremendous increase in the parent-child research literature has taken place in the past several decades. Several factors contributing to this trend can be discerned. First, Freudian emphasis on the importance of the early years—and especially the effect on later personality and behavior of the child's relationship with his parents during these years—led to a large body of research investigations. Although we certainly cannot dismiss Orlansky's * conclusion that most of the Freudian-inspired research has yielded negative or inconclusive results, nonetheless this early research set the pattern for a great many of the parent-child concerns to follow.

Second, an examination of historical trends in child research reveals an early interest in such variables as intelligence and physical growth. This can be attributed in part to the existence of reliable and valid measuring instruments. Early researchers devoted a great deal of effort to examining a number of correlates of physical and intellectual development: consistency over time; the relative influence of nature and nurture; and social class differences. Child developmentalists in the 1930's were concerned with mapping the terrain, so to speak, of a well-known, yet uncharted area. Following the accumulation of a considerable amount of data in the physical and intellectual domains, it was natural that interest would shift to personality development and to variables more complex and difficult to assess.

Third, the mental hygiene movement focused attention on prevention of mental illness, which in turn led to an interest in identifying antecedents of adult personality and adjustment. Causes of delinquency, schizophrenia, and a variety of antisocial behaviors received intensive examination.

Most college courses dealing with any aspect of personality involve some discussion of parent-child relations: child psychology, mental hygiene, behavior problems of children, abnormal psychology, and educational psychology. Many sociology and home economics departments also offer courses centering around the child in the family setting. While a number of books

* Orlansky, H. Infant care and personality. *Psychological Bulletin*, 1949, **46**, 1–48.

of readings in child psychology are available, the socialization process and the antecedents of personality development resting in the child's relations with his parents receive no more attention than a dozen other areas. Thus a book of readings dealing specifically with parent-child psychology seems appropriate. Moreover, although the present collection is limited to parent-child relations, its usefulness is broad, since parental influences are pervasive in their effects on numerous aspects of the child's development including various personality characteristics, cognitive functioning, school achievement, emotional stability, and the child's later behavior as a parent. Furthermore, instructors of traditional child psychology courses can vary the course emphasis by adopting different supplementary readings from time to time so that cognitive development may receive major emphasis one year, and attention may be focused on the socialization process later, and so on.

The parent-child literature is so extensive today that the task of sorting out and relating the various findings is difficult. The purpose of this book of readings is to present some of the more relevant research investigations in a systematic and coherent fashion so that the results of studies concerned with similar topics can be readily compared. This arrangement should enhance the overall meaningfulness of the data and make possible the drawing of some conclusions with regard to antecedent-consequent relations in this most complex area.

The studies are divided into six sections. Discussions of methodological problems and methodological procedures are included in the first section. The effects on the child of the two major parent variables, Acceptance-Rejection and Autocratic-Democratic behavior, are examined in Section II. Section III lists studies which have attempted to identify parental antecedents of a variety of child behavior dimensions. Investigations concerned with the concept of identification and children's perceptions of their parents make up the fourth section. The consequences of social class membership in terms of parental behavior are dealt with in Section V. The final section includes studies concerned with differences among cultures in various child-rearing practices and attitudes.

STATISTICS

Reports of research, including many of those found in this volume, often include statistical evaluation of results. Many of the students for whom the present volume is intended will not have had an extensive background in statistics. Since research articles nearly always include a discussion of the results obtained, the significance and contribution of each of the selections will be clear to the student even though some of the statistical terms used are not. However, some knowledge of these concepts should enhance the meaningfulness of the research reports.

Although a variety of statistical techniques were employed in the present collection of readings, two key concepts recur with considerable frequency: significance of a difference and correlation. Without trying to give the rationale or computational procedure for any specific statistical tool, I offer a few words about the meaning of these two concepts.

Test of Significance

In studying the results from two (or more) groups, the research worker usually wants to know whether there is a real difference in performance. To examine this question, he sets up the hypothesis that there is no true difference (null hypothesis), conducts a statistical test, and decides, depending on the outcome, to reject the hypothesis or to accept it. In general, if the obtained difference among groups is "small," he will accept the hypothesis; this means that if there were no true difference, a difference of the magnitude that he obtained could readily have resulted from sampling (chance) fluctuations. A difference of this kind is said to be one that has not reached the level of significance. If the difference is "large," he will reject the hypothesis. This is because he has determined that if there were no true difference, it would be very unlikely that chance fluctuations would produce a difference as large as the one he has obtained. This type of outcome is termed a significant difference.

In evaluating the result of a statistical test, we need some criterion to decide whether the discrepancy between groups is large enough to claim that a significant difference has been found. Usually, the researcher asks whether the obtained difference is so large that, if the hypothesis of no difference were true, it would occur less than 5 times in 100 by chance. If so, it is considered to have met the 5% level of significance (or confidence), and is declared to be a significant difference. Often a more stringent criterion is applied which requires that the result could be obtained by chance less than 1% of the time (1% level of significance). If this criterion is met, we can be still more confident that our difference is not due merely to chance. Sometimes research workers evaluate their statistical outcome by a notation in the following form: $p < .05$. This means that the "probability is less than .05," and indicates that the 5% significance level criterion has been met and that the hypothesis of no difference should be rejected.

Depending upon the nature of the data in a particular research investigation, any one of a number of tests of significance may be appropriate.

These include χ^2 (chi-square), t test, Mann-Whitney U test, F (analysis of variance), and the median test. The use of any one of these tests gives us essentially the same kind of information; it gives the basis for determining whether the difference between groups is significant or not. In the Bing study (Selection No. 19), for example, the t test was used to identify those interview and questionnaire variables that differentiated significantly between the high and low verbal children. The Mann-Whitney U test was employed in the Waters and Crandall study (Selection No. 28) to test the significance of difference of maternal behavior ratings for three time periods: 1940, 1950, and 1960. The χ^2 statistic was applied in the investigation by Schulman, Shoemaker, and Moelis (Selection No. 8) to test for the significance of the difference between conduct and nonconduct problem families on a number of parent behavior variables. Because a number of group means was involved, an analysis of variance (F test or F ratio) was used in the Jackson study (Selection No. 4) to test the significance of the difference between mothers and fathers in their coercion scores in response to eleven parent-child situations.

Correlation

The correlation coefficient describes the extent to which scores on two measures (for example, IQ of parent and IQ of child) tend to vary in an associated manner. The numerical value of this coefficient can range from -1 to $+1$. The closer the value is to one (in either direction), the closer the relationship. A coefficient of zero indicates no relationship. A negative coefficient indicates an inverse relationship. Thus, in a group of 100 twelve-year-old boys, we would expect measures of length of left arm and length of right arm to yield a very high positive correlation. In the same group of boys, intelligence test scores and reading achievement scores would be likely to exhibit a moderate positive correlation, whereas the correlation between level of intelligence and number of errors on an arithmetic test would be moderately negative. If we correlated length of right arm and intelligence, a coefficient close to zero would be expected. The most frequently used correlational technique is the Pearson product-moment correlation coefficient (r). The Pearson r was used in the Medinnus and Curtis study (Selection No. 10) to show the extent of the relation between maternal self-acceptance and child acceptance. In the Hurley study (Selection No. 11) Pearson r was used to describe the relation between parental acceptance and the child's IQ. In the Peterson et al. investigation of child adjustment (Selection No. 16), ratings of problem activity derived from interviews with mothers and fathers were correlated to determine the general accuracy of the ratings.

Sometimes the correlation coefficient is used to assess the internal consistency or reliability of a test. Thus in Selection No. 22 the test was split into two halves, and the correlation between these parts was obtained. A high correlation here indicates good internal consistency of the measuring instrument. A related use occurs when the correlation is obtained between test and retest on the same subjects. A high correlation indicates that the position of an individual within the group tends to remain stable over a period of time. Tests of significance frequently are applied to correlation coefficients to determine whether the magnitude of the coefficient is such that it differs significantly from zero.

ACKNOWLEDGMENTS

I am most grateful to the many authors and publishers who granted permission to reprint the journal articles included in the present collection. I would like to express my sincere appreciation to Dr. Edward Minium and Mr. Henry Sohn for assistance with the manuscript, and to Mrs. Dale Weese for an initial typing of the manuscript.

Gene R. Medinnus

June 1966

Contents

Contents xiii

READINGS IN THE PSYCHOLOGY OF PARENT-CHILD RELATIONS

Section I

Methodology

Introduction

Most research in the parent-child area operates on the assumption that there is a direct and discernible relation between parent variables (behavior, attitudes, personality) and child behavior and personality variables. But for several reasons this may well be an oversimplification. First, the causes of child behavior are complex, involving influences exerted by parent, siblings, peers, and others of psychological significance in the child's environment. It is not surprising that almost no research has considered all of these variables simultaneously. And even if such a study were attempted, it probably would be doomed to failure because it may not be a combination of these variables or even a weighted combination that is important; but perhaps the salience, in a psychological sense, of a single variable is most influential in affecting the child.

Second, parents and children influence each other in a mutual, two-way fashion although much of the research is based on a "one-tail" theory, as Bell (1964) has termed it. The infant helps to shape his environment just as he is shaped by it. Figure 1 illustrates these two ways of conceiving of the parent-child relationship.

Parental characteristics ⟶ Child characteristics

(a) All of child's characteristics attributed to parental treatment and handling

Parental characteristics ⟵⟶ Child characteristics
    behavior   physical appearance
    attitudes   health
    personality   sex of child
                              alertness
                              activity level

(b) Parent and child characteristics mutually interacting

Figure 1. (Adapted from Johnson and Medinnus, 1965, p. 238.)

1

The parent-child researcher who concerns himself with parent behavior is faced with the problem of deciding which child-rearing or child-training variables to examine. Stemming in large part from Freudian theory, early research dealt with such specific variables as weaning, feeding, and toilet training. The studies included in Section II suggest that more recent research has been concerned primarily with variables of a psychological nature rather than with specific behavioral variables.

A persistent concern of parent-child research has been with methodology. Five studies, each using a different technique, are listed in Part B. From an examination of these studies it seems safe to conclude that procedures for gathering data have reached a fairly sophisticated level. The data are readily quantifiable; operational definitions are stated with precision; and great effort is made to isolate, control, or eliminate extraneous variables.

The interview is the most frequently used method today, just as it has been throughout the history of parent-child research. Unfortunately a number of hazards are inherent in the interview method that are yet to be resolved. Typically, interviews require the mother to recall attitudes, training techniques, and child behaviors that occurred some time previously. Hoffman and Lippitt (1960) list several sources of verbal distortion in verbal report. For a variety of reasons some distortion is deliberate, stemming from the respondent's unwillingness to divulge certain information. Nondeliberate distortion may arise from sheer forgetting of seemingly trivial material, repression of threatening material, or lack of communication between interviewer and respondent.

Improvements have been made in the interview technique in order to ensure more objective information and to objectify the ratings of the information obtained. The early Fels research (Baldwin, Kalhorn, and Breese, 1945, 1949) involved lengthy interviews with mothers. Ratings of the psychological atmosphere of the home were then made on thirty variables. Although interrater reliability figures are available, the interview schedule has never been published and so it is difficult to determine the basis for the ratings. Also, recall on the part of the interviewer is required for the ratings. In contrast, in the comprehensive interview study of 379 mothers by Sears, Maccoby, and Levin (1957), the interview schedule is presented. Furthermore, the interviews were tape-recorded and then transcribed, and judges made ratings after reading the complete protocol.

By introducing several ingenious procedures, Hoffman has increased the accuracy of verbal report. In his research, parents are asked to give detailed descriptions of the parent-child interactions that occurred one day prior to the interview. Distortions due to long-term recall are eliminated, and the sheer task of recalling in great detail is so absorbing that personal relevance is reduced. Also, deliberate distortion can be detected because of minor incongruities and inconsistencies in the details reported.

In general it seems that the closer the researcher gets to the actual behavior and events, the more useful are his data and the more successful he will be in establishing linkages between parent and child variables. Thus, observations of parent-child interactions are superior to interviews, which in turn are better than attitude questionnaires. However, the observer is not without bias in interpreting the behavior observed, even though attempts have been made to develop symbols for recording the complexities of interaction sequences between two people (for example, see Moustakas, Sigel, and Schalock, 1956). Moreover, Smith points out that, compared with controlled observation, the interview method permits greater flexibility and allows for wider coverage.

Certainly the best method for collecting parent-child data depends in part on the specific variables with which a given investigation is concerned. A projective-type test might be most appropriate in one situation while direct observation is called for in another. Increasingly, too, the variables chosen for research in the parent-child area are derived from personality and learning theories. This should serve to increase the success of establishing antecedent-consequent relations, although methodological problems remain.

References

Baldwin, A. L., Kalhorn, Joan, & Breese, Fay H. Patterns of parent behavior. *Psychological Monographs*, 1945, **58**, No. 3.
Baldwin, A. L., Kalhorn, Joan, & Breese, Fay H. The appraisal of parent behavior. *Psychological Monographs*, 1949, **63**, No. 4.
Bell, R. Q. Structuring parent-child interaction situations for direct observation. *Child Development*, 1964, **35**, 1009–1020.
Hoffman, Lois W., & Lippitt, R. The measurement of family life variables. In P. Mussen (Ed.), *Handbook of research methods in child development*. New York: Wiley, 1960. Pp. 945–1013.
Johnson, R. C., & Medinnus, G. R. *Child psychology: behavior and development*. New York: Wiley, 1965.
Moustakas, C. E., Sigel, I. E., & Schalock, H. D. An objective method for the measurement and analysis of child-adult interaction. *Child Development*, 1956, **27**, 109–134.
Sears, R. R., Maccoby, Eleanor E., & Levin, H. *Patterns of child rearing*. Evanston, Ill.: Row, Peterson, 1957.

Part A   Methodological Problems

1. PROBLEMS OF METHODS IN PARENT-CHILD RESEARCH

Marian Radke Yarrow

Even most charitably, research in parent-child relations cannot be viewed as a field in which methodology is exemplary and in which evidence is firm and consistent. But even most critically or despairingly, this field cannot be dismissed as unimportant in behavioral or developmental theory. Despite or because of these facts, how parents bring up their children and how parental characteristics are infused into child personality are questions that continue to inspire research.

The motivations for this paper grow out of the feeling that critical and positive stocktaking can contribute toward better research on socialization processes. Two kinds of reviews need to go hand in hand. One is an evaluation of substantive findings on relations between maternal behavior and child characteristics, an accounting of relations that have stood up with impressive consistency. Unfortunately, there has been no recent general review of the extensive body of data on childrearing and associated child characteristics, the kind of review that is concerned with the extent to which relations have been replicated and discrepant reports reconciled. A second kind of review is needed which concerns itself with the methods by which data on childrearing are obtained and the nature of inferences about these data.

This discussion is concerned primarily with the latter issue—*how* research on socialization is done. Its starting point is the tremendous discrepancy which exists between the sophistication of theory and the sophistication of methods as they meet in research on parent-child relations. Hypotheses from psychoanalytic, learning, and cognitive theories are abundant and provocative regarding parental influences upon the child, but their fruits are in great measure lost on findings that rest on extremely shaky sources of evidence.

This paper shall follow two purposes: One is to examine the nature of our evidence, by taking a relentlessly critical point of view about a method and outlook characteristic of much of parent-child research and by considering ways of determining the soundness of present methods and evidence.

Reprinted from *Child Development*, 1963, **34**, 215–226, with permission of the author and the Society for Research in Child Development.

7

The second purpose is to look at possibilities of other research approaches to socialization problems, mainly direct observational methods.

Several research strategies are open to the researcher in this field. He may decide that relations between child and parent are far too complex to manage in research and that he had best abandon complexity. He chooses, therefore, to work with simpler laboratory variables, in programmatic succession, with the eventual but distant possibility of handling complicated sets of variables more nearly approximating socialization. Or he may follow another alternative, one which conceives of research in terms of the complex variables of family interaction and maternal characteristics. Historically and currently, the latter alternative has been followed most often in parent-child research. The ubiquitous interview and questionnaire on childrearing are examples. While neither strategy needs to be defended as the better and only one for all purposes, it is important in either case that the concepts and techniques employed are sound. It is in these terms that I should like to analyze the traditional approach in parent-child studies and to consider some of its basic weaknesses.

The classical form of study that is identified with parent-child research is the *interrogation of the mother,* through interview or inventory. She is asked about her practices in rearing her child and her attitudes and values relating to rearing. In the typical research interview, the mother is asked about numerous and widely different aspects of the rearing process. Devoting but a few minutes to questions and answers about each area, the interviewer extracts information on many complicated behaviors. The mothers seem willing to supply what is asked for. Though the childrearing dimensions on the interview are numerous, they have become an almost standard repertoire for research which can easily be predicted. Infant feeding, weaning, toileting history are likely to be treated. Mother's handling of the child's aggressive impulses, his dependency and independency needs, his achievement strivings, perhaps the sex role typing are included. Topics of authority and specific techniques of punishment and reward are emphasized, as well as affective relations—warmth-coldness and acceptance-rejection. In general, the variables studied have theoretical value, but our habitual focus on the same variables in study after study seriously restricts our theories and our knowledge of mother-child experiences. It becomes hard to conceive of different dimensions of maternal influence. Does one, for example, find research directed to kinds of sensory stimulation in the rearing environment or to the mother's handling of the child's needs for an individualized conception of himself?

When the objectives of parent-child studies extend beyond description and include investigation of the "effects" of the parent on the child, the typical study will again use the mother as the source of information, obtaining her reports of the child's behavior as well as her reports on herself. While there are variations in design (sometimes the grown child is asked to recollect his parents' practices), psychological studies of parent-child relations have placed their greatest emphasis upon and confidence in the research interview.

If we have hoped for the emergence of clearly discernible relations between parental variables and child outcomes by these methods, our efforts have led to rather more disappointment than evidence. Some encouraging sets of relations have been found that are consistent across studies and corroborative of theoretical predictions. But all who work or have worked in socialization are very familiar with clutching tenderly the correlation of $+.21$ or the one-tailed significance test at the 5 per cent level—barely holding out indications that "something is there." In defense of these methods and findings one could argue that we must be tapping significant relations through mothers' reports and that indeed the correlation of $+.21$ is meaningful if it comes through despite all the contaminants and all the nonmaternal influences affecting the child. I would like to take the position that we have probably defended this method too long and have relieved our misgivings too easily by telling ourselves that we have made the interview an "intensive" one and have made certain we have "good rapport with the respondent"—then proceeding upon many dangerous assumptions and gambles.

Stripped of all elaborations, mothers' interview responses represent self-descriptions by extremely ego-involved reporters. In addition, for the much-studied middle and upper-middle class mothers, these are self-reports in an area in which prescriptions and taboos have been dinned into the culture through *Ladies Home Journal* as well as Spock or Gesell or Children's Bureau. How well then can we expect the mother to report interactions of which she is a part and on which the culture has placed distinct values? When we ask the mother "What do you usually do when your child does something that pleases you?" or ". . . that you have forbidden him to do?" can we expect an accurate report, uncontaminated by the mother's particular needs and defenses, her values about parental and child behaviors, her class identifications and the childrearing mores attached to them? How strong are these influences in mothers' reports on research interviews we have not determined. There is probably no other area of psychology in which we have placed such heavy reliance upon self-report without exercising extreme caution in the interpretation of the data.

In addition to this most evident source of possible error in our data, the usual interview on childrearing requires very difficult discriminations and syntheses by a mother. In an hour or two we expect to learn the essence of the mother's relationship with her child and his reactions, in many dimensions and extending over a childhood span of years. In order to accomplish this, we ask the mother to formulate the principles which govern her rearing practices (although she may not have formulated them before). We ask for *modal* behavior, such as, "What do you generally do when your child asks for help?" or "How frequently does your child show affection?" or ". . . shyness?" But what of the important exceptions in the mother's behavior, and what of the regular variation in her behavior? What of the stimuli that evoke responses? By requiring the mother to place her behavior on a scale point of frequency and intensity, we may be creating illusions about childrearing environments and losing important variations. In reality, behaviors of a given parent and child may not have a simple modal level of occurrence. They may occur in patterns of intensity and frequency which are distinct and different according to the situation, the developmental level of the child, the psychological state of the mother, etc. I would suppose that few parents are uniformly nurturant or hostile or tolerant of a child's aggression. The significance of these dimensions of parental behavior may lie more in the *distribution* of their occurrence in relation to specific developmental stages and specific circumstances than in an "averaged" occurrence (though we need not ignore the "average"). Undoubtedly some variables of the rearing environment better than others can be described by modal categories and perhaps, therefore, can be reported more accurately.

There are other serious problems with the interview task that we impose on the mother. One arises from the fact that we ask her to rate herself and her child on relative scales. This requires that she have a frame of reference of other mothers and children against which her own situation can be compared. She may often not possess such referents, and, furthermore, the referents for different mothers are likely to vary considerably. For example, middle class mothers may be likely to think of "experts" advice as standards, whereas working class mothers may more often think in terms of the behavior of their own mothers.

The usual interview involves still another methodological problem: We expect mothers to *recall* their feelings and behaviors and those of their children for recent and more distant pasts. Such data are quite generally accepted at face value in studies of childrearing without much question as to their validity.

Most questionable of all our research practices is our general reliance upon the mother for data on herself (the presumed antecedent variables) as well as for data on her child (the presumed consequent variables). We find ourselves making the quick jump from mother's responses on questions ("What do you do when your child shows temper?" "What does he do?") to conclusions such as "Mothers using severe punishment of aggression have more aggressive children than mothers punishing mildly." I wonder if we should permit ourselves to speak of antecedent-consequent relations unless we have independent data sources or have most carefully built-in safeguards to protect against the obvious kinds of contamination.

I have tried to raise doubts about the mainstay sources of our information on parent-child relations in order to motivate investigators to undertake research that will determine how serious these problems are and will tell us what kinds of data *are* represented in mothers' reports. It may be that interviews are a better method of getting socialization data than has been allowed, but evidence is needed. The discussion which follows considers methodological research which could provide some answers to these questions.

The possibility of a selective and distorted quality in mothers' reports stands as a first hazard in the research interview on childrearing. Should we not set out systematically to analyze the concordance and discordance in assessments of mother-child data obtained from different sources? Suppose we obtain reports from the mother, father, child, and outside observer. If very similar inferences are drawn from the reports from these several sources, it should strengthen our faith in data which come simply and directly from the mother. On the other hand, if significant discrepancies appear, the picture of faith is shaken, and it becomes necessary to ask—how big are the discrepancies? What are the bases of these differences? How well do childrearing antecedents reported by the several informants predict child behaviors?

I am familiar with some data on this point in present research literature and there is undoubtedly other relevant evidence. Kohn and Carroll (5), using a standard type interview with mother, father, and 10-year-old child in 80 families, obtained parallel data from these three sources. In a published table dealing with the supportive roles of the parents (i.e., to whom is the child likely to turn for advice and reassurance), degree of consistency among the three sources is reported. In 46 per cent of the families, the same responses were given by all three family members; in 61 per cent father and mother agreed; in 48 per cent mother and child agreed; and in 51 per cent father and child agreed. When working class and middle class comparisons are made, the working class is somewhat lower in consistencies. In unpublished data from the same study agreement in parent-parent and parent-child reports ranges from 26 per cent to 72 per cent on a variety of items dealing with authority relations. This study, although not directed to the question for which we have used it, clearly alerts us to the rather considerable differences in the conclusions one would draw about families, depending upon the source of data.

A further interesting observation made by these investigators was that mothers' reports concerning the fathers' role in socialization differed for two groups of their subjects. Namely, mothers who knew that the father and child were also to be interviewed gave more favorable reports concerning the father than did mothers who knew that they alone were to be interviewed!

Certainly psychiatric work in which patients and their families are brought into therapy also makes us aware of the extreme differences in perceptions of family dynamics by different family members (11), although in these studies the discrepancies have been used mainly as they are helpful in diagnosis and treatment. Lack of agreement in reports from different family sources does not necessarily prove the mother's responses invalid.

It does, however, make one question how well interviews with mothers describe the effective maternal stimuli for the child, i.e., the stimuli communicated to the child and, therefore, the stimuli to be considered in investigating causal relations.

Further questions concerning agreement in sources of evidence involve research comparing inferences based on research interviews with inferences deriving from a series of psychotherapeutic interviews and comparing inferences based on interviews with inferences deriving from direct observations. We should remind ourselves that, if one is interested in comparing the information on childrearing which comes from interviews with that from observations, it is necessary to design studies which involve more than a line-up of (a) interview responses in which the mother has summarized her usual performance in the life of the child with (b) observations of mother-child interactions in a 5- to 30-minute play session in front of a one-way screen. Ideally the study should be designed so that observed mother-child interactions and mothers' reports of interaction refer to the same or more nearly the same samples of behavior.

It has been pointed out earlier that, when the mother serves as informant concerning her deeds and those of her child (as is so frequently found in the literature of childrearing studies), the problem of built-in correlations between socialization variables and child characteristics is created. A report published by the Fels group (1) describing parent behavior lends some concreteness to this possibility. Consider two mothers described by the Fels home observers. One mother (1, p. 23) is observed with her young daughter, saying "I suppose you're going to spill that down the front of your dress" (as her daughter eats an ice cream cone). As she sends the daughter upstairs to take a bath, "I suppose you're going to leave those dirty clothes all over the floor when you're through." "I suppose you're going to leave the screen open and let every fly in town into the house." In contrast, a second woman (1, p. 38) speaks of her child saccharinely as "my little sweetheart," "this little dumpling," "teacher's little helper." If one imagines interviewing these mothers about their daughters' aggression or dependency or response to discipline, it seems rather remote to believe that the reports obtained would be untinged by the mother's own feelings and practices. One would expect the mother who valued absolute obedience and who used severe punishment for any infringements to be highly attuned to aggressive behavior and to emphasize it in her conception of her child. The reverse might be anticipated for the permissive or indulgent mother. To clarify this issue, data on the child's characteristics are needed from independent sources for comparison with descriptions by the mother. Analyses of differences in relation to mothers' values, practices, and personalities should permit one to ferret out the likely imprint of different types of mothers upon their reports of the characteristics of their children.

One further problem of methodology concerns the use of retrospective data. Several methodological investigations already in the literature and others in progress are convincingly consistent in pointing to a large error in retrospective reports of childrearing. What mothers tell some months or years later about their weaning practices, their child's earlier responses, their own feelings and behaviors is often markedly different from data gathered at the time the events took place. A sampling of such findings follows. Marjorie Pyles *et al.* (6) in an early report on Berkeley longitudinal data found that by the time the infant was 21 months of age the mother's retrospective accounts of pregnancy and delivery were so unreliable as to have to be disregarded completely. Wenar (10) reinterviewed 25 mothers who 3 to 6 years earlier had brought their children to a therapeutic nursery school. When interview data obtained at the earlier time were compared with recall data, different inferences were drawn from the two sources in 43 per cent of the cases. Of the differences obtained, 40 per cent represented striking changes or even reversals in the two sets of "facts."

From a longitudinal study carried out by Skard in Oslo (4), initial and recall interview data from 19 mothers were compared. The authors were impressed, not only with the highly unreliable nature of these reports, but also with the tremendous variability from mother to mother in the degree of consistency in their reports. Degree of congruence between initial and anamnestic reports, as indicated by interclass correlations, ranged from .02 for attitude toward being pregnant to .83 for whether or not the parents planned to have a child. Correlations for items concerned with rearing variables were, with few exceptions, less than .40. Some mothers gave anamnestic reports that agreed reasonably well with reports given 6 to 8 years earlier (highest $r = .67$); anamnestic reports of some mothers were essentially random ($r = .04$). Robbins (7) also working within a longitudinal study similarly reports distressing inaccuracies in the recall of parents of 3-year-olds.

In our own research in progress,[1] mother's recall of socialization data is investigated in a college-educated and nonclinical sample of 200 families, presumably a group best able to supply accurate information on past events and relationships. Midstream in analysis there are suggestive trends. Data on disciplinary roles of mother and father show consistencies between initial and recall data in 50 per cent of the 54 cases used for preliminary analyses. In mothers' descriptions of child behavior (aggression, shy-withdrawn behavior, tenderness-sympathy) reasonably similar assessments occur at the two time periods in 60 to 75 per cent of the cases. It may be comforting to know that only in rare instances did the two data sets give completely opposite impressions of the child.

[1] This is a study entitled "The Validity of Retrospective Data on Parent-Child Relationships," being carried out by Marian Radke Yarrow, John D. Campbell, and Roger V. Burton of the National Institute of Mental Health.

More interesting than the gross comparisons of correspondence are the tantalizing indications of theoretically significant, subtler processes in the mothers' retrospections. For example, do initial and recall descriptions show the same amount and direction of discrepancies in mothers' reports on sons and daughters? There are suggestions that they may not, on certain dimensions. Thus, on descriptions of the child's aggression, 31 per cent of the mothers' reports on boys were rated identically from the initial and recall data, compared with only 15 per cent of the reports on girls. The tendency to recall boys as *more* aggressive and girls as *less* aggressive than described on initial measures appears but is not significant in the exploratory sample. There is another sex-linked trend: for their sons, mothers *recall* greater sharing by the father in the discipline role than was reported initially; for daughters the shift is to recall less sharing by the father than appeared initially. Should these tendencies hold up in the total analysis, are we discovering recollections that conform to differences in societal values for boys and girls, to differences in parental role expectations for the two sexes? If so, must we re-evaluate some of our research literature? In our analyses we are examining the possible systematic influences upon recall of other factors such as family size and sibling order, warmth of mother-child relationship, and present characteristics and achievements of the child.

From the methodological problems reviewed, several conclusions seem warranted as to the consequences of our methods for our knowledge of parent-child relations. First, though our second-hand data sources make us aware of considerable variations in important but limited dimensions of childrearing, these methods almost certainly minimize the "true" differences which exist. Second, our methods have introduced into the data a large quantity of error from diverse sources. Third, we have more information about the occurrence or nonoccurrence of particular socialization practices than about the nature of their distribution in what I shall call psychological space. That is, the characteristics of child, mother, and circumstance which evoke certain parental actions and interactions are virtually ignored. Another way of saying this is that we currently proceed with the unrealistic point of view of the *mother-doing-to-the-child,* although we know very well that mother does not respond machine-like, emitting rewards and warmth or independency training regardless of the stimuli to which she is responding. Fourth, the data we have gathered on parent and child are most often not in a form that permits inferences of causal relations.

These points put in focus some of the technical and theoretical problems for research. In a positive form they ask for research which (*a*) will deal with the *actual* behavior of mother and child (or better, of parents and child); (*b*) will search for a broader substantive base of childrearing variables by considering additional variables; (*c*) will concern itself with the genotypic similarities and differences in parental behavior; (*d*) will deal with *interactions;* and (*e*) will be designed to permit more defensible causative inferences. The remainder of the paper is devoted to considering the possibilities of realizing some of these objectives, particularly to considering the potentialities of observational data on parent-child relations.

There is, at present, much inclination to *want* to observe children and mothers. Although observation is not new in psychology, it is relatively new as a major approach to parent-child relations. It is often viewed as an approach which is impossible from a practical standpoint and which has the serious danger in it of destroying the "real" mother-child relationship by the process of peering at it. However, a fair number of studies using observations with parents and children have been done successfully (Schoggen [9], Rosen and D'Andrade [8], Barker and Wright [2]—to name but a few), and, in general, they have demonstrated the feasibility of making systematic observations in the home, in other than longitudinal research. Despite these successes it is not to be concluded that through observational data all the difficult problems of studying the mother-child relationship will be automatically solved. It is not to be discounted that the observational approach presents many problems of method which need to be worked out carefully. Observations do not necessarily yield valid data. They do so only to the extent that the phenomena to be observed have not been destroyed, missed, or misinterpreted by the observer. The avoidance of such calamities requires awareness by the investigator of new kinds of data-sampling problems, judicious selection of the categories and framework for observing, and the working out of a relation with the observed that is neither destructive nor unduly confining for the research. We have gradually to learn the answers to these issues. Sampling requirements of time to be covered by observations and of situational representativeness will vary with the research problem. Similarly we will have to experiment with the appropriateness of different kinds of observational lens, from one extreme of attempting recordings of minute movements in nonpsychological terms to the other extreme of psychodynamic interpretations that are relatively inattentive to the details of the interactions themselves. The artificiality introduced into the mother-child situation by the presence of an observer cannot be ignored (as it cannot also in other data gathering procedures). Problems from this source can be reduced, however, if the investigator lays sufficient ground work preceding his observations. This may be giving the time required for observees and observers to become accustomed to each other and to understand their relationship (something analogous to rapport in the interview). This may involve, too, creating the kinds of purposes or settings which make observations most reasonable, meaningful, and nonthreatening. For example, in work beginning in our laboratory, home observations of children with their parents are built into the expectations of the parents as part of the program of the nursery school, to be used by the school in its program for the child. The research purpose is not concealed, and the research activity has an immediate use and some feedback to the parent.

The forte of observation is, obviously, the firsthand nature of the data. Direct observations of behaving parents and children provide an opportunity for looking for *uncommon* socialization data, data not in the habitual focus of research. The investigator can try to *see* what is there, and thus to see other dimensions of parent-child interaction in addition to the salient ones of authority, aggression, dependency dimensions. For example, can one observe differences in mothers' handling of children's unhappiness, of children's failures and frustrations? Can one pin down differences in the ways of mothers in opening up the world to the young child, introducing him to conflicting demands, ugly realities, new concepts, etc.? There is much interest in finding roots of creativity. Can one discern differences in mothers' ways of inciting curiosity and in getting children to look for possibilities and explanations? Are mothers accountable for children's differences in following the "sure" and "tried" and unimaginative solutions or in thinking of the un-thought-of and seeing what others have not seen? We might discover through observation that mothers differ as much in their manipulation of the child's environment as in their manipulation of the child. Research has asked mainly questions of how parents handle the child when certain behaviors occur. Missing is information on parents' handling of the environment of the child by fostering or forestalling the occurrence of situations in which given experiences or behaviors of the child are likely to result. This seems particularly important in childrearing at early ages when the parent is in a position to control a great deal of the child's environment. Consider, for example, reported correlations between frequency of children's aggressive behaviors and severity of mothers' punishment. The differences in aggression may be a function of the kinds of situations which the mother creates or permits, i.e., whether of high or low aggression potential, rather than, or as much as, a function of specific techniques of handling the child's aggression when it occurs.

Just as the observational method may free research to look at new dimensions of socialization, it may also provide a fresh encounter with some old problems on which the interview has not been highly successful. As an illustration, one of these problems concerns the differences in socialization of boys and girls. Sex differences in personality, social behavior, interests, etc., appear persistently in psychological research, but research has not succeeded very well in identifying their childrearing antecedents. Perhaps mothers have been interviewed about the wrong areas of rearing to bring out differential relations with boys and girls, or perhaps mothers are unaware of differences, or the differences are subtle nuances which the questions do not distinguish. Explorations through observation would seem worthwhile for attempting to discern the not readily verbalized factors which create different learning environments for boys and girls. Direct observation should also have particular value in handling the questions that are truly questions of interaction. In *seeing* parent-with-child, it is harder to avoid a consideration of the contexts for particular parental behaviors, the circumstances in which the parent is autocratic, affectionate, nurturant, or rejecting. Also, the child's coercive role in eliciting parental behaviors may be too apparent to be ignored as readily as in an interview. Similarly, in observations we may be alerted to the importance of maternal characteristics others than techniques. In these ways it would seem that observational methods might help to refine variables of parent-child interactions.

Having disposed of the "verbal" mother as a reliable source of data on childrearing, she might be reconsidered as a data source in observational studies. The observer usually means the researcher. Under carefully specified conditions it might be possible to enlist the help of mothers. Only mothers have access to certain bodies of information, such as infrequently occurring events, particularly a sample of such events for the same child, or interactions in which dimensions of intimacy or crisis preclude the presence of the researcher. It would seem reasonable to explore the possibilities of asking mothers (even training mothers) to act as observers for data about these occasions as well as for data on the day-to-day rhythms of mother and child interactions. In a study of long ago, Goodenough (3) made some use of this approach for gathering data on children's temper tantrums. It was successful, yet it has not been developed to any extent. It appears quite as valid to obtain systematic observations from mothers as to obtain mothers' reports in interviews on their nonsystematic observations. This technique of using mothers as informants suggests several modified approaches which might be tried in parent-child research—(a) a modified interview-observational approach and (b) a coordinated data-gathering program in which parent and investigator become collaborators in a different-from-ordinary sense. In the interview, instead of attempting to cover a multitude of childrearing variables, suppose the focus were confined to a single variable, or at most to several variables for which interactive effects are hypothesized. If this were done, mothers might be cued to observe in advance of the interview, or even to recollect, specifically and systematically, one particular aspect of mother-child interaction. In this way the distribution of a given variable in the parent-child experience and the sequence of behaviors could be investigated with more thoroughness than in the usual interview.

On all but the rarest occasion in research the investigator tests his hypothesis or emerges with it on the basis of one type of research setting and one method. The possibility is seldom exploited of testing and retesting the hypothesis on the same sample of subjects, using several methods attuned to differing degrees of refinement of the same variables and relations. Suppose an investigator were conducting a series of laboratory experiments on the effects of different types of reinforcing stimuli or schedules of reinforcement on the 4-year-old's behavior. Having arrived at some conclusions, might it not be fruitful for him to attempt to obtain data on the same children, on the same relations, from observations in the natural or seminatural parent-child situation? Perhaps the mother could assume an experimenter role. In selected families it should be possible to create specific kinds of experiences by having the mother pursue a given policy or course of action with the child over an experimental period of weeks or months, thus creating a particular kind of socialization "history" through a series of contrived situations in the family setting. The mother's role might be varying shades of collaborator and "naive" participant for different problems. In this way, findings from laboratory and naturalistic settings could be seen in relation to one another.

In pursuing the coordinated research described, an investigator gives up, to a degree, his specialization in a particular method or technique of research. There may well be advantages in doing so. If the laboratory experimentalist, attuned to reinforcement schedules and shielded from many complexities, the ecologist, absorbed in behaviors of undisturbed Nature, and the interviewer, playing loosely with "behavior" of parent and child, could be persuaded to turn to other methods occasionally, even briefly, at critical points in their own research, they might be rewarded. The investigator might become sensitized to possibilities to which his favorite method had not alerted him, but which he could take back to his method and use creatively. Both he and parent-child research could be benefited.

REFERENCES

1. Baldwin, A. L., Kalhorn, J., & Breese, F. H. Patterns of parent behavior. *Psychol. Monogr.*, 1945, **58**, No. 3 (Whole No. 268).
2. Barker, R. G., & Wright, H. F. *Midwest and its children*. Row, Peterson, 1954.
3. Goodenough, F. L., *Anger in young children*. Univer. of Minnesota Press, 1931.
4. Haggard, E. A., Brekstad, A., & Skard, A. G. On the reliability of the anamnestic interview. *J. abnorm. soc. Psychol.*, 1960, **61**, 311–318.
5. Kohn, M. L., & Carroll, E. E. Social class and the allocation of parental responsibilities. *Sociometry*, 1960, **23**, 372–392.
6. Pyles, M. K., Stolz, H. R., & Macfarlane, J. The accuracy of mothers' reports on birth and developmental data. *Child Develpm.*, 1935, **6**, 165–176.
7. Robbins, L. C. Parent recall of aspects of child development and of child-rearing practices. Unpublished doctoral dissertation, New York Univer., 1961.
8. Rosen, B. C., & D'Andrade, R. The psychosocial origins of achievement motivation. *Sociometry*, 1959, **22**, 185–217.
9. Schoggen, P. Environmental forces in the everyday lives of children. *Studies of the stream of behavior*, in press.
10. Wenar, C., & Coulter, J. B. Reliability of mothers' histories. Paper read at SRCD symposium, Pennsylvania State Univer., March, 1961.
11. Wynne, L. C. The study of intrafamilial alignments and splits in exploratory family therapy. In N. W. Ackerman, F. L. Beatman, & S. N. Sherman (Eds.), *Exploring the base for family therapy*. Family Service Association of America, 1961. Pp. 95–115.

2. A RELIABILITY STUDY OF DEVELOPMENTAL HISTORIES

CHARLES WENAR AND JANE B. COULTER

This is a preliminary reliability study of the histories mothers give of their children's early development. In a previous article (4) the senior author contrasted the extensive use made of historical material in clinics and research with the relative paucity of data concerning its validity and reliability. In brief, we know little about the accuracy of mothers as observers of their children's behavior, the fate of these observations with the passage of time, and the effects of the information gathering techniques on the kind of information obtained.

In the present study, reliability is defined as consistency over time. Initially, three questions were posed: how reliable, in general, are mothers in recapitulating events in the first four years of their children's lives; what are the developmental areas of greatest and least reliability; and what personality characteristics of the mothers are associated with high and low reliability. The procedure consisted of reinterviewing 25 mothers who, three to six years previously, had brought their children to a therapeutic nursery school and comparing the historical material given on the two occasions.

PROCEDURE

Population

Table 1 summarizes relevant characteristics of the population used in this study.

Adopted children and those with organic brain pathology or severe intellectual retardation were not included in the research. The original plan was to limit the study to mothers who had only diagnostic interviews at the child guidance clinic; however, this proved impracticable and the influence upon reliability of subsequent treatment interviews is unknown.

Interview Procedures

A letter was sent to 60 mothers requesting their cooperation in a research project studying the initial interview. Although they were told that

Reprinted from *Child Development*, 1962, **33**, 453–462, with permission of the senior author and the Society for Research in Child Development.

Table 1   *Characteristics of Population*

MOTHERS $(N = 25)$

Age (at 1st interview)		Education		Race		Religion		Income	
Mean	32-6	Grade school	1	White	22	Protest.	2	Mean	$3,600
Range	23 to 44	High school	9	Negro	3	Catholic	5	Range	$0 to
		College	5			Jewish	18		$5,600
		Vocational	5						
		No information	5						

CHILDREN

Age (at 1st interview)		Sex		No. of Sibs		Position in Family		Diagnosis	
Mean	4-2	Female	8	None	5	First	15	No disorder	1
Range	2-6 to 6-6	Male	17	1	13	Middle	4	Situational disturbance	6
				2	4	Last	6	Neurosis	5
				2 +	3			Personality disorder	7
								Psychosis	3
								None made	3

INTERVIEWS

Time between Research Interviews		Number at Clinic		Interim Treatment	
Mean	4-4 years	Mean	17	Yes	16
Range	3 to 6-3 years	Range	1 to 51	No	9

the research included a review of historical material, this was mentioned casually so the mother would not try to reconstruct early events ahead of time. Twenty-five mothers were cooperative; 13 could not come for realistic reasons, such as moving out of state; four were too busy; three were disinterested; six had negative feelings about the clinic; five mothers accepted but failed the appointment, while there was no answer to four letters. Analysis of the group of uncooperative mothers indicated that there was no appreciable difference in their age, education, race, religion, income, and the number of interviews as compared with the cooperative mothers; there was also no difference in the ratio of boys to girls, and no over-all difference in the diagnoses of the children.

Both interviews followed a schedule of topics which was standard at the child guidance clinic where the initial interview was done. Before reinterviewing the mother, the social worker abstracted information relevant to this schedule from the case history and entered it on a specially prepared form. When this was done, she was prepared to ask a variety of questions designed to elicit material which could be compared with the data obtained earlier. In 16 of the 25 cases, the social worker had also done the initial interview at the child guidance center herself.

Both the initial interview and the research re-interview were conducted in a loosely planned fashion. The special form served as a guide to relevant areas of information, but the questions and sequence were not set. How this kind of interview procedure affects reliability is unknown; however, it resembles the procedure used in many child guidance clinics. Detailed notes were taken in the re-interview session, and these were subsequently recorded on a form identical to the one used for abstracting the initial interview. The information on these two forms served as the basic data for the analyses to be described in the following sections. Finally, it is important to mention that, whenever necessary, the mother was asked to remember what she had said during the initial interview rather than being asked to give her present evaluation of the situation: e.g., she was told to recall what her attitude toward the problem was when she first brought the child to the clinic, rather than what her present attitude might be. In all probability, this procedure increased the chances of consistency of report.

Scoring

Only items on which there was information in both the initial and repeat interviews were included in this study. It would also have been desirable to score information added to the second interview as compared with the first; since the interviews were not recorded verbatim, however, it was impossible to do this. For instance, there was no way of determining whether new information was given during the second session or whether such information had not been recorded during the first. There was another restriction placed on the data: an item on the interview schedule was not included in the final analysis of results unless at least 10 of the 25 mothers gave information which could be compared and scored. It was felt that conclusions based on less than 10 cases would be of dubious value.

The final list of items was as shown in Table 2.

There were 854 pairs of statements from the two interviews which could be scored as containing the Same (S) or Different (D) information. Numerical statements (such as age of weaning) presented no problem, since S could be defined as exact agreement and any numerical deviation could be scored D. Only 9 per cent of the statements were numerical, however, so the bulk of the scoring depended on the judgment of the investigators. Since the data were not verbatim recordings, statements were taken at face value and no effort was made to detect subtle shades of meaning or latent content; rather, the judgment was simply whether the same or different information was conveyed in both interviews. Average agreement between the two judges on S and D categories was 81 per cent, and the range was from 79 to 86 per cent.

Table 2

I.	V.	X.
Pregnancy	Speech development	School
Wanted or not		
Sex preference	VI.	XI.
Health	Toilet training	Sex
Morale	When begun & completed	
Father's feeling	How trained	XII.
	Regressions	Discipline
II.	Mother's feelings	
Labor and delivery		XIII.
	VII.	Relationships
III.	Health	With mother
Infancy	Illnesses	With father
Type of baby	Emotional aspects	With siblings
Breast or bottle fed		Other
Reason	VIII.	
Feeling of mother	Mannerisms	XIV.
Weaning	Expressions of feeling	General
Eating problems		Family situation
	IX.	Comments about child
IV.	Sleep	Attitude toward problem
Motor development	Infancy	
	Preschool	

In addition, the senior author undertook a further analysis of D scores, in terms of nature and direction of change. Five categories of change were derived empirically:

1. *Moderate change.* ("I felt a little anxious" vs. "Nothing worried me")
2. *Extreme change.* ("I was uncomfortable with an infection three weeks after his birth" vs. "I had mononucleosis and was over-worked and tense, very tense")
3. *Opposite or contradictory information.* ("I was unable to cut down gradually during weaning" vs. "I cut down gradually")
4. *Psychologizing after clinic contact.* Here, the mother used such professional explanations as "hostility turned inward," "passivity," and "birth trauma" when she had not done so previously.
5. *Discontinuous information.* Here, unlike the first three categories, statements are on two different continua. ("I thought he should learn in school without pressure from us" vs. "I thought he would be afraid of the teacher")

Whenever possible, the Ds were scored as Positive or Negative depending on whether the mother subsequently reported an item as less disturbing or stressful, more acceptable to her, more in line with normal development, or whether she reported the opposite. All categories were regarded as tentative and subject to modification in future studies, especially since no formal reliability measure was undertaken; however, they were retained because they furnished interesting leads as to the extent and direction of change.

Finally, the mothers were ranked in terms of percentage of S statements in order to determine which ones represented the extremes of accuracy and inaccuracy.

RESULTS

Extent and Nature of Change

Of the pairs of statements 57 per cent were judged as Same, and 43 per cent as Different. Sixty-eight per cent of the nonquantitative statements were S, while 47 per cent of the quantitative statements were S. However, it would be misleading to draw conclusions about comparative accuracy, since the units of the numerical scale are fixed while the units of the nonnumerical scale depend on definitions and judgments.

Turning to the nature of change of nonnumerical scores, 42 per cent were judged as Moderate, 21 per cent Extreme, 19 per cent Opposite, 5 per cent Psychologizing, 9 per cent Discontinuous, and 4 per cent Unclassified. Combining the Extreme and Opposite categories, it can be seen that 40 per cent of the Ds represent striking changes in content between the first and second interviews. In regard to direction of change, 59 per cent of the Ds could be scored Positive or Negative. Interestingly enough, there is no evidence that the direction of change was more one way than the other, there being 56 per cent Positive and 44 per cent Negative scores.

Areas of Change

The percentage agreement on all nonnumerical items was calculated, and the items arranged in order of decreasing accuracy. The results are presented in Table 3.

After the data were grouped, it was decided that items above 80 per cent agreement should be regarded as Accurate, while items below 55 per cent should be regarded as Inaccurate. The seven Accurate and six Inaccurate items thus include a little over one third of the total distribution.

Two further analyses were done. The first was to determine whether, among the different Accurate and Inaccurate items, there was a significant shift in either the Positive or Negative direction between the first and second interviews. There was no evidence of such a shift. The data were also analyzed to determine if the changes were more extreme on some items than on others. A chi square was run for Moderate vs. Extreme plus Opposite scores, but the p value failed to reach even the .10 level of confidence.

Analysis of Numerical Items

Since only six numerical items met the criterion of including at least 10 cases, the data could not be analyzed for Accuracy and Inaccuracy. However,

Table 3   *Agreement Between Interviews*

Item	Per-cent	Item	Per-cent
Breast or bottle fed	96	Emotional aspects of illness	69
Illnesses	93	Relation to sibs	69
Child wanted or not	93	Type of baby	65
Sleep in infancy	91	Expression of feelings	65
Sex preference	87	Father's feelings about pregnancy	61
Regression in toileting	83	Reason for breast or bottle	60
Motor development	82	Mother's feeling about breast or	
Labor and delivery	79	bottle	60
Sex	78	School	59
Eating problems	77	How toilet trained	56
Speech	76	Relation to others	56
General family situation	76	Comments	54
Weaning	75	Discipline	53
Sleep in preschool	75	Relation to mother	50
Mannerisms	72	Relation to father	50
Morale in pregnancy	69	Health in pregnancy	45
Mother's feelings about toileting	69	Attitude toward problem	35

a limited analysis of D scores could be done in terms of whether the second interview represented a significant shift in the direction of reporting events as happening at an earlier or later time. The principal significant difference was in the area of toilet training. Eight out of nine mothers reported starting training later in the second interview, which is significant at the .04 level of confidence using the two-tailed probabilities of the binomial test. Furthermore, the discrepancies ranged from 1 to 18 months, with a mean discrepancy of 8 months.

Mothers also reported their children as sitting up earlier in the second interview (all seven of the D scores were in the direction of precocity which is significant at the .016 level of confidence using the two-tailed probabilities of the binomial test); however, the discrepancy in six cases was 2 months or less, which hardly seems noteworthy.

Accuracy of Mothers

The mothers were ranked according to percentage of S statements. The range was from 52 to 87 per cent, with a mean at 67 per cent. The extremes of accuracy and inaccuracy were arbitrarily set at the upper and lower 25 per cent, but, because of tied scores, there were five cases in the former and seven cases in the latter. The five mothers with S between 75 and 87 per cent were called the High accuracy group, and the seven mothers with S between 52 and 58 per cent were called the Low accuracy group.

A number of comparisons of these two groups were done, but only a few positive findings were uncovered. There was no significant relation between the High and Low classifications and the number of statements scored for each mother. (The Mann-Whitney U test yielded a *p* significant at the .34 level of confidence.) In addition, the Mann-Whitney test yielded values well beyond the .10 level of confidence for most of the group differences tested: specifically, education of the mothers, income, number of children, number of therapy sessions, time between initial and research interviews, number of only children, age of children. The percentage of children in the different diagnostic categories was almost the same. The only significant finding concerned the age of the mothers. The mean age of the High mothers was 29, and the mean age of the Low mothers was 37, which, using the Mann-Whitney U test, is significant at the .03 level of confidence. In the interviews themselves, the percentage Extreme plus Opposite Ds was no different in the two groups (40 vs. 36), nor was the percentage change in the Positive direction (60 vs. 50). Finally, the social worker wrote personality sketches of all the mothers on the basis of her clinical impressions. This was done with no knowledge of which mother belonged in which group. In the Low group, five of the seven mothers were characterized as having high anxiety and being voluble talkers, but no consistent personality picture was found for the High mothers.

DISCUSSION

The results show that the initial question raised about mothers' histories —How reliable are mothers in reporting developmental information?—is too general. The answer that 43 per cent of the statements differed on the second interview and, of these, 40 per cent represented striking disagreements, has only limited value. The heart of the problem lies in the kinds of information which are reliably and unreliably given. In this respect, the second question raised by the study—What are the developmental areas of greatest and least reliability?—was incorrectly formulated. Accuracy and Inaccuracy did not follow developmental areas, and there was no tendency for extreme changes to occur in one area rather than another. The matter is more complex, and the present study furnishes only a few clues as to relevant variables.

To begin with, there is no evidence that inaccuracy is due to a general tendency to recall early events as less distressing and more pleasant as time passes; the tendency to see things as worse is as strong as the one to see them as better. Rather, accuracy seems to be more a function of the affective content of the information being reported. Whether the child was wanted or not, whether he was breast or bottle fed, and the parent's sex preference are all highly reliable. The mothers' responses to these items consist of statements of fact, of unadorned reports of events; the emotional aspects of the behavior or the motivations behind it are tapped by other items which, significantly, are not highly reliable. In a like manner sleep patterns during infancy, illnesses, and motor development were reported with little emotional involvement and a high level of accuracy. For instance, the illness item primarily consisted of a recall of disease and hospitalizations and not the emotional reactions of the mother or child; equally important is the fact that the item referring to emotional aspects of the illness was not highly reliable. (The accuracy of the regression in toilet training item will not be discussed, since three of the cases were still regressed on re-interview, and this makes reliability spuriously high.)

Examination of the Inaccurate items lends support to the hypothesis that reliability is, at least in part, a function of the affective content of the material. The relationship to mother item in particular is characterized by such words as scared, uncertain, furious, and hopeful. The same is true of discipline, attitude toward the problem, and relation to father, although the material here is more descriptive and less charged emotionally. The comment item is not so clearcut, although it might also fit the pattern. The data themselves most often consist of the mother's summing up of her child's personality apart from the symptom picture. Examples would include descriptions such as loveable, independent, and not all bad, which, implicitly if not explicitly, seem to be more affect laden than the impersonal reports of the Accurate items.

It is important not to put too great a strain on the affective content hypothesis, however. To begin with, not all the findings fit neatly into such a scheme. The mother's report of her physical health during pregnancy was as factual as the report of her children's illnesses; yet the former was Inaccurate while the latter was Accurate. A similar problem is involved in the finding that toilet training is reported as beginning on the average of 8 months later in the second interview. One might reason as Chess (1) does that mothers' distortions are in line with "socially acquired concepts of functioning"; what actually happened becomes distorted by the knowledge of what experts say should happen under normal or ideal conditions. Yet, why should this apply to reports of toilet training and not to reports of weaning or wanting the child, where pressures to sound acceptable are equally as great?

The second reason for not emphasizing one particular explanation is that others are equally plausible. For instance, relationships, general evaluations, and discipline are continuous features of the mother-child interaction, in contrast to specific events such as feeding or illness and to specific preferences or attitudes. It is possible, therefore, that a completed activity, regardless of its affective content, is more reliably recalled than one which is continuously present over long periods of time. The work in general psychology on remembering material which is homogeneous and material which is diverse in content is relevant here.

Regardless of how the findings are conceptualized, they point up a serious danger in the use of reconstructive information. It is not uncommon, in clinical evaluations, for feelings to be given more weight than objective facts, and relationships to be regarded as more important than descriptions of events. In research, too, much attention is paid to attitudes, affects, and relationships. (One need only to recall the many studies of schizophrenia which rely on the mothers' histories to reconstruct early attitudes and relationships.) Yet, it is just such data which are most susceptible to change with the passage of time and are therefore most suspect. This criticism becomes even more serious when one realizes that it applies only to consistency over time and says nothing of the accuracy or inaccuracy of the original observation itself. This does not imply that such data on relationships and feelings should be disregarded, since they still furnish important clues to understanding the mother's perception of herself, her husband, and her child; it is just that such data should not be regarded as historically accurate.

In regard to the characteristics of the mothers, the purely numerical finding that the High group was somewhat younger is difficult to explain. It is unreasonable to hypothesize that significant intellectual deterioration sets in between 29 and 37; on the other hand, there is no corroborative evidence in the histories that having children at a younger age indicated a more positive attitude toward pregnancy and motherhood.

The only clear finding concerning personality variables is that five of the seven Low mothers were extremely anxious, intense, voluble, and controlling. The fact that they talked more does not mean they gave more relevant information, since there was no correlation between number of scored items and reliability. One of the five mothers seemed extremely disturbed, was inconsistent and even a little bizarre in each of the separate interviews; thus, her unreliability was to be expected. The others were obviously distressed, but not to the point of severe pathology.

The remaining mothers conform to no clear-cut pattern. It is interesting to note that, while one of the Low mothers was described as coldblooded, evasive, and well defended, the other was seen as rather warm, sincere, and fairly comfortable. In the High group, one mother seemed open, easygoing, and phlegmatic, while another was pathologically bland, dense, and uninvolved. The only outstanding feature of the remaining mothers was that they did not fit into any traditional diagnostic scheme and there was nothing particularly noteworthy about their character structure. In these women neither pathology nor maternalism was outstanding. It would be interesting if further research showed that it was the unremarkable mother, rather than the warm one, who was most consistent in recall.

One final comment of a general nature: The research on reliability which has been reported so far seems to be "variable finding" rather than "hypothesis testing" in nature. Macfarlane (3) found a tendency for the mothers to make their children more precocious than they actually were, Chess (1) talks of distortion in line with socially acquired concepts of optimal functioning, and McCord (2) finds that parents tend to make their picture of family life conform to cultural stereotypes. These variables may be part of a more general need on the mother's part to make things look good and right, which is now being studied in clinical psychology under the heading of social desirability. The present study suggests that the affective content of the event being recalled and the mother's emotional state are two more important variables. Hopefully, future studies will uncover even more leads concerning significant variables, as well as refining and clarifying the ones already described.

SUMMARY

Twenty-five mothers were re-interviewed three to six years later in order to determine whether they would give the same (S) or different (D) developmental information. The results are as follows: (a) 43 per cent of the statements were judged as D, and 40 per cent of these represented extreme changes. (b) There was no tendency to give more positive and pleasant information in the second interview. (c) The most reliable items were: child wanted or not, sex preference, breast or bottle fed, motor development, regression in toilet training, illness, sleep in infancy. The least reliable items were: health in pregnancy, discipline, relation to mother, relation to father, attitude toward problem, and comments. The hypothesis was developed that reliability is, at least in part, a function of the affective content of the information reported. (d) Low accuracy mothers tended to be anxious, voluble, intense, and controlling. No consistent personality picture was found in the High accuracy group. The findings themselves suggest that clinicians and investigators should be cautious about regarding reports of relationships and feelings as factual.

REFERENCES

1. Chess, S., Thomas, A., Birch, H. G., & Hertzig, M. Implications of a longitudinal study of child development for child psychiatry. Amer. J. Psychiat., 1960, 117, 434–441.
2. McCord, J., & McCord, W. Cultural stereotypes and the validity of interviews for research in child development. Child Develpm., 1961, 32, 171–186.
3. Macfarlane, J. W. Studies in child guidance. I. Methodology of data collection and organization. Monogr. Soc. Res. Child Develpm., 1938, 3, No. 6 (Serial No. 19).
4. Wenar, C. The reliability of mothers' histories. Child Develpm., 1961, 32, 491–500.

3. A COMPARISON OF INTERVIEW AND

OBSERVATION MEASURES OF MOTHER BEHAVIOR

HENRIETTA T. SMITH

The study of parent-child relationships has been largely dependent upon indirect measures of behavior, including such techniques as rating scales (1), questionnaires, interviews, and case histories. Merrill (4) found that controlled observations of interactions between mothers and children could be used to isolate and correlate significant aspects of behavior with a high degree of reliability. The present study is an attempt to evaluate the adequacy of interviews as compared with such controlled observations of actual behavior.

The interview method is economical for it enables the investigator to collect data on past and present maternal attitudes and behavior, and it allows comparable measures of both maternal and child behavior. But it introduces the major problem of the mother's ability, or desire, to present a true picture of her actual behavior. Errors may arise from involuntary misconceptions, faulty perceptions, or inaccurate recall.

Moreover, the mother may feel anxious or insecure about her normal behavior and may be unwilling to report it fully or without modifications that seem to her more acceptable to society. This is a more serious problem in establishing the validity of verbal reports as a measure of actual events because there are not sufficient cues to allow either discrimination of the mothers who consciously report inaccuracies or differentiation of the areas in which such errors occur.

Observation of behavior, when properly controlled, shows consistency of behavior and can give data on actual behavior under specific conditions. But it also involves the problems of the relationship between controlled conditions and the natural home environment and of the reliability of the sampling of maternal behavior. While both of these can be minimized by various techniques, they can be neither fully estimated nor controlled.

For the present research, dependency shown by the child at home and during the observation session was used as the constant child variable because earlier studies have shown certain relationships between specific maternal behavior and dependency (2, 3, 5, 6, 7). Maternal feelings about and behavior toward displays of dependency are the focus of the study. Replication

Reprinted from the *Journal of Abnormal and Social Psychology*, 1958, **57**, 278–282, with permission of the author and the American Psychological Association.

of the findings of earlier studies will contribute to answering the two questions of primary concern here: (*a*) the relative adequacy and reliability of each method for studying maternal behavior; (*b*) the degree of similarity between reported and observed maternal behavior.

METHOD

Subjects

The *S*s were 30 mothers whose children, 18 girls and 12 boys, were enrolled in the Harvard Nursery School. The children's ages ranged from 3-0 to 4-1, with a mean age of 3-6. The mothers represented a highly selected group. Only four mothers had no college education; twenty-one had completed two or more years of college; five had completed one or more years of graduate work. It was expected, and found, that these mothers frequently would refer to publications on child rearing in order to explain their reasons for using a particular technique.

Procedure

The mothers were first observed for a 45-min. period while interacting with their children. Each mother was told that the *E* was interested in studying the child's play when she was present. She was reassured that no specific behavior was required and that she was free to do whatever she wished during the period. Both mother and child were then shown into the observation room, which was equipped with one-way vision windows, and the observer withdrew. After 30 minutes, the observer had the mother fill out a demographic questionnaire sheet in order to provide an experimental measure of her behavior toward the child's dependency solicitations when she was busy. As the observer withdrew again, the mother was told that there were 15 minutes remaining in the session.

At the end of the 45 minutes, *E* announced the end of this session and made arrangements for the interview. The interviews were conducted in the home by seven interviewers within two to four weeks after the observation session, and with only the mother present. Four interviews followed at longer intervals because of serious illness of mothers or children.

The training for the interviewers consisted of one month of intensive study of the interview schedule and the rating scales, as well as practice in actual interviewing. The practice interviews were criticized with reference to such factors as rapport with the mother, manner of interviewing, and adequacy of the answers when rated. The first few field interviews were also discussed with the interviewer. All interviews were recorded by means of an Audograph and scored directly from the records.

Equipment

The observation room contained a large table on which were several current magazines of various types, an upholstered chair, a child's table with two chairs, and a toy chest which could also be used as a bench or table. The toys were: (*a*) a set of finger paints and paper; (*b*) a set of small tools with thumbtacks and pieces of wood; (*c*) a set of colored blocks; (*d*) a jigsaw puzzle of a map of the United States; (*e*) a blackboard with erasers and chalk; (*f*) a partially dressed doll with the rest of its clothes; and (*g*) a set of interlocking blocks for building.

Scoring

To record the observed actions, a unit of behavior was defined as the equivalent of a simple sentence, although one element might be implied. The behavior of both the mother and the child was recorded on a scoring sheet containing a column for each category. The units were set down in rows in order of occurrence. Thus it was possible to indicate the sequence of interactions as well as the number and nature of elements scored for each person.

The child's dependency behavior was considered in terms of his stimulus and response activities; i.e., those actions which seemed to be primarily directed toward stimulating the mother to give help or attention which she did not volunteer, and actions that were primarily in response to situations which the mother seemed to set up. It was important to differentiate the conditions under which he sought help, the methods he used to solicit aid, and the kind of help or attention he desired. The mother's behavior was also thought of in terms of her stimulus and response actions, the latter being defined as behavior that resulted directly from specific stimulation by the child and served to end an on-going sequence. Although these actions might in turn stimulate further activity, they were differentiated on theoretical grounds from such maternal stimulus acts as degree of control exerted, specificity of control, and degree of contact imposed by the mother.

This conceptualization of the stimulus and response aspects of both child and mother behavior was used in the development of the categories for scoring the observed behavior. Table 1 presents the categories used for scoring both mother and child behavior. A category of positive social interaction was used to record verbal interchanges that were not concerned with dependency interactions, and therefore was given lowest priority in scoring and was not used in the final analysis of data. The observation session was timed and the end of each 15 minutes indicated on the scoring sheet.

Reliability was established with one other observer. Category reliability for those used varied from .75 to 1.00. Observer reliability for five sessions scored independently by the two observers ranged between .88 and .96, with a mean reliability of .94.

The interview consisted of 36 open-ended questions relating to such

Table 1 *Scoring Categories for Observed Behavior*

---

1. X—behavior in which the child engages to evoke the attention or affection of the mother; e.g., whining, leaning against her
2. Asking verbal help—asking for generalized directions or assistance; seeking information rather than direct aid
3. Asking material help—asking for specific physical help
4. Asking reward—asking for direct praise, reassurance, affection, or attention
5. Teaching—giving the child new information which is related to, but not dictated by, the situation; e.g., screwdrivers can be used to tighten screws or to lift out thumbtacks
6. Structurizing—giving generalized information from which the child may select his own behavior. The mother sets up the situation for the child, but gives him autonomy within it
7. Giving positive directions—giving specific directions or demands which are precise requirements for the child to meet
8. Giving negative directions—giving specific directions or demands which prohibit the child's on-going behavior, but which do not offer alternatives to it
9. Doing—physically carrying out of tasks by the mother for the child, usually preceded by some directions; an attempt to demonstrate to the child how the task should be done
10. 0—asking permission to help when the child has expressed no need for aid
11. Giving reward—giving attention, nurturance, praise, or affection at the end of an action sequence, or in response to the child's request
12. Comply—performance of a task which has been presented in the form of a demand, or verbal compliance to such a stimulus as the child's asking permission
13. Noncomply—lack of response to requested performance; including ignoring the demand
14. Punishment—verbal reprimands, physical punishment, disagreement, or derogation; usually comes at the end of an action sequence or serves to end a specific sequence
15. Leaves field—either participant indulges in activity or apparent thought which is unrelated to the other person, or to the total situation
16. Total observed dependency—summation of child scores under the first four categories; computed at the end of each session

---

variables as infant care and training, present demands made upon the child, amount and kinds of attention requested by the child at home, and the ways in which the mother responded to dependent behavior in the child. The scales on which ratings of mother behavior were made were grouped into the classifications of factual information, such as separations from the child, usage of "do" and "don't," and offering of help; information on feelings of the mother for the child, such as degree of warmth, nature of affectional relationship, and rejection by the mother; and information about the restrictions imposed upon the child, such as scheduling or feeding, restrictiveness of physical mobility, and overprotectiveness defined as excessive protection of the child in a majority of situations where the child might be considered capable of independent action.

Scales on child behavior were classified according to the nature of dependency solicitations (emotional, such as clinging or whining, or physical, such as wanting help while dressing), the conditions under which dependency occurs, and the areas in which the child strives for independence.

Interview scales which had a reliability of .60 or less were discarded and not used in analyzing the data. Since the remaining scales were divided into five points with 1 and 5 representing the extremes, and 3 the midpoint, two measures of rater reliability were used. The total rater reliability of the E and five other raters for nine interviews was .71 for complete agreement and .94 when one-point disagreements were included.

RESULTS

In comparing relative adequacy of these two methods, three measures were used: (*a*) consistency of observed behavior when a required task was interpolated; (*b*) replication of earlier findings on the antecedents of dependency behavior; and (*c*) similarity between observed behavior and reported behavior under similar conditions.

Table 2 presents the changes in behavior from the first 15 minutes of the session to the second 15 minutes, and from the first 15 minutes to the last. These are measured by the t test for the significance of differences between correlated means, and by product-moment correlations between the frequencies of each category for individual variability.

Table 2   *Changes in Mother Behavior During Three Parts of Observation Session* ($N = 30$)

| | Mean Frequencies | | | | | | |
Categories	First 15 min.	Second 15 min.	Third 15 min.	t_{12}	t_{13}	r_{12}	r_{13}
Teach	8.07	8.67	4.17	0.49	3.82***	.39[a]	.37[a]
Structurize	12.20	9.43	6.43	2.98[c]	6.14***	.64[b]	.36[a]
Give positive directions	23.53	24.27	22.07	0.43	0.85	.15	−.02
Give negative directions	3.10	3.83	4.23	1.43	2.02	.17	.38[a]
Give reward	13.67	10.23	15.23	2.92[c]	0.97	.30[b]	.25
Comply	9.17	8.70	10.00	0.46	0.73	.48[b]	.21
Noncomply	3.11	3.67	14.67	0.07	7.71[c]	.72[b]	.21

[a] $p \leqslant .05$.
[b] $p \leqslant .01$.
[c] $p \leqslant .001$.

Both *structurizing* and *giving reward* decreased from the first to the second 15 minutes, possibly as a result of the child's increasing ease in the situation or of the mother's decreasing feeling of any need to stimulate the child to new and better activities.

From the first 15 minutes to the last 15 minutes, there was a significant decrease in *teaching* and *structurizing,* along with a significant increase in *give negative directions* and in *noncompliance.* Thus, when busy, the mothers became less rewarding and more restrictive. In general, however, there is evidence that individual mothers tended to be consistent in their behavior.

Table 3 shows the correlations between five interview scales (selected because of their theoretical importance in the areas of warmth, frustration, and current restriction) and measures of dependency. Table 4 presents the correlations, in terms of r, between observed mother behavior and selected measures of dependency.

From Tables 3 and 4 the following significant relationships were found:

a. From interview data: *total dependency* is positively related to over-protectiveness; and *dependency* is positively related to rejection, especially in girls.

b. From observation data: *dependency* is negatively related to mother compliance and to mother giving reward, both of which are measures of lack of frustration; the more the mother *leaves the field* or *punishes* the child, the more frequently the child asks for material help, apparently to bring about an amicable close interaction; and the more the mother *complies* with the child's requests, the less verbal help or attention is requested.

c. From both observation and interview data: *dependency* in girls is positively related to warmth of the mother; and *dependency* is negatively related to amount of punishment given by the mother.

Table 3 *Correlations Between Interview Antecedents and Measures of Dependency*

Interview Antecedents	Total Dependency on Interview	Total Dependency on Interview		Total Dependency on Observation	
		Boys	Girls	Boys	Girls
Schedule feeding	−.13	−.13	−.08	.71[b]	.04
Severity of weaning	.08	.13	.04	.14	.24
Rejection	.51[b]	.27	.65[b]	.10	.18
Affectional relations	.27	−.06	.47	−.01	.46[a]
Overprotection	.49[b]	−.03	.11	.03	.28

[a] Significant at .05 level.
[b] Significant at .01 level.

Table 4 *Correlations Between Observation Antecedents and Measures of Dependency*

Observation Antecedents	Total Dependency on Interview	Total Dependency on Observation	Ask Material Help	Ask Verbal Help
Comply	.18	−.36[a]	.09	−.36[a]
Noncomply	.07	.02	−.29	.22
Give reward	.07	−.36[a]	−.18	−.16
Leave field	−.20	.29	.51[b]	−.14
Punish	−.39[a]	.10	.40[a]	−.18

[a] Significant at .05 level.
[b] Significant at .01 level.

These replicate earlier results found on the relationship between mother behavior and dependency in children.

Since ratings on the techniques preferred by the mothers in their interviews followed the definitions set up for categories of observed behavior, reports of behavior when mothers were busy were compared with their behavior during the last 15 minutes of the observation session by means of the *t* test. No significant results were found. Using the same test for the entire observation session and reported techniques, only two significant differences were found. The mean observed use of structurizing was higher, at the .01 level, for those mothers who reported its use than for those mothers rated as not using it; giving positive directions was higher at the .05 level.

It was found that 70% of the mothers reported using techniques which they were also observed to use. Thus, by the sign test, ratings on techniques from the interview were positively related to the total observed techniques at the .05 level of significance. The *t* test revealed that mothers reported more accurately their use of "don't" than of "do." The mean observed use of negative directions throughout the session was higher, at the .05 level, for mothers who reported high usage of "don't" than for those who reported high usage of "do." In contrast, the mean observed use of positive directions was not significantly different for those mothers who reported high usage of "do" than for those who reported high usage of "don't." This result seems to indicate that mothers were more conscious of actions that they considered "bad" and were therefore able to make better estimates of how frequently they occurred.

DISCUSSION

The general consistency of behavior during the first half-hour of observation seems to indicate that the mothers were giving a reliable sampling of their normal behavior under similar conditions at home. When this is contrasted with the increased individual variability of behavior during the last 15 minutes, it can be hypothesized that the introduction of the task not only changed the mothers' activities, but also changed their set within the situation. Thus, mothers who approached the situation with a definite set as to how they should, or would, act throughout the 45 minutes, could not maintain this behavior when the external conditions were changed. But this alone does not invalidate the reliability of the method.

To supplement this measure, it was assumed that the method which best replicated previous findings on the relationship between mother behavior and dependency in the child would be the more adequate. Since the Iowa study (5) replicated findings of earlier studies, it was used as the criterion in this area. Mother behavior from the interview data seems to contribute more of the significant findings that replicate the Iowa study. But when t's were computed on means of mother and child behavior during the last 15 minutes, it was found that increase in mother *noncomply* was positively related to increase in child *ask reward* at the .05 level, and mother *give reward* was negatively related to whining behavior at the .02 level. This relationship between warmth and whining is also similar to the Iowa report's finding on negative attention. Thus, the general results of this study replicated earlier findings on dependency, but neither method contributed more than the other.

A basic assumption for the study was that the observed behavior represented a criterion against which reported behavior could be validated. To test this, the mean and *SD* for changes in each observation category from the first to the last 15 minutes of the session were determined. The mothers whose scores on each category lay more than one *SD* from the mean were identified. Most of the mothers' scores lay outside this range for one or another category, but only six mothers showed such a deviation on 40% or more of the categories.

The introduction of a new task was constant; therefore, it was reasoned that those mothers who showed a change of behavior greater than that shown by four-fifths of the mothers were probably giving a less representative sample of their usual behavior during the first half-hour of observation than were the majority. Whether these six differed because of the degree and kind of motivation under which they took part in the study, or because they were more anxious and thus more defensive about their normal behavior was explored by testing the hypothesis that their answers on the interview would show higher conformity to a group mean, especially for questions which might be anxiety-arousing, than the other mothers' answers.

Using the t test, this group was compared with the 24 other mothers on 10 interview questions, 5 of which were judged to involve some anxiety and 5, selected at random, which were considered to be neutral. There were no significant differences found. When the means and *SD*s for these 10 scales were computed, it was found that the 6 mothers were consistently within one sigma of the mean; of the other 24 cases, from 8 to 12 mothers on each scale fell outside this range. It was not, however, a consistent group who did so. This seems supportive evidence that "defensive" mothers can, and do, give interview information which may be misleading in its very normality. In addition, they may not be discovered during a brief observation under constant conditions.

From the preceding results, there is little evidence for deciding that either interviews or controlled observations are better for securing valid measures of actual mother behavior. Since observed behavior is consistent for most mothers; since both measures yield results that replicate previous findings on the antecedents of dependency; and since most mothers report similar behavior to that observed, the interview seems to be the preferable method because it permits study of a wider range of behavior in a shorter time than can an observation session. It is important to remember, however, that "defensive" mothers can be more easily discriminated by the variability of their behavior under observation conditions than by their answers to interview questions.

SUMMARY

In order to compare the adequacy of interviews and observations as methods, 30 mothers were studied by means of individual interviews and controlled observation while interacting with their children. Neither method was found to be completely superior to the other by the measures used: consistency of observed behavior when a required task was interpolated, replication of earlier findings on the antecedents of dependency behavior, and similarity between observed and reported behavior. In general, it was concluded that the interview was a preferable method only because it allows coverage of a wider range of behavior than does an observation. However, it was found that observation of behavior discriminated "defensive" mothers better than did the interview.

REFERENCES

1. Champney, H. The variables of parent behavior. *J. abnorm. soc. Psychol.*, 1941, **36,** 525–542.
2. Gewirtz, J. L. Succorance in young children. Unpublished doctoral dissertation, State Univer. of Iowa, 1948.
3. Levy, D. M. *Maternal overprotection.* New York: Columbia Univer. Press, 1943.
4. Merrill, Barbara. A measurement of mother-child interaction. *J. abnorm. soc. Psychol.,* 1946, **41,** 37–49.
5. Sears, R. R., Whiting, J. W. M., Nowlis, V., & Sears, P. S. Child-rearing antecedents of aggression and dependency in young children. *Genet. Psychol. Monogr.,* 1953, **47,** 135–236.
6. Smith, H. T. A comparison of interview and observation measures of mother behavior. Unpublished doctoral dissertation, Radcliffe College, 1953.
7. Symonds, P. W. *The psychology of parent-child relationships.* New York: D. Appleton-Century, 1939.

Part B Methodological Procedures and Techniques

4. VERBAL SOLUTIONS TO PARENT-CHILD PROBLEMS

Philip W. Jackson

Children frequently cross the adult-defined boundaries which separate desirable and undesirable behavior. When this occurs, adults, especially parents, often take action aimed at the reduction of these "boundary-crossings." Study of this action promises to yield valuable information concerning the parent's concept of the parental role, his basic attitudes toward the use of authority, the nature of the child, etc. The importance of this action from the standpoint of its effect upon children is obvious. It is hardly surprising then that some of the earliest studies in the area of child development concerned an analysis of parental control and of children's attitudes toward that control (12).

Despite the importance of the problem, empirical investigations of parental reaction to a child's misbehavior have been less than successful. The obvious difficulty which confronts the researcher is the unpremeditated or spontaneous character of these events. He just cannot be there when it happens. If he is fortunate enough to be present, his very presence represents a variable which may affect quite drastically the events he hopes to observe. As a substitute for this "on the spot" observing, researchers have most frequently used two approaches. They have turned either to reports of parents or children concerning past parental action (4, 9, 14) or to some assessment of parental attitudes toward children (2, 3, 6, 10, 11, 13). The techniques used to accumulate this information have ranged from survey questionnaires to clinical interviews. Conclusions based upon data provided by these approaches assume that some relationship exists between the parent's verbal report and his action in the home.

That the two approaches cited above have been fruitful is clear. That they are not without serious limitations should be equally clear. It is imperative then that alternative approaches be used to verify the conclusions culled from parental reports and attitude studies. One such alternative might be to present the parent with a hypothetical problem situation which he is asked to "solve." This little-used technique provided the body of data reported in this paper.

It is the purpose of this paper (a) to describe a system of coding by

Reprinted from *Child Development*, 1956, **27**, 339–351, with permission of the author and the Society for Research in Child Development.

which the free responses of a group of adults to a series of hypothetical parent-child problems were classified, and (b) to report the substantive findings related to sex differences. Conclusions based upon these findings are compared with similar conclusions arrived at through different approaches.

SUBJECTS AND PROCEDURES

The subjects used in this study were 105 parents of freshmen and sophomore college students. Forty-five fathers and 60 mothers participated in the study. The mean age of the fathers was 45.2; of the mothers, 43.1. Socioeconomically, the group was judged to consist largely of middle and lower class parents. This judgment was based on information concerning the occupations and education of the subjects.

A questionnaire-type instrument, designed by the writer, was used to obtain the data of this study. The instrument was sent to the parents by mail. An accompanying letter requested the subjects to omit any identifying information in their responses. Although the parents believed their responses to be anonymous, identifying marks hidden in the body of the instrument provided the researcher with the identity of the respondent. Briefly, the subjects were asked to write free responses to the following situations:

Situation 1: You are seated in your living room when your twelve-year-old son enters. As he takes off his jacket, a pack of cigarettes falls from his pocket.

Situation 2: You return from a shopping trip one afternoon, and discover that your six-year-old daughter has cut off her beautiful curls.

Situation 3: You ask your adolescent son what time he came home last night. He tells you midnight, but you had been downstairs until one o'clock in the morning, so you know this is not true.

Situation 4: Looking out of the window, you see your seven-year-old daughter with some other children tying a string of cans to a dog's tail.

Situation 5: While playing with his building set, your five-year-old son hits his thumb with a hammer and he begins cursing loudly with fairly vile language.

Situation 6: Glancing into your bedroom, you notice your twelve-year-old daughter taking money from your purse.

Situation 7: After a delicious dinner is placed before him, your six-year-old son says he is not hungry.

Situation 8: You tell your four-year-old that he cannot have any candy before supper. He says, "I want some," and begins to strike you with his fists.

Situation 9: After telling your ten-year-old son that he can't go swimming with the boys, you hear him mumble a nasty description about you.

Situation 10: When told that one of her teachers has been seriously injured in a car accident, your thirteen-year-old daughter remarks, "That's good. I didn't like her anyway."

Situation 11: You have asked your sixteen-year-old daughter not to associate with a certain boy in her class. She tells you she is going to spend the evening at a girl friend's house, but, while running an errand in town, you see her stepping into a car with that boy.

Although no attempt was made to determine the real-life frequency of the situations depicted, it was assumed that each situation would appear somewhat realistic to the subject. This assumption was confirmed by the many comments of the this-is-exactly-what-happened-to-me variety which a group of college students made during a trial run of the instrument.

Codification of the Responses

Before the responses were examined, a trial set of categories was constructed. These categories resulted from an examination of the responses accumulated in the trial run mentioned above. The final categories were, with little change, those culled from the trial data.

An outline of the major categories used in the final classification appears below. For a more detailed listing of the categories the reader is referred to (7).

I. *Handling of Situation*

A. Acceptance
  1. Accept because nothing is wrong with behavior.
  2. Accept because a child did it.
  3. Accept because of infrequency.
  4. Accept under limited conditions.
  5. Accept to prevent deceit.
B. Explanation and/or Discussion
  1. Evaluate behavior and give reasons.
  2. Define conditions under which behavior might occur.
  3. Explain broad principles to child.
  4. Ask "loaded" question.
C. Natural Consequences
  1. Child will suffer enough from his own activities.
D. Information Giving
  1. Let child know that parent was aware of what was done.
  2. Evaluate behavior without explanation.
E. Bribery
  1. Promise reward for deterring.
  2. Call child's attention to a future pleasure.
F. Reprimand
  1. Scold, berate, argue.
  2. "Blow my top," "holler."
G. Assertion of Authority
  1. Urge the child "not to."
  2. Divert attention.
  3. Order, forbid, demand.
  4. Force to stop.

    5. Supervise child more closely.

    6. Alter situation so that it won't happen again.

H. Threat

    1. Of deprivation.

    2. Of natural consequences.

    3. Of physical punishment.

    4. Of loss of status, love.

    5. Of punishment (not elsewhere considered).

I. Compensation

    1. Have child do extra work.

    2. Have child pray for forgiveness.

J. Deprivation

    1. Remove privileges.

    2. Limit action, e.g., "Call indoors."

    3. Deprive child of social contact by ignoring.

K. Coercion to Repeat Behavior

    1. Noncorrection to get repeated natural consequences.

    2. Noncorrection to lead to guilt, shame.

L. Punishment (not otherwise specified)

M. Forced Admission of Error or Guilt

    1. Get word of honor.

    2. Get child to apologize.

N. Physical Punishment

    1. Spank, slap, whip, etc.

    2. Other, e.g., "Wash out mouth with soap."

O. Retribution

    1. Pay back in kind.

P. Creation of Shame

    1. Ridicule.

    2. Psychological pain, e.g., "Make child feel bad."

Q. Creation of Fear

    1. Create fear of natural consequences.

    2. Create fear of punishment.

II. *Elaboration of Situation*

X. Addition of Information

    1. Supplies facts (probable or definite).

    2. Supplies causes (probable or definite).

    3. Makes general statement, e.g., "All children do this."

Y. Search for Information

    1. Seeks facts.

    2. Seeks causes.

    3. Seeks general information, e.g., "I wonder if all children go through this state."

Z. Avoidance of Situation

    1. Denies possibility of situation.

    2. Expresses disapproval of behavior but does not act.

3. Places responsibility for action upon some other person.
4. Gives ambiguous reply, e.g., "So what?"

III. *Negation of Situation*

(In cases where the subject reported that he would *not* handle the situation in a given manner, the letter representing the method was placed in brackets with the following superscripts used to denote the reason for rejecting the method.)

( ) ^{0} No reason given.
( ) ^{1} Behavior not considered serious and/or frequent enough.
( ) ^{2} Method would be ineffective.
( ) ^{3} Method not appropriate to age of child.
( ) ^{4} Other.

Using the above categories it was possible to classify the major elements of extremely elaborate responses without wasting much of their richness. Due to space limitations, only two examples of this coding procedure will be given.

Response to situation 9: "First of all, this wouldn't happen to my son because I'd teach him to have a civil tongue. But if it did happen I would make him say the description out loud—he would feel pretty foolish. Then I would get the boy to come into the house and he would get the Ten Commandments read to him, especially 'Honor thy father and thy mother.' " Coded response: $Z_1K_2J_2B_3$.

Response to Situation 8: "I'd yell at him for hitting me but I probably wouldn't spank him since that might make matters worse. Then I'd explain to him that eating candy before dinner would spoil his appetite. I'd also promise him that he could have some candy after dinner if he stopped yelling." Coded response: $F_2(N_1)^2B_1E_2$.

In addition to the writer, an independent judge coded the responses of 20 subjects to the first four parent-child situations. The independent judge found 203 elements in these 80 responses as compared with 214 elements found by the writer. The two judgments were in perfect agreement on 181 or 84 per cent of the response elements.

Quantification of Coded Responses

As judged by five independent child psychologists, the methods of handling the situations are presented above in rank order: beginning with those which might place little pressure toward conformity upon the child and ending with those methods which might place great pressure toward conformity upon the child. The five psychologists ranked the methods on the basis of the amount of pressure toward conformity which they abstractly associated with each method. The coefficient of concordance (8) among the five independent judgments was .93. Using this agreement as a rationale, the writer conceptualized a continuum of coercion upon which these methods were thought to be located. Thus, Bribery would be considered "intrinsically" more coercive than Information Giving; Reprimanding would be more

coercive than Bribery, etc. Although it was impossible to locate logical steps
on this continuum of coercion, once the continuum was defined some
quantitative approximation of "degree" or "amount" seemed justified. Lacking the conditions which would make for a more sophisticated quantification,
consecutive numbers were assigned to the ranked methods. Following this
procedure Method A (Acceptance) was given the value of 1, Method B
(Explanation) a value of 2, etc. These values were identical with the rank
values given the methods by the group of psychologists.

Once the methods were assigned numerical values the possibility of
comparing the "coerciveness" of two responses seemed apparent. This possibility was complicated, however, by the fact that most subjects suggested
the use of more than one method of control in their response to a single
situation. Thus, Subject X in response to Situation 1 might suggest Information Giving, Deprivation, and Threat. The problem then was to find
some way of comparing X's response with that of Subject Y who in response to the same situation suggested the use of Physical Punishment and
Explanation. As a solution the response of each subject was represented by
two "scores." The numerical value of the *most* coercive method suggested
in the response was called "high coercion score." The corresponding value
of the *least* coercive method in the response was called "low coercion score."
By comparing the high coercion score of two subjects it was possible to
determine which of them suggested the most coercive method in response
to a particular situation. A comparison of their low coercion scores indicated
which of the two subjects suggested the milder method of control. By summing the high or low coercion scores of a number of subjects it was possible
to compare groups in the same fashion as described above.

A third value, the difference between the high and low coercion scores
of a subject, was given the term "coercion range." A subject who suggested
both very severe and very mild methods obviously would have a larger
coercion range than would a subject whose suggested methods clustered
around the middle of the continuum of coercion.

SUBSTANTIVE FINDINGS

The findings of this study which deal with differences between fathers
and mothers are twofold.

First, mothers suggested methods of control that were more coercive
than were those suggested by fathers. Comparison of the high coercion
scores of these two groups showed the mothers to be more coercive than
were the fathers in response to eight of the eleven situations. These differences are observable in Table 1 by comparing parallel cells in the first two
columns. Using an analysis of variance these differences yielded an F ratio
of 6.41 ($F_{95} = 4.96$).

While there was a tendency for the low coercion scores of women to

Table 1 *Mean High and Mean Low Coercion Scores of Fathers and Mothers*

Parent-Child Situation	Mean High Score		Mean Low Score	
	Fathers (N = 55)	Mothers (N = 60)	Fathers (N = 55)	Mothers (N = 60)
1	6.30	7.95	2.87	2.58
2	6.57	7.70	3.17	2.80
3	7.53	8.74	5.31	4.40
4	6.46	8.19	3.54	2.76
5	8.26	8.57	5.49	4.11
6	6.75	7.13	2.96	3.76
7	7.03	6.85	4.45	5.09
8	10.77	11.48	8.69	6.04
9	8.83	8.51	5.77	4.64
10	3.61	4.28	2.70	2.60
11	8.32	8.01	3.94	3.54

Note. Considering all situations, the mean high coercion score of mothers was significantly greater than that of fathers ($p < .05$). Differences in mean low coercion scores were not statistically significant.

Table 2 *Coercion Ranges of Fathers and Mothers*

Parent-Child Situation	Coercion Range of	
	Fathers (N = 55)	Mothers (N = 60)
1	3.43	5.37
2	3.40	4.90
3	2.22	4.34
4	2.92	5.43
5	2.77	4.46
6	3.79	3.37
7	2.58	1.76
8	2.08	5.44
9	3.06	3.87
10	.91	1.68
11	4.38	4.47

Note. Considering all situations, the coercion range was larger for mothers than for fathers ($p < .01$).

be lower than those for men, this difference was not statistically significant. The means of the low coercion scores for mothers and fathers are given in Table 1.

Secondly, in their responses to parent-child situations, mothers vacillated more between mild and severe methods than did fathers. A comparison of the coercion ranges of these two groups showed this value to be greater for mothers than for fathers in the responses to nine of the eleven situations. The size and direction of these differences are observable in Table 2. Using an analysis of variance these differences yielded an F ratio of 10.17 ($F_{99} = 10.04$).

In sum, the above findings suggest that mothers subscribe to the use of methods of control which are more coercive than those suggested by fathers. However, mothers are also more likely than are fathers to couple these highly coercive methods with some of the milder methods of control.

DISCUSSION

Few studies which concern parental action or parental attitudes fail to mention differences between the sexes. In general, the findings portray fathers as being more punitive, restrictive or authoritarian than are mothers, who tend toward the "warm," "permissive" end of the continuum. Although recent studies suggest that the fathers of today are less punitive than were their prototypes of a generation ago, they also suggest that both parents are moving toward the permissive end of the continuum without drastically changing their positions relative to each other (9). These findings agree in substance with the widely-held cultural standards of femininity and masculinity. Thus, the notion of a punitive, aggressive male and a loving, passive female are at least not contradicted by research findings. The results of this study, however, raise some questions concerning these traditional sex differences. Obviously, the findings reported above cannot be directly compared with the results of previous studies due to differences in the nature of the data. The conclusions, however, which seem to follow from these data are at variance with conclusions which were derived from other studies dealing with the general problem of parental behavior.

Although it would be interesting to speculate on why females are seen as being less punitive than are males when the measuring instrument is some type of an attitude questionnaire, no attempt will be made to do so here. An attempt will be made, however, to explain why this difference seems to reverse itself when the object of investigation is the written response of a parent to a hypothetical parent-child situation.

To offer an *a posteriori* explanation for the reported sex differences, it is necessary to consider the expectations which our society places upon the behavior of each sex in general as well as the differential role in child training which is expected of men and women. Considering the latter expectation first, it would seem that the mother is held more responsible for the child's behavior than is the father. This expectation results, in part, from the father's prolonged absence from the home as well as from his involvement in the more general task of "caring for" the family. Because of their reflection on her performance as a mother, acts of misbehavior would be more important to her than they would be to the father. The mother then would be more apt to use methods of control which would ensure the disappearance of the undesired behavior. Hence, we find in her solutions to hypothetical parent-child problems the suggested use of methods of control which are more coercive than those suggested by males.

However, in our society punitive or aggressive behavior is tolerated more in men than in women. The cultural concept of a punitive father and a warm, loving mother is one that tends to persist. Therefore, a woman is violating the societal concept of femininity to the degree that she behaves in an aggressive or punitive manner. Within the context of the parent-child relationship the pressing demands of being a "good mother" frequently may necessitate the use of methods which are decidedly aggressive. The mother may dilute these unfeminine actions, however, by coupling them with milder, more feminine methods. Thus it was found that in their solutions to parent-child problems women coupled severe methods with mild methods more so than did men.

The above explanation is in accord with recent formulations in role conflict theory. A concise statement of this theory follows:

> In certain situations *role conflicts* occur. That is, the situations are so ordered that an actor is required to fill simultaneously two or more roles that present inconsistent, contradictory, or even mutually exclusive expectations. The actor cannot realistically conform to these expectations. He is then forced to choose one of several alternatives: he may abandon one role and cling to the other, he may attempt some compromise between the roles, or he may withdraw either physically or psychologically from the roles altogether (5, p. 165).

Stated in terms of this study, the female respondents found it difficult to fill the roles of "mother" and "woman" simultaneously. Of the alternatives suggested in the above quotation, they predominately chose the second. Their attempt at a compromise between the demands of femininity and the demands of motherhood resulted in the patterning of responses described previously.

A final word should be said about the multiplicity of methods suggested in response to single situations. If these responses are at all related to the real life action of parents, this finding is important. It suggests that a one-to-one relationship between a problem situation and a method of control rarely exists. Parents are quite versatile. They do not threaten *or* scold *or* spank; rather, they are more likely to threaten *and* scold *and* spank. One possible reason for this multiplicity of action was discussed above. If it occurs in real life situations, the effect upon the child of this buck-shot approach remains a question worthy of further research.

SUMMARY

A content analysis technique was used to classify the written responses of 167 college students and 105 parents of these students to 11 hypothetical parent-child situations. A procedure for quantifying the classified responses was described.

Differences in the responses of fathers and mothers were found to be at variance with the popular stereotypes of a punitive male and a permissive female. Tentative explanations of these differences were offered within the framework of role conflict theory.

REFERENCES

1. Behrens, Marjorie L. Child rearing and the character structure of the mother. *Child Develpm.*, 1954, **25**, 225–238.
2. Block, J. Personality characteristics associated with fathers' attitudes toward child rearing. *Child Develpm.*, 1955, **26**, 41–48.
3. Coast, Louise C. A study of the knowledge and attitudes of parents and pre-school children. Researches in Parent Education, IV. *Univ. Iowa Stud. Child Welfare*, 1939, **17**, 159–181.
4. Cutts, Norma E., & Moseley N. *Better home discipline*. New York: Appleton-Century-Crofts, 1952.
5. Getzels, J. W., & Guba, E. G. Role, role conflict, and effectiveness: an empirical study. *Amer. sociol. Rev.*, 1954, **19**, 164–175.
6. Jack, Lois M., A device for the measurement of parent attitudes and practices. *Univ. Iowa Stud. Child Welfare*, 1932, **6**, 135–149.
7. Jackson, P. W. Verbal solutions to parent-child problems and reports of experiences with punishment. Unpublished doctor's dissertation, Columbia Univer., 1955.
8. Kendall, M. G. *Rank correlation methods*. London: C. Griffin, 1948.
9. Radke, Marian J. *The relation of parental authority to children's behavior and attitudes*. Minneapolis: Univ. of Minnesota Press, 1946.
10. Shoben, E. J. The assessment of parental attitudes in relation to child adjustment. *Genet. Psychol. Monogr.*, 1949, **39**, 101–148.
11. Staples, Ruth, & Smith, June Warden. Attitudes of grandmothers and mothers toward child-rearing practices. *Child Develpm.*, 1954, **25**, 91–97.
12. Stogdill, R. M. Experiments in the measurement of attitudes toward children: 1899–1935. *Child Develpm.*, 1936, **1**, 31–36.
13. Stogdill, R. M. The measurement of attitudes toward parental control. *J. appl. Psychol.*, 1936, **20**, 359–367.
14. Stott, L. H. Home punishment of adolescent. *J. genet. Psychol.*, 1940, **57**, 415–428.

5. TYPES OF REACTIONS IN PUNISHMENT SITUATIONS IN THE MOTHER-CHILD RELATIONSHIP

Patricia K. Morgan and Eugene L. Gaier

Figure 1. Card 6 of the Male Series of the Punishment Situation Index dealing with the lack of neatness in personal habits. [*Source:* Patricia K. Morgan and E. L. Gaier, "The Direction of Aggression in the Mother-Child Punishment Situation," *Child Development,* **27,** 447–457 (1956).]

In an initial study concerned with the direction of aggression in the mother-child punishment situation, the present authors (1) described a newly designed cartoon-type projective device—the Punishment Situations Index (PSI)—developed to assess characteristics of punishment responses in the mother-child relationship (Figure 1). The results of this investigation, interpreted within Rosenzweig's framework of reactions to frustration (2, 3),

Reprinted from *Child Development,* 1957, **28,** 161–166, with permission of the senior author and the Society for Research in Child Development.

indicated that the mother-child punishment situations are ones in which the major tendency was either to blame someone else (extrapunitiveness) or to blame oneself (intropunitiveness). It was also reported that the offense (e.g., lying, stealing, disobedience, destruction of parent's property) was infrequently a situation where punishment was evaded or the resulting frustration glossed over. When evasion of punishment did occur, it was most frequently related and described in the children's rather than the mothers' reports. In addition, the hypothesis was sustained that mothers seem more extrapunitive to children than they do to themselves. Mothers emerged as more extrapunitive and children more intropunitive according to both sources.

The present paper concerns itself with the types of reactions of mothers and their children in the punishment situation as they reported them.

SUBJECTS AND PROCEDURE

Each of the 10 pictures of the PSI (one series for boys, another for girls) was presented to 24 elementary school children, 14 girls and 10 boys, between the ages of 9 and 12, and their mothers. For each picture, an individual inquiry consisting of the following questions was conducted with the child and the mother and the answers were recorded verbatim by the interviewer:

1. Has this ever happened to you (with your child)?
2. What did your mother (child) *say* when it happened?
3. What did you *say* when it happened?
4. What did your mother (child) *do* when it happened?
5. What did you *do* when it happened?
6. How do you think your mother (child) *felt* about it?
7. How did *you feel* about it?

When the PSI is administered to both the child and the mother, four concepts of the punishment situation are obtained: from the child, his concept of himself (CC) and his mother (CM); from the mother, her concept of herself (MM) and her child (MC).

SCORING

The responses to the PSI were scored using the scoring factors developed by Rosenzweig (3). In this study we were particularly interested in the types of reactions in the punishment situation which, according to Rosenzweig, are: (*a*) obstacle-dominance (O-D), in which the barrier occasioning the frustration stands out in the response; (*b*) ego-defense (E-D), in which the ego of the subject predominates; and (*c*) need-persistence (N-P), in which the solution of the frustrating problem is emphasized. The scoring categories for obstacle-dominance (O-D) were E', I' and M'. Examples of actual responses given by the subjects are shown below:

E' is scored when the frustrating obstacle is insistently pointed out:

(CC) I never get any money to buy candy.
(CM) You could have gotten killed.
(MC) No use cleanin' it up, it'd get messed up again.
(MM) Look, you have broken my vase.

I' is scored when the frustrating obstacle is construed as not frustrating, or in some way beneficial, or, subject emphasizes the extent of his embarrassment at being involved in instigating another's frustration.

(CC) I was glad I got it cleaned up.
(CM) She'd be embarrassed about her little boy's taking apples from the store.
(MM) I thought it was just kind of cute.
(MC) She knew better the next time.

M' is scored when the obstacle in the situation is minimized almost to the point of denying its presence.

(CC) I felt fine, glad she didn't whip me and all.
(CM) She'd just feel neutral.
(MM) No particular thought of it at all.
(MC) She'd just forget about it.

The scoring categories for ego-defense (E-D) were E, I, and M.

E is scored when blame or hostility is turned against some person or thing in the environment.

(CC) I felt she was being mean to me.
(CM) My mother didn't know what she was talking about.
(MM) Will she *ever* learn to behave?
(MC) You're a clumsy little girl.

I is scored when blame and censure are directed by the subject onto himself.

(CC) I needed to be punished.
(CM) She would blame herself.
(MM) I would feel that I hadn't raised her right.
(MC) She would be terribly sorry.

M is scored when blame for frustration (punishment) is evaded altogether, the situation being regarded as unavoidable; in particular, the "frustrating" ("punishing") individual is absolved.

(CC) I didn't blame her very much.
(CM) She'd realize I had no money.
(MM) If he was in the right, I wouldn't do anything to him.
(MC) That's just like a little girl.

The scoring categories for need persistence (N-P) were e, i and m.

e is scored when a solution for the situation is expected of someone else.

(CC) Mother, help me get down.
(CM) She would tell me to get some clothes on.
(MM) Your report card is very bad; you'll have to improve it.
(MC) She would expect me to help her with it.

i is scored when amends are offered by the subject, usually from a sense of guilt, to solve the problem.

(CC) I'd pay for it.
(CM) She would let me watch TV.
(MM) I would pay for the window.
(MC) She would get her books and start studying.

m is scored when expression is given to the hope that time or normally expected circumstances will bring about a solution of the problem; patience and conformity are characteristic.

(CC) I would take the punishment like a man.
(CM) She says I'll get over it.
(MM) They seemed satisfied and I was.
(MC) She would do it without fussing.

RESULTS AND DISCUSSION

After scoring and tabulating the responses under the three categories, Fisher's matched-group t tests were computed between the six possible different combinations of *concepts* for O-D, E-D, and N-P. The results of the analyses, shown in Tables 1, 2, and 3, yielded the following conclusions:

1. *Ego Defense.* Table 1 indicates these significant relationships: (*a*) mothers report that children are more ego-defensive than mothers report

Table 1   *Ego-Defense Reaction in the Punishment Situation in the Mother-Child Relationship* ($N = 24$)

	M_1	M_2	t	Significance
MC > MM[a]	12.77	9.98	2.94	.01
CM > MM	15.06	9.98	3.97	.01
CM > CC	15.06	10.73	2.93	.01
CM > MC	15.06	12.77	1.67	N.S.
CC > MM	10.73	9.98	.67	N.S.
MC > CC	12.77	10.73	1.69	N.S.

[a] MM = Mother's self-concept; MC = Mother's concept of the child; CC = Child's self-concept; CM = Child's concept of mother.

Table 2   *Obstacle-Dominance Reaction in the Punishment Situation in the Mother-Child Relationship* $(N = 24)$

	M_1	M_2	t	Significance
MM > CM	4.54	2.23	3.52	.01
CC > CM	5.00	2.23	3.45	.01
MC > CM	5.06	2.23	4.44	.01
MC > CC	5.06	5.00	.07	N.S.
CC > MM	5.00	4.54	.53	N.S.
MC > MM	5.06	4.54	.72	N.S.

themselves to be; (*b*) children report mothers to be more ego-defensive than mothers report themselves to be; and (*c*) children perceive their mothers as more ego-defensive than children report themselves to be. Since Rosenzweig asserts that ego-defense reactions occur only under special conditions of ego-threat, it appears from our results that with ego threat there is a tendency to overestimate the ego-defense mechanism in other persons but not in the self. In this connection, it is noteworthy that in the previous study (1) it was found that children also conceived of mothers as being more extrapunitive than mothers conceived themselves as being.

2. *Obstacle-Dominance.* From Table 2 it may be seen that: (*a*) mothers report themselves as being more obstacle-dominant than children perceive mothers to be; (*b*) children report themselves that they are more obstacle-dominant than children report mothers to be; and (*c*) mothers report children as having more obstacle dominance than children report mothers as having. It would seem that the presence of the frustrating obstacle is more important to children in punishment situations than to mothers. And, furthermore, children do not clearly recognize or are unaware that mothers are also frustrated by obstacles in the situation as much as mothers recognize it.

Table 3   *Need-Persistence Reaction in the Punishment Situation in the Mother-Child Relationship* $(N = 24)$

	M_1	M_2	t	Significance
MM > MC	10.94	6.38	5.88	.01
MM > CM	10.94	6.85	4.14	.01
MM > CC	10.54	8.85	2.34	.05
CM > MC	6.85	6.38	.47	N.S.
CC > CM	8.85	6.85	1.83	N.S.
CC > MC	8.85	6.38	2.73	.02

3. *Need-Persistence.* The following conclusions appear to emerge from the findings presented in Table 3: (*a*) mothers report themselves to be more need-persistent than they perceive their children to be; and (*b*) mothers report themselves to be more need-persistent than their children perceive them. Need-Persistence is considered by Rosenzweig (2) to occur invariably after frustration; that is, the "fate of the frustrated need is considered." Need-Persistence implies a *solution* to the frustration. It is interesting to note that children do not feel that solutions have been found for the punishment situation as much as mothers believe they have. Perhaps this may point up many mothers' over-all frustration in adequately dealing with disapproved behaviors.

SUMMARY AND CONCLUSIONS

In an effort to assess the types of reactions occurring in the mother-child punishment situation, 24 children between the ages of 9 and 12 and their mothers were given the Punishment Situations Index. This index, a projective device recently developed to assess the direction of aggression in the punishment situations, consists of 10 cartoons (two series, one for boys and one for girls) depicting situations commonly leading to punishment of the child by his parent. On the basis of analysis made following Rosenzweig, the following conclusions appear warranted:

1. Where ego-threat is present, there is a tendency for both mothers and children to overestimate the ego-defense reaction in the other person, but not in the self.

2. Children appear to be more affected by obstacles in the punishment situations, but fail to recognize the extent of the importance of situational obstacles for their mothers.

3. Mothers regard themselves as seeking a solution to the situation more than children seem to realize they do, but they do not regard their children as seeking a solution as often as they do.

REFERENCES

1. Morgan, Patricia K., & Gaier, E. L. The direction of aggression in the mother-child punishment situation. *Child Develpm.*, 1956, **27**, 447–457.
2. Rosenzweig, S. An outline of frustration theory. In J. McV. Hunt (Ed.), *Personality and the behavior disorders.* New York: Ronald, 1944. Vol. I. Pp. 379–387.
3. Rosenzweig, S., Fleming, Edith, & Clarke, Helen Jane. Revised scoring manual for the Rosenzweig Picture Frustration study. *J. Psychol.*, 1947, **24**, 165–208.

6. AN INTERVIEW METHOD FOR OBTAINING

DESCRIPTIONS OF PARENT-CHILD INTERACTION

MARTIN L. HOFFMAN

Frequently in research it is desirable to obtain data on overt behavior in natural settings in which direct observation is difficult or might interfere with the activity being observed. In studies of parent-child interaction, in particular, it is important to know what occurs throughout the day. Some of these interactions are not accessible to observation because of the time of day at which they occur. Others do not take place in the home. Still others may be too intimate to remain unaffected by the presence of an observer.

Such considerations led us, in studying techniques parents use to modify their children's behavior, to develop an interview method which provides wider coverage than direct observation. With the interview we obtain a detailed description of the influence techniques parents use in the course of an entire day. The interview also yields detailed descriptions of the child's behavior which preceded the use of the technique, the child's response to the technique, and such contextual data as other people present, physical proximity of the parent and child, time, and place.

The purpose of this paper is to discuss briefly the main features of this interview method and to analyze their function in obtaining authentic reports.

The interview is begun by thanking the parent for agreeing to cooperate, giving him a general idea of the purpose and importance of the study, and asking a few factual background questions. After this the parent is asked in open-ended fashion to tell "in a few words what your child is like" and "what you would like him (her) to be like when he (she) grows up." These introductory portions of the interview mainly serve the function of establishing rapport and gradually preparing the parent for the personal details soon to be requested.

The main part of the interview consists of the parent's describing in great detail everything that took place between him and the child throughout the day preceding the interview. For mothers a randomly selected weekday is used, while for fathers both a work day and a Sunday are used. The interviewer's role is mainly as a guide for the parent, assuring the presentation of the chronological account of the day's events at the desired level of detail.

Reprinted from the *Merrill-Palmer Quarterly*, 1957, **4**, 76–83, with permission of the author and the Merrill-Palmer Quarterly.

He interrupts where necessary to probe for omitted material. This type of interview, in which the parent describes a complete behavior day, has been used by Nowlis [1] in the Iowa studies of aggression and dependency.

The use of such an interview is based on the assumption that the parent's behavior is more or less consistent from day to day, so that any day selected at random will be a representative sample which reflects his typical influence technique pattern. Thus, the major task is that of designing the interview so that it accurately portrays the actual parent-child interaction. To do this, it is necessary to minimize three potentially major sources of error: (a) forgetting due simply to the passage of time, (b) deliberate withholding or falsification of information, and (c) unconsciously motivated omissions and distortions, such as those due to repression and selective recall.

The first source of error, forgetting due to the passage of time, is handled by the selection of the day before the interview as the one which the parent describes. In this way we have been able to obtain highly detailed accounts. Recall is also facilitated directly by the interviewer's probes for omitted details. These details usually are readily given and appear to have been momentarily overlooked by the parent.

The second source of error, deliberate withholding or falsification, is handled as follows. First, the attempt is made to get the parents involved in the research by indicating in the introduction the ultimate usefulness and importance of the study for them and for all parents. Secondly, in order to keep them from feeling that their reports might reflect negatively on themselves, it is made clear that we do not make value judgments. This is done by indicating at the very start that we do not yet know the best ways to handle children and by maintaining a neutral attitude toward what is reported throughout the interview. For the same reason, the parent is given the opportunity to talk favorably about the child before getting into the description of the parent-child interaction. In addition, it seems likely that emphasis on behavioral details rather than opinions or beliefs results in very little need to withhold information. Thirdly, and perhaps more important than what is done to motivate the parents directly, is the continual pressure exerted on them to be logically and chronologically consistent. This pressure stems from the requirement to recall specific details in response to repeated probes of the interviewer. These probes deal with various types of minutae (e.g., details of the parent's and the child's behavior, the distance between parent and child, location of each interaction in the home, time of day, and others present) so that as complete a picture of the event as possible is presented. This seems to make it difficult for the parents to conceal or to falsify a particular bit of detail, as was brought out clearly in the pilot interviews in which some of the parents were asked if at any time they found themselves trying to make a good impression. The typical response was that they had all they could do to recall the details in their proper order, and that this task demanded all of their concentrated energy. Apparently, they became sufficiently engrossed in the task itself that the personal relevance of what was reported lost much of its salience. *Trying hard to remember details, then, seems to result in a certain amount of detachment, or a loss of self-consciousness.*

To fully appreciate this detachment it should be understood that probing is done very systematically. Verbatim statements are always asked for and probes are used consistently to obtain concrete referents for vague descriptive and feeling terms. What is first referred to by the parent as "suggestion," for example, may as the result of probing, emerge as a direct command, a request, a bribe, or perhaps a threat. Similarly, global statements like, "I got him to go upstairs," are invariably found through probing to mask a variety of specific behaviors. Even when terms like "holding" or "carrying" the child are used, the parent is asked just how he held or carried the child.

It becomes apparent that the interviewer has to try to visualize, and follow closely from what the parent tells him, just exactly what took place. This helps him to perceive gaps or seeming inconsistencies, at which points he probes for the omitted details or for clarification. Particular attention is paid to transitions from one situation to another. Probes at these points frequently bring out entire situations which were momentarily overlooked by the parent. The exact manner of probing varies somewhat from time to time. Most usually it takes the form of asking direct questions (e.g., "Can you recall just how you told him that he should share his toys with Jimmy?," "Can you remember just what words you used?," "How did you 'lay down the law'?"). Sometimes, however, non-directive reflections or pauses are used (e.g., "You say you suggested?"). The attempt is made at all times to keep probes from being suggestive or communicating in any way the interviewer's evaluation of the parent's method of handling the child. (Illustrations of probes in the context of interview excerpts are presented in the *Appendix.*)

This probing for exact detail appears to be a significant factor in minimizing not only the first and second, but also the third potential source of error, unconscious distortion. Our explanation of this is as follows. We assume that anxiety, guilt, or shame may be connected with something threatening in an event being reported. These motivational states if aroused could interfere with accurate recall either directly because of their disorganizing properties or indirectly by touching off such defenses as selective recall or repression of certain details. The threatening event presumably has some special meaning to the person in terms of his need system. If the event could lose this meaning, it should thereby lose its threatening quality. This would appear to be precisely the effect of having a set to recall highly specific details rather than meaningful wholes, a set which is reinforced by the interviewer's probes. *This set to recall details seems to result in a fragmentation of the event which weakens its gestalt properties and thus divests it of much of the emotional meaning it would otherwise have.* In this way anxiety seems to be avoided or at least reduced to a more controllable level. In psychoanalytic terms, a process of emotional isolation of the event takes place, the result being that the details of the event can reach consciousness without arousing anxiety. The details can then be reported by the parent, assuming that he is consciously motivated to co-operate with the study.

Lest the procedure we have described sound like our respondents are subjected to something akin to the third degree it should be pointed out that the interviewer probes only when appropriate and always attempts to be warm and accepting. He at times comments favorably on the quantity of detail in the parent's report and, where the parent shows some concern over his difficulty in recalling details, he reassures the parent by acknowledging that the task is difficult for all parents. It is also recognized that although the material is highly fragmented it may still at times be a source of anxiety, shame, or guilt to the parent. At such times the parent may be in part resorting to a defense mechanism when he uses vague rather than descriptive words, goes off on a tangent, omits details, or perhaps becomes excessively preoccupied with describing such irrelevant details as the objects in the room. When this appears to be the case, the parent is allowed to continue until he appears ready to be interrupted. At this time the attempt is made to gradually lead him back to where he left off and then he is asked if he can remember more of the details. In those few cases in which the parent continues to resist, probing for the particular bit of detail is ended and the parent asked to continue describing the rest of the day. In this way, by sacrificing a small amount of detail, it has always been possible to reorient the parent so that his descriptions again became appropriate. Fairly complete behavior day descriptions have been obtained from all parents.

Our general impressions, based on observation of the parents during the interview session and careful examination of the interview protocols, lead us to believe that the reports given by the parents are largely authentic, although gestures and tones of voice are not systematically obtained. The records are chronologically consistent and rich in the highly descriptive detail desired, even in situations which one might expect to be somewhat threatening to the parent. They provide us with a wide variety of influence techniques used in situations varying from brief momentary contacts with the child to highly complex and prolonged interactions. Their content varies from the casual and mundane to the intimate and what at times appears to be clinically significant. (Excerpts from the interviews illustrating the kind of material obtained are presented in the *Appendix.*)

In the interview session the parents show many overt signs of active and sincere cooperation. Rarely does their manner suggest concern for making a good impression. When this occurs it is only in the early part of the interview, particularly when the parent is asked to give a general description of the child. By the time the parent has started to describe the details of his interaction with the child he appears to be genuinely engaged in the task of trying to recall exactly what took place. On occasion details omitted earlier in the interview are spontaneously added later. Another indication of sincere cooperation is the fact that situations obviously handled badly by the parents are described as often as those handled well. In reporting some of the less pleasant situations, the parents appear to experience some discomfort in relation to certain of the details. But with very few exceptions this is kept under sufficient control for the situation to be adequately described. At times the parent will quite spontaneously acknowledge difficulty in handling a particular kind of problem, and, on, occasion, ask for advice, which by the way, is never given.

There are also subtle manifestations of emotional involvement in the situations being described—imitating the child's voice or imitating one's own voice when speaking to the child, changes in volume and voice tone when describing incidents with varying degrees of tension, and bodily movements appropriate to the situation being described, such as abortive hand movements when describing a spanking and nervous mannerisms when describing a tense situation. In making such responses the parents seem to be mildly re-experiencing the feelings of the situations described. In so doing they increase further our confidence in the authenticity of their reports.

The interview then, appears to be a very promising substitute for observation where observation is difficult or inappropriate. Even where observations can be made, this type of interview may at times be preferable because it is a more efficient way to obtain data. Generally, a two to three hour interview yields a highly detailed chronological account of what took place between parent and child during an entire day.

REFERENCES

1. Nowlis, V., The search for significant concepts in a study of parent-child relationships, *Amer. J. Orthopsychiatry*, 1952, **22**, 286–299.
2. Sigel, I., Hoffman, M., *et al.*, Toward a theory of influence techniques; preliminary report, *Merrill-Palmer Quarterly*, 1954, **1**, 4–17.

APPENDIX

Excerpts from the Interviews

FATHER 3-2

Parent: Well, we got to a point where he got bored with what we were doing and I was uncomfortable on the floor. So I got up and soon I left the room.

Interviewer: Did anything happen between the time you stopped playing with him and the time you left the room?

P. Oh yes. There was a little interplay about his fire engine ladder . . . because he's broken one already. And he seems to do anything more deliberately when you say something. You tell him not to do it, but he does it. There was a little interplay trying to get that situation straightened out.

I. Fine. Let's try to work on that situation. Can you remember just what he was doing?

P. He was playing with his fire engine.

I. How was he playing with it?

P. Well, he has a cane and a piece of rope and he ties the rope on the ladder and ties the rope to the cane. The cane is the hose and he walks around "shish, shish" with the hose. He didn't poke the cane at me yesterday, but we have cautioned him many times about poking sticks at people. There has been a lot of reprimand about that, but Sunday, no. He then started walking on the ladder, sort of balancing on it, standing on it. And he wears cowboy boots. He likes to, he has other shoes but he likes to wear those most frequently and they are big, heavy, clodhoppers with hard heels on them. Well, the ladder is made of aluminum and it won't take too much. It won't take a 35 pound boy stomping on it. It's going to bend. And I know I told him quite strongly, trying to let him know that he was not to step on the ladder and break it or crush it. And for a while, I don't know, it seemed a sort of deliberate "I'll show you," and he stood on it and we picked him off. This wasn't all exactly pleasant. I mean it wasn't all in an even tone. But I said, "G——, you are going to break it up and you won't have it." It didn't register, so I slid the ladder into the fire engine and G—— corrected me. He said, "Fire engines have them hanging on the side." Then I said, "Some of them do but this one has a very special slot where you are supposed to slide them into the fire engine, and many of them carry their ladders there." Well, that was alright. But he was very sure that most fire engines have their ladders hooked to the sides.

I. What did he do after that?

P. I think he walked away from the fire engine for a while.

I. Let me ask you some more questions about that fire engine situation. You see, what I am trying to do is to get all the details of each situation. About how close were you to him during that interplay about the fire engine?

P. Well, I was right beside him. The room is small to begin with. I was sitting in a chair beside the desk and he was playing right in front of me and my wife was sitting at the card table. And he was playing between us and the card table.

I. You were sitting all that time. Is that it?

P. I was, but when he stood on the ladder I think that I got up and pushed him off the ladder and picked the ladder up and tried to explain to him that he could break the ladder, destroy it. I think he said something about he didn't care whether he destroyed it or not.

I. Can you recall how you pushed him off the ladder?

P. Physically.

I. Around the waist?

P. Yes, I don't know. Just moved him. (I. I see.) Just moved him away. He didn't bounce off the far wall (laugh). But he wasn't getting off of it on his own. I don't think that it was exactly a natural thing for a child to obey a command. I wasn't exactly commanding. He didn't hop off immediately and I guess I sort of noticed that he didn't do it quickly and I pushed him off and picked it up. It's a very good fire engine by the way, and he is rough on it and it has stood the test so far and we would like to help him keep it if we can.

I. You say that he didn't obey. Did he react in any way to your request?

P. Stubbornly, in a sense. He just looks at you dumbly and doesn't do anything.

I. Uh huh. He didn't continue to jump or anything.

P. Oh, no. He just stood there and looks at you (laugh).

FATHER 9-3

P. Now, they sneak off into the dining room. I got a day-bed where the older boy sleeps, in the corner there, in the dining room, and they both get up there and they start to rassle. I can see W—— when he's on his knees there rassling with R——, he'll kinda look over. Now he already knows that whatever program comes on the television, that I says, I want it quiet, and I didn't want to miss none of that. And, uh, I didn't want no interruption. Now, he remembered that much, that he, evidently he knew that he was making a little bit too much noise, because he took time out to stretch around the archway and look to see how I'm reacting to the noise, if I'm setting on the couch. And I'm letting on like I didn't see him, see, and I'm looking straight ahead. I'm looking at the television, but yet I can see him. So, it looks to him like ah, I'm not paying no attention to them, too deeply wrapped up in the television. Well, the game gets a little rougher on the daybed. I mean W——'s really tearing in there, to the older one and it got pretty loud, and I says, "Fellas," I says, "What did I say to you about ten minutes ago?" W—— crawled off and had R—— straddled with his knees dug down into the couch. He was setting on the older boy, the older boy was laying sideways there, and he kinda got off him, looking at me dumbfounded like over here. And I says, "Remember what I told you W——. Now don't forget." And as soon as I look at the television, he's sneaking over. He's, oh, I can see that that's what he's up to, I know I'm gonna pull my strap off and I'm gonna give him a lick or two and give the other one a lick or two. And I got hold of the strap, watching the television, not to let them know that I'm pulling my strap out real quick, and then fold it up and put my hand down to my side. W—— takes one more peep in and to him it looked like the coast was clear, and he dug into R—— again as they were rassling. And just then I jumped off the couch and W—— had his little hind end sticking up and I came down with the strap, and then before the older one knew what was coming off, why I let him have one, I let both of 'em have one a piece. I says, "What'd I tell you guys?" Well, they scatter just like wild fire then, and after I hit both of 'em once. . . .

MOTHER 3-10

P. So we went upstairs again and, ah, played. He has a plastic track and some little cars that wind up and run on it, and ah, he asked me to help him put the track together and I did. And his little brother, C——, was uncooperative and pulled it apart as fast as we put it together. And he was quite perturbed at C—— and I explained that C—— wasn't big enough to know that he, I mean that that wasn't the way to play with the track, but that C—— really wanted to play too. And we finally got it together and they each got a car and pushed it around.

I. How did he show that he was perturbed?

P. Oh, he ah, he said, "C——'s a bad boy" and "I'm gonna spank him a little" and he'd just touch him, very, very gently, not to hurt him but, ah, he does that to C—— sometimes and then . . . well, I said, ah, I tried to explain to him that C—— really wasn't a bad boy. I mean, I wanted to get across the point that he wasn't, that he was just a little boy and that, that ah, he was learning, but that he hadn't learned that, that wasn't the way to put a track together.

I. Can you remember the exact words you used?

P. I said, "You see, C——'s trying to put the track together and help us do it . . . but we're gonna have to show him how to do it." And, ah, oh, we've been working on this for weeks and months and at the beginning it wasn't as easy as it is now. He used to be quite perturbed and he'd throw things at C—— and really hit C—— and hurt him sometimes, and ah, I think we feel that we have been very, fairly successful and that he's learning that C—— can be fun too, and ah, that if we show C—— how to do things, then the next time he might know a little better.

7. THE MEASUREMENT OF MATERNAL CARE

Harriet L. Rheingold

Maternal care is commonly assumed to have an effect upon infant behavior, but experimental verification of the assumption is still only sketchy. Of general notions about possible relationships between maternal care and infant behavior there is no dearth, nor are suitable measures of infant behavior lacking. Rather, it is measures of maternal care which are needed before statements concerning the effects of maternal care upon infant behavior can be drawn in a more precise, and hence testable, form.

Questionnaires, interviews, and case histories have customarily been used to obtain assessments of the mother's personality traits and attitudes and to obtain reports of her child rearing practices. But personality assessments and retrospective accounts are several steps removed from the actual care the infant receives (2) and, furthermore, do not easily lend themselves to the kinds of exact measures needed for statements of association.

The purpose of this paper is to describe a method of measuring maternal care in terms of the actual operations the mother performs in caring for the infant. It is a method which gives direct access to many of the important environmental events of the infant's life and thus establishes more closely the rationale for relating maternal care to infant behavior; at the same time it should be possible to gain clues to the mother's attitudes and personality traits from her caretaking behavior. The method employs the technique of time-sampling maternal care as it occurs in its natural setting. As demanded by the technique (1), both the items of behavior to be recorded and the time schedule of observations are exactly specified in advance. The details of the method will be illustrated by an account of a study in which the care given three-month-old infants in their own homes was compared with care given by an institution. The results obtained will be presented and then used to evaluate the method's success in providing the needed measures.

METHOD

Subjects

Ten infants were the subjects of study; five of them were home infants, and five were residents of an institution. The mean age of the home Ss

Reprinted from *Child Development*, 1960, **31**, 565–575, with permission of the author and the Society for Research in Child Development.

was 3.4 months (range, 3.2 to 3.7), of the institution Ss, 3.5 months (range, 3.2 to 3.8). Age was the only criterion used for choosing the Ss in the institution. In addition to age, home Ss had to be "only" infants of parents of better than average socioeconomic status, requirements which it was expected would increase the probability of finding a difference between home and institutional care. The home Ss were located by word of mouth, and requests for cooperation were made by telephone. It was necessary to ask only six mothers to find the five Ss; one refused on the plea of personal illness. All Ss were females except for one male in the institutional group.

Description of Homes and Institution

The Ss and their parents lived without other relatives in small houses or apartments which were simply but imaginatively furnished. Each S had his own room.

The Ss in the institution, resident since birth, lived in a large room which housed 19 infants. The caretakers included the Sister in charge, who was a trained nurse, attendants, and volunteers. In general, the caretakers were sensitive to the needs of the infants, while the infants themselves appeared to be well-developed, active, and responsive.

Procedure

The checklist. On the basis of observation and trial (3) a checklist composed of 42 items was drawn up, 30 for mothering activities and 12 for infant activities (Table 1 gives the items). Of the 30 mothering items six recorded the location of S in his environment, four the number of people in his room, and four the number of people within six feet of him.

The remaining 16 items recorded activities more closely related to mothering. "Caretaking" was an all-inclusive item which was checked if at the moment of observation someone was doing something for S while in proximity to him. "N of caretakers" recorded the number of different caretakers who cared for S during the eight-hour period of observation. The last 14 items were sufficient to cover all the caretaking operations performed by people in caring for three-month-old infants at the level of analysis selected for study here. Although all items were defined in detail, the behaviors included in them need no comment, with a few exceptions. "Talks" was checked when the caretaker talked to anyone and not specifically to S; her speech could be thought of as providing auditory stimulation for the infant. "Plays" included both social play of caretaker and infant *and* caretaker's initiating infant's play with toys. The item "Other" had to be used very infrequently; it covered such caretaking activities as giving S vitamins and weighing him.

It should be noted that the caretaking activities were not considered as mutually exclusive. Rather, all the activities occurring at any moment of observation were checked; thus, a caretaker could be bathing the infant, looking at his face, and talking to him on the same observation.

Table 1   *Means and Ranges of Maternal Care and Infant Activity*

N of Infants in Each Group = 5
N of Observations for Each Infant = 1280

Item	Home Mean	Home Range	Institution Mean	Institution Range
Caretaking [d]	475.2	347– 617	105.8	74– 144
N of caretakers [d]	1.4	1– 2	6.0	5– 8
Looks at face [a, d]	140.2	109– 173	28.4	6– 36
Talks [d]	55.8	26– 105	7.8	0– 19
Talks to infant [d]	166.2	51– 310	17.0	12– 22
Pats [d]	26.2	9– 44	2.0	1– 4
Shows affection	3.6	0– 14	0.2 [b]	0– 1
Plays [c]	11.8	4– 25	0.8 [b]	0– 4
Holds [d]	285.4	196– 394	45.6	11– 70
Diapers [d]	37.4	27– 57	5.6	1– 10
Bathes	35.2	0– 103	8.8	6– 11
Feeds [d]	154.4	72– 198	28.6	4– 43
Dresses	11.2	0– 28	16.2	6– 31
Adjusts position [d]	6.8	0– 11	2.2	1– 4
Rocks	37.2	0– 138	2.2	0– 4
Other	14.2	8– 20	11.4	3– 18
Location of Infant				
In crib	787.0	667– 908	908.4	699–1081
In arms	258.6	179– 391	46.2	8– 76
Seated	0.0		260.0	128– 530
Bathinette	86.0	27– 139	41.2	19– 70
Other location	148.2	2– 327	24.2	0– 112
Out of own room	304.4	153– 391	43.0	21– 77
N Adults in Room				
0	690.0	466– 899	263.0	178– 352
1	534.8	372– 814	464.4	416– 568
2	34.8	0– 136	246.0	182– 329
3+	20.0	0– 99	304.2	210– 361
N Adults within 6 Ft.				
0	755.5	652– 919	1062.6	1022–1093
1	492.2	361– 621	161.0	130– 213
2	12.8	0– 38	45.0	33– 68
3+	19.5	0– 78	11.4	5– 18
Infant Activities				
Awake	847.4	565–1081	928.6	647–1042
Vocalizes	54.2	22– 81	38.4	1– 76
Vocalizes to mother	9.6	1– 30	3.0	0– 5
Protests	14.4	5– 21	20.6	1– 59
Fusses	31.4	14– 46	43.6	19– 71
Cries	23.6	2– 64	14.8	0– 47
Finger in mouth	103.8	0– 312	69.0	10– 111
Bottle in mouth	54.4	0– 146	298.8	170– 435
Plays with toy	62.8	9– 168	18.2 [b]	0– 91
Plays with hand	8.4	2– 20	41.6	1– 117
Plays with dress	0.0		8.4	2– 20
Bursts of activity	32.6	13– 78	46.0	18– 92

[a] Caretaking items not mutually exclusive.
[b] Mean based on one case.
[c] Difference between groups significant at .05 level, two-tailed test.
[d] Difference between groups significant at .01 level, two-tailed test.

Although the purpose of the study was to measure the caretaker's activities, a number of infant activities which served to delineate maternal care were also included.

Time of observation. For each S a period of eight hours was sampled according to the following schedule: O looked at S for a full second and then recorded on the checklist what he was doing, if someone was caring for him, the nature of the caretaking act, where he was, and how many other people were in his environment. O could take as long as 14 seconds to complete the record, but in any case she did not look up again until the 15th second when she again observed S for a full second. In this fashion, four observations were made in each minute for a total of 10 minutes. After a break of five minutes another sample of 10 minutes was observed. Thus, the first 10 minutes of each quarter hour were sampled for four consecutive hours, that is, from 9 A.M. to 1 P.M. on one day and from 1 P.M. to 5 P.M. on the next day, to make a total of eight hours. There were three Os in all, but only a pair for each infant, one observing the first four hours, and the other, the second four.

Observers' behavior. The Os endeavored to put the mothers and the attendants at their ease by being friendly and by conspicuously making the infant the focus of observation. The O, for example, stayed in the room with S, whether he was asleep or awake, and continued to make observations. The readiness with which Os were accepted was reassuring, as was the extent to which people went about the business of caring for S as though they were not being observed. Mothers, on questioning subsequent to the period of observation, said that O's presence inhibited only their more "foolish" behavior with the infant, e.g., using nonsense syllables, singing, etc. The effect of O's presence will be raised again in the Discussion.

Scoring. The score was the frequency of occurrence of each item over the eight-hour period for each subject. From these scores a mean score for each item was derived for each group of five Ss.

Since 40 observations were made during each 10-minute period, the total number of observations for the eight-hour period was 1280. Dividing the mean scores by 1280 could give percentages of occurrence; and, since the observations were systematically distributed throughout time, the mean score could also be translated into hours and minutes.

Observer-agreement. To check the reliability of the observations, Os made independent simultaneous observations during 64 10-minute periods. Thirty-five of the periods occurred before the study began, the rest at intermediate points as the study progressed, in order to insure continuing agreement. The observations were made on seven Ss, four in the institution and three in homes, none of whom were subjects in the study.

The amount of observer-agreement for each item was calculated by two different methods. In the first, a percentage of agreement was obtained by dividing the number of agreements by the combined number of agreements and disagreements. Here an agreement was a tally identical in both records; that is, both *O*s agreed not only in *identifying* the item but also in the *timing* of the item; agreement on the absence of an activity was *not* counted as an agreement. The median percentage of agreement for all items was 89.8 (range 16.7 to 100.0). As one might expect, there was some tendency for *O*s to agree more often on frequently occurring items. (The rank-order correlation between percentage of agreement and frequency of items was .71, $p < .01$).

In the second method, observer-agreement was calculated by correlating the frequencies obtained for each item. The median of the product-moment correlations was .97 (range .35 to 1.00).

On the basis of these findings the method was judged to have sufficient observer-agreement to warrant a measure of confidence in the results obtained by its use.

RESULTS

Table 1 gives the means and the ranges of the scores for the items of maternal care and infant activities.

Because the variances of the data on caretaking were not homogeneous, a finding to be discussed later, the nonparametric Mann-Whitney test was used to assess the significance of the differences between the means of the two groups. (The results obtained by this test paralleled very closely those obtained by a *t* test with reduced degrees of freedom.) Two-tailed tests seemed indicated because what was at test was the power of a method to differentiate between two groups.

Caretaking

Amount of caretaking. The range of frequencies for "Caretaking" in the two groups not only did not overlap but were in fact widely separated. Home infants were cared for on 37 per cent of the observations to the institution infants' 8 per cent. Thus, they received care 4.5 times as often.

Number of caretakers. Most commonly the mother was the only caretaker for the home infant during the period of observation. In one home, however, a father, and in another, an aunt, gave some caretaking. The institution infant, on the other hand, was cared for by six different caretakers during the eight-hour period of observation.

Caretaking activities. Table 1 shows that the home infant received more of every caretaking activity than the institution infant, with the exception of "Dresses." While the home infant received care 4.5 times as often, the differences in amounts of different kinds of caretaking were even greater. He was looked at 4.9 times as often, fed on 5.4 times as many observations, held 6.2 times as often, and talked to 9.5 times as often. Some less frequent kinds of caretaking occurred even more often in the home. For example, the home infant was patted 13.1 times as often, played with 14.8 times as often, rocked 16.9 times as often, and shown affection 18.0 times as often.

The results also reveal that in most caretaking activities the differences were so great that there was no overlapping of scores between the two groups. All the differences were statistically significant, except those for "Shows affection," "Bathes," "Dresses," "Rocks," and "Other."

Amount vs. kind. The difference between care in the home and in the institution appeared to be not in the kinds of caretaking activities (as defined here) but rather in the amounts of the different kinds. First, every activity performed by a mother in the home was performed, however infrequently, in the institution. Second, there were marked similarities between home and institution in the caretaking activities occurring most frequently. For the home, the activities in order of magnitude were "Holds," "Talks," "Talks to," "Feeds," and "Looks at face"; in the institution the order was "Holds," "Feeds," "Looks at face," "Talks to." And lastly, the ratio of each caretaking activity to the total amount of caretaking was similar for home and institution. Differences, therefore, tended to be differences in amounts and not in kinds.

Location of infant. The infant in the institution spent more time in his crib than the home infant, but the difference was not significant. When the home infant was out of his crib, he was most often in his mother's arms; in contrast, the institution infant, when out of his crib, was most often seated in a swing. "Other location" occurred significantly more often for the home infant and included play pen, parents' bed, and sofa. The home infant also spent much more time out of his own room. The comparison, however, is not entirely appropriate: the institution infant's room was often as large as, or larger than, the entire apartment of the home infant; and different parts of his room were used for different purposes and hence were furnished differently.

Number of people in the environment. The institution infant spent less time alone, with no one in his room, than the home infant. Furthermore, there were more often two or more adults in the room with him. But, because the room in the institution was so large, these people were often at a distance from him. Thus, on the one hand, the institution infant saw and heard more people upon occasion, while, on the other, he more often had no adult in his *near* environment. The home infant had far fewer persons in his environment, but these few (most often, the mother, of course) were more often with him.

Variability of caretaking activities. Not only did the means for maternal care differ in the two groups, but, as has been noted earlier, the variances also differed widely. On 14 of the 16 mothering items, the ratio of home variances to institution variances was greater than 1.0, the median ratio being 19.5. Only for the items, *"N* of caretakers" and "Other," were the institution variances greater.

The differences in the variances present more than a statistical problem. They suggest that the care home infants receive may vary a great deal from one home to another, while the care given in an institution may be more similar from infant to infant. If this conclusion is warranted, and if maternal care does affect infant behavior, then one might expect home infants to differ more among themselves, institutionalized infants to differ less. Of course, repeated measures of maternal care in the same homes would be needed before definitive statements could be made about the variability of care between individual mothers. One might also find by means of repeated measures in the institution whether some infants elicit more care than others.

Infant Activities

Contrary to the findings on caretaking activities, measures of infant activities showed much smaller differences between the two groups, as may be seen in Table 1. In only three activities, "Bottle in mouth," "Plays with toy," and "Plays with dress," were the differences large enough to achieve statistical significance. All three were activities which reflect differences in the caretaking practices of the two environments rather than in infant behavior; the institution infant's bottle was propped; he had few, if any, toys in his crib; and he wore a short, loose shirt. If "Plays with toy" is combined with "Plays with hand" and "Plays with dress," the difference between the groups becomes negligible. One can conclude that, in the absence of toys, the infants in the institution played an equal amount, but with their hands and their clothes, that is, with what the environment offered.

Some differences in other infant activities were large, to be sure, but the variability within the groups was also large. The following statements of difference may be presented, but only tentatively, because they do not possess statistical significance: the home infant slept more, vocalized more, protested and fussed less, but cried more often, than the infant in the institution. He more often had a finger in his mouth and was physically less active.

Variability of infant activities. It will be recalled that the variability in caretaking activities was much greater in the home than in the institution. One might therefore have expected a similar difference in variability to appear in the infant activities. The data, however, did not support the expectation, for the variances of infant activities in the two groups of infants were similar.

Part vs. Whole Measures

Now that differences in maternal care in institution and home have been demonstrated for samples of eight-hour periods, it may be asked whether shorter samples would have yielded differences of the same magnitude. To answer the question the results for the first four hours (9 A.M. to 1 P.M.) were compared with those for the second four (1 P.M. to 5 P.M.).

Specifically, the differences between the means for home and institutional care in the morning and between the means for home and institutional care in the afternoon were tested for statistical significance by the Mann-Whitney test. On 38 of the 42 items the differences were of the same magnitude, the 38 including all the caretaking activities. In fact, the means for caretaking in the home were identical for morning and afternoon (237.6), while in the institution they were 51.6 for morning and 54.2 for afternoon. A four-hour sample of maternal care then would have been adequate to obtain most of the differences yielded by the eight-hour sample.

CONCLUSION AND DISCUSSION

Two separate topics may be considered here, the results of the comparison of maternal care in two environments and an evaluation of the method. The first will be discussed only briefly because the comparison was made primarily to illustrate the method.

Results of the Study

The results showed that the home infant had many more contacts with a mother than the institution infant with a caretaker. Not only was more done for him but he was brought into contact with more things. He had a richer life, a more complex environment. At the same time, one can speculate, his life was probably more the same from day to day. To the extent that a mother gave care in her own way, his life would lack the kind of complexity brought about by many different and frequently changing caretakers.

While the contrasts in care were noteworthy, so too were the similarities. The results showed, for example, that caretaking activities were similar in kind and in order of frequency, whether in home or in institution.

That no differences of statistical significance were found in the infant activities (that is, in those not dependent on caretaking practices) raises several questions. It may be that, infrequent as the institutional care was, it was neverthless sufficient at this age to arouse and maintain behavior similar to that shown by home infants. Indeed, the very infrequence and variableness of the institution's schedule of reinforcement, in contrast to the home's more regular schedule, may have accounted for its potency in shaping and maintaining selected acts of behavior. Interesting as such speculations are, however, it must be pointed out that the method was designed to measure maternal, rather than infant, behavior.

To look, further, for association between caretaking activities and infant behaviors in the results obtained is tempting but, once again, caution is in order; had differences been found, they could not have been attributed to differences in maternal care alone.

Evaluation of the Method

The results of the study demonstrate that a set of maternal care variables can be specified, defined, and measured. Clear and unequivocal differences in these variables were found in two environments; as a consequence, exact, quantitative statements can now be made about the extent of the differences.

Limitations of the method. Implicit in the method are characteristics which some might regard as limitations. The presence of the observer is one of these characteristics, and, admittedly, it may alter the mother's usual behavior. Although the observer can by his deportment do much to reduce the extent and the nature of the distortion, this limitation, more generally, will need to be considered afresh for each task set the method. In the present case, for example, there is no reason to believe that all the mothers were similarly stimulated by the observer's presence to give *more* care than they usually did or all the caretakers in the institution to give *less* care. It need only be mentioned in this connection that mechanical recorders may pose still other problems.

It should also be obvious that the measures yielded by the method are discrete and discontinuous; the 14 seconds between the observations are silent. Thus, the method offers no information about the sequence of stimulus and response between mother and infant.

Research implications. With exact measures of maternal care at hand it should be possible to reproduce, experimentally, environments offering certain kinds and amounts of maternal care, thereby gaining a measure of control.

Without revision the method could be used, also, to answer a number of questions. How does maternal care vary from mother to mother? How does it differ with the socioeconomic status of the home? What are the characteristics of maternal care in different cultures? How does maternal care vary with the age or birth order of the child?

Given only the requirement that the items of behavior and the schedule of observations be defined in advance of measurement, the method will be seen to possess considerable flexibility. In the present study only one of the possible sets of maternal care variables has been used; other sets of variables, for example, one employing finer discriminations of behavior, come to mind.

Finally, it is probably not enough to demonstrate that maternal care can be measured. In the end, the measures will gain validity only to the extent to which they can be shown to enter into predictable relationships with infant behavior.

SUMMARY

The purpose of this paper was to describe a method of measuring maternal care in terms of the actual operations a mother performs in caring for an infant. The method employed the technique of time-sampling, with both the items of behavior to be recorded and the time schedule of observations specified in advance. The method was illustrated by comparing care given three-month-old infants in their own homes with care given in an institution.

On a checklist containing 30 items of mothering activities and 12 items of infant behavior, the observer recorded what both mother (or caretaker) and infant were doing on any second of observation. Observations were made every 15th second for the first 10 minutes of every consecutive quarter hour for a period of eight hours. A record for an infant therefore consisted of 1280 observations systematically distributed over eight hours.

The results showed that the home infants received care 4.5 times as often as infants in an institution; the differences in some specific caretaking operations were even greater. The differences, however, tended to be differences in amounts of caretaking and not in kinds (as defined here). Measures of infant activities, on the other hand, yielded only small and, in general, not reliable differences.

The results demonstrate that a set of maternal care variables can be defined and measured. As a consequence, it may now be possible to formulate and test quantitative statements about the relationships between maternal care and infant behavior.

REFERENCES

1. Arrington, Ruth E. Time-sampling in social behavior. *Psychol. Bull.*, 1943, **40,** 81–124.
2. Bell, R. Q. Retrospective attitude studies of parent-child relations. *Child Develpm.*, 1958, **29,** 323–338.
3. Rheingold, Harriet L. The modification of social responsiveness in institutional babies. *Monogr. Soc. Res. Child Develpm.*, 1956, **21,** No. 2 (Serial No. 63).
4. Rheingold, Harriet L. A method for measuring maternal care. *Amer. Psychologist*, 1958, **13,** 319. (Abstract)

8. LABORATORY MEASUREMENT OF PARENTAL

BEHAVIOR

ROBERT E. SCHULMAN, DONALD J. SHOEMAKER, AND
IRVIN MOELIS

Lacking adequate internal measures of child personality functioning, clinicians have traditionally turned to an attempted analysis of the parent-child interaction in order to understand the etiological factors involved in the development of maladjustive behavior in children. The primary methods utilized in such clinical investigation have been the interview and psychological testing of the parents. While some studies have suggested that a sufficiently controlled interview can yield predictively useful information (Fitzgerald, 1954; Putney, 1947), the defensive tendencies in interviewees leading to inadequate report and distortion are generally recognized by those utilizing the method. Psychological tests have as yet demonstrated few consistent relations between test scores of the parents and the occurrence of problems in their children.

An obvious alternative to the reliance on questionable data obtained in an interview is the use of a home visit. This method of obtaining information regarding parent-child interaction patterns has been used by social workers and in more intensive psychological research, but is rarely seen as a routine procedure in psychological or psychiatric clinics. The obvious reasons for its relative disuse are expense and lack of quantifiable measurement techniques.

Another alternative, one utilized as a part of a larger investigation of parent-child relations conducted by one of the present writers and other staff members of the University of Illinois Psychological Clinic, is the measurement of parent-child interaction in the clinic playroom situation. In utilizing this method, either one or both of the parents have been invited into the playroom with the child, with the instructions either to play freely with the child or to interact with the child on some predetermined task. Various measures of the observed interaction have been obtained, and attempts to relate these measures to child behavior *outside* the playroom have been made. Although this method is similar to that utilized by Bishop (1951) and Moustakas, Sigel, and Schalock (1956), it differs in that the primary focus is on the relation existing between parent-child behavior in the playroom and child

Reprinted with slight abridgement from the *Journal of Consulting Psychology,* 1962, **26,**
109–114, with permission of the senior author and the American Psychological Association.

behavior in the general life situation. If such relations can be demonstrated, then the possibility arises of using the parent-child interaction in the clinic to help locate factors in the general parent-child interaction that are related to child maladjustment.

The present study focused on one aspect of child behavior (aggression) and two aspects of parental behavior (frustration and model) that, on the basis of previous research (Leton, 1958; Levin and Sears, 1956), were hypothesized to be related to aggression in children. In considering frustration, we were concerned with the parents' excessive limiting or controlling of the child's behavior with resulting frustration to the child. In considering the parents as a model for aggression, we were concerned with the example for aggressive behavior that the parents might present to the child in the interaction with each other in the child's presence. The hypotheses tested were (*a*) the parents of conduct problem children will exhibit significantly more control over the behavior of the child than will parents of nonconduct problem children and, (*b*), the parents of conduct problem children will exhibit significantly more aggression between themselves than will the parents of nonconduct problem children.

METHOD

Delineation of the Variables

On the basis of pilot study, nine behavior rating categories were specially constructed for use in the present research. Four of the categories deal with the aggressive model variables, five deal with the parental control variables.

Control variables
   pd: Parental domination—Parent dominates the task, and restricts the child's behavior.
   pr: Parental rejection—Parent rejects child's behavior in the task situation.
   pt: Parent takes over (literally)—Child stands aside while the adult goes ahead to do the task.
   ph: Parent hostile to child—Not physically, but is overcritical, forbids certain behaviors, does not reward child for his effort.
   ps: Parent subtle direction—Parent offers aid if child will do it a certain way and gives child information which tends to bias child in parent's direction.

Aggression model variables
   a: Parents argue—Parents disagree between themselves over how the task should be done.
   d: Dominance—One parent attempts to dominate and control the behavior of the other.
   h: Hostility between parents—One or both parents are aggressive towards the other, not physically, but through remarks and gestures.
   cr: Criticism—One parent criticizes and corrects other parent's behavior.

These categories were scored by two trained observers in 10-second blocks of time. An automatic timing device flashed a light on every 10 seconds; at that time the observer recorded the behavior that had occurred in the last 10 seconds. Behavior was rated by the two observers for 45 minutes or 270 10-second blocks of time. While the parents were engaged in many activities, and since the experimenter was interested in relatively few behaviors, the pertinent behavior did not arise in every 10-second block.

In addition to the behavior rating categories, several six-point rating scales were included to give additional information concerning the overall effectiveness of the family unit, cooperation and hostility between the parents, rejecting behavior by the parents, a love-hostility dimension, and an autonomy-control dimension. The two observers rated each family on these scales immediately after the 45-minute observation period.

The interrater reliability coefficients, for each observation and rating scale (Tables 2 and 3 respectively), were determined by computing a Pearson r between the scores of the two raters for each family.

Subjects

Forty-one males, 8 through 12 years old, and their parents served as subjects. Twenty children who were exhibiting conduct problems were selected upon the recommendation of psychologists and social workers who were working with them psychotherapeutically. As further verification of a conduct problem, the mother of each child filled out the Peterson Problem Check List which provides a measure of the conduct and personality problems seen in a child by others. The nonconduct problem children were drawn from the public schools by having teachers select children who were not behavior problems in school. Mothers of this group also filled out the Problem Check List.

Materials

The parent-child interaction took place in a carpeted playroom equipped with one-way mirror and microphone. Directly in front of the mirror was a table on which the experimenters had constructed a plywood garage, school, church, and house of the type normally used in play therapy. These were all one-story buildings with no roofs, so the children could easily manipulate small dolls and doll furniture in the buildings. The doll figures consisted of two adult males, two adult females, a girl, a boy, and a baby. In addition to these materials directly associated with the task presented to the family, the room also contained numerous toys considered highly desirable by most children. These included a small wading pool with boats, a drum set, blackboard and chalk, doctor's set, Lincoln logs, beads, and a small football and baseball. These toys were chosen because they were generally much more desirable than the task materials. Through the use of these desirable toys and the instructions to the parents (see next section) which stressed the importance of keeping the child working with the task materials, the experimenters intended to create a situation analogous to the socialization process in which the parent, reacting to social pressure, must attempt to guide the child away from activities that might be more intrinsically desirable toward activities that are more "constructive" or socially acceptable. In this way it was hoped that the playroom situation would mirror, even if only to a mild degree, interaction situations normally occurring in the home, thus strengthening the relation between playroom and home interactive behavior. Observation suggested that the experimenters were successful in creating a mild conflict in the child as to whether to cooperate with the parents on the task or to play with the extraneous toys.

Playroom Task

The mother and father were asked to construct verbal imaginative stories using the scene set up in the playroom. The parents were given the beginnings (story leads) of 10 stories which they and the boy were to complete. In making up the stories, it was the parents' job to keep the child interested in the task. The task equipment could be used in any way the parents and child wished. The following story leads are typical of those given to the parents; (a) The boy is outside playing. His parents have just called to him to come inside . . . . ; (b) The family is in the house getting ready to go on a picnic . . . .

Experimental Procedure

All families were treated in the same manner. At the time of the appointment, the first experimenter (E_1) met the families in a waiting room. He knew their names but not their group identity. E_1 gave the instructions to the family, then sent the child back to another room, and gave the parents the additional information that they were going to be observed. After this the family and E_1 entered the experimental playroom. A practice stem was then worked on in the presence of E_1. E_1 assisted the family in getting started and spending the correct amount of time on the story. After this practice, E_1 left the room and entered the observation room where the second experimenter (E_2) had been. E_2 did not know the names of the people in the playroom. E_2 started the tape recorder and timing device during the practice story. E_1 and E_2 sat at individual tables in the observation room separated by a cardboard partition. At the light signal, scoring of behavior was started. After the observation period, E_1 took the boy and administered a short form of the WISC. E_2 at this time obtained from the parents their occupation, the boys' birth date, and answered questions the parents had. At this time, E_2 indicated that he did not know who the parents were and they were not to tell him. In this way E_2 was able to tally the frequency counts still unaware of the group identification of the family.

Table 1 *Intercorrelation Matrix of Control Variables*

Variable	Pr	Ph	Pd	Pt	Ps
Pr					
Ph	.77 [a]				
Pd	.07	−.01			
Pt	−.15	−.17	−.62 [a]		
Ps	.03	.00	−.30 [a]	−.07	

[a] Significant beyond the .05 level of confidence for a 2-tailed test.

RESULTS

Before considering the results relevant to the major hypotheses, it is necessary to point out that, as the intercorrelations in Table 1 indicate, the five control variables apparently were not measuring the same thing. Parental rejection and parental hostility appear to be measuring a common variable of love-hostility and seem to be independent of the other three control variables. While the categories of parent domination (pd) and parent takes over (pt) are negatively correlated, they show a low positive relation to an autonomy-control rating scale (.19). This suggests that these two variables may be mutually exclusive or incompatible methods of parental control. In their reaction to the situation, parents may show either pd or pt, but not both. In considering the results, therefore, it is necessary to be aware that we are dealing with two dimensions, love-hostility and control, rather than a single dimension of control.

The control variables and the parent interaction variables were analyzed by use of the median test (corrected for continuity) as described by Siegel (1956). The two raters' frequency scores for each variable were combined into a joint frequency score for each family on each variable. Each rater's score for a category was actually a combination of both mother and father behavior. In rating the family behavior each parent was rated individually, but the main interest was on the combined behavior pattern of the parents as they related to the child in the standard situation.

The results of the chi square analyses are presented in Table 2. The measures of parental rejection and hostility were both significant beyond the .01 level, indicating that the C group parents were more hostile and rejecting than the NC group parents. The correlation between pr and ph was .77.

In addition to these behavior ratings, the scores on the six rating scales were divided into high (4, 5, and 6) and low (1, 2, and 3) for each scale and analyzed by use of a 2 × 2 contingency table (Table 3) corrected for continuity (Siegel, 1956). Two of these scales showed significant chi squares; the rejecting behavior continuum, and the love-hostility continuum. These results again indicated that the C group parents were more hostile and rejecting of

Table 2 *Difference Between Conduct and Nonconduct Problem Families*

Behavior category	C	NC	χ^2	Rater reliability
Parental domination			.216	.92
above	9	12		
below	11	9		
Parental rejection			7.077 [a]	.93
above	15	6		
below	5	15		
Parent takes over			.216	.98
above	9	12		
below	11	9		
Parent hostile to child			7.077 [a]	.90
above	15	6		
below	5	15		
Parent subtle direction			.026	.96
above	11	10		
below	9	11		
Parents argue			.021	.87
above	10	12		
below	10	9		
Dominance			2.061	.93
above	14	9		
below	6	12		
Hostility between parents			.026	.86
above	11	10		
below	9	11		
Criticism			.616	.85
above	12	9		
below	8	12		

[a] Significant beyond the .01 level of confidence for a 2-tailed test.

their children than the NC group parents. These two rating scales were correlated .78.

If no scorable activity took place during a 10-second scoring period, a check mark was entered into the scoring box. This provided an indication of the general activity level in the playroom situation.

There were no difference between the average combined (for both raters) number of check marks between the two groups. The NC group had a mean of 182.95 with a sigma of 71.98 and the C group had a mean of 181.05 with a sigma of 58.15.

As an overall measure of reliability, the percentage agreement between the two raters was calculated. Agreements were counted when both raters scored the same behavior, and in the same time sequence within a box. The average percentage agreement for the C group families was 74.02% with a sigma of 6.86. For the NC group it was 76.79% with a sigma of 5.29.

Table 3   *Group Differences on Rating Scales*

Scale	C	NC	χ^2	Rater reliability
Rejecting behavior			13.535 [b]	.85
high	16	5		
low	4	16		
Cooperation between parents			3.640	.78
high	3	10		
low	17	11		
Hostility between parents			.005	.66
high	4	3		
low	16	18		
Overall effectiveness			.767	.68
high	5	9		
low	15	12		
Love-hostility			7.077 [a]	.74
high (hostility)	15	6		
low (love)	5	15		
Autonomy-control			1.389	.40
high (control)	15	11		
low (autonomy)	5	10		

[a] Significant beyond the .01 level of confidence for a 2-tailed test.
[b] Significant beyond the .001 level of confidence for a 2-tailed test.

DISCUSSION

The results of this study indicate that, in this situation, the parents of conduct problem children exhibit significantly more hostile behavior toward their children than do the parents of nonconduct problem children. These parents also reject their children significantly more than do parents of nonconduct problem children.

On the basis of these results, it is tempting to assume that we have shown a cause and effect relationship, whereby rejection and hostility on the part of the parents lead to aggressive behavior in children. The results of this study, however, can only indicate what kind of parent behavior might be expected in families where there is a child who is manifesting some form of a conduct problem. One of the purposes of this work, it will be recalled, was to make a first attempt at using measurement of parent-child interaction in the playroom situation as a diagnostic procedure. In light of this, the inability to infer a causal relation between parent and child behavior does not lessen the value of this technique as a diagnostic procedure.

Before examining the diagnostic implication of this procedure, it is necessary to consider why several of the variables were not significant. Considering that the task of the parents was to elicit the help of the child in making up stories, a wide range of behaviors was not available to the parents, whether the child was a conduct problem or not. Thus, for C group families, one way of coping with the situation was to manipulate the materials, to make up stories without the child, and to ask questions of the boy whenever possible. It was expected, however, that the NC families would give the boy more freedom. This was not the case, and in terms of three of the control variables, pd, pt, and ps, the NC families were as controlling as the C families. Coincidentally, a chi square analysis ($\chi^2 = 1.95$; $df = 1$) of the combined pd and pt scores was completed. This suggested that the NC parents may have been more controlling than the C parents. The probability level ($.20 > p > .10$) achieved, however, does not allow us to feel certain in regard to this relationship. It may well be that the C parents wanted to control their child, but could temper this, in attempting to "look good." The C parents could not, however, control their hostile and rejecting feelings. As Becker, Peterson, Hellmer, Shoemaker, and Quay (1959) have demonstrated before, parents of conduct problem children are themselves more maladjusted and more freely exhibit their hostilities. However, given the problem of interesting the child in the task, both groups of families manifested similar types of behavior.

Since the variables which were significant were highly correlated in both the case of the behavior categories and the rating scales, it is possible that we are dealing with a single factor upon which hostility and rejection have high loadings.

Finally, both groups were equally active in the playroom, yet differed significantly on two major variables. This suggests, of course, that hostility and rejection are overtones which enter into the general and more inclusive relationship which parents of conduct problem children have with their offspring.

It was hypothesized that conflict and hostilities between the parents perhaps furnished a model for the conduct problem child's behavior. Contrary to expectations, there was no difference between the two groups of parents on the parent interaction variables. Actually, in neither group was there very much interaction between the parents. Since both parents were engaged in the task of keeping the boy interested in the job at hand, perhaps hostility that might have been felt for each other was directed toward the task and the boy. This would be particularly true of the C group parents, who seem to have a need to express hostility in an uncontrolled fashion.

This may be exactly what happens in the home. While both parents may in their own interaction present a model of aggressive and hostile behavior for the child, when they interact with the child they direct this hostility towards the child. In one sense, the child serves as a scapegoat.

The most unique aspect of this research is the fact that in an observed situation, those aspects of parental hostility and rejection which have been talked about and studied for the most part in an indirect manner have been observed directly. Apparently, the fact of being observed does not inhibit the parents' behavior to such an extent that primary differences between parental groups disappear. This observational technique demonstrates the possibility of relating parental playroom behavior with child behavior *outside* the playroom, and therefore becomes potentially important as a diagnostic technique.

At its present level of development, the fixed playroom diagnostic procedure is an excellent adjunct to other diagnostic techniques, and may aid the diagnostician in gaining a sharper picture of family dynamics.

SUMMARY

The particular focus of interest in this study was on differences in behavior between parents of conduct problem children (C) and parents of nonconduct problem children (NC). Two predictions were made:

1. In families in which the child can be considered a conduct problem, the expectation is that the parents will exhibit significantly more control over the behavior of the child than will parents of nonconduct problem children.

2. In the conduct problem children's families, the expectation is that there will be significantly more aggression between the parents than there will be between parents of nonconduct problem children.

Forty-one males, 8 through 12 years old, and their parents served as subjects. The parents and their child were told that they were to construct stories to a scene which included a variety of buildings and people. While the parents and their child performed the task, two experimenters rated the parents' behavior.

A chi square analysis of the parent behavior rating scales indicated that the C group parents were significantly more rejecting and hostile toward their children than were the NC group parents.

The implications of these results were discussed as they pertain to a cause and effect relation between parental hostility and rejection and aggressive behavior in children. In addition to this, the merits of this playroom technique as a diagnostic instrument were presented.

REFERENCES

Becker, W. C., Peterson, D. R., Hellmer, L. A., Shoemaker, D. J., & Quay, H. C. Factors in parental behavior and personality as related to problem behavior in children. *J. consult, Psychol.*, 1959, **23,** 107–118.

Bishop, Barbara M. Mother-child interaction and the social behavior of children. *Psychol. Monogr.*, 1951, **65,** No. 11 (Whole No. 328).

Fitzgerald, B. J. The relationship of two projective measures to a sociometric measure of dependent behavior. Unpublished doctoral dissertation, Ohia State University, 1954.

Leton, D. A. A study of the validity of parent attitude scales. *Child Develpm.*, 1958, **29,** 507–514.

Levin, H., & Sears, R. R. Identification with parents as a determinant of doll play aggression. *Child Develpm.*, 1956, **27,** 135–154.

Moustakas, C. E., Sigel, I. E., & Schalock, H. D. An objective method for the measurement and analysis of child-adult interaction. *Child Develpm.*, 1956, **27,** 109–134.

Putney, R. W. Validity of the placement interview. *Personnel J.*, 1947, **26,** 144–145.

Siegel, S. *Nonparametric statistics for the behavioral sciences.* New York: McGraw-Hill, 1956.

Warner, W. L., Meeker, Marian, & Eells, K. *Social class in America.* Chicago: Science Research Associates, 1949.

Wechsler, D. *Wechsler Intelligence Scale for Children.* New York: Psychological Corporation, 1949.

Section II

Parent Attitude and Behavior Variables

Introduction

A great number of dimensions have been employed to describe the psychological atmosphere of the home. Ratings are made on 30 variables in the Fels research, and these were selected from a list of some 150 original items. Because of the difficulty of dealing either conceptually or in research with such a large number of variables, attempts have been made to identify a few basic dimensions. Table 1 lists some major dimensions which have been uncovered through factor analysis. Schaefer (1959) notes that two principal dimensions are apparent in all studies of maternal behavior: Love vs. Hostility and Autonomy vs. Control. These are remarkably similar to the two dimensions presented by Symonds (1939) twenty years earlier: Acceptance-Rejection and Dominance-Submission. Moreover, a nearly identical pair of factors was extracted in a factor analytic study (Zuckerman, Ribback, Monashkin, and Norton, 1958) of a parent attitude test: Authoritarian-Control and Hostility-Rejection. It must be pointed out, however, that these two dimensions are psychological in nature and are concerned primarily with effects on the child's personality development. In a study of dimensions of early maternal care, Yarrow (1963) found high correlations between the infant's IQ at six months and ratings of the mother on a variable termed "Stimulus-learning conditions." Thus the child's cognitive development is affected by parental achievement pressures and intellectual stimulation, which may be correlated only slightly with the two dimensions mentioned above.

The selections in this section are grouped according to the main parental dimensions. Although the Acceptance-Rejection continuum certainly is as

86   Parent Attitude and Behavior Variables

Table 1   *Major Parent-Child Dimensions*

Investigators		Psychological Dimensions
Symonds (1939)	Dimensions:	Acceptance-rejection Dominance-submission
Baldwin, Kalhorn, and Breese (1945)	Syndromes:	Democracy in the home Acceptance of child Indulgence
Baldwin, Kalhorn, and Breese (1949)	Clusters:	Warmth Adjustment Restrictiveness Clarity Interference
Roff (1949) [a]	Factors:	Concern for child Democratic guidance Permissiveness Parent-child harmony Sociability-adjustment of parents Activeness of home Nonreadiness of suggestion
Lorr and Jenkins (1953) [b]	Factors:	Dependence-encouraging Democracy of child training Organization and effectiveness of control
Milton (1958) [c]	Factors:	Strictness or nonpermissiveness of parent behavior General family interaction or adjustment Warmth of the mother-child relationship Responsible child-training orientation Parents' attitude toward aggressiveness and punitiveness
Schaefer (1959)	Dimensions:	Autonomy-control Love-hostility
Zuckerman, Ribback, Monashkin, and Norton (1958)	Factors:	Authoritarian-control Hostility-rejection

[a] Based on the Baldwin, Kalhorn, & Breese (1945) data.
[b] Based on the Baldwin, Kalhorn, & Breese (1945) data and Roff's (1949) factor analysis.
[c] Based on the Pattern data (Sears, Maccoby, & Levin, 1957).
Source. Adapted from Johnson and Medinnus, 1965, p. 284.

important as the Autocratic-Democratic one in terms of its effects on the child's personality development, the research is relatively meager and less clear-cut. Undoubtedly this stems from the methodological difficulties encountered in assessing parental acceptance of the child. Kinstler (Selection #9) employed judges' ratings in constructing a scale to assess covert and overt aspects of maternal rejection and acceptance of the child. Medinnus and Curtis (Selection #10) operationally defined maternal acceptance as the distance between the mothers' ratings of "my child as he really is" and "my child as I would like him to be" on twenty pairs of bipolar adjectives. Hurley's study (Selection #11) raises a question concerning the relation between acceptance and punitiveness, since his acceptance index is based largely on parental responses to punishment-type situations.

The first selection in Part B suggests a relation between the mother's authoritarian attitudes toward child rearing and her behavior in the maternal role in terms of disciplinary techniques employed. The Hoffman (Selection #13) and Watson (Selection #14) investigations list a variety of personality and behavioral consequences in the child stemming from autocratic parental behavior.

The fact that research has been successful in showing relations between child behavior and the autocratic-democratic parental dimension points strongly to the usefulness of this dimension in further parent-child research. Although less research evidence is available concerning the effects of parental acceptance or rejection on child behavior and personality, a great many clinical reports have dealt with this variable. The development of a valid measure for assessing parental acceptance is an important research task for the future.

References

Baldwin, A. L., Kalhorn, Joan, & Breese, Fay H. Patterns of parent behavior. *Psychological Monographs,* 1945, **58,** No. 3.

Baldwin, A. L., Kalhorn, Joan, & Breese, Fay H. The appraisal of parent behavior. *Psychological Monographs,* 1949, **63,** No. 4.

Lorr, M., & Jenkins, R. L. Three factors in parent behavior. *Journal of Consulting Psychology,* 1953, **17,** 306–308.

Milton, G. A. A factor analytic study of child-rearing behavior. *Child Development,* 1958, **29,** 381–392.

Roff, M. A factorial study of the Fels Parent Behavior Scales. *Child Development,* 1949, **20,** 20–45.

Schaefer, E. S. A circumplex model for maternal behavior. *Journal of Abnormal and Social Psychology,* 1959, **59,** 226–235.

Sears, R. R., Maccoby, Eleanor E., & Levin, H. *Patterns of child rearing.* Evanston, Ill.: Row, Peterson, 1957.

Symonds, P. M. *The psychology of parent-child relationships.* New York: Appleton-Century-Crofts, 1939.

Zuckerman, M., Ribback, Beatrice B., Monashkin, I., & Norton, J. Normative data and factor analysis on the Parental Attitude Research Instrument. *Journal of Consulting Psychology,* 1958, **22,** 165–171.

Part A   Acceptance-Rejection
Dimension

9. COVERT AND OVERT MATERNAL REJECTION IN STUTTERING

DONALD BUTLER KINSTLER

Parental acceptance or rejection of the child is believed by a number of speech clinicians to be a primary factor in the etiology of the stuttering symptom. Although the direct actions of parents toward their children are unquestionably critical, perhaps far more important for the children's mental health are the parents' underlying feelings and attitudes. Symonds (14, p. 13) has stated this very precisely: "The essence of parent-child relations . . . lies more in how a parent *feels* than in what a parent *does*." Baldwin, Kalhorn, and Breese (1), in a detailed observational study of parent-child relationships, reached the conclusion that "acceptance-rejection is the fundamental dynamic: it is the amount of acceptance which determines and delimits the other aspects of parental behavior."

Horney (6, p. 80) has described the covert or subtle rejection of the child as essentially devastating. She says that, in the childhood history of neurotic patients, she finds that "the basic evil is invariably a lack of genuine warmth and affection" and that this is all the more shattering if this lack is hidden or disguised.

Clinical observation based upon individual and group psychotherapy with stutterers suggests that one of the strongest feelings of many stutterers is the feeling of covert or hidden rejection by the mother. Judging from the reports of stutterers in therapy, overt or undisguised rejection on the part of the mother is less damaging.

Parental attitudes containing rejection as a hidden element constitute more of a trap for the child than outright rejection, which would allow him to hate his parents for their unfair behavior. The parents do not give love, but at the same time they either cannot see this or they do not allow themselves to recognize it. They pretend to be acting in the child's best interests and thus allow him no legitimate or justifiable outlet for his aggression. He is constantly frustrated, but he may not express the resulting hostility. He is forced to repress his aggressive feelings and, having learned that speech can be a weapon, he must withhold this most natural vehicle for the expression of his feelings. This might result in no speech at all, which in our culture is

Reprinted with abridgement from the *Journal of Speech and Hearing Disorders,* 1961, **26,** 145–155, with permission of the author and the American Speech and Hearing Association.

nearly impossible for any appreciable length of time, or it could result in a partial involuntary withholding of speech—stuttering.

A number of studies deal with parental attitudes and their influence upon personality development. Witmer (15) found that parental attitudes were useful as an index of probable success in clinical work with children. Symonds (14, pp. 18–28) reported correlation between child behavior and parental rejection. Levy (7) described relationships between the child's pattern of adjustment and maternal overprotection.

In the field of speech pathology there have been very few reported attempts to measure parental attitudes in the etiology of stuttering. Darley (4, pp. 142–143), comparing the responses of parents of stutterers with a control group, found only minute differences in the attitudes of the two groups. Moncur (10) attempted to evaluate the parental domination of the child as a possible factor in the development of stuttering, with somewhat inconclusive findings. Duncan (5) used the Bell Adjustment Inventory to analyze the general relationships within the home of the stuttering child and found that the home adjustment of the stutterer is comparatively poorer than that of the child with normal speech. McCarthy (8) found that the parents of stutterers tend to be "tense, perfectionistic parents . . . whose overprotectiveness is often a disguise for real rejecting attitudes."

In spite of the fact that there has been surprising agreement among authorities as to the relevance of parental attitudes to the emotional difficulties of children, there have been very few studies dealing with attempts to devise scales or measuring devices in order to evaluate these attitudes. Merrill (9) and Brody (2) employed the method of direct observation which, while of demonstrable value for research, offers little practical help for the practicing clinician. Champney (3) developed the Fels Parent Behavior Scale which provides a more readily usable measuring instrument but has the limitations of being time-consuming and expensive and of requiring the use of trained personnel. The inventory questionnaire as used by Darley (4), Shoben (12), Stogdill (13), and Sears, Maccoby, and Levin (11) seems to offer a number of advantages, ease of administration, economy, and comprehensiveness of information obtained.

PROBLEM

This study was formulated in an attempt (a) to create a usable scale which would differentiate between the attitudes of mothers of stutterers and .the mothers of children with normal speech and (b) to test the clinical hypothesis that the mothers of stutterers reveal a greater degree of covert or hidden rejection than do the mothers of normal speakers. Corollary hypotheses were that the mothers of stutterers display less overt or manifest rejection, less covert or hidden acceptance, and more overt acceptance than do the mothers of normal speakers.

This formulation was based upon a concept of covert rejection, the implication of which was that the mother may not and will not openly reveal her lack of love for the child. Therefore, it was hypothesized, she will avoid rejecting her child openly and will display much overt or manifest acceptance while she withholds the covert or implicit acceptance which depends upon her basic satisfaction with the child and respect for his individuality.

PROCEDURE

It was decided to create a scaling model in the form of a self-inventory questionnaire. A projective questionnaire was constructed which consisted, in its final form, of 92 statements combining general statements of opinion and statements more directly revealing the subjects' own practices. Subjects were required to make a forced choice expressing "agreement" or "disagreement" with each item on a six-point scale ranging from "strongly agree" to "strongly disagree."

The following items comprise the U.S.C. Maternal Attitude Scale used in this study. Items 59 and 78 were omitted.

1. I'd prefer not to have any more children.
2. I believe parents need to have holidays from children.
3. Children should be told to say, "I love you."
4. I should listen to my child whether interested in what he's saying or not.
5. I feel better when I buy my child a gift.
6. A child should be made to feel what he should do without my having to order him to do it.
7. I should always act as if I love my child even if I don't.
8. I try not to express anger with my child openly.
9. I always try to do what's best for the child's sake whether he likes it or not.
10. A mother should sacrifice her own desires for what is best for her children.
11. A mother should help her children even if they don't request help.
12. A child should be a good reflection on his parents.
13. I feel it is my duty to show my child that what I want is for his sake.
14. Any parent should be proud to have a child who is almost always well-mannered.
15. Any parent should be proud to have a child who keeps himself neat and clean.
16. Any parent should be proud to have a child who hardly ever is noisy and quarrelsome at home.
17. Any parent should be proud to have a child who does what he is told most of the time.
18. Any parent should be proud to have a child who has rarely shown any sexual curiosity.
19. Any parent should be proud to have a child who was toilet-trained early.
20. Any parent should be proud to have a child who rarely cries.
21. Any parent should be proud to have a child who is weaned early from the bottle.

22. Self-control and self-sacrifice are two of the most desirable traits of a good mother.

23. A baby can be spoiled if he is picked up whenever he cries.

24. A child will be spoiled if he gets his own way too much when he is small.

25. A mother should stop nursing her baby if her doctor tells her he is big enough for a bottle.

26. I find my child exceptionally attractive.

27. A mother should be proud to have a baby who is weaned early from the breast.

28. It's quite normal for a mother to be relieved when her children start school.

29. Children restrict the social activities I would like to have.

30. Children should learn not to upset a neatly kept house.

31. It is better for a child to learn to leave things alone than to have to put things out of his reach.

32. Playing with children should wait until the housework is done.

33. It is better for a mother to hold in her anger when upset by her child's conduct.

34. A mother should intervene in children's quarrels if there is a possibility that one might be hurt.

35. The older child should be held responsible in his play with younger children.

36. A baby should never be neglected, even if it makes the older child resentful.

37. A mother should encourage her child to follow the example of another child's good behavior.

38. It disturbs me when my child is not superior to other children.

39. I rarely forgot the feeding hour.

40. I more often punish the child by confinement to his room than by spanking.

41. I more often punish by removal of privileges than by spanking.

42. Much delinquent behavior could be eliminated if parents taught their children control by stronger disciplinary measures.

43. The alarming growth in juvenile delinquency may be attributed in part to lax methods of discipline.

44. Most juvenile delinquency could be avoided if young people were kept busy.

45. I have often wished that I were single again.

46. Parents can control children by giving them gifts for good behavior.

47. If a child is warned enough about bad behavior, he may not have to be punished so much.

48. Turning over discipline to my spouse is often more effective than handling it myself.

49. Deliberate disobedience should be punished severely, especially if it might lead to endangering the child's health.

50. A good scolding seems to work better with my children than spanking.

51. I often have to "keep after" my child to get him to do things.

52. The reason more "gifted" children are from upper-class families is that these families have higher standards.

53. It is impossible to "spoil" a baby by too much indulgence.

54. I am unconcerned when my child makes a mess around the house.

55. Neatness and orderliness are taught by early training.

56. There are many occasions when children should be seen and not heard.

57. A good way to increase a child's motivation to do better in school is to offer him a prize for improved grades.

58. I would be satisfied if my child made "D" grades at school.

59. I should hear my child just as soon as he starts to cry at night even if I am asleep.

60. I pay little attention to my child's expression of "mean" or hostile feelings.

61. I would like to have a trustworthy baby sitter two or three times a week.

62. I don't like children to play together if they don't get along with each other.

63. Parents should lavish their children with praise for their achievements at school.

64. My child is generally capable of making decisions for himself.

65. A child should be given music, dancing, or swimming lessons, even if he is not interested.

66. A parent should feel responsible for seeing his child do his homework.

67. A parent should expect his child to behave better in public than at home.

68. I frequently try to help my child by correcting his mistakes.

69. I don't like my child to eat dirt or grass.

70. I like to hold my child whether he is dirty or clean.

71. I am apt to be impatient if my child interrupts me when I'm speaking to adults.

72. I spank my child when he is disobedient.

73. I always permit my child to have a light burning or his door open at night if he wants it.

74. I do not permit my child to climb tall trees.

75. I try to discourage my child from playing in mud and dirt.

76. I punish temper tantrums firmly and promptly.

77. It is easy for me to tell my child that I love him.

78. I feel that some of my child's friends are a bad influence on him.

79. I generally insist that my child eat what I believe to be best for him.

80. I dislike changing my child's dirty diapers.

81. A child should be disciplined when he soils his pants after he starts toilet training.

82. Parents should be disturbed if their child fails to progress at the rate they know he should.

83. Children should be allowed to fight freely with their brothers and sisters.

84. I do not allow my child to say, "I hate you."

85. I allow my child to eat pretty much what he wants.

86. If my child sucked his thumb, I would try to discourage him by some form of discipline.

87. Children should be permitted to talk whenever they wish.
88. It is better to let a baby cry it out than to pick him up every time he cries if there seems to be nothing wrong with him.
89. I am greatly annoyed when my child whines or cries for long periods.
90. I don't let my child use crying as a device to get out of a bad situation.
91. I meet my child's demands for attention with firm but moderate discipline.
92. Mothers should feel free to work outside the home if they can find a good baby sitter for their children.

The subjects of this study were 60 white urban mothers, of whom 30 mothers of stuttering children comprised the experimental group and 30 mothers of children with normal speech comprised the control group.

The two groups were matched as closely as possible for age, education, socioeconomic status, and incidence of psychological counseling or therapy. Age and sex of children, number of children, religion, and education of husbands were also matched although it was believed that these factors were not critical.

A description of the attitude universe is necessary in order to determine whether a scale measures this universe. One method of determining whether a scale does measure its universe (or is intrinsically valid) is to study the judgments of a group of experts. To judge the individual items, 26 experts were selected, including clinical psychologists, psychiatrists, professors of speech pathology, professors of psychology, and speech pathologists in private practice. Each judge was requested to evaluate the scale as if a subject had answered the questionnaire with all 'agree' responses or as if all responses had been "disagree." The judges' ratings were tabulated and the modal trend for each item was considered to be the valid rating for that item in terms of overt or covert rejection, or overt or covert acceptance.

RESULTS

The results of the pairings with the covert rejection category are shown in Table 1. The total number of responses favoring covert rejection was considerably greater for the experimental group (56 to 23) with the largest

Table 1 *Responses Favoring Covert Rejection when Paired with Covert Acceptance, Implied Acceptance, Overt Rejection, and Undifferentiated Acceptance*

Group	r-A	r-a	r-R	r-a/A	Total
Experimental	15	24	12	5	56
Control	11	10	0	2	23
Total	26	34	12	7	79

Table 2 *Responses Favoring Overt Rejection when Paired With Covert Acceptance and when Paired with Overt Acceptance.*

Group	R-a	R-A	Total
Experimental	0	3	3
Control	4	4	8
Total	4	7	11

difference between the two groups falling in the covert rejection-overt rejection category (12 to zero) and the next largest difference in the covert rejection-covert acceptance category (24 to 10). Grouping those responses favoring overt rejection is shown in Table 2. The total number of responses favoring overt rejection was greater among the control group (eight to three) with the largest difference in the overt rejection-covert acceptance category (four to zero). Reversing the pairings in order to measure covert and overt acceptance is shown in Table 3.

The experimental group showed more accepting responses only in the categories of covert acceptance-overt rejection (four to zero), and overt acceptance-overt rejection (four to three). When acceptance was paired with overt rejection, the experimental group tended more to choose acceptance, but when the acceptance was paired with covert rejection the experimental group tended more toward covert rejection. These pairings of responses are consolidated in Table 4.

Chi-square test for significance, when applied to these responses, yielded a value of 28.65. Since for four degrees of freedom p is 13.277 at the .01 level of confidence, these responses may be considered to be significant at far better than the .01 level of confidence.

This result was based upon the differences in proportion of response to each category for each group, derived by the method described earlier, and included all items which exhibited small differences which were discriminative

Table 3 *Selection of Covert Acceptance when Paired with Covert Rejection and Overt Rejection, of Overt Acceptance when Paired with Covert Rejection and with Overt Rejection, and of Undifferentiated acceptance Paired with Covert Rejection*

Group	a-r	a-R	A-r	A-R	a/A-r	Total
Experimental	10	4	11	4	2	31
Control	24	0	15	3	5	47
Total	34	4	26	7	7	78

Table 4   *Total Responses Favoring Covert Rejection, Overt Rejection,
Covert Acceptance, Overt Acceptance, and Undifferentiated
Acceptance. The Scale Originally Contained 92 Items. One
Item Was Dropped Because the Judges Could Not Agree upon
Its Evaluation and One Item Did Not Discriminate between
the Two Groups, Bringing the Total to 90 Items.*

Group	r	R	a	A	a/A	Total
Experimental	56	3	14	15	2	90
Control	23	20	24	18	5	90
Total	79	23	38	33	7	180

and constituted trends toward agreement with the category, as well as those
items which discriminated at the higher levels of confidence.

Consolidation of all acceptance and rejection responses is show in Table
5. These responses are significant at the .02 level of confidence (chi square is
5.8, one degree of freedom) with the experimental group favoring rejection
very nearly twice as often as it favored acceptance, in contrast to the control
group's approximate 52 per cent acceptance and 48 per cent rejection.

DISCUSSION

The hypothesis that this study was designed to test, that the mothers of
young male stutterers tend to reject their children in a covert or hidden
fashion more than do the mothers of young nonstuttering males, was based
upon clinical observations made by the experimenter and by others practicing
in the field of speech pathology. Although many clinicians have long suspected
that rejection is an element in the mother-child relationship which might
contribute to the phenomenon of emotional disorder in the child, relatively
few have investigated the significance of the kind of rejection involved.
Clinical work with male stutterers has often revealed the apparent paradox
that many male stutterers, while seemingly incapable of recalling any specific
rejective acts or rejective attitudes on the parts of their mothers, have nevertheless described a vague intuitive awareness of being rejected.

Table 5   *Consolidation of Acceptance and Rejection
Responses*

Group	Acceptance	Rejection	Total
Experimental	31	59	90
Control	47	43	90
Total	78	102	180

It was suspected that this vaguely felt rejection was real and that the mother did reject the child in ways which were not easily perceived or understood by him. The corresponding 'acceptance' of the child would then, at least hypothetically, tend to be of an obvious socially approved type while the more subtle or hidden acceptance which grows out of complete inner satisfaction with the child would be lacking or in relatively short supply. In so far as the U.S.C. Maternal Attitude Survey is a valid measure of the arbitrarily labeled concepts of covert and overt rejection and covert and overt acceptance, this theory seems to be substantiated by the results obtained.

The total number of responses in which covert rejection was favored was much greater for the experimental group. The experimental group mothers tended to favor covert rejection in 56 items as compared to 23 items in which the control group mothers favored this type of rejection. This is a ratio of almost two and one-half to one. The implication of this finding is that, although the mothers of young male nonstutterers also reject their children in a hidden fashion, they tend to reject in this way much less frequently than do the mothers of young male stutterers. This may account for the belief expressed by some stutterers that they feel rejected but cannot pin-point the source of this feeling or recall specific rejective actions which may justify or explain it.

The paired categories, between which the choices had to be made by the subjects, clearly affected their responses. When covert rejection was paired with the alternative of overt or open acceptance, the experimental group mothers chose covert rejection in 15 items as compared to 11 items chosen by the mothers of the control group. In this grouping there was only a slight tendency toward more covert rejection by the experimental group. This is possibly due to the tendency of these mothers to choose obvious and socially approved manifestations of love which can be perceived readily by the people about them. This "acceptance" may be a means by which the mother's anxiety about her child can be alleviated.

In contrast, when covert rejection was paired with covert acceptance, the experimental group preferred covert rejection in 24 items while the control group preferred covert rejection in only 10 items. The ratio, again, is almost two and one-half to one in favor of covert rejection by the experimental group. The experimental mothers tended to choose rejection when the alternative was implicit or hidden acceptance, which is not highly visible and which depends upon a basic internal satisfaction with the child and respect for him as an individual.

Perhaps the most dramatic difference occurred in the pairing of covert rejection with overt rejection. The experimental mothers chose covert rejection in all 12 items while the control mothers chose overt rejection for all 12. This finding seemed to substantiate the clinical observation that the mothers of stutterers were, at least superficially, nonrejecting in their relationships with their children. Straightforward and undisguised rejective acts may not be performed by the mothers of the experimental group, although they tend to reject their children in subtle hidden ways of which they themselves may not be aware.

The experimental group mothers differed very little from the control group mothers when overt rejection was paired with overt acceptance, choosing overt rejection in three items as compared to the choice of four items by the control group. The allure in overt acceptance for the experimental group is clearly demonstrated in this choice contrasted with its choice of no items favoring covert acceptance when paired with overt rejection.

Consolidating the acceptance responses, the experimental group chose acceptance in 31 items as compared with the control group's selection of acceptance in 47 items. The ratio is about one and one-half to one in favor of acceptance by the control group, but again the critical difference is apparent in the distribution of the categories. In the choice of overt acceptance there is little to choose between the two groups, but in the choice of covert acceptance the difference is marked. The control group chose covert acceptance in 24 items and the experimental group chose covert acceptance in only 14 items, a ratio of about eight to five. If the undifferentiated acceptance items (which are probably closer to covert than to overt acceptance in that they are not readily seen to be overt acceptance and thus not clearly socially approved) are grouped with the covert acceptance responses, the result is a score of 29 acceptance responses for the control group and only 16 acceptance responses for the experimental group. The ratio is then nearly two to one for the control mothers' selection of covert acceptance over the experimental group's choice.

Several generalizations based upon these findings may be stated: (a) Mothers of young male stutterers tend more to reject their children covertly than do mothers of young male nonstutterers. (b) Mothers of young male stutterers tend to avoid overt or obvious rejection of their children. (c) Mothers of young male stutterers tend to accept their children in overt, socially approved ways only slightly less than do the mothers of young male nonstutterers. The mother of the stutterer is seen by the casual observer to be a 'good' and accepting parent. (d) Mothers of young male stutterers tend less frequently to accept their children in the covert or hidden ways which are the expression of the mother's inner satisfaction and contentment than do the mothers of nonstutterers.

Predicated upon the assumption that the judges employed in the study were truly expert in their evaluations of the categories and upon the assumption that the population tested was a representative one, the central hypothesis—that the mothers of young male stutterers tend to reject their children covertly rather than overtly, and that their accepting attitudes tend to consist more in open or manifest acceptance than in covert or implied acceptance—appears to have been rather directly corroborated.

The dynamics involving these concepts which are operative in the mother-child relationship might be hypothesized somewhat as follows: If a mother rejects her child in a hidden fashion, never giving him a reasonable justification for the hostility which inevitably arises from his frustrated needs for warmth and affection, she thereby lays the foundation for a basic insecurity. If she compounds this insecurity by manifestly accepting him in many of the socially approved ways while withholding the implicit acceptance which depends upon trust in him and respect for his identity, she cannot help but add to the unexpressed and inexpressible feelings of hostility within him. Because he can find no plausible justification for his surges of anger against an apparently blameless and devoted mother, his rage is accompanied by feelings of guilt which not only make it more difficult for him to vent his anger but add immeasurably to his misery. If, in addition, these events occur at about the time that he first learns that speech can be used as a weapon, it seems quite possible that this insecure and frustrated child, in his fear of expressing dangerous feelings, might find stuttering a relatively safe and anxiety-reducing symptom.

Undoubtedly the hypothetical case outlined, which is based upon a particular psychological viewpoint, is not a definitive explanation, and probably other elements contribute equally to produce the stuttering symptom. It may, however, serve to illustrate one fairly reasonable possibility in an area characterized by great uncertainty, diametrically opposed theories, and endless speculation.

The implications of this study should be of value in the treatment of stutterers, and in the guidance and counseling of the parents of stutterers. It is also possible that these implications may have a wider scope and that the same factors believed to be operative in the etiology of stuttering may apply to other emotional disorders growing out of disturbances in the mother-child relationship.

SUMMARY

An experimental group of 30 mothers of young male stutterers and a control group of 30 mothers were matched for age, education, size of family, age of children, socioeconomic status, religion, psychological guidance, and education of spouses. Both groups were administered a projective-type questionnaire designed to measure covert rejection, overt rejection, covert acceptance, and overt acceptance. The results yielded significant differences in the pattern of responses. Chi-square analysis yielded a value better than the one per cent level of confidence. Conclusions derived from this study include the following: (*a*) Mothers of young male stutterers reject their children covertly far more but overtly far less than do the mothers of normal speakers. (*b*) Mothers of stutterers accept their children covertly less and overtly only slightly less than do the mothers of normal speakers. (c) Mothers of stutterers reject their children more than they accept them while mothers of normal speakers accept their children more than they reject them.

REFERENCES

1. Baldwin, A. L., Kalhorn, J., and Breese F. H. Patterns of parent behavior. *Psychol. Monogr.*, 1945, **58**, 1–75.
2. Brody, S. *Patterns of mothering: maternal influence during infancy.* New York: International Univ. Press, 1956.
3. Champney, H. The variables of parent behavior. *Abnorm. (soc.) Psychol.*, 1941, **36**, 525–542.
4. Darley, F. L. The relationship of parental attitudes and adjustments to the development of stuttering. In W. Johnson (Ed.), *Stuttering in children and adults*, Minneapolis: Univ. Minnesota Press, 1945.
5. Duncan, M. H. Home adjustment of stutterers versus non-stutterers. *J. Speech Hearing Dis.*, 1949, **14**, 255–259.
6. Horney, K. *The neurotic personality of our time.* New York: W. W. Norton, 1937.
7. Levy, D. M. Maternal overprotection. *Psychiatry*, 1938, **2**, 99–128.
8. McCarthy, D. Language disorder and parent-child relationships. *J. Speech Hearing Dis.*, 1954, **19**, 514–523.
9. Merrill, B. A measurement of mother-child interaction. *J. abnorm. (soc.) Psychol.*, 1946, **41**, 37–49.
10. Moncur, J. P. Parental domination in stuttering. *J. Speech Hearing Dis.*, 1952, **17**, 155–165.
11. Sears, R. R., Maccoby, E. E., and Levin, H. *Patterns of child rearing.* Evanston: Row, Peterson, 1957.
12. Shoben, E. J. The assessment of parent attitudes in relation to child adjustment. *Genet. Psychol. Monogr.*, 1949, **39**, 101–148.
13. Stogdill, R. M. Attitudes of parents, students, and mental hygienists toward children's behavior. *J. soc. Psychol.*, 1933, **4**, 486–489.
14. Symonds, P. M. *Dynamics of parent-child relationships.* New York: Columbia Univ. Press, 1949.
15. Witmer, H. L. Parental behavior as an index to the probable outcome of treatment in a child guidance clinic. *Amer. J. Orthopsychiat.*, 1933, **3**, 431–444.

10. THE RELATION BETWEEN MATERNAL

SELF-ACCEPTANCE AND CHILD ACCEPTANCE

Gene R. Medinnus and Floyd J. Curtis

Assessment of parental attitudes has received a tremendous amount of attention in research concerned with factors influencing the child's personality development. While the content of most current parent attitude tests focuses on the parent's attitude toward a number of aspects of child rearing, of at least equal importance is the parent's attitude toward the individual child in terms of an acceptance-rejection dimension. In case studies of emotionally disturbed children, the inference frequently is made that one or both of the parents reject the child. Support for the emphasis on the importance of parental acceptance comes also from factor analyses of parent behavior ratings (Schaefer, 1959) and of parent attitude scales (Zuckerman, Ribback, Monashkin, and Norton, 1958). In both analyses, an acceptance-rejection factor appeared in addition to an authoritarian-democratic one.

A number of personality theorists have suggested that the attitudes held toward the self are reflected in the attitudes held toward others. Fromm (1939), for example, maintains that self-love and the love of others go hand in hand. He notes that a failure to love the self is accompanied by a basic hostility toward others. Horney (1950) feels that the person who does not love himself is incapable of loving others. Rogers (1951) argues that when a client enters therapy he typically holds a negative self-concept; he is unable to accept himself. However, once the client becomes more accepting of himself, he begins to be more accepting of others.

The attitudes which a child holds toward himself, especially those dealing with self-esteem and self-worth, play an important role in his personality development. The extent to which a child develops a positive self-concept depends crucially upon the extent to which he is accepted by the "significant others" (typically his parents) in the early years.

While numerous studies could be cited showing a relation between self-acceptance and acceptance of others, a majority of these have used as subjects college students or individuals receiving counseling or therapy. There is almost no research evidence for the relation between parental self-acceptance and acceptance of the child, though several investigations have described the effects on the child's personality development of parental nonacceptance.

Reprinted from the *Journal of Consulting Psychology*, 1963, **27**, 542–544, with permission of the senior author and the American Psychological Association.

Most of this research has dealt with clinic populations, however, and the research involving normal parents and children is meager and less confirmatory.

HYPOTHESIS

The purpose of the present investigation was to test the hypothesis that there is a significant positive relation between self-acceptance and child acceptance in a nonclinical group of mothers of young children.

METHOD

Subjects

Fifty-six mothers of children enrolled in a parent-participating cooperative nursery school served as subjects. The mothers ranged in age from 25 to 45 years with a mean of 32; years of education ranged from 11 to 18 with a mean of 14. The children in the nursery school on whom the mothers made the ratings ranged in age from 3 to 5 with a mean of 4 years.

Procedure

Two measures of self-acceptance and one measure of child acceptance were administered during two consecutive meetings of the mother group. The self-acceptance measures were the Bills Index of Adjustment and Values (Bills, Vance, and McLean, 1951) and a semantic differential scale of 20 bipolar adjectives in which the distance (D) between the mothers' ratings of "Me (as I am)" and "Me (as I would most like to be)" was defined operationally as the extent of self-acceptance. The child acceptance measure consisted of the same set of bipolar adjectives with the distance between the mothers' ratings of "My child (as he is)" and "My child (as I would most like him to be)" defined as the extent of maternal acceptance of the child.

RESULTS AND DISCUSSION

The intercorrelations among the three self-regard scores and the child acceptance measure are provided in Table 1. All of the coefficients are in the expected direction; the negative correlations are due to the method of scoring the tests. On the Bills self-acceptance measure, the higher scores indicate greater self-acceptance while the Bills adjustment scores and the semantic differential self-acceptance scores are discrepancy scores with the higher scores denoting less favorable self-attitudes. The findings strongly support the hypothesis of a significant positive relation between maternal self-acceptance and child acceptance.

It is likely that the present sample of mothers was restricted in terms

Table 1 *Correlations Among Maternal Self-Acceptance and Child Acceptance Measures*

Measures	Bills Self-Acceptance	Bills Adjustment	Semantic Differential Child Acceptance
Semantic differential self-acceptance	−.57 [b]	.53 [b]	.33 [a]
Bills self-acceptance		−.57 [b]	−.48 [a]
Bills adjustment			.28

[a] $p < .05$.
[b] $p < .01$.

of the child acceptance dimension. The mothers were concerned and interested enough in their children to spend the considerable time and effort which is involved in participation in the cooperative nursery school. Since moderate correlations were obtained in this rather restricted range of subjects, one might expect higher correlations to emerge in a study of mothers randomly selected from the general population.

The validity of the measure employed to assess child acceptance remains to be established. Subsequent research may show that factors in the parent-child relationship other than acceptance are reflected in this instrument. However, the fact that positive results were obtained in the present study suggests that the semantic differential approach holds promise as an instrument for assessing the dimension of parental acceptance of the child. The technique is easy to administer and score, and its purpose in assessing child acceptance appears to be somewhat disguised.

The present findings suggest that the area of parental self-acceptance merits intensive study in any attempt to identify antecedents of child acceptance, an important element in the child's self-acceptance and in his personality development in general.

REFERENCES

1. Bills, R. E., Vance, E. L., & McLean, O. S. An index of adjustment and values. *J. consult. Psychol.,* 1951, **15,** 257–261.
2. Fromm, E. Selfishness and self-love. *Psychiatry,* 1939, **2,** 507–523.
3. Horney, Karen. *Neurosis and human growth.* New York: Norton, 1950.
4. Rogers, C. *Client-centered therapy.* Boston: Houghton Mifflin, 1951.
5. Schaefer, E. S. A circumplex model for maternal behavior. *J. abnorm. soc. Psychol.,* 1959, **59,** 226–235.
6. Zuckerman, M., Barrett-Ribback, Beatrice, Monashkin, I., & Norton, J. Normative data and factor analysis on the parental attitude research instrument. *J. consult. Psychol.,* 1958, **22,** 165–171.

11. PARENTAL ACCEPTANCE-REJECTION AND CHILDREN'S INTELLIGENCE

John R. Hurley

Broad evidence of the enduring impact of early experience upon subsequent behaviors and the young child's plain dependence upon adult nurturance for sheer physical survival suggest that parental child care beliefs, attitudes, and broad predispositions should relate importantly to children's behavior. Prominent among the facets of children's behavior which have most interested psychologists are those subsumed under the rubric of intelligence, despite the ambiguities of this concept (Liverant, 1960). Perhaps salient among the major dimensions of parental child-rearing practices is the "acceptance-rejection" (A-R) variable empirically identified by Baldwin, Kalhorn, and Breese (1945) as a principal dimension undergirding observers' ratings of parental reactions to children within the home. A similar variable, "hostility-rejection," was later cited as the most unambiguous major factor (Zuckerman, et al., 1958) in the independently developed Parental Attitude Research Instrument (Schafer and Bell, 1958). The A-R variable seems identifiable in several other major investigations of parental behavior patterns (Radke, 1946; Sewell, Mussen, and Harris, 1955; Sears, Maccoby, and Levin, 1957; Milton, 1958) as well as highly pertinent to, but not identical with, Bowlby's (1952) concept of maternal deprivation as a subvariety of the "masked deprivation" (Prugh and Harlow, 1962) or "distorted mothering" (Yarrow, 1962) case.

For present purposes, acceptance is conceptualized as representing one extreme of a bipolar continuum, epitomized by parental behaviors oriented toward encouraging the child to interact fully and freely with the environment within a context of parental approval and support, with minimal reliance upon techniques of coercive control. Rejection, representing the opposite pole of this continuum, is viewed as defined by parental behaviors oriented toward constricting and limiting the child's inclinations to freely explore the physical, interpersonal, and ideational aspects of the environment and communicated by a heavy parental commitment to coercive techniques such as intimidations, punishment, and other fear-inducing behaviors. While this abstraction plainly sidesteps other major variables influencing the child-parent relationship—and ignores the likely prospect that both accept-

Reprinted with slight abridgement from the *Merrill-Palmer Quarterly*, 1965, **11**, 19–31, with permission of the author and the Merrill-Palmer Quarterly.

ance and rejection may have many important subdimensions—such complexities are beyond the scope of this paper.

It is intriguing that the relationship between children's intelligence and parental A-R has remained so obscure as to be generally skirted by writers of contemporary Child Psychology textbooks (Watson, 1959; Mussen, Conger, and Kagan, 1963) despite the apparent significance of the A-R variable. This vacuum does not seem attributable to a dearth of relevant theory. Parental rejection of the child, whether expressed subtly and indirectly due to parental fears of social disapproval, or more overtly manifested through general negligence or even by direct punishment and attack on the child, would seem to carry a common core of unpleasant affective experience for the child. These unhappy experiences, particularly when delivered by persons controlling the child's food and love supplies, might commonly be expected, according to general behavior theory (Dollard and Miller, 1950), to result in the extinction of approach responses toward environmental objects associated with such persons and the simultaneous acquisition of avoidance responses, perhaps including the "stopping thinking" response. It seems only a minor restatement of this formulation to suggest that such aversive conditioning by the principal persons in the child's life would commonly generalize to related environmental objects and tasks. Within the realm of cognitive operations, the child experiencing such rejection might typically be expected to show a decreased curiosity in exploring and manipulating the world of people, objects, and ideas—due to a prepotent general state of inhibition and discouragement, resulting from prior traumatic encounters and subjectively correlated expectations that further harassment will result from any new "misbehaviors."

Methodological obstacles may have obscured an earlier grasp of this phenomenon. It seems reasonable that the impact of parental A-R would be most apparent during the early years of childhood, when dependency upon parents is greatest and confounding contacts with peers, teachers, and other adults are more limited. Before the age of about six years, however, conventional intellectual measures are of dubious validity (Bradway, 1944; Pinneau, 1962). It is not until children become of school age that intellective measures possessing well-substantiated predictive validity become available.

It is near this very point in the child's development, however, when the sex-typing and identification phenomena assume major importance as boys tend to switch allegiance from maternal to paternal role-models while girls generally continue to identify with their mothers. Given the much greater contact between mother and child than between father and child which characterizes U.S. culture, the net effect of these identification processes would suggest at least the continuation and perhaps strengthening of high daughter-sensitivity to maternal behaviors and feelings, during this period when male children are typically identifying more closely with their fathers and becoming less sensitive to maternal controls. This formulation is empirically supported by the recent findings of Eron (1961), and those of Adams and Sarason (1963).

The following hypotheses seem consistent with these considerations.

1. During the early school years children's intelligence should be enhanced by parental acceptance and diminished by parental rejection.

2. Given greater contact between mother and child than occurs between father and child, children's intelligence during the early school years should relate more highly to maternal A-R than with paternal A-R.

3. The inverse relationship between parental A-R and the child's intelligence should be greater between mother-daughter pairs than in the case of mother-son, father-son, or father-daughter pairs.

Due to pervasive evidence of relationships between socio-economic status (SES) and such behavioral variables as intelligence (Wechsler, 1958) and child-rearing practices (Miller and Swanson, 1960), findings consistent with these hypotheses will be further scrutinized to see if they may be readily attributed to the influence of SES and level of parental education.

PROCEDURE

Acceptance-Rejection Indices

Two distinct methods were utilized to provide A-R measures. One was a postal questionnaire requesting the mothers and fathers of the third graders to react independently to separate copies of a series of items dealing with child-rearing practices. Its principal component was a set of 30 items concerning the general inclination of parents to endorse a "tough" disciplinary policy toward children. Called the Manifest Rejection (MR) index, this measure utilized a variation of the "reversed subscales" procedure shown effective in restraining the influence of the acquiescence (Zuckerman, 1959) and social desirability (Taylor, 1962) response sets. The questionnaire format required endorsement of one of the following choices for each item: strongly agree, mildly agree, neither agree nor disagree, mildly disagree, and strongly disagree. An important feature of the MR index was that extreme scores could only be obtained by systematically "agreeing" with certain items and by "disagreeing" with their counterparts. Representative items with high item vs. total MR correlations were: (1) "When parents speak, children should obey." (2) "It is good for children to sometimes 'talk-back' to their parents."

Two separate measures of one's tendency to punish children were obtained from most of these parents, from among many specific pieces of information acquired within several months of the postal questionnaire, through an individual pre-coded interview of about ninety minutes duration (Walder, Eron, Lefkowitz, and Toigo, 1962). One of these measures, called the Punishment index (PUN) (Eron, 1961, p. 25), consisted of 24 items categorized under physical punishment, love-withdrawal, restraint, isolation, shame, threat, and corrective reasoning. Only direct parental acknowledgments that they might employ the described punishment with their own third-grade child were scored positively. Representative items were: (1) "If (child's name) got very mad at you, would you slap him/her in the face?" (2) "Would you tell (child's name) you don't love him/her for getting very mad at you?"

The other interview-based A-R index was somewhat projective in character. It required parents to indicate how they viewed a series of common punishments, such as "giving (child's name) an angry look," along a numbered scale with anchoring points of "very mild" (No. 1) and "very harsh" (No. 8). Total scores on this judgment of punishment (JP) index represented the sum of numerical scores over a series of thirteen such items.

Socio-Economic Status and Level of Parent Education

Prior research indicates that father's occupational status is as meaningful an index of social class as any combination of other measures (Kohl and Davis, 1955; Lawson and Boek, 1960). Father's occupation, derived from parent interview data, was classified according to Census Bureau levels (U.S. Bureau of Census, 1950) of ten occupational categories and employed as the SES index. In this system the highest father's occupational level (professional technical) carried a numerical rating of zero, and the lowest (nonfarm laborer) a numerical rating of nine.

Children's Intelligence

Several months before their parents received the postal questionnaire, all third-grade students were administered the California Test of Mental Maturity (CTMM), 1957 S-form, in their regular classrooms. The CTMM has been shown to correlate highly with such standard individual intelligence tests as the WISC (Altus, 1955) and Stanford-Binet (Sheldon and Manolakes, 1954). With third-grade children, the CTMM has an internal consistency reliability coefficient of .75 (California Test Bureau, 1957). Seven children in this postal sample missed school on the day the CTMM was administered. Their I.Q. scores from first-grade school intelligence tests were substituted.

Sample

Voluntary return of the mail-out questionnaire concerning child-rearing practices, largely constituted of MR index items, was obtained from 143 families. The return represented about 20 per cent of some 695 families of children from all third-grade classrooms of a rural upstate New York county reachable by mail addresses obtained from the schools. This investigation represented one phase of a broader study of the psycho-social correlates of aggressive behavior in children, drawing upon a total sample of 875 third-graders, which has been previously described by Eron and Walder (1961). The present sample was markedly constricted by the requirement that at least one parent in each family must voluntarily return the postal questionnaire. Two additional restrictions were imposed to limit the influence of variables judged likely to obscure the findings. Adoptive and foster parents, totaling 8 mothers and 6 fathers, were excluded so as to control at least roughly the duration of parent-child contact. Also excluded were those parents rated by the interviewers as "faking good" in their responses (14 mothers and 14 fathers), as it seemed likely that the questionnaire responses of these persons would have been similarly slanted. The resulting "restricted" sample contained data from a total of 128 different families, 83 mother-father pairs, 33 mothers, and 12 fathers. In a few instances parents returning the questionnaire could not be interviewed, so the exact number of cases varies slightly according to the completeness of the data. All findings are based upon the maximum data available from these 128 families.

FINDINGS

A-R Measure Intercorrelations

To ascertain that the A-R indices were related empirically as well as conceptually, Pearson product-moment correlations were computed among these measures. These correlations, all significant at beyond the .05 level, were MR vs. JP = .15 (N = 194); MR vs. PUN = .46 (N = 194); and JP vs. JUN = .14 (N = 194). Despite their differing origins in questionnaire and interview items, the largest communality is plainly between the MR and PUN indices. The projective character of the JP index may be responsible for its limited relationship to the other measures. Information concerning the reliability of parents reports was derived by correlating the scores of mother-father pairs. These product-moment correlations were: MR r = .58 (N = 80); PUN r = .46 (N = 77); and JUP r = .31 (N = 77).

Parental A-R vs. Children's I.Q.

Given in Table 1, these data show that all 12 correlations between parental A-R indices and children's I.Q. were in the hypothesized direction.

SES and EL as Related to Intelligence and A-R Indices

The relationships of SES to parental A-R scores and to children's I.Q. are indicated by the following Pearson product-moment correlations:

Table 1   *Product-Moment Correlations Between Parent Acceptance and Child's I.Q.*

(N's given in brackets)

	Sons			Daughters			All Children		
	MR	PUN	JP	MR	PUN	JP	MR	PUN	JP
Fathers	− .08	− .26	− .15	− .29	− .41 [a]	− .30	− .17	− .34 [b]	− .23 [a]
	(51)	(47)	(47)	(39)	(39)	(39)	(90)	(86)	(86)
Mothers	− .23	− .03	− .16	− .46 [c]	− .41 [b]	− .40 [b]	− .35 [c]	− .21 [a]	− .25 [a]
	(61)	(58)	(58)	(53)	(50)	(50)	(114)	(108)	(108)
All Parents	− .16	− .12	− .15	− .38 [c]	− .41 [c]	− .33 [b]	− .27 [c]	− .26 [c]	− .24 [c]
	(112)	(105)	(105)	(92)	(89)	(89)	(204)	(194)	(194)

[a] $p < .05$.   [b] $p < .01$.   [c] $p < .001$.

MR vs. SES $r = -.30$ ($N = 185$); JP vs. SES $r = -.11$ ($N = 181$); PUN vs. SES $r = -.23$ ($N = 181$); and children's I.Q. vs. SES $r = .07$ ($N = 112$). Parental EL tended to correlate more highly with these variables than did SES, despite a substantial correlation ($r = .59$; $N = 184$) between EL and SES. The EL vs. A-R index correlations were: MR vs. EL $r = -.37$ ($N = 195$); JP vs. EL $r = -.10$ ($N = 196$); PUN vs. EL $r = -.31$ ($N = 196$); child's I.Q. vs. EL $r = .16$ ($N = 197$).

Since EL related so importantly to the parental A-R indices, it seemed worthwhile to identify EL's impact upon the Table 1 correlations more precisely. Holding out EL, partial correlations were determined for the four parental A-R vs. I.Q. correlations which surpassed the .05 significance level in Table 1. These resulting partial correlations (McMemar, 1949), all remaining significant at beyond the .05 level, were: father's PUN vs. daughter's I.Q. $r = -.39$ ($N = 39$); mother's MR vs. daughter's I.Q. $r = -.42$ ($N = 53$); mother's PUN vs. daughter's I.Q. $r = -.34$ ($N = 50$); mother's JP vs. daughter's I.Q. $r = -.36$ ($N = 50$).

DISCUSSION

The findings offer unqualified support for the hypothesized inverse relationship between parental A-R and children's I.Q. scores. An independent partial confirmation of this finding seems to have recently been described by Digman. He reported an $r = -.31$ between factors of "child's intelligence and parental attitude: Harshness vs. Permissiveness" (Digman, 1963, p. 55) based upon teachers' ratings of 102 Hawaiian first- and second-graders. The relationship between A-R and I.Q. appears largely independent of such possible confounding variables as parental educational level and SES.

Not clearly supported by present data was the hypothesis of stronger linkage between children's I.Q. and mothers' A-R than between the former and fathers' A-R. While four of the six (three A-R indices x sex of child) relevant comparisons of differences between the Table 1 correlations were in the anticipated direction, none of these differences closely approach statistical significance. Perhaps the combined influence of the substantial inter-parent A-R correlations and the crudity of the A-R indices worked against making a sensitive test of this hypothesis. However, the current findings do not support the conclusion that mothers' A-R type behaviors are more highly associated with children's I.Q. than are fathers' A-R behaviors.

Broadly supported is the hypothesis that mother-daughter pairs have a special sensitivity to the A-R vs. I.Q. phenomenon. No correlations between the father-son, father-daughter, or mother-son pairs exceeded the corresponding relationship between mother-daughter pairs. Only the tied correlations ($-.41$) between daughters' I.Q. and the PUN scores of mothers and fathers prevented the mother-daughter pairs from exceeding the other pairs in all nine possible comparisons. Aside from this tie, the likelihood of the mother-daughter correlations exceeding those of the other pairs in the eight remaining comparisons, again using the two-tailed significance test, would be 1 out of 256. Also interesting was the general tendency for the "all parent-daughter" A-R vs. I.Q. correlations to exceed the magnitude of the comparable "all parent-son" correlations, although the .05 significance level was reached only with the PUN index.

Parental SES does not seem to play a critical role with respect to the A-R vs. children's I.Q. phenomenon. Partialling-out the influence of EL did not materially reduce the significant relationships between child's I.Q. and parents' scores on any of the A-R measures. Nevertheless, both the MR and PUN indices correlated significantly with SES and EL. As expected, higher degrees of parental rejection were associated with lower levels of parental SES.

The substantial magnitude of the correlations found between the three A-R indices and children's I.Q. may seem surprising in view of two major influences which attenuated the magnitude of these relationships. One of these attenuating factors was the limited internal consistency of both the CTMM I.Q. scores and A-R indices. Assuming that the A-R measures had internal consistency comparable to that of the CTMM—which is doubtlessly erring in the direction of overestimating the internal consistency of the former indices—correcting the average correlation of about $-.42$ between the three mothers' A-R scores and daughters' I.Q. for this type of attenuation produces a corrected estimated correlation of $-.55$. Further upward revision of this estimate would seem justified on the basis of under-representation of lower SES families in both the postal sample and in the larger interview sample.

Speculation about possible underlying mechanisms seems warranted by both the substantial magnitude and method independence of this linkage between parental A-R and the intelligence of children. Three major lines of interpretation are apparent.

A. Less intelligent children elicit more rejecting behaviors from parents than do more intelligent children;
B. Parental rejection produces lower intelligence in children;
C. Other, as yet unidentified, variables play the vital causal roles undergirding the described A-R vs. I.Q. correlations.

Interpretation "A" seems likely to possess general validity within the context of highly competitive and industrialized societies, where "slow learning" children may threaten parental social status ambitions. Yet, the present data offer little support for this view. Assuming that parents from upper educational levels would be most ambitious for their children and, therefore, more likely to react rejectingly toward slow learners, the findings suggest that the A-R vs. I.Q. relationship is keener among parents of lesser education. Despite this contrary evidence, more definitive information, perhaps derived from longitudinal studies or from families having children who differ sharply in I.Q. would be required before this interpretation could be more definitively assessed.

The notion that parental rejection, irrespective of its origin, may adversely influence the intelligence of children appears consistent with data based on lower species (Hebb, 1949; Hymovitch, 1952; Thompson and Heron, 1954) which indicate that restrictive early-life experiences antedate ineffective performance in problem-solving tasks. Hunt's (1961, p. 108) suggestion that early experiences should have a greater impact upon later performance in species with greater association area to sensory area ratios leads to the expectation that A-R experiences, to the extent to which they structure the child's perceptual and conceptual worlds, should have a marked impact upon subsequent development. Too numerous to be reviewed here are the many strands of evidence suggesting that punitive, coercive, and repressive interpersonal experiences have a brutalizing and intellectually impoverishing influence upon humans.

Baldwin et al. (1945) have previously linked acceptant parental patterns with children's I.Q. increments and rejectant parental behaviors with I.Q. losses. Fitting comfortably into this perspective, the present findings supplement prior reports (Hurley, 1959; Hurley, 1962) of important relationships between the intellectual performance of children and child-rearing attitudes. These findings clearly imply that rejectant-parental behaviors within the normal range of contemporary U.S. child-rearing practices may have a substantial and damaging impact upon children's intellectual development.

The possibility that these parental A-R vs. child's I.Q. relationships may be wholly or largely attributable to other, as yet unidentified, variables cannot be entirely discounted. This prospect appears importantly diminished, however, by the method-free character of the present evidence in that the A-R indices, while related conceptually, were based upon different measurement techniques. More plausible is the prospect that further research will provide a more complete identification of the A-R phenomenon. At present there is no convincing empirical evidence that the so-called A-R indices are actually related to measures employed in earlier studies which gave birth to the acceptance-rejection concept. Thus, the currently implied linkage is entirely definitional and necessarily tentative. It remains possible that the findings described may eventually prove more compatible with an interpretation having little to do with either acceptance or rejection but simply linking parental punitiveness to the child's I.Q. The validity of the offered conceptualization of punitiveness as intrinsically related to acceptance-rejection can only be verified by further research.

Both advantages and disadvantages seem to accrue from the several sample selection criteria used. Prominent among the advantages is the probability that psychological phenomenon may sometimes be more accurately defined by cooperative, well-educated, candid, and more articulate persons than by individuals who are indifferent, less-educated, distorting, and probably less verbally expressive. Although in themselves these restrictions doubtless served to sharpen the findings, it should be noted that using data based upon the total postal return sample might have led to equally clear results. One limitation of the sampling procedure was that the participating parents clearly scored higher in acceptance, or lower in rejection, than did the large county-wide sample.

An urgent need for further research seems strongly implied by this unambiguous evidence of a substantial linkage between the child's cognitive functioning and parental behaviors. It seems likely that some varieties of cognitive operations, perhaps those more dependent upon interpersonal trust and cooperation, may prove to be more closely associated with A-R than would more impersonal kinds of cognitive functions. Examination of those A-R measure items which correlated most highly with I.Q. scores may help to identify the mechanisms involved more precisely. Various kinds of laboratory studies may also be envisioned which would cast further light upon this vital area of contemporary ignorance.

SUMMARY

Evidence was described of a substantial inverse relationship between the I.Q. scores of third-grade children and their parents' responses to one questionnaire and two interview measures conceptually related to the parental behavior variable of acceptance-rejection. As anticipated from theory and prior research findings, this phenomenon was most clearly visible

between the A-R scores of mothers and their daughters' I.Q. The same
general pattern of inverse relationships between A-R scores and children's
I.Q. was observed among both parents. Fathers' and mothers' A-R scores
were not differentially related to their children's I.Q. scores, although
daughters' I.Q. tended to be more closely linked to parental A-R than did
sons' I.Q. The data suggest that parental A-R differences may account for
more than 30 per cent of the variance in the I.Q. scores of eight-year-old
girls. It is not clear that socio-economic status and level of parent education
are associated with the A-R vs. I.Q. relationship, except for suggestive
evidence that this phenomenon may be even more marked among families
with lower levels of parent education.

REFERENCES

Adams, Elsie, B. & Sarason, I. G. Relation between anxiety in children and their parents. *Child Develpm.*, 1963, **34**, 237–246.
Altus, Grace F. Relationships between verbal and nonverbal parts of the CTMM and WISC. *J. consult. Psychol.*, 1955, **19**, 143–44.
Baldwin, A. L., Kalhorn, Joan, & Breese, Fay H. Patterns of parent behavior. *Psychol. Monogr.*, 1945, **58**, No. 3 (Whole No. 268).
Bowlby, J. Maternal care and mental health. WHO *Monogr.*, 1951, No. 2.
Bradway, Katherine P. IQ constancy on the revised Stanford-Binet from preschool to the junior high school level. *J. genet. Psychol.*, 1944, **65**, 197–217.
California Test Bureau. Technical report on the California Test of Middle Maturity, 1957 edition. Monterey, Calif.: Author, 1957.
Digman, J. M. Principal dimensions of child personality as inferred from teachers' judgments. *Child Develpm.*, 1963, **34**, 43–60.
Dollard, T. & Miller, N. E. *Personality and psychotherapy.* New York: McGraw-Hill, 1950.
Eron, L. D. Progress report: Psychosocial development of aggressive behavior, Project M1726 USPHS. October 13, 1961.
Eron, L. D. & Walder, L. O. Test burning: II. *Amer. Psychol.*, 1961, **16**, 237–244.
Hebb, D. O. *The organization of behavior.* New York: Wiley, 1949.
Hunt, J. McV. *Intelligence and experience.* New York: Ronald Press, 1961.
Hurley, J. R. Maternal attitudes and children's intelligence. *J. clin. Psychol.*, 1959, **15**, 291–292.
Hurley, J. R. Achievement pressure: an attitudinal correlate of college course grades. *Psychol. Rep.*, 1962, **10**, 695–702.
Hymovich, B. The effects of experimental variations in early experience on problem solving in the rat. *J. comp. physiol. Psychol.*, 1952, **45**, 313–321.
Kohl, J. A. & Davis, J. A. A comparison of indexes of socio-economic status. *Amer. socio. Rev.*, 1955, **20**, 317–326.
Lawson, E. D. & Boek, W. E. Correlations of indexes of families' socioeconomic status. *Soc. Forc.*, 1960, **39**, 149–152.
Liverant, S. Intelligence: a concept in need of re-examination. *J. consult. Psychol.*, 1960, **24**, 101–109.
McNemar, Q. *Psychological statistics.* New York: Wiley, 1949.
Miller, D. R. & Swanson, G. E. *Inner conflict and defense.* New York: Holt-Dryden, 1960.
Milton, G. A. A factor analytic study of child-rearing behaviors. *Child Develpm.*, 1958, **29**, 381–392.

Mussen, P. H., Conger, J. J., & Kagan, J. *Child development and personality.* New York: Harper & Row, 1963.

Pinneau, S. R. *Changes in the intelligence quotient: infancy to maturity.* New York: Houghton-Mifflin, 1962.

Prugh, D. C. & Harlow, R. G. "Masked deprivation" in infants and young children. In *Deprivation in maternal care,* Geneva: WHO, 1962. Pp. 9–29.

Radke, Marian J. The relation of parental authority to children's behavior and attitudes. *Univer. Minnesota Inst. Child Welf. Monogr.,* 1946, No. 22.

Schafer, E. S. & Bell, R. Q. Development of a parental attitude research instrument. *Child Develpm.,* 1958, **29**, 339–361.

Sears, R. R., Maccoby, E. E., & Levin, H. *Patterns of child rearing.* Evanston, Ill.: Row, Peterson, 1957.

Sewell, W. H., Mussen, P. H., & Harris, C. W. Relationships among child training practices. *Amer. socio. Rev.,* 1955, **20**, 137–148.

Sheldon, W. D. & Manolakes, G. A comparison of the Stanford-Binet revised form L and the California Test of Middle Maturity, S. Form. *J. educ. Psychol.,* 1954, **45**, 499–504.

Taylor, J. B. What do attitude scales measure: the problem of social desirability. *J. abnorm. soc. Psychol.,* 1961, **62**, 386–390.

Thompson, W. R. & Heron, W. The effects of restricting early experience on problem-solving capacity of dogs. *Canad. J. Psychol.,* 1954, **8**, 17–31.

U.S. Bureau of Census. Classified index of occupations and industries, U.S. Gov't Printing Office, 1960.

Walder, L. O., Eron, L. D., Lefkowitz, M., & Toigo, R. The relationship between social class and parental punishment for aggression and of both to an independent measure of child aggression. Unpublished manuscript, 1963.

Watson, R. I. *Psychology of the child.* New York: Wiley, 1959.

Wechsler, D. *Measurement and appraisal of adult intelligence.* Baltimore: Williams & Wilkins, 1958.

Yarrow, L. J. Maternal deprivation: toward an empirical and conceptual reevaluation. *Psychol. Bull.,* 1961, **58**, 459–490.

Zuckerman, M., Ribback, B. B., Monasakin, I., & Norton, J. A., Jr. Normative data and factor analysis on the parental attitude research instrument. *J. consult. Psychol.,* 1958, **22**, 165–171.

Zuckerman, M. Reversed scales to control acquiescence response set in the parental attitude research instrument. *Child Develpm.,* 1959, **30**, 523–532.

Part B Autocratic-Democratic Dimension

12. MATERNAL CHILD-REARING PRACTICES AND AUTHORITARIAN IDEOLOGY

I. HART

This study was an attempt to investigate maternal preferences in techniques for controlling child behavior as a function of socialization situations and a particular aspect of maternal personality. The basic hypothesis was that patterns of child-rearing preferences can be predicted from personality trends expressed in ideological form; specifically, authoritarianism. As a test of this hypothesis, specific predictions were formulated, derived from the clinical insights and descriptive statements of Adorno et al. (1) and Levinson and Huffman (4). These predictions were tested in terms of the socialization model of Whiting and Child (7).

Writers on the authoritarian personality have contended that certain child-rearing practices are both antecedents and consequents of authoritarianism. The authoritarian parent is said to emphasize discipline that takes the form of "bodily harm, social isolation and/or shaming, rather than the loss of love, since the giving of love and the establishment of strong affectional ties are not likely to be primary issues in an autocratic setting" (4).

Whiting and Child's analysis of the punishment techniques customarily used by parents in socializing their children bears considerable congruence to the range of behaviors that Levinson and Huffman attribute to high and low authoritarian parents. One phase of Whiting and Child's analysis rests on the assumption that punishments differ in the extent to which they contribute to maintaining the child's orientation to the goal of parental affection. Thus they distinguish three kinds of discipline as "love-oriented," i.e., serving to maintain the child's striving for parental love: denial of love, threats of denial of reward, and threats of ostracism. In contrast to these techniques, they propose three kinds of discipline as having the overall effect of establishing tendencies in the child to avoid the parents. These "nonloved-oriented" punishment techniques are: physical punishment, threats of physical punishment, and punishment by ridicule. Whiting and Child did not include actual denial of rewards and actual ostracism in either the love-oriented or the nonlove-oriented categories because these techniques were considered to contribute potentially both to striving for parental affection and to the de-

Reprinted with slight abridgement from the *Journal of Abnormal and Social Psychology,* 1957, **55,** 232–237, with permission of the author and the American Psychological Association.

119

velopment of avoidance tendencies. These latter punishments were described as "ambiguous." On the basis of the descriptions of Adorno *et al.* and of Levinson and Huffman, low and high authoritarian parents might be expected to select love-oriented and nonlove-oriented disciplinary techniques, respectively.

METHOD

One hundred and twenty-six mothers, who had children between the ages of $2\frac{1}{2}$ and $5\frac{1}{2}$, were studied by means of intensive but structured interviews in which each mother was asked to indicate her most probable response to her own child's behavior in specific situations. Free responses were submitted to three independent raters (psychology graduate students) for coding appropriate to the Whiting and Child categories of disciplinary techniques, according to agreement of two out of the three raters. The subjects (Ss) were white, native born, Christian Americans ranging in age from 23 to 43. Mean mother's age was 30.8; mean age of the children was 4.1.

In an attempt to keep the effects of education and socioeconomic level as constant as possible, the sample was restricted to middle-class mothers who had completed at least one year of college. The fathers were predominantly college graduates, and for the most part were engaged in either professional or higher level managerial occupations. The Ss were recruited by asking interviewees to suggest mothers who could participate in the study. Almost all of the Ss were able to suggest others; 95 per cent of those who were asked participated.

The interview schedule contained 38 items depicting various child behavior situations, and a modified version of Whiting and Child's categorization of punishment techniques, combined in questionnaire form. The behavior situations were chosen on the basis of a priori judgment and some brief preliminary research, in the expectation that they would occur rather frequently and tend to elicit some form of discipline rather than reward from parents of children in the age range sampled. It was further intended that each situation represent an instance of behavior in one of the following six areas:

1. Feeding and oral activities: e.g., "insists on eating with fingers," "seldom finishes meal," etc.

2. Cleanliness-toilet training: e.g., "frequently has toilet accidents because won't interrupt play."

3. Sex: sexual curiosity, sexual and obscene remarks, handling genitals, body exposure.

4. Aggression: Items involve insolence and impudence, hitting and pushing, temper tantrums, explicit disobedience, willful property damage.

5. Dependence: These items attempt to depict behavior suggesting that the child lacks self-reliance, is attempting to gain parental support, etc., e.g., "whines or begs for help unnecessarily."

6. Independence: This area includes situations that are intended to suggest that the child is showing initiative, curiosity, assertiveness, e.g., "insists on own way with other children," "wanders away from home," etc.

In addition to the structured interview phase, each mother was asked to describe her three biggest problems concerning her child, to answer two open-end projective-type questions, and to fill out a combined version of the short-form (TFI) scale (4) and F scale (1). The scores thus obtained (M, 3.70; *SD*, 1.09) provided the measure of authoritarian personality. The interviews took from 1½ to 2½ hours.

RESULTS

Authoritarianism was found to be unrelated to each of the following variables: age of the mother, age of the child, sex and birth order of the child, and number of children in the family. The behavior situations included in the interview schedule were quite comparable to and representative of the kinds of behavior problems reported by the *S*s.

The main results are described below with reference to three experimental predictions.

1. *The selection of nonlove-oriented disciplinary techniques should be a positive function of maternal authoritarianism score.* To test this prediction, a product-moment correlation was computed between each mother's authoritarianism score and the number of situations for which she selected nonlove-oriented techniques. The correlation thus obtained was .63 ($p < .001$).

For a more detailed analysis, the distribution of authoritarianism scores was divided into thirds, with cutoff scores for highs and lows falling at 4.1 and 3.2, respectively. The relationship between mothers' authoritarianism and preferred disciplinary techniques may be observed in the right-hand marginal column of Table 1. The body of Table 1 lists the percentages of type of discipline selected by mothers of a given authoritarianism level, in the various behavioral areas. Mothers at all levels of authoritarianism in general selected more love-oriented than nonlove-oriented control measures. However, it will also be seen that as authoritarianism level increases, nonlove-oriented techniques are preferred increasingly, and that as authoritarianism level decreases, the tendency to select love-oriented techniques increases. Since practically all of the previous research concerning authoritarianism has employed only the extremes of the distribution, the confirmation of this prediction also lends support to the contention that authoritarianism is an intrinsic continuum, not merely a dichotomous or trichotomous aggregate of traits.

2. *High authoritarians in comparison with low authoritarians, should select relatively more nonlove-oriented responses for the sex and aggression areas respectively, than for the remaining areas.* This prediction was based

Table 1   *Mean Percentage of Mothers at Each Level of Authoritarianism Who Select Each Type of Discipline*

Type of Discipline and Level of Authoritarianism	Behavior Area						
	Independence	Dependence	Cleanliness	Feeding	Sex	Aggression	Overall Mean
Love							
High	30.33	65.12	59.52	47.29	70.26	18.64	48.53
Medium	27.90	69.52	69.64	58.93	80.57	23.14	54.95
Low	45.05	84.76	88.69	83.31	89.12	42.52	72.24
Mean	34.43	73.13	72.62	63.18	79.98	28.10	
Nonlove							
High	60.55	23.10	33.93	30.57	20.62	69.40	39.69
Medium	53.02	16.45	26.19	20.48	11.17	47.57	29.15
Low	47.60	7.36	8.93	8.81	8.14	41.88	20.45
Mean	53.72	15.64	23.02	19.95	13.31	52.95	
"Ambiguous"							
High	9.12	11.78	6.55	22.14	9.12	11.96	11.78
Medium	19.08	14.03	4.17	20.59	8.26	29.29	15.90
Low	7.35	7.88	2.38	7.88	2.74	15.60	7.31
Mean	11.85	11.23	4.36	16.87	6.71	18.95	

on the supposition of authoritarian personality theory that children's sexual and aggressive behavior are especially unacceptable to authoritarian parents, and especially subject to control by discipline.

If nonlove-oriented measures are the characteristic disciplinary techniques of high authoritarian parents, and if children's sexual and aggressive behavior is especially unacceptable to them, then it might be expected that authoritarian parents would select more nonlove-oriented responses for these areas than for the other areas. To test that portion of the prediction pertaining to aggression, each high and low authoritarian mother was given a score based on the differences between the percentages of nonlove-oriented responses in the aggression area and the combined value of the remaining areas (minus sex). The t ratio of 1.8 between the mean scores of the highs and lows, was close to significance at the .05 level.

The failure of the data to attain an acceptable level of significance may reflect the arbitrary grouping of genotypically different items in the particular categories adopted. The behavior situations classed under aggression included items differing markedly from each other in interpersonal significance.

Perhaps behaviors embodying threat to authority relationships may be more germane to the authoritarian personality dimension than the particular situations chosen for inquiry. For example, one group of aggressive behaviors that may be interpreted as predominantly involving threat to parental authority discriminated significantly between highs and lows in an individual situation analysis, while the remainder did not. Aggression (and other areas of problem behavior as well) may require finer analysis to yield satisfactory categories in terms of interpersonal significance.

Not only did the data fail to support that part of the prediction pertaining to sex, but as Table 1 indicates, the differences between highs and lows in the selection of nonlove responses were smaller in the sex area than in any other area. It might be speculated that this finding indicates considerable enlightenment in the attitudes of the sample studied towards sexual behavior in their children. The writer was impressed with the casualness and acceptance which the mothers displayed concerning sexual manifestations in their children. Many of the mothers indicated that their own mothers would have been shocked by such behavior, and would not have been so tolerant. While this suggests a cultural trend toward increased leniency in middle-class attitudes toward the expression of sex, it also is very likely in considerable part a reflection of the cultural sophistication of the sample. Moreover, sexuality per se was generally not recognized nor accepted as intrinsic in the particular behavior, but the behavior was generally equated to intellectual curiosity, or otherwise rationalized as part of the childhood learning process.

As may be observed in Table 1, the class of behavior control techniques preferred varied with behavior area. To determine if these variations exceeded chance probability, analyses of variance were computed in which the six behavior areas and the three authoritarianism levels were the independent variables and the classes of disciplinary techniques were the dependent variables. The data summarizing the analysis of variance for nonlove-oriented disciplinary techniques are presented in Table 2. Since love and

Table 2 *Analysis of Variance of Preference for Nonlove-Oriented Disciplinary Techniques*

Source	df	SS	MS	F	P
Levels of authoritarianism	2	46796.62	23398.31	33.52	.01
Subjects within levels	123	85864.80	698.09		
Behavior areas	5	217209.28	43441.86	137.07	.01
Level × Area	10	7014.05	701.41	2.21	.05
Area × Subjects within levels	615	194917.34	316.94		
Total	755	551802.09			

nonlove response frequencies are essentially mirror images of each other, the results of the analysis of variance for love-oriented discipline were substantially the same. Since the distributions were heterogeneous in variance and form, the F ratios were interpreted as inflated. While the very large F ratio (137) suggests that it would be quite safe to assume that the main effect of behavior areas is significant, the comparatively small F ratio (2.2) for interaction effects does not warrant the conclusion of a significant interaction. This finding corresponds to the nonsignificant results for Prediction 2.

Inspection of Table 1 indicates that nonlove-oriented responses were selected most frequently in the independence and aggression areas, and least frequently in the sex and dependence areas. One possible explanation is that the independence and aggression areas depict behaviors that are more threatening to parental control and authority. However, many of the mothers explained their choice of response to the independence items referring to certain behaviors as potentially dangerous to the child by indicating that threat to their child's safety was the one time they did not hesitate to resort to physical punishment. It might be surmised that aggressive behavior on the part of the child might provoke parental aggressive retaliation. The most frequent reason advanced by the mothers for their reluctance to select nonlove-oriented responses for dependency behavior was fear that these techniques might cause the child to feel rejected.

3. *The low authoritarian's description of her child-rearing philosophy and related attitudes should contain more attitude statements with the judged consequence of maintaining the child's approach tendency to her, than should the high authoritarian's.* The high authoritarian's "philosophy" is expected to be judged as more likely than the low authoritarian's to produce and strengthen an avoidance tendency in the child. For the purpose of testing this prediction, each mother was asked the following open-end questions: "What is your philosophy of child-rearing?" and "What do you think are the most important things to take into consideration when dealing with child behavior problems?" To reduce the scope of the task of rating, only the protocols of the mothers with the 30 highest and lowest authoritarianism scores were used in the statistical test. These protocols were submitted to two additional judges who rated them in terms of the anticipated effect the depicted behavior would have on the tendency of the child to approach or avoid the mother. The protocols were in no way identified with regard to authoritarianism and, in fact, the judges were unacquainted with authoritarian theory or the hypotheses of the study. Each protocol was divided into meaningful, coherent idea units on a purely a priori basis, in an attempt to facilitate comparability of ratings. The task of the judges was to sort each unit of the mother's statements into an "approach" category, i.e., behavior thought to strengthen the child's approach tendency; an "avoidance" cate-

gory; or a "miscellaneous" category. Although the number of units in the protocols varied, the mean number of units of the highs was close to that of the lows. However, as a precaution and in an attempt to compensate for unequal length of protocols, the score for each protocol consisted of the summed approach rating minus the summed avoidance rating. Thus, the final score for each protocol is a discrepancy score and is assumed to represent the relative excess of approach over avoidance (or vice versa).

Fairly high interrater agreement is reflected in the product-moment correlation of .72 for the lows and .73 for the highs. It was concluded that there was sufficient reliability in the judges' ratings to warrant their combination in mean judgments. The mean discrepancy score of the lows was 36.1, SD, 7.6; that of the highs 30.5, SD, 6.42; each case representing an excess of approach over avoidance judgments. The t test computed to determine the significance of the difference between the scores of high and low authoritarians yielded a value of 3.08, $P < .01$, in support of Prediction 3.

The confirmation of this prediction suggests that the structured interview schedule has construct validity (2), and that the socialization techniques differentially preferred by high and low authoritarians have conceptual significance in terms of approach and avoidance principles.

DISCUSSION

These findings emphasize a conclusion that many have long taken for granted. They show that the choice of behavior control techniques, in a variety of socialization situations, is to a significant extent conditioned by measurable personality factors in the mother. Whiting and Child (7) have argued that parental personality is one critical link in the mediation of culture from generation to generation. The present study, like theirs, was not designed to clarify the antecedents and consequents involved in this process. However, the results do suggest that different emphases or alternative customs of the culture are mediated as a function of maternal personality.

The significance of the present results for authoritarian personality theory depends rather critically on the status of one assumption: that the authoritarian mother's relative preference for nonlove-oriented punishment is a cause as well as an effect of authoritarianism. Assuming that the children of authoritarians themselves tend to be authoritarian, one can speculate about the role of avoidance tendencies in the etiology of authoritarianism. It may be that the child of authoritarian parents is highly ambivalent toward them (and other authorities) because of a heightened avoidance gradient, resulting in more closely balanced approach and avoidance tendencies. His later behavior toward superordinates typically reflects "coping techniques"—such as emphasis on the maintenance of social distance, interaction between formal roles rather than persons as individuals, etc.—designed to manage this ambivalence. But, as many writers on authoritarian personality have contended, there remains an underlying resentment and hostility toward authority that is revealed in such displaced forms as scapegoating and prejudice.

The speculative tenor of the above remarks could be avoided if the child's actual behavior toward and perception of his parents, and reaction to different forms of socialization pressure, were determined by direct and indirect means in subsequent research.

SUMMARY

The primary purpose of this study was to investigate the way in which the mother's authoritarianism affects her selection of behavior control techniques in a variety of socialization situations. Specific predictions were formulated in an attempt to combine the hypotheses and insights of authoritarian personality theory (1) with the socialization model suggested by Whiting and Child (7). One hundred twenty-six mothers of preschool children responded in a structured interview to 38 behavior situations which commonly arise and call for maternal decisions about mode of control. These items were classified as relating to feeding, cleanliness and toilet training, sex, aggression, dependence, and independence; the preferred response of the mother could in turn be classified as love-oriented, nonlove-oriented or "ambiguous."

The main results of the study may be summarized as follows:

1. As predicted, authoritarians show a consistent tendency to select more nonlove-oriented and fewer love-oriented responses than nonauthoritarians. When the middle-range authoritarians are included, inspection indicates the relationship is linear.

2. There are significant variations in the proportion of love- and nonlove-oriented responses selected as a function of the behavior area involved. Thus, aggression and independence involve behaviors that provoke more nonlove-oriented responses, whereas sex and dependency behaviors call forth fewer nonlove-oriented responses.

3. There is no significant interaction, however, between authoritarianism and behavior area. That is, in terms of the a priori classification of items into six different areas, authoritarianism does not discriminate significantly better in one area than in another. It is quite possible, though, that different item arrangements (in terms more precisely relevant to authoritarianism) would show that the authoritarian's relative preference for nonlove responses is to some extent conditioned by the situation.

REFERENCES

1. Adorno, T. W., Frenkel-Brunswik, Else, Levinson, D. J., & Sanford, R. N. *The authoritarian personality*. New York: Harper & Bros., 1950.

2. Cronbach, L. J., & Meehl, P. E. Construct validity in psychological tests. *Psychol. Bull.*, 1955, **52**, 281–302.
3. Hart, I. Maternal child-rearing practices and authoritarian ideology. Unpublished doctor's dissertation, Duke Univer., 1956.
4. Levinson, D. J., & Huffman, Phyllis E. Traditional family ideology and its relation to personality. *J. Pers.*, 1955, **23**, 251–273.
5. Lindquist, E. F. *Design and analysis of experiments in psychology and education.* Boston: Houghton Mifflin, 1956.
6. Sears, R. R., Whiting, J. W. M., Nowlis, V., & Sears, Pauline S. Some child-rearing antecedents of aggression and dependency in young children. *Genet. Psychol. Monogr.*, 1953, **47**, 135–234.
7. Whiting, W. M., & Child, I. L. *Child training and personality: A cross-cultural study.* New Haven: Yale Univer. Press, 1953.

13. POWER ASSERTION BY THE PARENT AND

ITS IMPACT ON THE CHILD

Martin L. Hoffman

Power is an ingredient of many social situations. If we consider power as the potential an individual has for compelling another person to act in ways contrary to his own desires, we can see that there are a variety of situations in which power exists. The parent-child relationship is one of these. The purpose of this paper is to analyze the effects of the use of power by the parent on the personality of the child. First, it is necessary to define the concept of power as it is here used.

The potential for compelling unmotivated behavior in another person is, aside from idiosyncratic personality factors, largely a function of how much control one is given over the administration of punishment and the allocation of supplies needed by the other person, as well as the amount of freedom permitted by the larger social unit to the exercise of control. (Examples of societal restraints are regulations delimiting the conditions and the manner in which power may be asserted, and the existence of agencies of appeal for low-power persons.) Power may be manifested overtly in a class of social behaviors called influence techniques, which are defined as on-the-spot attempts to modify another person's behavior.

The kinds of influence techniques a person may reasonably use is determined in large part by his power position. Thus, in those areas of life where the power structure applies, the high-power person is able to choose between (a) techniques which assert his power, i.e., apply external pressure; and (b) techniques which attempt to gain "voluntary" behavior change by inducing internal forces. The low-power person, on the other hand, is more limited to the latter types of techniques. This difference in amount of choice applies to the initial techniques used to change the other's behavior and, perhaps even more so, to those used in reaction to noncompliance.

When the parent-child relationship is examined in this context, it is clear that the parent has a great deal of power in all areas of the child's life. The parent possesses and controls the material and emotional supplies needed by the child. As the controller of these supplies, and with his greater physical strength, he is in the position to punish the child at will, either physically or through deprivations. He can potentially force any behavior

Reprinted with abridgement from *Child Development,* 1960, **31,** 129–143, with permission of the author and the Society for Research in Child Development.

on the child, within the latter's biological and physical limitations, e.g., it is not possible to force a child directly to move his bowels or to fall asleep. Furthermore, the parent's treatment of the child—outside of extreme neglect and cruelty—is subject to little, if any, legal restraint. Probably in no other relationship does a person in our society have such complete power over another.

Because of his strong power position, the parent is free to choose influence techniques which, in varying degrees, assert power or attempt to induce the child to change his behavior voluntarily. The most power assertive techniques that might be used—as initial techniques or as reactions to noncompliance—are those which, without qualification, put direct coercive pressure on the child to change his entire ongoing pattern of behavior immediately. These techniques, exemplified by direct commands, threats, deprivations, and physical force, we refer to as *unqualified power assertion.*

The same techniques become less power assertive when qualified. One type of qualification is an explanation which attempts to justify or legitimize the required behavior change in terms of something outside the parent's control, e.g., the welfare of the child, the parent, or someone else; the physical, temporal, or spatial demands of the situation; or the socially prescribed norms of child behavior. Another type of qualification is some form of compensatory gratification for the child which permits him a certain amount of closure before requiring compliance or indicates that closure will be possible soon after compliance. Or the parent might temper the power assertiveness of a technique by providing a substitute, making the required behavior more attractive, or expressing supportive understanding of the child's desire to continue what he is doing.

Techniques, on the other hand, which do not assert power are those which invoke no parental authority but instead rely for their effectiveness primarily on the child's own internalized standards and good judgment. Such techniques communicate to the child the behavior change desired but also, with varying degrees of explicitness, indicate that he has the choice of complying or not.

Our concern here is with the parent's use of unqualified power assertion and its implications for the child's personality development.

THEORY

Any influence technique the parent uses to modify the child's behavior in a direction not desired by the child is apt to communicate, explicitly or implicitly, some degree of dissatisfaction or displeasure with the child's ongoing behavior. The child cannot readily ignore such discrepancy of will between the parent and himself because of his low-power position in the home and his total dependence on the parent. It follows that any influence technique tends to interrupt the continuity of the child's behavior and thought processes and to present him with a conflict. The amount and type of conflict depends on the specific technique employed by the parent and the child's motivational state at that time.

Unqualified power assertive techniques convey that the parent feels strongly about the behavior at issue; that despite the child's wishes of the moment he must, without question, stop what he is doing and do what the parent wants of him. The parent does not attempt to explain nor to justify his demand, nor does he attempt to compensate the child for having to alter his behavior. In using these techniques, especially in reaction to the child's noncompliance, the parent appears to impose his personal will rather than legitimize the demand and to override the child's wishes and involvements of the moment. Neither the child's wants nor his internalized controls are called upon to help change his behavior. Unqualified power assertion relies for its effectiveness primarily on the high degree of external coercive pressure it puts on the child to comply.

From the standpoint of the child the demand for unconditional surrender of his own interests and involvements in such an arbitrary manner not only frustrates his momentary need for task completion but also constitutes an assault on his autonomy as well. Opposition tendencies and feelings of hostility should therefore be aroused in response to the parent's use of unqualified power assertion as an initial technique or as a reaction to the child's noncompliance, especially the latter. It follows from this brief analysis of the immediate impact of unqualified power assertion on the child that its frequent use by the parent, especially in reaction to the child's noncompliance (to be called "reactive unqualified power assertion"), should lead to the accumulation of hostile tension, needs to be power assertive toward others, and heightened autonomy needs—all of which may be displaced in more permissive situations. The development of a power-assertive orientation toward others may also be facilitated by the child's identification with the parent model, i.e., his introjection of the parent's power assertiveness.

In addition to the above, the use of unqualified power assertion gives the child no explicit information that may help him develop internalized controls or draw upon those that already exist. Because of the threatening and punitive aspects of unqualified power assertion, the main basis for controlling unacceptable impulses that may be learned is expediency and fear of the consequences of noncompliance, especially from authority figures. The child may also become sensitized to the power aspect of social relationships because the use of unqualified power assertion highlights the power structure existing in the home. Frequent experiences like these should result in the child's acting out of his hostile and other impulses more toward low-power than toward high-power persons. Whether or not these impulses are acted out toward high-power persons at all would depend on how permissive they are.

It should be emphasized that this theory pertains to the *excessive* use of unqualified power assertion. There are undoubtedly many situations in which these techniques may be quite appropriate, e.g., when there is external danger to the child with no time for explanations and when physical restraint is necessary in order to keep the child with inadequately developed controls from being overwhelmed by his own impulses. Even in more ordinary situations, the *occasional* use of unqualified power assertion may help instill the sense of urgency in the child that might be necessary for learning certain limits. If used sparingly, unqualified power assertion may even contribute to the child's development of a sense of identity, i.e., being openly confronted with interpersonal conflict should result in a heightened sense of self. The total avoidance of unqualified power assertion might therefore contribute to a dulling of the borderlines between self and not-self. Its excessive use, however, should have the negative social effects described in the above theory.

HYPOTHESES

On the basis of the above theoretical approach it was hypothesized that the parent's use of unqualified power assertive techniques, initial or reactive, would relate positively to the following characteristics of children: *hostility toward other children; power assertiveness toward them;* and *resistance to their influence attempts.* It was also hypothesized that the parent's use of unqualified power assertion would relate to the child's expression of these characteristics toward permissive authority figures, but to a lesser extent than toward children.

Stronger relationships were expected for (*a*) *reactive* than for *initial* unqualified power assertion because both parent and child become more involved and the interaction presumably becomes more psychologically significant once the child displays resistance to the parent; and (*b*) mothers' unqualified power assertion than for fathers', because of the greater amount of contact the mother has with the child.

Social Class and Unqualified Power Assertion

The literature on social class differences in child rearing (1) suggests that working class parents have a more traditionalistic approach than middle class parents. This approach is characterized by the more or less unreflective application of handed-down notions and places great stress on obedience. To a greater extent the middle class orientation involves a more self-conscious and deliberate attempt to apply the principles currently advanced by leaders in various child-rearing fields. It is less concerned with obedience and more oriented toward considering the child's needs whenever possible. It was therefore hypothesized that working class parents use more unqualified power assertion than middle class parents.

METHOD

Sample

The sample consisted of 10 working class families and 12 middle class families having a child in attendance at a half-day nursery school in an urban industrial community. The working class children were in a community sponsored school while the middle class children were in a private laboratory-like nursery school. All the families were intact, nonclinical, and white; the fathers were employed full time; and the mothers were housewives with no outside employment.

The working class parents were mostly Roman Catholics of East European descent and, except for two mothers and one father, native born. They averaged 11 years of formal education. Occupationally, the fathers were mainly skilled and semiskilled industrial workers.

The middle class parents were mostly Protestants who were native born, except for one mother and one father, and whose parents were born in this country or in Western Europe. They all attended college and all but three received degrees. The fathers were professionals, executives, salesmen in large corporations, or owners of middle-sized businesses.

Parental Measures of Unqualified Power Assertion

Influence technique data were obtained from tape-recorded interviews in which each parent reported in detail an account of his interaction with the child on the day before the interview. The day described was a randomly selected weekday for the mothers and both a weekday and a Sunday for the fathers. Intensive probing elicited highly detailed material on each parent-child interaction—including, for example, the initial influence technique used by the parent, the child's behavior prior to the technique, the child's response to the technique, and the parent's reaction to the child's resistance. The use of this type of interview is based on the assumption that the parent's behavior is more or less consistent from day to day. Thus, a day selected at random may be taken as a representative sample of his influence technique pattern.

Since so much rests on the parent's narration, accuracy of reporting becomes crucial. Attempts were made to design the interview so as to minimize three potential sources of error in the parent's report: forgetting (unmotivated distortion), deliberate falsification, and unconsciously motivated distortion. Forgetting is handled simply by focusing on the day before the interview and by probes which are made by the interviewer when gaps appear in the parent's account. Deliberate withholding or falsification of material is handled in part by getting the parent positively interested in the study and giving him ample opportunity to talk favorably about the child at the outset of the interview. The parent was also assured that no attempt would be made to evaluate his role as a parent and that the interview's focus was on behavioral details rather than beliefs or opinions. The requirement to recall specific details in response to frequent interviewer probes (e.g., for verbatim statements and other concrete referrents instead of vaguely descriptive terms), besides helping to motivate the parent, also seemed to force him to be logically and chronologically consistent. Our pilot interviewees typically remarked after the interview that the task of recalling so many details in their proper order required all of their concentrated energy. Some added, in response to questioning, that this concentration distracted them from interpersonal aspects of the interview situation and that as a result they were not concerned about the impression they were making. Trying to remember details, then, may result in a certain amount of detachment and loss of self-consciousness.

The third potential source of error, unconsciously motivated omissions and distortions, may also be minimized by the interview's focus on factual description. Thus, the set to recall specific details rather than meaningful wholes seems to result in the fragmentation of the event described, by weakening many of its gestalt properties. Thereby the event is divested of much of the emotional meaning it might otherwise have. In this way, any anxiety or guilt which may be associated with an event and which, if aroused, could interfere with actual recall by touching off a variety of defenses is perhaps avoided or at least considerably reduced. In psychoanalytic terms there may be an "isolation" of the event which allows details to reach consciousness without arousing painful emotional states.

The first step in processing the interview material was to have it transcribed. Then, in order to prevent any personality-relevant material, like the parent's thoughts and feelings about the event, from influencing the coding, the purely overt behavioral interaction sequences between parent and child were abstracted. The influence technique codes were then applied to these behavioral interactions by an assistant who was hired specifically for this purpose and knew nothing about the theory or hypotheses of the study.

All influence techniques used by the parent to change—prevent, terminate, initiate—the child's overt behavior were coded, regardless of what the behavior was. The only requirement was evidence that there was a discrepancy between what the parent desired and what the child wanted to do or continue doing. The parent's *initial unqualified power assertion score* (initial UPA) was the percentage of initial techniques he used which fit the category of unqualified power assertion. Similarly, the parent's *reactive unqualified power assertion score* (reactive UPA) was the percentage of the techniques employed when the child did not comply initially, fitting the category of unqualified power assertion. Percentage scores were used in order to control for volume.

Child Measures

The child data were obtained from three half-hour running account observations of each child as he behaved in the nursery school group over a two-month period, about the same period of the interview. The attempt was made, with the aid of stick figure drawings and a form of shorthand, to record everything the child did and said. The raw observation material was dictated immediately afterwards and eventually typed for purposes of coding.

The child measures were as follows:

Hostility. The percentage of all social contacts made by the child in which he expressed physical or verbal hostility.

Power assertiveness. The percentage of all influence attempts made by the child that fit our definition of unqualified power assertion. The same definition was used here as with the parents.

Resistance to influence. The percentage of all influence attempts directed at the child which he responded to in a noncompliant manner.

Separate scores were obtained for each of these measures for the child's behavior toward the teacher and toward the other children. A "difference" score for each measure was also obtained by subtracting the "teacher" score from the "children" score.

To avoid contamination, it was made certain the persons having contact with the child material knew nothing about the parents; and the persons in contact with the parent material knew nothing about the children.

RESULTS AND DISCUSSION

Class Differences in the Use of UPA

Working class fathers, as expected, used initial UPA and reactive UPA to a greater extent than middle class fathers. Significant differences between the working and middle class mothers were obtained only in initial UPA.

A possible reason why the mother differences are less clear cut than the fathers' is that the working class mothers are more influenced than their husbands by current child-rearing notions regarding disobedience and as a result their behavior is somewhat closer to the middle class norms. That these mothers do have more contact with expert opinion than their husbands is indicated by their spontaneous references to what they had learned from the nursery school teacher and by some of the reasons given in the interview for the techniques they used. They also gave less traditional responses than their husbands to a questionnaire on child-rearing ideology ($p < .1$).

With the data combined for social class most of the hypotheses were confirmed. Significant correlations were found between the mother's reactive UPA and the child's hostility toward children, power assertiveness toward children, and his resistance to children's influence attempts; his resistance to the teacher's influence attempts; and his being more hostile and more resistant toward children than toward the teacher (Table 1). The remaining correlations were also in the expected direction but not significant.

The reason for the many high correlations supporting the hypotheses involving reactive UPA, in contrast to the paucity of relationships for initial UPA, may be that the mother's influence behavior has more lasting effects when the techniques are employed in situations of heightened conflict and involvement. These conditions probably arise mainly in situations in which the mother is reacting to the child's noncompliance. Further, the child's noncompliance may reflect the decision to assert his autonomy and challenge the authority of the parent. This may very well change the interaction from a relatively casual one for the child into one in which his integrity and self-

Table 1

*Correlations Between Mother's
Reactive UPA and Child's
Hostility, Power Assertiveness,
and Resistance to Influence
(Middle and Working Class Data
Combined)*

Child Variable	Correlation ($N = 19$)
Hostility	
Toward Children	.60 [b]
Toward Teacher	.17
Difference	.51 [a]
Power Assertiveness	
Toward Children	.48 [a]
Toward Teacher	—
Difference	.31
Resistance to Influence	
By Children	.68 [c]
By Teacher	.42 [a]
Difference	.54 [b]

[a] $p < .05$.
[b] $p < .01$.
[c] $p < .001$.
Note. The "within-groups" procedure outlined by Hills (2) was used to obtain correlations based on the combined data because the Ss were from intact groups.

esteem become more the issue rather than some specific desire of the moment.

It seems probable that these effects of reactive UPA would become less apparent as the child grows older. For one thing, the parent's current influence behaviors very likely become less important to the child because of the increased stabilization of his personality and patterns of interacting with the parent as well as his decreased dependence on the parent. Further, one of the assumptions underlying our hypotheses, i.e., that the child immediately responds to unqualified power assertion in terms of its arbitrary and frustrating quality and with little or no intervening ego process, becomes less tenable as the child grows older. With increasing age the child may come to realize that, although the mother does not often explain her demands, she usually has realistic bases for them, and eventually the child is able to seek out and find the reason for himself. The interposition of such cognitive responses, in addition to the guiding standards the child will have begun to internalize, should reduce his tendency to perceive unqualified power assertion in purely coercive and arbitrary terms. His reactions to these techniques might then become more similar to his reactions to other techniques. Further research is obviously needed before this view can be adequately assessed.

The Role of the Father

Although less had been expected of the father predictions as compared to the mother predictions, the lack of a consistent pattern that might provide at least some support for the hypotheses was surprising. Perhaps we underestimated the importance of the father's being away from home during most of the child's waking hours and the resulting monopoly of most of the child's time by the mother. With few exceptions, the interviews of both parents indicate that the only times the father generally spends alone with the child, other than in play activities, are during those short periods when he is at home and the mother is otherwise occupied in or out of the home, and occasionally when he puts the child to bed—most of these interactions occurring during the weekend. Furthermore, when both parents are present, the mother is usually the agent of influence and discipline. It should therefore not be surprising if the accumulated effects of the father's use of reactive UPA do not approach the effects of the mother's daily repeated use of these techniques. Perhaps the child must attain a certain level of cognitive development before the father's techniques can have important effects despite his absence from the child's immediate life space for most of the day.

Although the father's behavior may thus not have a direct effect on the child—at least with respect to the variables here under investigation—there is evidence that the father does have an important indirect role. The relevant findings were obtained in another phase of the study, that which dealt with personality factors underlying the parent's use of UPA. Briefly, our expectations were that the parent's authoritarianism and power needs would relate positively to the use of UPA. In the working class group this proved to be true for the fathers but not for the mothers. In addition, the fathers' F scores related significantly and positively to *their wives'* reactive UPA ($r = .60; p < .05$). These findings in combination were interpreted to mean that the authoritarian father in this group manifests his authoritarianism toward his wife; the wife resents this and takes it out on a "safer" target, the child. There is more dramatic support for this hypothesis that the mother's reactive UPA is, to some degree, a response to her husband's authoritarian behavior toward her. A very high relationship was obtained between the extent to which the husband is more authoritarian than the wife (husband's F score minus wife's F score) and the wife's reactive UPA ($r = .84; p < .01$).

A similar pattern of findings were obtained in the middle class, not with the F scale but with a projective measure of power needs previously validated with middle class subjects (4). Thus, in the middle class the fathers' power need scores related positively to their wives' reactive UPA ($r = .73; p < .01$), while the wives' power needs did not relate to their own reactive UPA. Here, too, the mother's use of reactive UPA toward the child seems to be partly a displaced reaction to her husband's power-relevant behavior toward her.

Although these personality findings were brought into the discussion in order to place the role of the father in proper perspective, they are also important from another standpoint. The fact that the mothers' authoritarianism and power need scores did not relate to their use of reactive UPA raises a serious question about one of the assumptions often made in parent-child research, i.e., that it is sufficient to obtain parent data at the personality level since this underlies overt behavior.

What Is Antecedent and What Is Consequent?

In this study, like many others, the variables hypothesized as being antecedent and consequent are measured concurrently rather than sequentially. The findings relating the mother's reactive UPA to the child variables (Table 1) might therefore be explained by other interpretations in which the causal sequences are the reverse of those hypothesized. Thus, it might be argued that (*a*) mothers tend to use reactive UPA with children who are already hostile, power assertive, and rebellious; and (*b*) the child's nursery school behaviors are merely reflections of these same characteristics rather than displaced responses to the mother's reactive UPA. Although this explanation appears to rest on less solid theoretical ground than the assumption underlying our hypothesis and interpretation of the data, i.e., that parental discipline procedures are more apt to be determiners of child personality than consequences, it poses a challenge that should not be ignored. Some of our findings have direct relevance here.

Firstly, it would follow from the alternative interpretation that the child's tendency to resist the mother (*a*) predisposes the mother to use reactive UPA and (*b*) is consistent with the child's behavior outside the home. This leads to the hypotheses that the child's resistance to the mother relates positively to the mother's use of reactive UPA and to the child's resistance to others in the nursery school. These hypotheses could be tested since it was possible to obtain from the interview a score for the child's resistance to the mother's influence attempts, i.e., the percentage of initial techniques the mother used which were resisted by the child. The correlations obtained were all low and not significant ($r = .19$ between resistance to mother and mother's reactive UPA; $r = -.07$ between resistance to mother and resistance to teacher; $r = -.23$ between resistance to mother and resistance to children). *This suggests that the child's rebelliousness and resistance to control does not underlie the mother's use of reactive UPA.*

Secondly, the significant findings involving the hostility and resistance "difference scores," i.e., the relationships between mother's reactive UPA and child's being hostile and resistant *more toward children than toward teacher,* cannot readily be explained by the alternative view here being examined.

Additional evidence against this view is obtained when the relationships mentioned earlier, between the mother's reactive UPA and the father's authoritarianism and power needs, are examined. These relationships are relevant because they demonstrate that to some extent the mother's use of reactive UPA results from how her husband treats her. *Consequently, her use of reactive UPA cannot be attributable solely to the child's personality or behavior.*

It seems reasonable to conclude that mother's reactive UPA is very likely the antecedent variable and child's hostility, power assertiveness, and resistance to influence are the consequent variables.

SUMMARY AND CONCLUSIONS

The parent-child relationship was viewed as one in which the parent, by virtue of his greater physical strength, his complete control over the child's material and emotional supplies, and the existence of little external restraint, has a great deal of power (potential for compelling another to behave in a certain way) in all areas of the child's life. Because of his strong power position, the parent is free to choose influence techniques (attempts to change the child's overt behavior) which in varying degrees assert his power or attempt to induce the child to change his behavior voluntarily. The most power-assertive techniques, those which without any qualification demand immediate compliance, are referred to as unqualified power assertion (UPA). These techniques were assumed to conflict with the child's closure and autonomy needs. It was therefore hypothesized that the parent's use of UPA either as initial attempts to change the child's behavior (initial

UPA) or as reactions to his noncompliance (reactive UPA) relates positively to the child's hostility toward other children in the nursery school, his attempts to assert power over them, and his tendency to resist their influence attempts; and that these same relationships also exist *vis-a-vis* the teacher but to a lesser extent. It was also hypothesized that working class parents use more UPA than middle class parents.

The sample consisted of 12 middle class and 10 working class families having a child in attendance at a half-day nursery school. The parental UPA data were obtained from interviews in which the parent gave a fully detailed account of his interaction with the child the day before the interview. The interviews were coded for the parent's influence techniques and percentage scores were obtained for initial UPA and reactive UPA. The child data were obtained from three half-hour running account observations of each child in the nursery school. The observations were coded for hostility, power assertiveness, and resistance to influence attempts.

Working class fathers were found to use more initial and unqualified power assertions than middle class fathers. Differences between working and middle class mothers were obtained only in initial unqualified power assertion. Reasons were given for thinking this might reflect greater susceptibility to expert opinion by the working class mothers as compared to their husbands.

As regards effects on the child's personality development, the findings indicate that unqualified power assertion plays an important role when used by the mother under conditions of maximum involvement, i.e., after the child has already resisted a previous influence technique. Considerable support is given the hypotheses that the frequent use of unqualified power assertion under these conditions contributes to the development of hostility, power needs, and heightened autonomy strivings which the child displaces toward peers and, to a lesser extent, toward permissive authority figures.

Although a direct relationship between the father's use of unqualified power assertion and the child variables was not obtained, the findings suggest that the father does have an indirect effect on the child in that his power assertiveness toward his wife contributes to her power assertiveness toward the child. That is, her power assertiveness toward the child is partly a response to her husband's power assertiveness toward her. At least with respect to the variables and the age level dealt with here, then, the father appears to function like a catalyst in affecting the mother's influence behavior toward the child, this behavior in turn affecting the latter's personality development.

An important implication of this research is that studies of the effects of child-rearing practices should, whenever possible, include data on the parent's actual overt behavior toward the child. It is insufficient to measure just personality variables and assume these are related to overt behavior. The findings also suggest that studies of the antecedents of parental behavior should include data on the husband-wife relationship. Perhaps thinking of the entire family as a system of functionally interdependent relationships may be a fruitful guide even in research which focuses only on one dyadic relationship, e.g., mother and child.

REFERENCES

1. Bronfenbrenner, U. Socialization and social class through time and space. In E. E. Maccoby, T. M. Newcomb, & E. L. Hartley (Eds.), *Readings in social psychology.* New York: Holt, 1958. Pp. 400–425.
2. Hills, J. R. Within-groups correlations and their correction for attenuation. *Psychol. Bull.,* 1957, **54,** 131–134.
3. Hoffman, M. L. An interview method for obtaining descriptions of parent-child interaction. *Merrill-Palmer Quart.,* 1957, **4,** 76–83.
4. Veroff, J. Development and validation of a projective measure of power motivation. *J. abnorm. soc. Psychol.,* 1956, **54,** 1–8.

14. SOME PERSONALITY DIFFERENCES IN CHILDREN RELATED TO STRICT OR PERMISSIVE PARENTAL DISCIPLINE

Goodwin Watson

A. INTRODUCTION

In controversies over parental discipline of children, few of the arguments advanced for more permissiveness or for more strict adult control have yet been empirically tested. Does early indulgence "spoil" children or does it give them a foundation of "security" to meet life's stress and strain? Does firm and consistent discipline by the parents create in children inner hostilities, anxieties, and self-rejection or does it relieve anxiety and foster more successful self-discipline? Psychologists, psychoanalysts, teachers, parents, grandparents have often spoken with strong conviction on one or the other side of these issues, but the evidence has usually come from personal experience, clinical cases, plausible theories, or unconscious bias.

A generation ago this writer made a first effort at empirical study of this problem, comparing the self-reports of 230 graduate students who rated their home discipline during childhood along a continuum from the most strict to the most lenient. Those who came from the strictest quartile of homes reported: (a) more hatred for and constraint in relation to parents; (b) more rejection of teachers; (c) poorer relations with classmates, more quarrels, and shyness; (d) more broken engagements and unsatisfactory love affairs; (e) more worry, anxiety, and guilt feeling; (f) more unhappiness and crying; (g) more dependence on parents; but (h) better school grades and stronger ambition. Two cogent criticisms should be made of this study. First, the "strict" category included homes where there was severe punishment and quite possible rejection. The "lax" category included possible indifference and neglect along with genuine concern for freedom. Second, since all data came from the student's self-reports, a generally negative or optimistic outlook may have permeated both the reports on home discipline and the present self-evaluation.

A few years later (1938) Carpenter and Eisenberg (4) reported findings leading to similar conclusions. Among 500 college women, the 50 rated as

Reprinted with abridgement from *The Journal of Psychology,* 1957, **44**, 227–249, with permission of the author and The Journal Press.

most "dominant" reported a childhood in which their own "freedom" and "individuality" had been stressed. The more "submissive," like the shy, dependent, anxious students in our 1929 study, came almost entirely from adult-dominated homes. Those who "had to have parents permission to do practically everything" turned out at college age to be "submissives" (21%) rather than "dominants" (2%).

Studies attempting to relate specific early child-rearing practices (e.g., breast feeding, self-demand feeding, method of toilet training, etc.) to child personality seem to have been inconclusive [Cf. Sewell (11) and review by Orlansky (9)]. Those which center upon the general social climate in the home, on the other hand, reveal marked and generally consistent differences. One exception is Myers (8) who, in 1935, reported that a pupil adjustment questionnaire and high school teacher ratings on quality of personality adjustment were unrelated to strictness of home discipline.

Hattwick (5) in 1936 found that "over-attentive" homes which "favor" the child or "revolve around" the child were positively correlated (.2 to .4) with tendencies of nursery school pupils to be babyish in such matters as "cries easily," "asks unnecessary help," and "avoids risk." On the other hand, these same over-indulged children were less likely to take the property of others or to mistreat animals.

Ayer and Bernreuter (2) in 1951 reported on another study of the personality traits of nursery school children in relation to their home discipline. Significant correlations appeared between physical punishment at home and a tendency of children not to face reality ($r = .35$) and between permissiveness of parents (letting children learn from the natural consequences of their acts) and a more "attractive" personality in the child ($r = .33$).

Symonds (13) matched 28 parents who "dominated" their children in an authoritative way with 28 who permitted the child much freedom and who usually acceded to child wishes. He found the children from stricter homes more courteous, obedient, and neat, but also more shy, timid, withdrawing, docile, and troubled. The more permissive parents brought up children who were more aggressive, more disobedient, and who had more eating problems, but who also were more self-confident, better at self-expression, freer, and more independent.

Anderson (1) identified a group of junior high school pupils who had been brought up with warm affection but little adult dominance. He found these children marked by a high degree of maturity, poise, cheerfulness, coöperation, obedience, and responsibility.

Lafore (7), using techniques of direct, on-the-scene observation, made two half-hour visits in the homes of 21 nursery school children, and reported that:

> Parents who presented the largest number of instances of dictating (to) and interfering with their children, received the largest number of expressions of hostility from their children. . . .

Parents who showed large numbers of instances of blaming, hurrying, punishing, threatening and interfering had children who presented large numbers of crying. . . .
Children who were frequently threatened scored high on fearfulness. . . .
Children who were cautioned most often scored low on resourcefulness.

Radke's study (10) is in some ways closest to the one to be reported here. She studied 43 children of nursery school or kindergarten age, giving the parents a questionnaire and observing the children in free-play and picture-interpretation test situations. Children from more restrictive and autocratic home discipline showed less aggressiveness, less rivalry, were more passive, more colorless, and less popular. They did not get along so well with other children. The children from homes with freer discipline were more active, showed more rivalry, and were more popular. Radke found that parents who were "democratic" in their disciplinary methods, giving more respect to the youngsters, fostered children who themselves showed more consideration for others.

Baldwin (3) in 1948, reported on a study of 64 four-year-olds, showing that parents who were strict and undemocratic in their methods of control were likely to have children who were quiet, well-behaved, unaggressive, but restricted in curiosity, originality, and imagination.

Shoben (12) found that when parents of "problem children" (defined as: referred for clinical help, or brought into custody of juvenile authorities at least twice) were given an attitude scale they were more apt than were parents of non-problem children to agree with statements approving strict discipline and demand for obedience. Bi-serial correlation was .80 on the original group and .62 on a validating group for this variable which Shoben called "Dominating."

There is considerable convergence among the findings of these studies. There seems to be reason to suppose that firm, strict adult domination will produce the conforming, obedient child but will handicap him in initiative and probably burden him with shyness and a sense of inadequacy. More permissive treatment seems, in these studies, to result in more independence and aggressiveness on the part of the child. These children are less docile but in some studies appear to be more popular and more considerate of others. Shoben's results challenge a popular belief that juvenile delinquency is associated with lack of punishment by parents.

B. SELECTION OF SUBJECTS

This study was conducted under the auspices of The Guidance Center, a child-guidance clinic in New Rochelle. Associated with the Guidance Center was a positive program of education in mental health and of community service, reaching hundreds of parents of "normal" children in the eastern part of Westchester County. Subjects for this study were limited to normal children in school from kindergarten through sixth grade. Only "good" homes where children were wanted, loved, and well cared for were included. Any children who had ever been referred for psychological or psychiatric treatment were excluded. Nominations were sought from parents, teachers, and social workers, to find good homes that were known to be clearly "strict" or "permissive."

During a preliminary period, social workers visited the recommended homes and talked with these parents about their practices in child-raising. On the basis of the interviews a multiple-answer questionnaire was constructed and printed under the title, *How I Am Bringing Up My Child*. The instrument asked about parental reaction to each of 35 fairly common situations, such as children's eating, sleeping, toilet training, dressing, keeping clean, caring for toys, quarreling, anger at parents, sex curiosity, attendance at school and church, choice of television programs, friends, etc. Each situation was followed by three kinds of possible response: (*a*) a clearly permissive reaction, (*b*) a middle-of-the-road or "sometimes this and sometimes that" answer, and (*c*) a reply characteristic of the parent who sets standards and enforces strict obedience. The responses were assigned weights of 5 for the most permissive, 3 for the neutral, and 1 for the strict reaction. There was opportunity for parents to write in a response to each situation in their own words if none of the proposed answers seemed to fit well enough. If a parent's qualified answer fell between "strict" and "middle-of-the-road" it was given 2 points; if it fell between "middle-of-the-road" and "permissive" it was given 4 points. Consistent choice of the "strict" responses would result in a score of 35; consistent "middle-of-the-road" responses would give a total of 105; consistent "permissiveness" would bring a total score of 175. The actual range was from 55 to 158.

A range of 20 points on either side of the neutral point of 105 was arbitrarily set as representing the area of common practice—strict about some things at some times and more lenient on other matters or at other times. Although we had made special efforts to reach the more extreme groups— the permissive parents with scores of 125 or over, and the strict parents with scores of 85 or less—more than half (53%) of our responses fell in the 40 point middle range and were not used in this study.

The home discipline for 34 of the children was rated by fathers independently of the mother's rating. Fathers usually reported a less permissive attitude than did mothers. For these cases, fathers averaged a score of 105 and mothers 115. In only seven instances did the mother's report indicate a stricter attitude than that of the father. Correlation between mother's rating and father's was .61. For the sake of consistency, since mother's rating was available in all cases and since in suburban communities today the mother is more directly and more frequently responsible for discipline in the type of situation listed, our classification into strict or permissive is based only on the mother's report. In no instance would a child's classification have moved from one extreme category to the other if the father's questionnaire had been used instead of the mother's.

Responses of children to questions on home discipline as they saw it, usually confirmed the answers of the parents. Interviews and questionnaires, independently administered by Dr. Norris E. Fliegel, indicated that children from strict homes concurred with their mothers on 86 per cent of the items, and children from permissive homes agreed with mother on 91 per cent of the items. It is interesting also that the children almost invariably approved the form of discipline they were receiving. Those from permissive homes believed it was best to give children freedom to make their own decisions; those from strict homes felt that parents knew best and should exercise firm control.

C. PROCEDURE

Parents whose questionnaire score was extreme, falling under 86 (strict) or over 124 (permissive), were visited by a trained social worker who conducted an interview designed to check both directly and indirectly on the reported attitudes and practices, to evaluate the general climate of the home, and to obtain the parents' perception of their child's strength and weaknesses. The social workers were not informed as to whether the home to be visited had been reported as permissive or as strict but the differences were so marked that this was seldom in doubt. In the few (3) instances in which the social worker felt that the questionnaire classification was questionable because the home really belonged in the middle-of-the-road category rather than at the extreme, the case was not included in our comparative study. Thus every case which was included met both the criteria: extreme score on the questionnaire, and confirming judgment of a social worker who had independently observed parent and child in the home.

Children included in our study were voluntarily brought to the Guidance Center by their parents for an hour or two of psychological testing which included a free play period, a Rorschach test, selected pictures from the TAT, a figure-drawing test, and a performance test (Alexander Passalong) which gradually became too difficult and so gave opportunity to study reaction to stress or frustration.

We endeavored to get school behavior ratings for all the children, but this proved impossible in some cases. Wherever they cooperated, teachers or school guidance officers rated the children on a scale which provided intervals from 1 to 5 on: (*a*) level of activity; (*b*) initiative; (*c*) independence, spontaneity, self-reliance; (*d*) confidence, good adjustment; (*e*) friendliness and popularity; (*f*) cooperation; (*g*) self-control; and (*h*) persistence. In the case of 16 of 36 children rated by teachers a trained worker from the Guidance Center made an independent appraisal using the same scale. Agreement of the teacher and the outside observer is represented by a correlation of .77. Of 121 parallel judgments, 59 per cent agreed exactly; 31 per cent differed by only one scale step; and 10 per cent were two steps apart. Thus 90 per cent assigned the same or an adjoining category.

D. RESULTS

1. *Permissiveness Is Rare*

The first surprise of the study was our difficulty in finding parents who were fairly consistently permissive. Perhaps this should have been anticipated.

Whiting and Child (15) have estimated the over-all indulgence or severity of child training in 47 societies studied by competent anthropological observers. The aspects of discipline which they included in their index were: (*a*) earliness and severity of weaning; (*b*) toilet training; (*c*) repression of sexual activity; (*d*) repression of aggression; and (*e*) effort toward child's independence. They found only two of the 47 cultures as severe on the younger child as is the typical American middle-class white family described by Davis and Havighurst. No culture in the records is less permissive with children than we are. The short-shift given to "progressive education" in this country might further have warned us.

We had been led to believe, however, that in certain sub-cultures of the United States the ideal of respecting the child and of permitting him great freedom to mature in his own way and at his own good time had taken root. We knew that psychoanalytic concepts were commonly heard in upper-middle class Westchester child-study groups and that "mental hygiene" was looked upon as favorably as Divine Grace once had been. Some teachers complained that children were being given too much freedom at home and writers in popular journals freely listed lack of firm parental discipline as a major cause of juvenile delinquency. It was easy to find citizens who thought that some of their neighbors were overly-permissive parents.

We set the modest goal of 50 cases—25 boys and 25 girls—from child-centered, permissive homes. After strenuous search, with the cooperation of the Guidance Center, the Child Study Association, the Mental Hygiene Association, social workers, clergymen, teachers, pediatricians and P.T.A.'s; and after extending our quest for an extra year and modifying our qualifying scores a step or two downward toward the middle, we eventually located 38 permissively brought-up children—21 boys and 17 girls.

2. *Plan of Personality Study*

Children who are strictly brought up will be compared with children who are treated much more permissively, on each of nine dimensions of personality as follows:

Overt Behavior
1. Independence—dependence.
2. Socialization—egocentrism.

3. Persistence—easy discouragement.
4. Self-control—disintegration.
5. Energy—passivity.
6. Creativity—stereotyping.

Inner Feelings

7. Friendliness—hostility.
8. Security—anxiety.
9. Happiness—sadness.

In each instance the null hypothesis—that there is no significant difference between the two groups—will be statistically tested.

a. *Independence—Dependence, Hypothesis 1.* Is there no difference between children from strict and those from permissive homes in the personality dimension of independence—dependence?

Five measures bearing upon this hypothesis have been combined to give an index of independence. One is a rating by the psychologist of the child's behavior as he was brought into the playroom, shown the toys, games, puzzles, craft materials, etc., and told he might play with them in any way he chose. A rating of "5" is assigned to those children who promptly sized up the situation and went to work on their own responsibility with no further demands on the adult. The low extreme of the scale, a rating of "1," is assigned to those children who were unable to get going despite repeated instruction and reassurance. This rating correlates .70 with the composite index.

The second measure is a rating of the child's evident need for adult attention during the later activities of the testing period. Those children who independently judged their own performance with little reference to cues from the psychologist are at the high (5) end of the scale; those who were so dependent on adult approval that without definite reassurance their behavior was disrupted are given a rating of 1. This measure correlates .71 with the composite.

The third rating is based on a period of free play with doll figures representing a family. If the examiner was asked to make decisions for the child, the rating is low; high ratings represent independent, self-reliant structuring of the interpersonal play. This measure has the highest correlation (.76) with the composite index.

The fourth measure is based on the story interpretations which the child assigned to several TAT and CAT pictures. If the figures with whom the child seemed to identify most were self-reliant, acting on their own responsibility, the rating is 5. The lowest rating, 1, means that the identification figures were generally passive, helpless, or dependent. This correlates only .51 with the composite.

Our fifth rating is derived from Rorschach responses. Whether M (movement) responses were active and extensor or passive and flexor, or absent; whether the balance of C, CF, and FC tended toward or away from control, and the content of food and adult-child relationships were all taken into account. The Rorschach estimate correlates .67 with the composite.

Although some children from each type of home were found at every level of independence but the null hypothesis—that no real difference will be found—must be rejected. Differences (based on χ^2 with Yates' correction) are significant at better than the .01 level. The highly independent children include 29 per cent of our permissive sample, but only 5 per cent of the strictly disciplined children. The very dependent children represent 6 per cent of those from permissive homes and 21 per cent of those from strict homes. We find, therefore, a marked tendency for greater freedom in the home to show itself in greater independence in the child's behavior outside the home.

b. *Socialization—Egocentrism, Hypothesis 2.* Is there no difference between children from strict and those from permissive homes in the personality dimension of socialization—egocentrism?

Differences between the two groups show markedly better cooperation by children from permissive homes. Differences are statistically significant, being large enough to have a probability of chance occurrence, less than .01. The highest level of mature cooperation is found among 32 per cent of the children from permissive homes but only 9 per cent of the children strictly disciplined. The null hypothesis must be rejected and so also must the "spoiled child" or "little monster" tradition. Exceptionally permissive disciplined seems on the whole to be associated with better socialization and more effective cooperation with others. At the same time, it should be remembered that children from each type of home can be found at every step of the socialization scale.

This study does not demonstrate that the higher average level of independence reported earlier, or of cooperation reported here, is produced by the permissive discipline. It may be true—and the data on freedom from hostility to be reported later made this plausible—that the more relaxed home atmosphere is responsible for the observed differences in personality. Alternative explanations cannot, however, be excluded. Perhaps the kind of parents who choose the permissive role transmit, via heredity or via associated cultural influences, a different temperament or pattern of living. It should not be assumed that if parents who have heretofore practiced strict discipline were simply to change over to great permissiveness, their children would thereby become more independent or cooperative. They might, or might not. A correlational study cannot satisfactorily answer questions of causation.

c. *Persistence—Easy Discouragement, Hypothesis 3.* Is there no difference between children from strict and those from permissive homes in the personality dimension of persistence versus being easily discouraged?

All subjects were given the Alexander Passalong test which begins with easy problems in block movement and arrangement but proceeds to those which, although they seem workable, are impossibly difficult. The psychologists noted how long the child persisted at the task and also the effect of increasing difficulty and frustration upon personality organization and ability to make intelligent use of experience.

The null hypothesis can be accepted here since the two groups cannot confidently be regarded as from different statistical distributions. The null hypothesis is likewise supported by teacher ratings (for 38 cases) on persistence at school tasks which showed similar distributions for children from strict and from permissive homes.

If our hypothesis were revised to state that permissive discipline is associated with a moderate degree of persistence, while strict discipline is associated with either unusually persistent or easily discouraged behavior, this *post hoc* revised hypothesis would be supported by the psychological test data as better than the .01 level of significance. The revised hypothesis makes good psychological sense. Since we already know that the children from permissive homes are more inclined to act independently and on their own initiative, we might expect them to make a try at a very difficult problem, but to use their own judgment in giving it up when no progress is made. In contrast, the children accustomed to firm adult control might more readily feel helpless, or, if instructed to keep on trying, persist in their vain efforts. The data on intellectual quality of the continued effort will be helpful in assessing this expectation.

As the task grew more difficult, some children became frustrated and deteriorated in their learning process. Others continued to study the problem, did not repeat errors, and evidenced growing insight into the difficulty. Type of home discipline does seem to be related to quality of behavior under difficulties. Serious deterioration in intellectual quality of response was found in 13 (32 per cent) of the children with strict up-bringing, but in only 2 (6 per cent) of the children given greater freedom.

The hypothesis that home discipline is unrelated to persistence-discouragement should probably be rejected. The observed differences certainly do not sustain the popular fear that children who are allowed their own way much of the time at home will collapse when faced by difficult tasks. Apparently—with due allowance, again, for the fact that some children from each type of home can be found at every level—there is some tendency for permissive discipline to foster the type of personality which makes a reasonable effort, continues effective intellectual attack upon problems, but is unlikely to persist indefinitely against odds. Differences in school work are not significant.

d. *Self-Control—Emotional Disintegration, Hypothesis 4.* Is there no difference between children from strict and those from permissive homes in the personality dimension of self-control versus emotional disintegration?

Closely related to the quality of intellectual attack upon a difficult problem is the emotional response during frustration. The psychologist's rating of the child's emotional reactions as the Passalong test became too difficult for him showed that the null hypothesis is acceptable; observed differences are not statistically significant. A further test of the hypothesis may be made, using teacher's ratings for 37 of the children. Again, differences fall within what might well be expected by chance.

Our data do not support the view that children given firm control at home are better able to withstand frustration; neither do they support those who argue that strict parental control interferes with the development of the child's self-control.

e. *Energy—Passivity, Hypothesis 5.* Is there no difference between children from strict and those from permissive homes in the dimension of energetic versus passive personality?

Three ratings are applicable to testing of this hypothesis. One is a rating by the psychologist of the apparent energy level of the child. Scores range from 1 for "inert, uninvolved" manner during play and testing, through 2 for subdued activity, to 5 for very lively participation. This variable refers to focused personality energy, not to merely physical, muscular activity.

The second rating is derived wholly from the Rorschach performance, taking account of total number of responses, number of content categories, number of wholes, and amount of movement.

The third estimate is based on an exercise in which the child drew a man, a woman, and himself.

Average intercorrelation of the three ratings is .46; predicted reliability for the three combined is .72. The differences between groups are not significant and the null hypothesis is acceptable.

"Activity level" has also been rated by the teachers of 38 of our children. High (4 or 5) ratings are given to 15 (63 per cent) of 24 children from strict homes as compared with only 5 of 14 children (36 per cent) from permissive homes. Differences between the two distributions are significant at a probability level between $P = .02$ and $P = .05$, with higher ratings for the children from stricter homes. That pupils from strictly disciplined homes are seen by teachers as more energetic and active may be related to their more ready acceptance of teacher direction. This point came out earlier in connection with teacher ratings on "independence." The sex difference again raises a question about what the typical teacher means by "energetic." High ratings on activity and energy were assigned to 67 per cent of the girls but to only 43 per cent of the boys.

Neither the data from the psychological tests nor those from the classroom would support the view that strict home discipline typically represses impulses to such an extent as to make children inactive. In the test situation no difference is apparent, at school the well-disciplined children appear, on the whole, more active along approved lines.

f. Creativity—Conformity, Hypothesis 6. Is there no difference between children from strict and those from permissive homes in the personality dimension of creativity versus conformity?

Five measures of this variable are available. One is based on the child's behavior, ranging from free and imaginative to stereotyped and monotonous, during a free play period. A second has been similarly observed during a period of play with a full family of dolls. The third estimates originality and imagination in stories composed as responses to CAT and TAT pictures. The fourth comes from Rorschach responses and the fifth from human figure-drawing. The average intercorrelation of these measures is .53 and the predicted reliability for the combined rating is .85.

The differences between the two groups are the most impressive of any in our comparisons, and compel rejection of the null hypothesis. High creativity characterizes 11 (33 per cent) of the children brought up with unusual freedom, but only 2 (5 per cent) of those from strict homes. The more firmly disciplined children are most apt to be found near the middle of the range in this variable.

The first six variables—independence, socialization, persistence, self-control, energy, and creativity—have focused on more overt, and directly observable behavior. The remaining three turn attention to the inner life of the child.

g. Friendliness—Hostility, Hypothesis 7. Is there no difference between children from strict and those from permissive homes along the dimension of friendly versus hostile feelings toward others?

Our psychological testing yields four projective indications of inner hostility. One is based on observation of free play with dolls. Hostile contacts or avoidance of contacts is rated 1; friendly interaction is rated 5.

The second is based on the TAT and CAT stories. The low end of the scale (rating 1) is assigned to stories of violent conflict, death, and destruction. High scores represent stories of friendly interaction.

The third rating is based on such Rorschach signs as content items interpreted as aggressive weapons, mutilated human or animal bodies, and aggressive or hostile M or FM.

The fourth has been drawn from analysis of the figure-drawing test and responses during the drawing.

Intercorrelations among these tests range from .50 to .74 averaging .60; the predicted reliability for the four combined is .87—the highest of any of our measures.

When the hostility versus friendliness scores of the two groups are compared, the null hypothesis should be rejected. More hostility is evident in those children who have been strictly disciplined; more positive feelings toward others are expressed by children whose parents have been permissive; these differences are consistent through the distribution and are statistically significant. At the same time, it should be remembered that neither group has a complete monopoly on positive, friendly feelings toward others or on inner hostility.

Reactions to frustration on the Passalong Test make possible another rating which has in it a high component of hostility for some children. Half of the TAT story-completion test was administered before the frustrating experience of failure on the too-difficult block test. The other half was given immediately after the somewhat annoying defeat. For a few children, the consequence was that the stories in the latter part of the test were briefer, the child was less cooperative and gave more evidence of hostility. This behavior characterized six (15 per cent) of the 41 children from strict homes; but only one (3 per cent) of the 32 children from permissive homes. This difference was not statistically significant, but its direction is in accord with the evidence indicating that strict discipline does leave a residue of inner hostility.

Supplementary research by Dr. Norris E. Fliegel, in which the Blacky Test was administered to 47 of our subjects, showed only one significant difference in the emotional life of the 24 adult-dominated as distinguished from that of the 23 self-regulating children. "Children from strict homes did not feel free to express their hostility, but had to inhibit it." As reported earlier, the children from strict homes did not openly resent adult control; indeed, they endorsed it. But on projective tests it was clear that they fancied that even a little puppy should submit to what is expected of him and never get angry at those who push him around.

h. Security—Anxiety, Hypothesis 8. Is there no difference between children from strict and those from permissive homes in the personality dimension security-anxiety?

Five different ratings compose our measure of anxiety. One is the psychologist's general impression of the overtly confident or insecure behavior of the child. Three are based on projective tests: one on Card 9 of the CAT, one on the Rorschach, and one on the figure drawing test. The fifth measure is the anxiety evident during failure on the Passalong test. These five measures have an average intercorrelation of .33; the combined index would have a predicted reliability of .71 which is not high but would suffice if the groups turn out to be markedly different.

Here two groups are not clearly distinguished. The null hypothesis is acceptable. Half a dozen children from each type of discipline show marked evidence of anxiety—another half-dozen from each category behave in an easy, secure manner. What makes for anxiety in a child must be something other than unusually strict or unusually lax parental control.

i. Happiness—Sadness, Hypothesis 9. Is there no difference between children from strict and those from permissive homes in the personality dimension of happiness versus sadness?

Three measures are related to general level of happiness. One is a rating of the overt manner and apparent mood of the child during his play and testing periods. Scores range from 5 for the most euphoric to 1 for the most depressed. A second measure is derived by analysis of the imaginative stories given in response to CAT and TAT pictures. Predominantly optimistic and enjoyable events result in high ratings; stories in which distress, sadness, and unhappiness come to the leading figures result in a low score. The third measure is based upon Rorschach test responses. Predominant use of black, and perception of figures as torn and broken, are used as indicators of depression.

Intercorrelations among the several indices (except for overt behavior and the Rorschach which correlate .54) are low, averaging .28 and giving a combined predictive reliability of .54.

Results conform to the null hypothesis. While our data show a slightly larger proportion of permissive discipline subjects in both the "happy" and the "unhappy" categories, the differences are unreliable.

E. SUMMARY

Forty-four children brought up in good, loving, but strictly disciplined homes are compared with 34 children from the same community and also brought up in good loving homes but with an extraordinary degree of permissiveness. Two periods of psychological testing, supplemented (in 38 cases) by teacher ratings, have yielded measures of nine dimensions of personality. On three of the nine, no statistically significant difference is found: these are the dimensions of self-control, inner security, and happiness. Factors making for anxiety, emotional disorganization, and unhappiness are found about equally often under either type of home discipline. No difference in activity and energy level was observed during the psychological testing, but teacher ratings indicate higher activity level of an approved sort, at school for the children accustomed to stricter discipline.

On persistence, teachers observe no differences, but on a psychological test children from strict homes are more apt to fall in extreme categories, being either unusually persistent or very easily discouraged. A moderate persistence is more characteristic of the children from permissive homes. These children maintain a better quality of intellectual activity under difficulty than do the children from strict homes.

On the four remaining variables (which are also those most reliably measured, with predicted r's from .80 to .87) significant differences in each instance are in favor of the children from permissive homes. Greater freedom for the child is clearly associated with: (*a*) more initiative and independence (except, perhaps, at school tasks); (*b*) better socialization and cooperation; (*c*) less inner hostility and more friendly feelings toward others; and (*d*) a higher level of spontaneity, originality, and creativity.

None of the personality differences applies to all cases; some from per-

154   Parent Attitude and Behavior Variables

missive homes may be found at every level on every characteristic tested. It is impressive, however, to find no clear personality advantage associated in general with strict discipline in a good home. Where differences do emerge, these are consistently to the credit of the more permissive upbringing. This study cannot distinguish the extent to which the advantages associated with permissiveness are due to that procedure alone and the extent to which more permissive parents may convey hereditary or cultural assets with which the permissive attitudes happen to be correlated.

REFERENCES

1. Anderson, J. P. *The relationships between certain aspects of parental behavior and attitudes of junior high school pupils.* New York: Teachers College, Columbia University, 1940.
2. Ayer, M. E., & Bernreuter, R. A study of the relationship between discipline and personality traits in young children. *J. Genet. Psychol.,* 1937, **50,** 165–170.
3. Baldwin, A. L. Socialization and the parent-child relationship. *Child Devel.,* 1948, **19,** 127–136.
4. Carpenter, J., & Eisenberg, P. Some relationships between family background and personality. *J. of Psychol.,* 1938, **6,** 115–136.
5. Hattwick, B. W. Interrelations between the preschool child's behavior and certain factors in the home. *Child Devel.,* 1936, **7,** 200–226.
6. Hattwick, B. W., & Stowell, M. The relation of parental over-attentiveness to children's work habits and social adjustment in kindergarten and the first six grades of school. *J. Ed. Res.,* 1936, **30,** 162–176.
7. Lafore, G. Practices of parents in dealing with preschool children. *Child Devel. Monog.,* 1945, **31,** 3–150.
8. Myers, T. R. *Intrafamily relationships and pupil adjustment.* New York: Teachers College, Columbia University, 1935.
9. Orlansky, H. Infant care and personality. *Psychol. Bull.,* 1949, **46,** 1–48.
10. Radke, M. J. *The relation of parental authority to children's behavior and attitudes.* Minneapolis: Univ. Minnesota Press, 1946.
11. Sewell, W. H. Infant training and the personality of the child. *Am. J. Sociol.,* 1952, **58,** 150–157.
12. Shoben, E. J., Jr. The assessment of parental attitudes in relation to child adjustment. *Genet. Psychol. Monog.,* 1949, **39,** 101–148.
13. Symonds, P. M. *Psychology of parent-child relationships.* New York: Appleton-Century-Crofts, 1939.
14. Watson, G. A comparison of the effects of lax versus strict home discipline. *J. Soc. Psychol.,* 1934, **5,** 102–105.
15. Whiting, J. W. M., & Child, I. L. *Child Training and Personality.* New Haven: Yale Univ. Press, 1953.

Section III
Parental Antecedents of Certain Child Behavior Dimensions

Introduction

Much of the research in the previous section was designed to identify the consequences for the child of parental attitudes and behavior. The research in this section has sought to trace back and attribute to the parents differences among children on various dimensions. The research in both sections has been primarily correlational in nature, subject to all the hazards involved in attempting to draw cause-and-effect conclusions from data which only show a relationship to exist between two variables. For example, no researcher has manipulated parental rejection by instructing a group of parent subjects to reject their children and then measure the behavioral consequences in the child, with all other variables held constant. Similarly, few experimental studies have attempted to establish antecedents of aggression or anxiety by manipulating behavior in such a way as to create these emotional states.

Thus, parent-child research data suffer from the danger of attributing child behavior C to parent behavior A when C actually was the result of parent behavior B, which almost invariably accompanies A. Or, to use another kind of example, the child's low self-acceptance may be due to parental rejection, or both of these may be the result of parental self-rejection, as illustrated below.

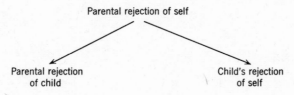

Included in this section are seven studies. In the first selection a variety of maternal behaviors are related to several personality and emotional characteristics in the child. One study is concerned with parental factors related to aggression in boys, and another compares parental attitudes of disturbed versus normal children. Two investigations deal with school behavior—one with the child's early adjustment to school and the other with cognitive functioning. Antecedents of dependency and conscience development are examined in the two remaining selections.

Interestingly, the studies dealing with aggression and emotional disturbance agree in showing the importance of the father's role in the development of these behaviors. The mother, on the other hand, seems to play the predominant role in the appearance of dependency. Parents as role models, as well as the role each parent plays in relation to the child, may account for this situation. The father, representing the male role, serves as a masculine role model and is probably the chief frustrating agent in the home. The mother's closer contact and stronger emotional relation with the child might be such as to lead to dependency in the child if there is any disruption of this relationship.

15. MATERNAL BEHAVIOR AND PERSONALITY

DEVELOPMENT: DATA FROM THE

BERKELEY GROWTH STUDY

Nancy Bayley and Earl S. Schaefer

This report is concerned with one segment of an investigation of social interaction patterns as they were observed in a longitudinal study, and as they bear on several aspects of the development of a group of normal children. This part of the research is an exploration into interactions between the child and his mother, as they bear on the formation and establishment of emotional and attitudinal patterns of behavior in the child. The study involves both the development of *conceptual schemes* of relevant maternal and social-emotional child behaviors and a preliminary empirical testing of them. Our empirical data are from the Berkeley Growth Study (3), and our conceptual schemes have, to a considerable extent, grown out of these same empirical data.

SAMPLE AND OUTLINE OF STUDY

The main emphasis in the Berkeley Growth Study has, until recently, been directed toward the mental, motor, and physical growth of this group of children who were seen first as healthy neonates. But in the thirty-year records of their growth we have accumulated much information about their emotions, attitudes, and ways of coping with their environments. The evident relevance of these social-emotional behaviors to the other aspects of growth, as well as the importance for study of these processes of growth themselves, have led us in the last several years to try a new approach to the Berkeley data. Some of the resulting studies have already been reported by Schaefer, Bell and Bayley, and are published or in the process of being published (1, 4, 5, 6). A brief review here of these preliminary studies seems in order, to set the background for the material we wish to present today.

The children of the Berkeley Growth Study have been observed at the Institute of Child Welfare at frequent intervals from the time they were born in Berkeley, California in 1928 and 1929 (3). The criteria for their inclusion in the study were that they be full-term, healthy infants of white, English-

Reprinted with abridgement from *Psychiatric Research Reports*, 1960, **13**, 155–173, with permission of the authors and the American Psychiatric Association.

speaking parents who were willing and able to cooperate in the planned series of tests and measurements. The babies were born in two Berkeley hospitals and were first seen by the pediatrician in the study at about four days of age. In a six-month period 61 babies (31 boys and 30 girls) were registered in the study. A few of these dropped out and a few replacements were made. Of the total, there are fairly complete records on 54 of the children through at least their first six years, and on 48 of them to adult or almost adult status.

In addition to the measurements of mental, motor, and physical growth, a variety of ratings and notes were made on the children's emotional and attitudinal behaviors. Also, among the records are some fairly extensive descriptions of the mothers' behaviors as observed during the children's first three years, when the mothers were present while their babies were being tested and measured (usually about 20 visits during this period). For 34 of the mothers there is an additional set of descriptive characterizations that are based on interviews made when the children were between the ages of nine and 14 years.

We have converted descriptive notes on both the mothers and the children into scores that can be treated statistically. These, together with various ratings made at the times of observation and with other measures and scores, have been intercorrelated and further analyzed statistically. From these data we have derived patterns of maternal and child behaviors and have been able to study some of their interrelations and their consistencies over time.

MATERNAL BEHAVIORS

The maternal records were converted into objective scores by Schaefer and Bell, who devised what they have called a Maternal Behavior Research Instrument (6). This is a series of rating scales for 32 variables representing those maternal behaviors that were considered to be theoretically relevant, and that also could be judged from the available material in the notes. They then adapted 28 of the scales and applied them to the descriptions that had been made of the mothers at the preadolescent (9-14 year) interviews. Schaefer has found that most of these maternal behavior rating scales can be arranged in a circular order with two reference dimensions of Autonomy-Control and Love-Hostility. This circumplex reveals a sequential ordering of scales according to a law of neighboring (2).

Utilizing the two circumplex orderings and other published data on maternal attitudes and behaviors, Schaefer (4) has developed a theoretical circumplex model of maternal behavior, shown in Figure 1. Most of the relevant mother-child personal-social interactions seem to fall into this two-dimensional space. We have based our further ordering of maternal and child behavior on hypotheses derived from this model. Intercorrelations between behaviors can be arranged into sequential orders of neighboring, and often

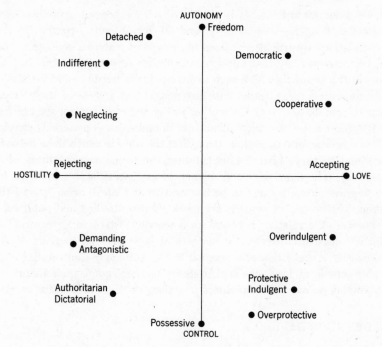

Figure 1. A theoretical model for the circumplex of maternal behavior. (*Source:* Schaefer, 1959, page 232.)

into fairly complete circumplexes. With this procedure, we may explore patterns of interaction by relating one ordered set of variables (*e.g.*, maternal behavior) with another ordered set (*e.g.*, child behavior).

One of our first explorations has been a study of the consistency over time of maternal behavior. Presumably those characteristics that are more stable will have a greater, cumulative effect on the children and their behaviors. It was possible to correlate the maternal traits that appeared to be very similar as they had been rated from the protocols obtained at the two periods, roughly 10 years apart (5). These correlations show rather high consistency for items in the Love-Hostility dimension, but low intercorrelations for those in the Autonomy-Control dimension. That is, the mothers of children under three years who were seen to be affectionate and warm in the testing situation were usually also seen by an independent interviewer as affectionate in their attitudes toward their young adolescents. However, the other dimension, Autonomy-Control, was not stable, as here measured. These differences in consistency may be summarized in the cluster correlations: That is, when the ratings representing love *vs.* hostility and those representing autonomy *vs.* control are combined into two sets of scores for the two sets of data, behavior toward infants is correlated with expressed attitudes toward preadolescents .68 for love-hostility, and .26 for autonomy-control. If these two correlations are true descriptions of degrees of maternal consistency over time, then we may say that affectional attitudes tend to be stable, but that factors in the age of the child, such as his needs for freedom, and his abilities to exercise autonomy, together with the mothers' awareness of these factors, appear to operate to change the mother in the degree of control she exercises.

Before we leave this description of the organization of maternal behaviors, we should note several conditions that affect the ways in which these behaviors were found to vary. First, let us consider the socioeconomic status of the mother (1). The more educated, higher socioeconomic-status mothers tend more to grant autonomy and to be cooperative and equalitarian toward their children. The low-status mothers are more often controlling and punitive.

Further, the relation between socio-economic status and maternal behavior is consistently greater for mothers of boys than for mothers of girls. There is even a suggestion of a reversal in the Autonomy-Control dimension: For this sample at least, the higher-status mothers grant their infant sons more autonomy and their daughters less than do the lower-status mothers.

CHILDREN'S BEHAVIORS

Given these characterizations of the mothers, what information have we on the children which we can relate to maternal behavior? The most readily available scores on child behavior are a series of ratings that had been made by the examiner (most often Bayley), immediately after the child's visit. These ratings were all made on seven-point scales; they are concerned with emotional and attitudinal aspects of the children's behavior in the testing-measuring situation. Three different rating forms were used (each appropriate for the child's age), and the ratings included all ages between nine months and 12 years. In order to have a measure of the children's adolescent behavior, we utilized descriptive notes that were written after each examination, but it was necessary first to convert them into a meaningful array of scores. Ratings (seven-point) were made from these notes on 96 adjectives that covered a wide range of personality variables.

We have thus, in the form of ratings, some evaluations (more or less restricted in nature) of the children throughout almost their entire period of growth. We should emphasize that we are dealing with observed overt behaviors, and can thus make no direct tests of underlying conflicts or motivations.

In working with these ratings we have found sufficient evidence of sex differences, both in the mothers' treatments of their children and in the children's behaviors, that it has been necessary to make our analyses for the sexes separately.

A. THE MOTHERS' BEHAVIORS TOWARD THEIR INFANTS RELATED TO CHILD BEHAVIOR

a. The Child from 10–36 Months

Figure 2 shows the correlations between mothers' behaviors and their sons' happiness (or non-irritability). In this chart, for each maternal variable there are 4 correlations, for the 4 age levels within the 10 to 36 months period. Although many of the *r*'s are not, when taken alone, statistically significant, there is a definite order in their pattern. This order becomes impressive as it is seen in series after series of the correlation charts.

The correlational trends show a tendency for the loving mothers to have calm, happy sons, the controlling, hostile mothers to have excitable, unhappy sons. Similarly, sons' positive behaviors tend to go with loving mothers and negative behaviors with anxious, intrusive, irritable mothers.

Responsiveness to persons and shyness show no significant relations to these maternal behaviors. These two behavior traits appear to be in a neutral position in the order of neighboring in the matrix of maternal-child interrelations.

There is a shift in relations as we move from the emotional to the activity variables. The loving mothers tend to have inactive babies, up through 15 months, while for the same ages the hostile mothers have active babies. For the later ages (18–36 months) the correlations are abruptly reduced or possibly even reversed. Speed of movement presents a very similar picture.

The mother-daughter relations are essentially similar. For the girls the pattern of relations looks even stronger for the "emotional-tone" variables (calmness, happiness, positive behavior), but is less clear for the activity variables. Here again is a suggestion of a possible sex difference.

b. The 2½ to 12-Year-Old

With some exceptions, the mother-son relations are similar at all ages between 2½ and 8 years. In general, the boys show a fairly clear pattern in the four observed areas of behavior as they relate to the Maternal Behavior circumplex. Friendly, Cooperative, Attentive, and Facile scores tend to go with maternal scores that are high in Autonomy, Positive Evaluation, Equalitarian Treatment, and Expression of Affection; while the sons of the hostile mothers tend to score low in these four traits. There is no relation to scores in the area of maternal control. There are, however, some shifts in correlation with age. Between 33 to 54 months all of the correlations are reduced, so there is no clear pattern of relations, but only slight tendencies in the expected directions. The pattern is evident again by six years. Figure 3, for age 90–96 months is illustrative of these mother-son correlations.

For the girls, the pattern of mother-child relations undergoes a definite

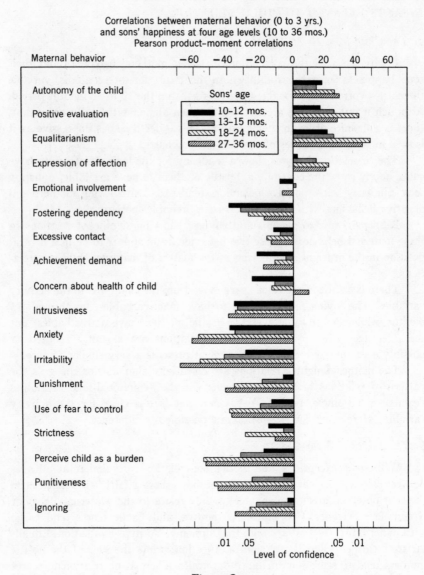

Figure 2.

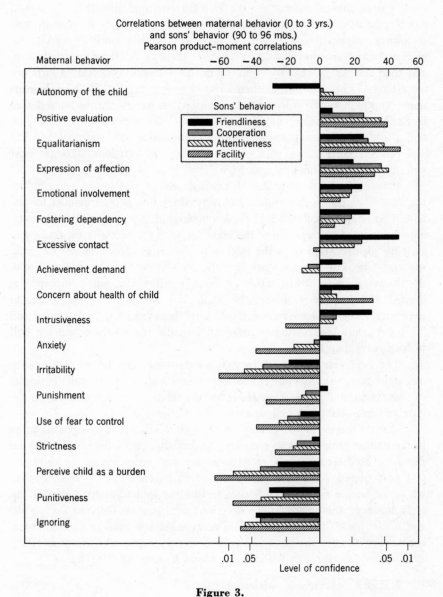

Correlations between maternal behavior (0 to 3 yrs.)
and sons' behavior (90 to 96 mos.)
Pearson product-moment correlations

Figure 3.

change with age, most marked in Friendliness and Cooperation. Age-runs of these correlations show an orderly shift in size and direction. At 27–30 months the daughters of accepting (loving) mothers tend to be friendly and somewhat cooperative, while the daughters of hostile mothers tend to be unfriendly and uncooperative. But with age these correlations approach zero, and then reverse, so that by eight years, the friendly, cooperative girls are more likely to have hostile mothers. The change is most marked for Friendliness. In the more test-oriented behaviors (Attentiveness and to some degree in Facility) there is more stability in the correlations. For the most part, we find a fairly constant pattern of negative correlations with maternal hostility and positive correlations with maternal love, the relations showing most strongly between 42 and 60 months.

It is interesting to note that this period around four to five years is just the time when the mother-child pattern of correlation is least evident for the boys. One might speculate about the importance of this age-period in developing identification with parent of the same sex, with the necessity for the boy to shift his identification from the mother to the father. However, we can only speculate; because our cases are few, the correlations, by the very nature of the behaviors under investigation are mostly rather low, our information is limited, and we have no information about father-child relationships. But at their face value, we have evidence that girls' behaviors are more related and boys' behaviors less related to maternal warmth around three and one-half to four years than at other ages.

The 9–12 year ratings are very similar to those made between 27 months and eight years. And the pattern of correlations with maternal traits is similar to that found at adjacent ages. However, the relations are less evident for the girls and in general less clear than for the earlier ages.

During this period of latency or neutral childhood, there appears to be in the mother-child relations stability for the boys and a systematic shift for the girls. Mothers who were rated as loving and accepting in the children's 0–3 year period, have sons who continue to be classified as well-adjusted, while the hostile mothers tend to have the less well-adjusted sons. For the girls, however, these correlations drop as the girls grow older so that at the end of the period there is practically no relation and even the possibility of some reversals. For the boys, the relationship is lowest when they are three and one-half to four and one-half years, and it then builds up again.

c. Children's Behaviors at Adolescence

We should expect some changes in mother-child relationships during the period of adolescence. This is notorious as a time when children rebel against parental controls and often experience strong emotions in the process of adjusting to adult status.

How do these adolescent traits relate to early maternal behavior? Among the girls, the correlation charts show only hints of resemblance between their behavior-tendencies and the way their mothers treated them as infants. The r's are so low that we are not justified even in speculating. The boys, however, as usual show some clear patterns.

In the mother-son relationships, it appears that the Love-Hostility dimension is less important, although positively evaluating equalitarian mothers more often had well-adjusted sons. It is the early maternal pattern of autonomy-control that is most clearly correlated with adolescent extraversion-introversion. That is, the pattern of correlation coefficients shows that autonomy-granting, ignoring (and to some extent punitive) mothers more often had sons who at adolescence were reserved, timid, and tactful. The mothers who were close, involved, and controlling toward infant sons (emotionally involved, fostered dependency, made excessive contact, demanded achievement, and were concerned about their sons' health) had adolescent boys who were more often characterized as rude, irritable, impulsive, and independent. In other words, the adolescent revolt appears to be strongest in those boys whose mothers were closely interacting and involved with them as infants.

CONCURRENT MOTHER-CHILD INTERACTIONS AT ADOLESCENCE

So far, we have talked about children's behavior as related to the maternal behavior when they were infants. When we turn to the mothers' attitudes toward their children at a later age we again find sex differences in correlation. The ratings of mothers made from interviews when the children approximated 12 to 13 years show similar concurrent correlational patterns toward both daughters and sons, but they are much clearer for the daughters. The adolescent girls, who evidence little carry-over from the influences of early maternal behavior, seem to be well attuned to their mothers' present attitudes. Although there are only 13 girls on whom we have the later maternal ratings, many of the correlation coefficients are high enough to reach statistical significance. Girls who are maladjusted, (*i.e.*, rated as gloomy, unhappy, sulky, and hostile) more often have mothers who are hostilely controlling (*i.e.*, punitive, irritable, controlling, isolating, and make excessive contact with their daughters).

Girls who are rated as popular and not nervous, and who on the adolescent behavior circumplex are well-adjusted, show high correlations with mothers who are social, and outgoing, and on the maternal circumplex grant their daughters autonomy, are equalitarian, and evalute them positively: That is, these mothers' scores tend to fall in the upper right quadrant of the maternal circumplex (Autonomy-Love), and themselves are somewhat extraverted.

The 13 boys for whom we have the 9–14 year maternal ratings more often show maladjusted tendencies (hostile, cold, not courteous) if their mothers are hostile (primarily punitive, ignoring, and intrusive). None of the other r's are significant, but they in general tend to support this relation and to indicate a probable relation between well-adjusted (friendly, sociable) boys and loving mothers.

We may summarize these concurrent mother-child interactions at adolescence by noting the tendency which is stronger for girls, for well-adjusted children to have mothers who are autonomy-granting and loving, and for maladjusted children to have mothers who are hostile and controlling.

SEX DIFFERENCES IN MOTHER-CHILD PATTERNS OVER TIME

As was noted earlier, the behaviors of mothers toward their infant sons continued to show significant relations to these boys' characteristics even through adolescence. The only exception is a brief period around three and one-half to four and one-half years when the correlations dropped very low. However, the mother-daughter correlations that were strongly clear in infancy, faded out as the girls grew older.

When we reverse the picture and compare the ratings on the mothers made when the children were around 12 to 13 years old with the children at all ages, we again find the sex differences in constancy over time. The boys' scores at adolescence show a moderate pattern of correlations in the predicted directions with these concurrent maternal scores. And also the patterns of correlation are present retrospectively and often rather strongly clear back to the 10–36 month ratings. Again the relations drop out briefly around three and one-half to four and one-half years. With this exception, the boys appear to establish early certain characteristic behaviors or attitudes and inter-actions with their mothers that persist over time.

The mothers' later scores, as we have noted, show a marked pattern of correlation with the girls' scores at adolescence. But there is no correlation with the girls at younger ages. The mother-daughter interactions appear to be strong, but continuously changing over time, so that for them it is the present that determines the nature of their interpersonal behavior. It is as though the girl is attuned to adapt to the important aspects of her present interpersonal milieu rather than to persist in an established set of habit patterns.

In reviewing these patterns of correlation there appears to be at least one area of incompatibility of findings. Comparisons of the children's own scores over time indicate somewhat greater consistency in girls than in boys. But when we turn to mother-child relations the boys' behaviors are the ones that maintain the clearer relations to maternal behaviors whether the mothers are rated before or after the boys' ages at comparison. Perhaps these two conditions are not mutually exclusive. There is still room for freedom in correlations of the magnitude under consideration here. It is also possible that, in the close mother-daughter ties the daughter's behaviors have considerable effect on their mothers' concurrent behavior. The boys, on the other hand, might show in later childhood and adolescence close relations to their fathers, if such data were available to us.

INDIVIDUAL PATTERNS OF INTERACTION

In this presentation, so far, we have treated these mother-child interactions entirely by manipulating correlations between groups. The question arises whether, and to what extent, we can apply these findings to individual cases.

To explore this question, we have plotted individual scores for mothers and adolescent children on circumplex charts. The analyses of these cases has not yet been completed. But in looking them over it is evident that although many of the cases fit the expected pattern of relations, a fair number do not. For example, Jim's mother is hostile and controlling toward him, both as an infant and as a preadolescent. Jim was an unhappy, and unfriendly, little boy, and a hostile and maladjusted adolescent. For comparison, the mother of another boy, Tom, is also somewhat controlling but is definitely loving and not hostile. Her son Tom has at adolescence a very similar profile to Jim's, though he is even more hostile. It is difficult to explain these discrepant relationships, but some information about the boys may be relevant. For one thing, these boys are brothers. The same woman has obviously different attitudes and behaviors toward her two sons, so much so that she was never recognized by the raters as the same person. We might have expected Tom to be less hostile and in general better adjusted than Jim. In the senior author's personal experience with Tom, it is her belief that he is better adjusted, but less inhibited and freer to express his hostility. Also there was evidence in his behavior that Tom tried hard to emulate his older brother. But there are, of course, also many other relevant factors that must be called into the picture for an adequate understanding of these boys' similarities and differences.

Another mother was loving and autonomy-granting toward Dan, her first-born. Dan was a calm, happy baby and a friendly, social, attentive little boy. As an adolescent, he is extraverted, with no clear-cut evidence for either poor or good adjustment.

The mother of Anna is loving and controlling toward her infant daughter. As her daughter approached adolescence, she has shifted from control to autonomy-granting, remaining loving. Anna is a well-adjusted, friendly adolescent.

Let us now select on the basis of some characteristic of the child. Morgan has had serious problems as an adult, having been hospitalized briefly after 21 years with a diagnosis of catatonic schizophrenia. The ratings on his mother show some congruence between her controlling behavior and theories of schizophrenogenic mothers. Morgan himself, as an adolescent, was maladjusted, though his scores are not extreme.

Another boy who was in a mental hospital briefly is Elbert. His mother is rated consistently as loving and autonomy-granting. One would never suspect maladjustment in her son. We do not have ratings on Elbert at adolescence because he was so upset by having to go through the physical examinations that he refused to come in for any tests. In retrospect, he is remembered as a quiet, rather withdrawn, sensitive, painfully self-conscious adolescent who was also very small and slow in maturing physically. It may be relevant to note that both Morgan and Elbert became ill while in the armed services, and both boys, though very different from each other, would (in the Examiner's opinion) have problems in adapting to the gregarious and conforming army life. With two such different mothers, we must look to some of these other factors as precipitating causes of their difficulties.

Nora and her mother make an interesting pair. The mother was very involved and controlling, more affectionate at first, then later a little more punitive. As an adolescent Nora was very hostile and extraverted. Her behavior appears to be a strong rebellion against maternal control. The impression Nora gave the examiners at this period was that she now controlled her parents. For example, she obtained from them written consent to marry at 16. When she came in for tests at this age, she gave the name and a description of her fiancé. Three days later there was a newspaper account, with picture, of Nora's marriage to an obviously different man. This is only a small episode in Nora's history. But her behavior has always been extraverted, tending after her first eight or 10 years toward hostile extraversion.

These are only meager samples of data from a few cases. When all the case studies have been worked out in more detail, we shall be able more adequately to evaluate the meaningfulness for individuals of the correlational patterns of mother-child relations. At present, our case studies point up the need for caution. We must not make hasty generalizations from the trends in mother-child correlations. After all, these correlations are only moderate: There is ample room for the effects of other variables (genetic and environmental) in determining behavioral tendencies in individual children.

What we do have is some evidence for trends in mother-child relations for a group of normal children. These trends show both sex differences and changes over time as the children grow older. The boys in this study tended to do well if their mothers were loving at an early age and at adolescence also granted autonomy. The girls appear to be a little more consistent in their own behavior patterns, and also to show more correlation with their mothers' concurrent maternal behavior. From our data we can not say whether the mother-child interactions are determined primarily by the behavior tendencies of the mother or the child.

REFERENCES

1. Bayley, Nancy, & Schaefer, E. S. Relationships between socioeconomic variables and the behavior of mothers forward young children. *J. Genet. Psychol.*, 1960, **96,** 61–77.
2. Guttman, L. A new approach to factor analysis: The Radex. In P. F. Lazarsfeld (Ed.), Mathematical thinking in the social sciences. Glencoe, Ill.: Free Press, 1954.

3. Jones, H. E., & Bayley, Nancy. The Berkeley growth study. *Child Developm.*, 1941, **12**, 167–173.
4. Schaefer, E. S. A ciccumplex model for maternal behavior. *J. Abnorm. Soc. Psychol.*, 1955, **59**, 226–235.
5. Schaefer, E. S., & Bayley, Nancy. Consistency of maternal behavior from infancy to preadolescence. *J. Abnorm. Soc. Psychol.*, 1960, **61**, 1–6.
6. Schaefer, E. S., Bell, R. Q., & Bayley, Nancy. Development of a maternal behavior research instrument. *J. Genet. Psychol.*, 1955, **95**, 83–104.

16. PARENTAL ATTITUDES AND CHILD

ADJUSTMENT

Donald R. Peterson, Wesley C. Becker, Leo A. Hellmer, Donald J. Shoemaker, and Herbert C. Quay

Many contemporary personality theories attach great importance to the role parents play in determining the personality characteristics of children. Such emphasis is wisely placed. The primacy, the intimacy, and the extensive protraction of parental influences are likely to render them crucial to the formation of personality tendencies among children. In view of these considerations, there is a clear need for research in which important aspects of parental influence are examined, the behavior of children concurrently appraised, and relationships between the two sets of variables determined.

It is neither possible nor necessary to review here the mountainous literature on parent-child relationships which has emerged over the past 30 years, but certain remarks concerning that literature can and should be made. A good deal of it consists of "expert" advice whose content changes with fashion (13) and whose factual basis is obscure. Much of the rest is theory, which is sometimes a product of keen observation and closely reasoned thought, but which is seldom buttressed by carefully gathered, rigorously evaluated empirical data. There remain a number of excellent investigations on parent-child relationships, among which the works of Radke (10), Baldwin and his collaborators (3, 4), and Sears et al. (12) seem particularly outstanding, but it is no disparagement of these and similar studies to note that they leave large areas of the domain almost entirely untouched. A major hiatus exists, for example, in regard to the attitudes of fathers and their part in the formation of personality tendencies among children. A review of the literature on parent-child relationships over the years 1929 to 1956 revealed at least 169 publications dealing with relationships between mothers and their children. Available information on father-child relationships, by contrast, was encompassed in 10 articles, one convention address, and one book. This imbalance has ordinarily been justified through reference to an assumption that mothers play a more important part than fathers in the development of child personality. Levy's statement is typical: "It is generally accepted that the most potent of all influences on social behavior is derived from the social experience of the mother" (8, p. 3). The present study permits evaluation of the va-

Reprinted with abridgement from *Child Development*, 1959, **30**, 119–130, with permission of the senior author and the Society for Research in Child Development.

lidity of this assumption through examination of both parents and assessment of their relative influence on the behavior of children.

An analogous sampling restriction obtains in respect to most available investigations of child behavior. Attention has ordinarily been limited either to problem behavior or to "normal" activity. To our knowledge, there has been *no* research in which both fathers and mothers have been studied and their attitudes related to the behavior of disturbed as well as "normal" children, although the methodological advantage to be gained through expansion of variance among children is obvious. In this investigation, the families of both problem and nonproblem children have been examined. The study has two specific purposes. The first is to assess differences between parental attitudes in two groups of families, one in which the children display certain adjustment problems, and another in which they do not. The second is to establish, within the group of families where the children have problems, differential attitudinal patterns associated with two major dimensions of child behavior difficulty.

SUBJECTS AND PROCEDURES

Thirty-one families were selected for investigation from the clientele of a guidance clinic. All the children were from 6 to 12 years of age, of Caucasian extraction, and manifested difficulties in adjustment of sufficient severity to warrant treatment. Cases of known organic brain damage or other serious physical defect, families in which the parents were separated, and cases of intellectual retardation were excluded. We shall refer to this sample henceforth as the *Clinic* group. They were compared with 29 *Nonclinic* families in which the children had been judged by teachers to display acceptable adjustment tendencies in school. Age was again restricted to the range 6 to 12. Since no children with organic disturbances or intellectual defect appeared on the lists submitted by teachers, exclusion in terms of these criteria was unnecessary.

The groups do not differ significantly in respect to any of the dimensions examined (age and IQ of child, SES, and age, IQ, and education of mother and father), though there is an unequal representation of boys and girls in the Clinic group which approaches statistical reliability. The proportion of boys to girls in the latter sample is more than $2:1$, while there are only a few more boys than girls in the Nonclinic group. Such disparity is typical of most clinic populations, but its possible effect on the results of this study will receive later comment. The discrepancy in child IQ also approaches significance ($.10 < p_t < .20$), but the fact that the IQs of parents were not reliably different (means for Clinic parents were in fact numerically superior to those for the Nonclinic group) suggests that the lower functional intelligence of the Clinic children is part and parcel of the adjustment difficulty, and constitutes an interesting trend in its own right.

On the basis of a one-hour interview, parents were rated on 17 of the 30 Fels Parent Behavior Rating Scales (3). The 17 scales were selected on the basis of Roff's factor analysis (11) in such a way that each factor was represented by at least two of the most heavily saturated rating scales.

Four staff psychologists and one advanced graduate student in clinical psychology performed the ratings immediately after each interview. Methodological ideals would have been most neatly met by rigorous structuring of the interview, but the need to allow parents of disturbed children to discuss problems in their own terms prevented such standardization. Rather free discussion was therefore permitted through much of the interview, but certain standard questions were asked, as needed, to insure collection of data relevant to the ratings. Distributions of scores on each of the attitudinal factors were then formed separately for fathers and mothers, and χ^2 analyses of discrepancy between the Clinic and Nonclinic groups conducted. Cutting points were set as close to the first and third quartiles as the distributions would permit, thus segregating the groups into those manifesting high, average, and low scores on each factor, and χ^2 calculated in accordance with the procedure suggested by McNemar (9) for analysis of $2 \times k$ tables.

Information pertinent to reliability of the attitudinal factors was obtained by recording three interviews and comparing judgments made by the five interviewers after listening to the recordings. Over all comparisons, the judges were in agreement more than 80 per cent of the time in classifying subjects as high, average, or low on the factors, and *no* radical disagreements were found, i.e., in no case did a single judge regard a case a high on a given factor when another judge assigned the subject a low score. Such agreement seems quite remarkable in the light of commonly expressed views about the unreliability of clinical judgments. It appears that if raters are asked to judge certain well-defined variables at an appropriate level of differentiation, and are given enough information to do so, they can perform the rating task in a thoroughly acceptable way.

During the interviews with parents, information was also obtained about the nature of the problem which each child displayed. A rating schedule derived from Himmelweit's analysis (7) of Ackerson's data (1) on problem children was employed. The schedule required 3-point ratings of 8 behavior characteristics loading on a *personality problem* factor (sensitivity, absent-mindedness, seclusiveness, day-dreaming, inefficiency in work, inferiority feelings, changeability of mood, and nervousness), and 11 tendencies loading on a *conduct problem* factor (truancy from home, truancy from school, stealing, fighting, lying, destructiveness, swearing, disobedience, rudeness, selfishness, and temper tantrums). Unit weights were assigned, and the two factor scores derived by direct addition of the appropriate elemental scores. The child problem scores were then correlated with each parent attitude factor to determine the kinds of attitudes associated with each problem dimension.

This analysis was performed separately for mothers and fathers, and was restricted to the Clinic group. To reduce contamination, attitudes of mothers were correlated with judgments of child behavior based on the reports of fathers, and attitudes of fathers correlated with judgments based on the mothers' reports of child behavior.

Reliability of ratings on problem activity was estimated by correlating scores derived from the interviews of mothers with those based on the accounts of fathers. Correlations of .40 and .83 emerged for personality problem and conduct problem, respectively. Evidently the open behavior involved in conduct problems can be judged with fair accuracy, but the fine discriminations required in judging the severity of internalized difficulties, within such a homogeneous group as the present one, are too difficult to permit close agreement.

It is of methodological interest to note that gross classification of children into those manifesting personality problems and those manifesting conduct problems could be done in a highly reliable way. When classification was made simply by noting which of the two problem scores was higher, and designation based on father report compared with that based on mother report, only one case of actual disagreement was found. Classification was impossible in four cases, because the scores were equal, but independent judgments were in accord for the remaining 26 cases (84 per cent). Insufficiency of N in the two groups of problem children prohibited direct comparative study, and required use of the correlational analysis of dimensions described above, but investigators can be encouraged by the possibility of attaining respectably high agreement, not only in rating parental attitudes, but in rating child behavior, when variables are defined with proper care and the differentiations required are appropriate to the sensitivities of the judges.

Configural analyses of inter- and intraparental patterns were considered, but on the basis of two pilot studies (5, 14) rejected in favor of the simpler, more straightforward, and evidently more powerful statistical techniques described above. A factor analysis drawn from the same basic data pool as the present one but dealing with a differently constituted set of variables is reported elsewhere (4).

RESULTS

Results of comparison between the Clinic and Nonclinic parents are given in Table 1. Both mothers and fathers of problem children were judged to be less well adjusted and sociable, more autocratic, and to experience more disciplinary contention than were the parents in the Nonclinic group. No other reliable discrepancies were found for mothers, although a tendency for Clinic mothers to be either very strict or very permissive in disciplining their children approached significance. Fathers, however, differed reliably in respect to two dimensions which did not differentiate between the Clinic and Non-

Table 1   *Comparison between Clinic and Nonclinic Parents*

Parent Attitude Factor	Mothers				Fathers			
	Clinic	Non-clinic	χ^2	p	Clinic	Non-clinic	χ^2	p
1. Concern for child			1.92	< .50			5.40	< .10
high	10	5			12	6		
average	15	16			9	17		
low	6	8			10	6		
2. Democratic guidance			8.58 [a]	< .02			10.25 [a]	< .01
high	5	11			4	13		
average	13	15			15	13		
low	13	3			12	3		
3. Permissive-ness			4.79	< .10			1.17	< .70
high	8	6			8	9		
average	11	18			14	15		
low	12	5			9	5		
4. Parent-child harmony			21.13 [a]	< .001			19.03 [a]	< .001
high	2	11			4	13		
average	15	18			13	16		
low	14	0			14	0		
5. Sociability-adjustment			18.09 [a]	< .001			7.14 [a]	< .05
high	2	14			5	10		
average	15	13			14	16		
low	14	2			12	3		
6. Activeness			1.04	< .70			8.21 [a]	< .02
high	10	6			10	4		
average	15	16			11	21		
low	6	7			10	4		
7. Readiness of sugges-tion			2.20	< .30			7.69 [a]	< .05
high	10	5			13	3		
average	15	15			13	18		
low	6	9			5	8		

[a] Significant at or beyond .05 level.

clinic mothers. The fathers of problem children were more prone to make suggestions than were the fathers of children without known problems, and were either highly active and rigidly organized or relatively inactive and disorganized in the conduct of their affairs. They also tended toward extremes in regard to concern for their children, but discrepancy along this dimension did not quite reach the level usually demanded for assertion of statistical significance.

In erecting hypotheses for study in future research, it is often fruitful to consider not only statistically significant results, but more modest data trends as well. If this is done by considering all parent attitudes for which r exceeds .20, the following patterns emerge. Personality problems seem largely independent of maternal attitude, but related to dictatorial attitudes and a lack of genuine concern among fathers. Conduct problems are related chiefly to maladjustment among mothers, and to democratic attitudes and heightened feelings of parental concern among fathers. Both parents appear overly permissive, and characterization of the fathers of children who present conduct problems as generally weak and ineffectual may not be far wide of the mark. Democratic qualities are esteemed in our culture, but when they are combined with laxity, unwillingness to issue orders, exaggerated concern for children, and a tendency to shelter them in the face of day-to-day problems the seeds of conduct disorders may be sown.

DISCUSSION

Probably the most significant finding to emerge from this study is that the attitudes of fathers are at least as intimately related as maternal attitudes to the occurrence and form of behavior problems in children. The popular choice of mothers as a focus of research attention and the general clinical tendency to offer psychotherapy to the mothers rather than the fathers of disturbed children are usually rationalized by noting that mothers generally spend more time with their children than fathers do, and by speculating that mother-child relationships are more intimate affairs than those between fathers and children. Whatever the validity of these assumptions, only the final effect is of fundamental concern, and we now have reason to believe that the emphasis in this effect is not as one-sided as it has previously appeared.

The extent to which the present results were affected by sex disparity among children is difficult to assess. Surely the presence of twice as many boys as girls in the Clinic sample could have a bearing on any findings related to relative influence of the two parents on child behavior, and we may only have demonstrated that fathers play a more vital role in influencing the behavior of *boys* than has previously been assumed. Even this, however, would be a result worth noting, and, while there is an obvious need to find out whether the present results can be repeated in a study involving more nearly equal representation of boys and girls, the necessity for examining paternal influence remains as vital as before. The practical difficulties involved in securing the cooperation of fathers for a study such as this are considerable, but they can be overcome, and it is now clear that they must be overcome if the social environment, in its relationship to personality development in children, is ever to be understood.

The various relationships, as we have reported them, are probably better estimates of "true" association than some theory and previous research would lead one to expect. We have eliminated at least a little of the contamination-generated spuriousness of many earlier investigations, and as a consequence, relationships between parental attitudes and child behavior appear with generally lower magnitude. We would be the last to deny the importance of the relationships we have presented, no matter how small they seem, and in evaluating the importance of our results feel justified in agreeing with Sears et al. (12), who regard the location of any real (i.e., replicable) influence, however low its magnitude, as a contribution to knowledge. "If our general assumption is correct—i.e., that any given behavior is the product of many influences—it would be quite impossible to obtain high correlations between single child-rearing dimensions and the measures of child behavior" (12, p. 456). But the results pointedly indicate the operation of many factors other than the ones we chose to examine. Though certain general statistical tendencies emerged, we still found families in which the parents appeared maladjusted, evidently didn't get along, and exhibited the most abhorrent kinds of attitudes toward their children, but the children appeared to be getting along beautifully. We saw parents whose attitudes and other characteristics were in nearly perfect congruence with the stereotype of the "good parent," but whose children displayed problems of the most severe order. The need to expand the scope of studies on personality development, and to examine other parental characteristics, relationships with such influential adults as teachers, interactions with siblings and peers, in sum, a more complete matrix of social factors, is patently clear.

It is our belief, however, that even if all social influences could be encompassed, and absolutely perfect measurement of them attained, a sizeable share of the variance in child behavior would still be unexplained. Parents frequently reported that their children had displayed certain behavior consistencies very early in life, and that these tendencies had remained stable in the face of what often appeared to be very extensive changes in social environment. In a study of parent-child relationships of the present kind, we are not dealing with unidirectional causalities; we are dealing with interactions. We have reported a number of correlations and other relationships between parental attitudes and child behavior, and have sometimes implied that the former caused the latter. This inference seems the most likely of the several which might be made, but the tenability of other interpretations cannot be denied. To explicate the second most likely inference, it is often just as reasonable to assume that personality tendencies on the part of the children, appearing very early in life and possibly of constitutional origin, have engendered modification of parental attitudes. The parents of a stable, predictable, sensible child can afford to be democratic. As Escalona (6) has suggested, the parents of an erratic, difficult, peculiar child may become apparently inconsistent out of sheer desperation. The direction of a causal relationship can only be established through determination of temporal priority, and the need to examine children *very* early in their development, and to explore the effects children may have on parents, is logically as critical as examination of the kinds of relationships with which this study is primarily concerned.

The extent to which the results have been influenced by rater bias is unknown. The interviewers made a conscious effort to avoid such bias, and it is entirely possible that estimates of "true" relationships were reduced rather than magnified through the operation of the systematic error such an effort could conceivably entail. In the correlational analysis, contamination was reduced by relating parental attitudes as measured on interview with one parent to child behavior as independently assessed by the clinician who saw the other parent. Throughout the study, however, interviewers knew which parents belonged to which group, they had rather firm ideas about the kind of behavior disturbance each child in the Clinic group presented, and there is a real possibility that some of the "significant" results reported above are spurious. Certain of the results were contrary to expectation, no obvious "bias factor" emerged on factor analysis of these and other data (4), and both considerations suggest that obtained associations were not completely generated by the preconceptions of the raters. Still the actual effect, even the probable direction of the effect of bias, is indeterminate, and will remain so until the appropriate methodological improvements are made. The need for direct, independent, objective measurement of parental attitudes and of child behavior is obvious. Much of our current effort is addressed to the development of such measures in the conviction that their proper application can determine some of the facts so urgently needed for adequate explanation, accurate prediction, and successful modification of developing personality trends in children.

SUMMARY

This study was designed to furnish information about relationships between parental attitudes and child behavior. It began with two purposes. The first was to assess differences between parent attitudes in two groups of families, one in which the children displayed certain adjustment problems (Clinic group, $N = 31$), and another in which no such problems had been observed (Nonclinic group, $N = 29$). The second aim was to establish differential attitudinal patterns associated with two major dimensions of child behavior disturbance. On the basis of interviews with mothers and fathers, ratings pertinent to seven parent attitude factors were made. Attitudes in the Clinic group were then compared with those in the Nonclinic group, separately for mothers and for fathers, and correlations were computed between the measures of parent attitude and indirect but independent evaluations of child problem behavior. The following results emerged:

1. Contrary to general assumption and our own original expectation, the attitudes of fathers were found to be at least as intimately related as the attitudes of mothers to the occurrence and form of maladjustive tendencies among children.

2. Both mothers and fathers of children who displayed adjustment difficulties were judged to be less well adjusted and sociable, less democratic, and to experience more disciplinary contention than the parents of children with no manifest problems.

3. In addition, Clinic fathers were regarded as more prone to offer suggestions, and tended toward extremes along a dimension of activity and organization in the conduct of their affairs.

4. Personality problems among children in the Clinic group were found to be relatively independent of maternal attitudes, but appeared to be related to autocratic attitudes and lack of parental concern among fathers.

5. Conduct problems were associated with general maladjustment among mothers in the Clinic group, and with evident permissiveness and disciplinary ineffectuality on the part of fathers.

Some rather impressive research has been done on mother-child relationships. But there is an equally urgent need to examine other social factors, as well as constitutional predispositions, in personality development, ideally through the application of objective measures. The need to study fathers, as crucial components of the social-environmental matrix from which child personality tendencies emerge, seems especially vital.

REFERENCES

1. Ackerson, L. *Children's behavior problems.* Chicago: Univer. Chicago Press, 1942.
2. Baldwin, A. L. The effect of home environment on nursery school behavior, *Child Develpm.,* 1949, **20,** 49–62.
3. Baldwin, A. L., Kalhorn, Joan, & Breese, Fay H. The appraisal of parent behavior. *Psychol. Monogr.,* 1949, **63,** Whole No. 4.
4. Becker, W. C., Peterson, D. R., Hellmer, L. A., Shoemaker, D. J., & Quay, H. C. Factors in parental behavior and personality as related to problem behavior in children. *J. consult. Psychol.,* in press.
5. Cepenas, Ina. Maternal attitudes and child behavior. Unpublished B.A. thesis, Univer. of Illinois, 1957.
6. Escalona, Sibylle. Some considerations regarding psychotherapy with psychotic children. *Bull. Menninger Clinic,* 1948, **12,** 127–134.
7. Himmelweit, Hilde T. A factorial study of "Children's behavior problems." Unpublished manuscript, Univer. of London, 1952. Cited in Eysenck, H. J. *The structure of human personality.* London: Metheun, 1953.
8. Levy, D. M. *Maternal overprotection.* New York: Columbia Univer. Press, 1943.
9. McNemar, Q. *Psychological statistics.* New York: Wiley, 1949.
10. Radke, Marion J. *The relation of parental authority to children's behavior and attitudes.* Minneapolis, Minn.: Univer. of Minnesota Press, 1946.
11. Roff, M. A factorial study of the Fels Parent Behavior Scales. *Child Develpm.,* 1949, **20,** 29–45.

12. Sears, R. R., Maccoby, Eleanor E., & Levin, H. *Patterns of childrearing.* Evanston, Ill.: Row, Peterson, 1957.
13. Stendler, Celia B. Sixty years of child training practices. *J. Pediat.,* 1950, **36,** 122–134. (1950).
14. Zimmerman, Marie. Paternal attitudes and child behavior. Unpublished M.A. thesis, Univer. of Illinois, 1958.

17. FAMILIAL CORRELATES OF AGGRESSION IN NONDELINQUENT MALE CHILDREN

WILLIAM McCORD, JOAN McCORD, AND ALAN HOWARD

Conservative social philosophers from Hobbes through Ortega y Gasset have had a profound suspicion of the motives and capacities of the "mob." Their dislike for the mass has been premised on a series of assumptions concerning human nature. One of the most fundamental of these axioms has been the conviction that man is innately aggressive. Hence, in the opinion of these theorists, the instinctive cruelty and barbarism of mankind must be kept under the strict control of a more enlightened "élite"—a class, who, through long training in the ways of civilization, has inhibited its own aggressive impulses.

This jaundiced view of human motivation has been buttressed by the Freudian belief that aggression is a universal outcome of the "thanatos instinct." In Freud's view—at least, in one of its several versions—all men strive not only for libidinal satisfactions, but also for return to a state of nothingness, of "nirvana." Freud argued that aggression, a desire to destroy, was the "natural" energy emerging from the death instinct; a drive which makes its appearance in infancy and is either fused with "Eros," directed toward the destruction of others, or aimed at self-annihilation.

On a general level, this view of aggression as an inevitable element in the make-up of man has been challenged by such writers as Fromm, Horney, Allport, and Maslow. These observers have put forward the position that aggression is the result of specific types of social milieu, rather than being an instinctual drive.

In an empirical fashion, other investigators have produced evidence which —at least, implicitly—contradicts the conservative Freudian opinions about aggression. Many analysts have demonstrated the variability of the level and expression of aggression in response to various environmental conditions (cf. Weiss and Fine, 1956). Others have concentrated on the child rearing antecedents of extremely aggressive antisocial behavior. For example, the Gluecks (1950), examining a lower class sample, and Bandura and Walters (1959), concentrating on a middle class group, have independently produced a similar portrait of the backgrounds of such individuals. Both studies found

Reprinted with abridgement from the *Journal of Abnormal and Social Psychology*, 1961, **62,** 79–93, with permission of the senior author and the American Psychological Association.

that the aggressively antisocial person emerged from an environment characterized by parental rejection, familial discord, punitive discipline, and inconsistency.

Perhaps the most comprehensive study of the early determinants of aggression can be found in the work of Sears, Maccoby, and Levin (1957). From carefully executed interviews with 379 New England mothers (and other sources of data) these researchers concluded that aggression in small children—defined as "behavior intended to hurt or injure someone"—was associated with such environmental antecedents as parental permissiveness for aggression, the use of physically punitive discipline, and maternal lack of self-esteem. These results led the investigators to reject the instinctual view of aggression and, instead, to affirm: "Today, with our better understanding of the ruling influence of culture as a source of behavioral universals, we are inclined to suspect that the determination of which stimuli will arouse rage, and the focusing of the emotion into an actual *desire and intent* to hurt others (or the self), are products of learning experiences begun in early infancy" (p. 222).

The purpose of this paper is to report a study which supports the view that aggression is a form of behavior which is learned by the child during his early experiences within the family. This research, concerned with 174 boys and their families, differs from certain of the previous studies: none of the subjects were known delinquents; the sample was drawn from a relatively lower class, urban environment; and the information on child rearing practices and on the boy's aggression was gathered through direct observation of both parents and child over more than a 5-year period. Each of these differences is important in assessing the significance of the research:

1. The fact that delinquents were excluded from the sample means that this study of "normal" aggression is not obscured by a simultaneous examination of the causes of delinquency.

2. The fact that the sample is drawn in disproportionate numbers from the lower class has two advantages: the sample serves as counterbalance to those findings which have emerged from analyses of primarily middle class children; and, at the same time, it counterbalances studies of delinquency which have usually concentrated on lower class samples.

3. The fact that the material was gathered through direct observation eliminates the difficulties that hamper studies based on interviews, experimental situations, or therapeutic sessions.

BACKGROUND OF THE RESEARCH

The opportunity to investigate the genesis of aggression came from the Cambridge-Somerville Youth Study of the 1930s. This extensive project, aimed primarily at the prevention of delinquency, has been described in numerous other publications (McCord, McCord, and Gudeman, 1960; Mc-

Cord, McCord, and Zola, 1959; Powers and Witmer, 1950); consequently, we will outline its history only briefly.

Six-hundred and fifty boys, referred by their teachers, ministers, or by social agencies, were chosen for participation in the experiment. At the time of selection, the boys averaged 9 years in age and were drawn primarily from lower class districts in Cambridge and Somerville, Massachusetts. In composition, the sample contained a relatively high proportion of Catholics and recent immigrants, approximately 25% of the families were on relief during the depression, and only 4% of the parents had attended college. It should be noted, in passing, that these "peculiarities" of the sample did not generally affect the results. Neither social class, immigration patterns, ethnic group, nor paternal occupation was significantly related to the child's aggression.

Since the subjects were selected from a restricted socioeconomic level, the lack of association between the child's behavior and more general social factors is hardly surprising.

Half of the boys were selected because they were judged potentially delinquent, "maladjusted" children; the remaining cases were regarded as "normal," nondelinquent boys.

Between 1939 and 1945, 325 children (composed equally of delinquent and normal boys) were given medical, educational, and social aid; all of these boys were assigned to a counselor who visited and advised both the boys and their families. The remaining 325 cases, closely matched to those who received treatment, formed a control group.

In the process of the study, the boys were subjected to physical, psychiatric, psychological, and intelligence examinations. Reports on the boys and their families were systematically gathered from social agencies, the schools, and various community agencies. Detailed reports on the behavior of the boy and of his family were recorded by the staff after each contact.

In 1956, the authors and their colleagues initiated a re-evaluation of the Cambridge-Somerville project, aimed at the solution of three problems:

1. What effect did the treatment have on the adult behavior of the subjects?

2. What correlations could be detected between the early familial experiences of the boys and their later behavior as adults?

3. What relationships could be noted between the familial environments and the boys' behavior in childhood?

As a first step toward resolving these issues, the cumulative case histories of the subjects were read by a trained staff (who did not have knowledge as to the adult behavior of the boys). A rating system concerned with 150 aspects of the boys' families, physical status, general social condition, and personality was developed. Each category as far as possible was defined in terms of observable behavior.

The Measure of Aggression

"Aggression" is an amorphous term. It has been used to describe such seemingly disparate phenomena as gossip, jokes, suicidal tendencies, hostile fantasies, as well as directly destructive acts. A simple event—slapping a person on the back—can be viewed by one observer as a hostile attack, while another individual, aware of the context surrounding the action, would regard it as evidence of exuberant friendship. Thus, the first task in any study of aggression is to define the concept in behavioral terms which can be replicated by other investigators. For the purposes of this research, we followed Sears, Maccoby, and Levin in defining aggression as "behavior intended to hurt or injure someone." The word "intention" is, itself, tricky; it is notoriously difficult to establish the underlying desires which prompt an action. Consequently, we sought to limit the term aggression to those acts which, objectively, "hurt or injured someone."

Fortunately, the staff of the Cambridge-Somerville study had ample opportunity to observe the boys' behavior. Counselors visited their homes and neighborhoods and watched their behavior in relation to parents, friends, neighbors, and siblings. The psychiatrists, physicians, and psychologists submitted reports on the boys' reactions under relatively stressful conditions. The boys' teachers and other school officials were systematically questioned concerning the children's activities. Camp counselors, social agencies, ministers, police, YMCA directors, and employers submitted additional information. Not only did the information come from diverse sources, but it was gathered over an average period of 5¾ years—thus making it possible to observe the boy under different conditions, at different ages.

From these various sources of information, the 174 boys were placed into one of three categories.

Twenty-five boys were consistently and overtly *aggressive*. These individuals participated in the whole range of aggressive acts; they were involved in fist-fighting, bullying of smaller children, attacks on their teachers, or destructive actions in camp or in the community. They frequently threatened other children with violence—and often carried out their threats. In response to almost any form of frustration, they reacted with verbal abuse, open rage, and attempts to destroy the frustrating object.

Ninety-seven boys were, by the norms of American society, normally *assertive*. They participated, at times, in fights, acts of destruction aimed at other children or adults, occasional battles with teachers or other community officials, and bullying of weaker children or girls. They differed from the openly aggressive boys, however, in that their hostile responses were sporadic exceptions to the general pattern of their lives. Normally, in the face of frustration, they responded realistically; sometimes with anger, but seldom with aggressive actions. In the classroom, they sometimes created disciplinary problems for the teacher, but usually they conformed to the standards of the school.

Fifty-two boys were consistently *nonaggressive*. Outbursts of rage and directly aggressive attacks were exceptionally rare in their lives; and, indeed, in some cases, nonexistent. In the classroom, they did not actively participate in aggressive disturbances. In relations with other children, they were placid and friendly. They could absorb the usual frustrations of childhood —failure in school, loss of a game, discipline from an adult—with apparent calm and realism. Thus, this categorization of aggression is descriptive not only of isolated acts, but of the entire *pattern* of the child's behavior over a period of 5 years.

Two raters, independently categorizing the behavior of 30 cases randomly selected from the sample, reached 86.7% agreement in their judgments of aggression.

The Measures of Family Environment

Our task was to assess the relevance of the child's early environment in determining whether he became "aggressive," "assertive," or "nonaggressive." To achieve this goal, the "raw" information gathered by the staff in their 5 years of direct observation of the families was systematically categorized into a set of variables, descriptive of the child's environment. These ratings ranged from such relatively objective matters as the occupation of the parents, their education, and ethnic group, through more subjective judgments concerning emotional relationships within the family. Categories were developed concerning the parents' attitudes toward one another, their role in the family, their affective relationship with the son, and their personality. The parental methods and consistency of discipline were considered, as well as the specific values which they wished to inculcate. The child's physical status and aspects of his behavior, other than aggression, were also evaluated. (It should be noted that none of the measures of the child's physical status— the conditions of his birth, neurological or glandular disorder, early childhood diseases, body deformities, etc.—was significantly associated with the level of aggression.)

Although the specific definitions and reliability of each category will be discussed in the following pages, certain general characteristics of the ratings should be mentioned:

1. The observations were made in the home of the child, over an average period of 5¾ years, by a number of different people (usually, each child was exposed to at least three counselors). These observers did not know that their material would be used for a study of aggression; hence, the possibility of conscious bias or of a "halo effect" was minimized.

2. The raters who, between 1956 and 1958, recategorized this information were also unaware that the data would be used for a study of aggression and were not acquainted with the hypotheses to be tested.

3. These ratings have previously been used in follow-up studies of those boys who became criminals, alcoholics, and psychotics in adulthood. The

ratings successfully differentiated between these deviants and the nondeviant cases in the sample. Thus, in terms of certain forms of deviant behavior, the "predictive validity" of the categorizations has been established (cf. McCord, McCord, and Gudeman, 1960; McCord, McCord, and Zola, 1959).

RESULTS

We assumed, as the basic premises of this research, that early environmental experiences might affect a child's level of aggression in four conceptually distinct ways:

1. Emotional relationships between the boy and his parents would be fundamental in two ways: first, by affecting the child's level of frustration (and, thus, indirectly, his aggressive desires) and secondly, by molding his conception of the nature of human interaction.

2. The parental methods of disciplining and controlling the child would affect his willingness to inhibit whatever aggressive desires he felt.

3. The example of the parents (regardless of their direct relationship with the son) would affect the son by offering him an immediate, intimate model of human reactions to frustration.

4. The degree to which the parents reinforced each other's values would affect the "intensity" with which the son internalized parental demands (that is, we believed that parents who disagreed on a variety of issues, including the behavior which they expected of the child would be likely to produce a confused, relatively uninhibited child).

Let us examine the actual effects of each of these four general influences.

The Instigation of Aggression

Direct parental attacks on the boy—whether manifested in physically punitive discipline, the frequent use of threats, or constant unfavorable comments on the boy's worth—were strongly associated with a high level of aggressive behavior. Presumably, this kind of parental behavior is highly frustrating to the boy's dependency needs; parental rejection teaches him early in life that other human beings are threatening and aggressive. One indication of this relationship between parental punitiveness and aggression among the sons can be found in an examination of parental methods of discipline. Some of the parents employed "nonpunitive" means of disciplining their children; they reasoned with the son, withdrew certain privileges, or indicated their verbal disapproval. Other parents depended on directly "punitive" techniques: if the child disobeyed, they responded with angry abuse, slaps, or beatings. A significantly lower proportion of the nonaggressive boys than of the aggressive or assertive children were raised by "punitive" mothers. (Throughout the paper, the Scott π reliability coefficient was used to estimate interrater reliability. Reliability on judgments of maternal punitiveness was .772, on father's punitiveness, .581. A comparison of the nonaggressive boys to the others in terms of maternal punitiveness was significant at the .025 level; $\chi^2 = 5.09$; $df = 1$. A comparison of the effects of the fathers' techniques was not significant. Throughout the paper, the chi square test, two-tailed, was applied.)

Another indication that parental attacks on the child led to more aggressive behavior was that those parents who frequently threatened the child, who verbally frightened him with dire consequences if he disobeyed, were more likely to produce aggressive sons than were parents who rarely threatened the boy ($p < .05$; $\chi^2 = 6.11$; $df = 2$; Scott π reliability = .734).

As one might predict from the preceding evidence, those parents who generally disliked and rejected their sons were most likely to produce aggressive boys. In terms of their overall emotional relationship with the boy, the parents in the study were described as either "affectionate" or "rejecting." Affectionate parents were individuals who talked of their love for the son, who never voiced overtly rejecting statements about the son, and who demonstrated (at least, to some extent) their regard for the boy through kisses, hugs, gifts, proud statements about his accomplishments, etc. Rejecting parents, in contrast did not hesitate to express a fundamental dislike for their sons; they sometimes mentioned that they wished that the boy had never been born; they treated the boy either with open cruelty, neglect, or an erratic alternation between demonstrations of affection and blatant dislike.

The parents of the aggressive boys had an emotionally meager, cold relationship with their sons: The great majority of the aggressive boys, 95%, were raised in homes where at least one parent was emotionally rejecting; the majority of the assertive boys and of the nonaggressive children were raised by affectionate parents ($p < .001$; $\chi^2 = 22.28$; $df = 1$; Scott π reliability on mothers was .757, on fathers, .710).

The variables which we have discussed up to this point—parental rejection, punitiveness, and parental threats—have certain features in common. These attitudes and actions are all, presumably, direct attacks on the child's sense of security; they all tend to undermine the boy's conception of himself as a person of worth and significance; and they all carry the implication that the world is a dangerous, hostile environment. It would seem reasonable to suppose that these influences serve to arouse pervasive aggressive tendencies in the child; he is not only extremely frustrated by these attacks but he is implicitly taught that aggression is the "way of the world." If one views these variables in combination, an expected pattern appears: the aggressive children usually came from environments where several "drive-instigating" influences were present, while the assertive and nonaggressive children typically emerged from relatively "positive" homes.

Thus, 80% of the aggressive boys, 50% of the assertive boys, and only 33% of the nonaggressive boys had been exposed to two or more "negative" influences ($p < .001$; $\chi^2 = 15.12$; $df = 2$). It should be noted, in passing, that the delinquents were usually exposed to at least three "negative" conditions.

In summary, this evidence leads to the conclusion that:

1. The aggressive boys and the assertive boys were more likely to have been disciplined in a punitive fashion by their mothers than were the nonaggressive boys ($p < .025$).

2. The aggressive boys were more likely to have been frequently threatened by their parents than were the assertive boys and the nonaggressive boys ($p < .05$).

3. The aggressive boys were more likely to have been raised by parents who rejected them than were the assertive or the nonaggressive boys ($p < .001$).

4. The three types of boys differed significantly in the total number of "aggression-instigating" elements in their backgrounds ($p < .001$).

The Direct Instillation of Controls

The preceding evidence suggests that a high level of aggression was originally instigated by parental rejection, punitiveness, and threats. Another general set of factors—the extent to which the parents exerted immediate controls over the boy's behavior—also played an important part. We assumed that such factors as the kind of demands imposed on the child, the degree to which his actions were supervised by the parents, and the extent to which the parents imposed their values in a consistent fashion could serve to modify the boy's expression of aggressive urges. Even a child who was plagued by intense aggressive urges, we assumed, might not express these desires overtly, if he was subjected to consistent controls by his parents. Several measures revealed the influence of this aspect of the boy's environment in the molding of aggressive behavior.

The parents differed strikingly in the kinds of demands which they imposed on their sons. In some families, the parents placed "high demands" on the child for conformity; the son was expected to clean his room, do chores around the house, perform well in school, be polite, attend Sunday school—in other words, to conform to the dominant customs of American society. In other families, the parents did not require this high degree of "polite behavior." In some cases, they simply ignored the child; in other cases, they demanded a high level of performance in one area of behavior (e.g., wearing clean clothes) but gave the child complete freedom in other ways (e.g., behavior in the classroom).

The nonaggressive boys were more likely than either the assertive or the aggressive children to emerge from families that placed high demands on them for "polite," "responsible" behavior ($p < .005$; $\chi^2 = 9.09$; $df = 1$; Scott π reliability $= .535$).

As in the kind of demands imposed on the child, the families also differed in the degree to which they directly supervised the boy. Some of the parents (or other adults) kept a close eye on the boy's activities; they did not hesitate to advise the child or to intervene directly in behavior which they disapproved; they wished to know where he was and what he was doing most of the time. They were anxious to hear reports of his behavior away from the home. Other parents provided little, if any, supervision over the child; he was allowed to roam at will, to choose his own activities and friends. The nonaggressive children were significantly more likely to have been closely supervised ($p < .05$; $\chi^2 = 4.0$; $df = 1$; Scott π reliability = .710).

Another measure, a rating of the mother's control of the child, was also related to the level of aggressive behavior. The boys' mothers were divided into three categories: those who "overcontrolled" their children (who demanded that the boy should be close to the mother at all times and submit completely to her direction); those who exerted "normal controls" over the child (women who were concerned with the boy's activities but gave him freedom in certain areas, such as the choice of playmates or the type of clothes which he would wear); and those who "subnormally" controlled the boy (such mothers frequently were neglecting or unconcerned with the child's behavior). The aggressive boys tended to be either "overcontrolled" or "subnormally controlled" by their mothers; the assertive boys were raised in approximately equal proportions by each type of mother; and the nonaggressive children were most often reared by mothers who "overcontrolled" or "normally controlled" them ($p < .005$; $\chi^2 = 15.46$; $df = 4$; Scott π reliability = .771).

One other element, the consistency of parental discipline, deserves attention. The majority of the parents in the study disciplined their children in an "erratic" fashion: for the same action, the child was sometimes severely punished while, at other times, he was allowed (or even encouraged) to continue in his behavior. In these inconsistent families, parental discipline was strongly affected by swings in mood or by the immediate situation. Other parents were relatively consistent; the child could be sure that if he was caught committing a certain action, he would receive punishment. The nonaggressive children were raised by parents (particularly by mothers) who used consistent methods of discipline, while the converse tended to be true of the assertive and the aggressive boys (interrater reliability on ratings of parental consistency was .772, for the mothers, and .581 for the fathers. Comparison of nonaggressive boys to others in terms of consistency of maternal discipline was significant at the .01 level; $\chi^2 = 7.03$; $df = 1$; in terms of paternal consistency, the comparison was not significant).

It is clear that those variables which deal with direct parental control over the child—the kind of demands that they imposed on the son, the degree of supervision that they gave him, and the consistency of their discipline—have an important relation to the boy's aggression. These influences in the child's environment are only theoretically distinct from those factors which are related to the instigation of a high degree of aggression. In practice, for example, one would expect that parental rejection would usually be combined with a lack of direct parental supervision. It is useful, therefore, to view the impact of these conditions in combination. In Table 1, one can observe the interaction between one factor that seems to be primarily related to the instigation of aggression (parental punitiveness) and another factor that appears to be principally related to the instillation of controls (parental demands on the child).

Both factors seem to be relevant to the expression of aggression. The aggressive boys tended to come from homes in which at least one parent was physically punitive and the demands on the child were low: 67% of the aggressive boys, 55% of the assertive children, and only 22% of the non-aggressive cases emerged from this type of family ($p < .001$; $\chi^2 = 17.74$; $df = 2$). Nonaggressive behavior appears to be associated with a lack of punitiveness on the parents' part *and* with the imposition of high demands. Of those children who came from homes in which both parents were non-punitive and placed high requirements on their children's behavior, 56% were nonaggressive. At the opposite extreme (homes in which both parents were punitive and did not impose high demands), only 15% were nonaggressive ($p < .05$; $\chi^2 = 6.63$; $df = 2$). In general, if demands were high, a lack of aggressive behavior resulted; if demands were low, parental punitiveness tended to increase the level of aggressive behavior.

Table 1 *Parental Punitiveness, Parental Demands on the Child, and the Boy's Aggression (in percentages)*

	Aggressive Boys ($N = 24$)	Assertive Boys ($N = 95$)	Nonaggressive Boys ($N = 49$)
The families imposed high demands on the child and:			
Both parents were punitive	4	3	8
One parent was punitive but the other parent was nonpunitive	8	14	18
Neither parent was punitive	4	6	19
The families imposed low demands on the child and:			
Both parents were punitive	13	21	8
One parent was punitive but the other parent was nonpunitive	54	34	14
Neither parent was punitive	17	22	33
	100	100	100

In summary, this material has indicated that:

1. The aggressive and the assertive children were more likely to have been raised by parents who did not impose high demands on them than were the nonaggressive boys ($p < .005$).

2. The aggressive boys and the assertive boys were less likely to have been closely supervised by their parents than were the nonaggressive boys ($p < .05$).

3. More often than the assertive boys, the nonaggressive children were raised by mothers who "overcontrolled" them while the aggressive boys tended to be reared by mothers who either "overcontrolled" or "subnormally" controlled their sons ($p < .005$).

4. The nonaggressive boys (and to a lesser extent, the assertive boys) were more likely to have been disciplined by their mothers in a consistent fashion than were the aggressive children ($p < .01$).

5. The aggressive boys and the assertive boys were more likely than the nonaggressive boys to have been raised by parents who were both punitive and placed low demands on their sons ($p < .001$).

The Parental Model

It would seem reasonable to expect that highly aggressive parents would be likely to produce aggressive children. Presumably, a boy exposed to a father who consistently reacted with aggression to crises in his home, his work, or his neighborhood would tend to emulate the parental model. Surprisingly, the data do *not* confirm this "common-sense" prediction. Although there was a slight tendency for aggressive parents to produce aggressive children, this trend was not statistically significant at the 5% level.

Three measures—ratings of the father's aggression, his reaction to specific crises, and his role in the family—were used to estimate the effect of the parental model on the boy's behavior.

In terms of the same definition that was applied to their sons, the fathers in the study were divided into "aggressive," "assertive," and "nonaggressive" men. Fifteen percent of the aggressive boys were raised by aggressive fathers, but so were 18% of the assertive children, and 10% of the nonaggressive children. At the opposite extreme, 10% of the aggressive boys, as opposed to 6% of the assertive and 18% of the nonaggressive cases, were reared by nonaggressive fathers (Scott π reliability = .619).

Judgments were also made concerning the reactions of the fathers to specific crises: loss of a job, failure to gain a promotion, loss of "face" in the community, legal involvements, etc. Most of the fathers responded "realistically" by attempting to correct the situation in an effective fashion. Other men reacted in an "escapist" way: they went on a drinking or eating binge or withdrew into total passivity. A third set of fathers responded with overt "aggression" (verbal or physical attacks on the source of their frustration).

Although one might expect that the aggressive fathers would "teach" their sons to respond in a similar fashion, this did not occur: almost equal proportions of the aggressive, assertive, and nonaggressive boys were raised by fathers who responded aggressively to crises (17%, 16%, and 11%, respectively). "Realistic" fathers, on the other hand, tended to have non-aggressive children; 33% of the aggressive boys, 39% of the assertive, and 56% of the nonaggressive boys were raised by such men ($p < .05$; $\chi^2 = 3.84$; $df = 1$; Scott π reliability $= .678$).

The fathers differed, too, in terms of their role within the family. Some fathers were "dictators"; they made all the decisions in the family and ruled the home with an iron grip; others were passive, ineffectual men, who left the guidance of the family to the mother; and still others were "leaders"— they made the basic decisions for the family, but only after consultation. Although one might expect that the aggressive boys would come most often from "dictatorial" fathers, this did not prove to be the case. Nineteen percent of the aggressive boys, as compared to 8% and 7% of the assertive and non-aggressive boys were reared by dictatorial fathers; 38% of the aggressive boys, as opposed to 51% of the assertive and 55% of the nonaggressive were raised by fathers who played the role of the leader; the remainder came from passive fathers (Scott π reliability $= .632$).

One can draw a general conclusion from these data: paternal aggression did not significantly heighten the son's aggression; rather, it would appear that any form of paternal "deviance" whether expressed in aggression, "escapism," or an eccentric role within the family—tended to be associated with a higher level of aggression in the son. The nonaggressive boys were more often reared by nonaggressive fathers who responded to crises in a realistic fashion and acted the role of "leader" within the family; one can assume, therefore, that these children were offered a parental model of responsibility and relatively stronger control over deviant impulses. The aggressive children often lacked such a paternal model of inner control; it would seem to be this deficiency in their background (rather than a specific example of aggression) that may have contributed to their unrestrained behavior.

Two other pieces of data support this interpretation. Many of the fathers in the study participated in various forms of deviant behavior (criminality, alcoholism, psychoses, desertion, sexual promiscuity, etc.). Only rarely was this behavior directly aggressive in nature. The deviant men, however, were relatively uninhibited, escapist, and irresponsible; they failed to offer their sons an example of moderation. The aggressive boys and the assertive cases were more often raised by such deviant fathers; 48% of the aggressive boys, 52% of the assertive cases, and 39% of the nonaggressive children were reared by deviant fathers ($p < .05$; $\chi^2 = 3.84$; $df = 1$; Scott π reliability $= .827$).

The strength of religion within the family may also have played a part. The nonaggressive boys were more often reared in homes which were "strongly" religious (that is, families in which the parents attended church at least once a week and gave other signs of devotion to their faith). Forty-eight percent of the nonaggressive children, as compared to 34% of the assertive and only 21% of the aggressive boys, were raised by strongly religious mothers ($p < .10$; $\chi^2 = 5.68$; $df = 3$; Scott π reliability for father $= .856$, for mother, .676). The specific religious affiliation of the family did not significantly affect the level of the boy's aggression. The strongly religious parents were people who, in general, valued inner control, conformity, "humility," and nonaggressiveness more than did those who were simply nominal members of a religious faith. Thus, one can assume that the strongly religious parents more often offered a model of inner control to their sons.

These data suggest that a parental model of conformity and inner control (whether expressed in realistic reactions to crises, the fulfillment of a mature role within the family strong adherence to a religious faith, or a lack of obvious deviance) may be associated with a low level of aggressive behavior on the son's part. More strikingly, the material indicates that an aggressive parental model is, in itself, no more productive of aggression in the child, than are other "milder" forms of parental deviance, irresponsibility, or escapism.

Even these tentative generalizations should be further qualified. Within the sample, there is a general correlation between parental deviance and such other factors as parental rejection, punitiveness, and lack of control of the child. Thus, the slight association between parental deviance and the boy's aggression may well be simply a reflection of these other factors.

Parental Agreement on Values

One final set of conditions within the home, the amount of agreement between the parents concerning their basic values, has bearing on understanding the origins of aggression. In some homes, the parents were in constant conflict about each other's attitudes and actions or were fundamentally dissatisfied with their place in the family; in other words, such parents tended to undermine, rather than to reinforce the attitudes of one another. We assumed that a child raised in such an environment would tend to become confused concerning parental expectations and would be likely to "write off" parental demands. Thus, if would seem reasonable to assume that these children would be less governable by their parents, and, specifically, less inhibited in the expression of their aggressive urges.

The data support this interpretation. The parents' relation to one another, as well as their immediate relation to the child himself, had bearing on the boy's level of aggression. As a group the aggressive boys more often came from homes that were disordered by parental conflict, lack of respect of the parents for each other, disagreement within the family concerning methods of child rearing, and antagonism between the child and his relatives. The aggressive boys were, therefore, often raised in a milieu in which one parent undermined (or directly attacked) the other; an environment which was not conducive to the establishment of a consistent set of values.

A variety of measures, all tapping the same phenomena, suggested that the aggressive children came from homes which were fundamentally disrupted by parental disagreements. The specific figures are presented in Table 2.

In summary, these conclusions can be drawn from the material:

1. The aggressive and the assertive children came more often from families characterized by "intense" conflict between the parents—constant bickering, recriminations, and, at times, overt physical attacks ($p < .005$; $\chi^2 = 9.16$; $df = 1$; Scott π reliability $= .647$).

2. The aggressive and the assertive children more often came from families in which one parent held the other in "low esteem." These were homes in which the parents expressed, with complete openness, their lack of respect for the other person ($p < .005$; $\chi^2 = 8.65$; $df = 1$; Scott π reliability $= .833$).

3. The aggressive boys more often came from homes in which both parents were dissatisfied with their role in life. In these families, the mothers complained of the burdens of being a housewife and mother and the fathers expressed their disgust with their job, their role in the home, and their relation to society ($p < .02$; $\chi^2 = 8.37$; $df = 2$; Scott π reliability $= .679$).

4. The aggressive boys were more likely to come from homes in which the parents disagreed concerning methods of child rearing ($p < .10$; $\chi^2 = 3.67$; $df = 1$; Scott π reliability $= .620$).

5. The aggressive boys were more likely to come from homes in which the parents were *not* demonstratively affectionate toward one another ($p < .05$; $\chi^2 = 4.64$; $df = 1$; Scott π reliability $= .631$).

Taken together, these various measures of the "milieu" of socialization reveal that the aggressive boys (and, to a lesser extent the assertive children) were reared in families that had been disorderd by a high degree of parental conflict and antagonism. The nonaggressive boys, in contrast, more often emerged from environments in which the parents respected one another, agreed on basic issues (including the ways in which their sons should be raised), and were relatively satisfied with their lot in life.

A natural effect of such parental conflict would be that the son tended to reject his family and the values that the parents represented. As one would expect, the aggressive boys more often chose a "reference group" (delinquent gang, neighborhood group, etc.) outside of their home. Thirty-two percent of the aggressive children, as contrasted to only 14% of the assertive boys and 6% of the nonaggressive boys consciously oriented their behavior to an "outside" reference group rather than to their parents' wishes ($p < .02$; $\chi^2 = 6.58$; $df = 1$).

This tendency for the aggressive children to separate themselves from their families was also revealed in their attitudes towards their siblings. Only

Table 2 *Parental Relationships and the Boy's Aggression (in percentages)*

	Aggressive Boys	Assertive Boys	Nonaggressive Boys
Parental conflict:	(N = 21)	(N = 83)	(N = 43)
Intense	38	36	12
Some	38	27	47
None	24	37	31
	100	100	100
Parental esteem:	(N = 20)	(N = 81)	(N = 38)
High mutual esteem	50	52	79
One parent disrespected the other parent	25	20	13
Mutually low esteem	25	28	8
	100	100	100
Parental role satisfaction:	(N = 20)	(N = 84)	(N = 42)
Both parents dissatisfied	45	26	12
One parent dissatisfied	5	25	19
Neither parent dissatisfied	50	49	69
	100	100	100
Parental conflict about the child:	(N = 21)	(N = 76)	(N = 41)
Intense conflict	24	10	10
Some conflict	38	30	24
No conflict	38	60	66
	100	100	100
Parental affection for each other:	(N = 20)	(N = 83)	(N = 39)
Affectionate	15	38	44
Sporadically affectionate	40	27	36
Indifferent	10	8	10
Antagonistic	35	27	10
	100	100	100

42% of the aggressive children had a cooperative, friendly relationship with their siblings. In contrast, 70% of the assertive boys and 66% of the non-aggressive boys had an affectionate regard for their brothers and sisters ($p < .02$; $\chi^2 = 5.56$; $df = 1$).

CONCLUSIONS

In this paper, we have argued that three major elements in a child's environment affect his subsequent level of aggressive behavior:

1. The emotional relationship between the boy and his parents (the degree to which the family treats the child in a punitive, threatening, or rejecting fashion).

2. The direct controls exerted by the parents over the boy's behavior (the degree to which the parents guide the child in a consistent, rigorous fashion).

3. The pervasive milieu of the family (the extent to which the parents reinforced or undermined the values and significance of one another).

A fourth factor—the conformity or deviance of the parental model—may also be weakly associated with the child's level of aggression.

The data presented in this study—data gathered from the direct observation of 174 nondelinquent boys and their families over a period of more than 5 years—indicate that "aggressive," "assertive," and "non-aggressive" boys emerged from radically different environments.

These contrasts in background can perhaps best be viewed as summarized in Table 3.

These variables in the child's environment are not, of course, completely independent. We have treated particular conditions in the home, such as parental rejection of the child, as primarily related to the instigation of aggressive desires. Clearly, however, a factor such as parental rejection has other effects: it offers the child a model of aggression and it presumably weakens the child's desire to follow the demands of his parents. Certain other variables, however, do not seem to have this many-faceted influence. The degree to which the child has been subjected to adult supervision, for example, would seem to have direct relevance to controlling the boy's expression of aggression, but little or no bearing on the original establishment of aggressive desires.

To construct a comprehensive picture of the origins of aggression, one must view these various conditions in the child's environment in terms of their total impact. In an attempt to develop a general portrait of the origins of aggression, 10 variables in the background of every child in the study were categorized.

First, the children were divided according to the number of "aggression-creating" factors in their environment. For this purpose, five variables were

Table 3 Backgrounds of Aggressive, Assertive, and Nonaggressive Boys

Environmental Conditions	Aggressive Boys	Assertive Boys	Nonaggressive Boys
Parents' emotional relationship with the boy	Rejecting	Affectionate	Affectionate
	Punitive	Relatively punitive [a]	Nonpunitive
	Frequent use of threats	Infrequent use of threats	Little use of threats
Instillation of direct controls	Overcontrolled or subnormally controlled by mothers	Normally or subnormally controlled by mothers	Normally or overcontrolled by mothers
	Low demands on the child	Low demands	High demands
	Lack of supervision	Relatively little supervision of the child [a]	Firm supervision of the child
	Inconsistency in discipline	Relatively inconsistent in discipline [a]	Consistent in discipline
Parental model	Socially deviant	Relatively deviant [a]	Socially conformist
Parental relationship to each other	A high degree of general conflict	High degree of general conflict	Low degree of general conflict
	Lack of mutual esteem	Relatively low mutual esteem [a]	High mutual esteem
	Dissatisfaction with role in life	Relatively dissatisfied with role [a]	Satisfied with role
	Unaffectionate	Affectionate	Affectionate

[a] In comparison to the background of nonaggressive boys.

used: paternal attitude toward the boy, maternal attitude toward the child, paternal punitiveness, maternal punitiveness, and parental use of threats. For each factor that was present in the child's home, a "negative" score of one was given. Thus, the child who was rejected by both parents, who was treated punitively by both parents, and was subjected to frequent threats received a score of "−5." At the opposite extreme, the child who had not been subjected to any of these influences received a score of "0." If we did not possess sufficient information on a particular variable, this factor in the child's background was, *de facto*, considered as "positive."

Secondly, five variables relating to the general milieu of the home, the parental model, and the controls exercised by the parent over the child were considered—in other words, those factors which were presumably related to modifying the expression of aggressive desires. These conditions included parental supervision of the child, maternal consistency of discipline, parental demands on the boy, the strength of the maternal religion, and the level of general conflict between the parents. Each factor was given a "positive" weight of one; thus, the boy who came from an environment characterized by maternal consistency, firm supervision, a strong religious faith, high demands, and parental agreement was awarded a score of "+5." If we did not possess sufficient information on a particular condition, the factor was considered as "negative."

Since we knew that each of these 10 variables was independently related to aggression, our supposition was that their combined influence would account for much of the variation in aggressive behavior. We assumed, in particular, that the aggressive boys would be most likely to emerge from an environment that simultaneously instilled a high level of aggressive urges and failed to provide the conditions for controlling aggression. The nonaggressive boys, in contrast, would be expected to come from homes characterized by a high level of controls and a low degree of aggression-creating influences. These expectations were generally fulfilled.

In a general sense, therefore, we can argue that the *aggressive boys* were most likely to have been raised by parents who (*a*) treated the boy in a rejecting, punitive fashion; (*b*) failed to impose direct controls on his behavior; (*c*) offered him an example of deviance; and (*d*) were often involved in intense conflict.

The *nonaggressive boys* came from a strikingly contrasting environment—a home in which they were (*a*) treated in an affectionate, nonpunitive manner; (*b*) guided by a consistent set of controls; (*c*) exposed to examples of social conformity; and (*d*) reared by affectionate, satisfied parents.

The *assertive boys* generally resembled the nonaggressive children in that they were reared by relatively affectionate, nonthreatening parents; thus, they were not victimized by the rejection characteristic of the families of aggressive boys (51% came from families which were nonpunitive and affectionate as opposed to only 20% of the aggressive boys). They resembled the aggressive boys, however, in that their parents (*a*) often failed to impose consistent controls; (*b*) were deviant models; and (*c*) often were in open conflict. (64% of the assertive boys came from an environment where these conditions were present.)

It would appear, therefore, that the aggressive boys had a high level of aggressive urges and were uncontrolled; the nonaggressive boys had a low degree of aggressive desires and, in addition, were well-controlled; the assertive boys had a few basically aggressive urges but were relatively uncontrolled individuals.

It is encouraging to note that the results of this study, despite methodological differences, are in fundamental agreement with the conclusions which have emerged from prior research. For example, Bandura and Walters (1959) have studied the childhood antecedents of adolescent aggression. Their sample, drawn from a group of middle class, antisocial, delinquents differed strikingly from the boys studied in this research (in age, in social class, in geographic area, and in illegal behavior). Yet the results are basically similar; the antisocial, aggressive boys came from homes in which they were rejected and treated in an inconsistent fashion.

Again, the results achieved by Sears, Maccoby, and Levin (1957) in their recent investigations of childhood aggression bear a basic resemblance to the findings of this research. Among other relationships, Sears and his colleagues found that aggression in childhood was associated with the use of physical punishment, low esteem of the mother for the father, a high degree of permissiveness for the expression of aggression, disagreement between the parents, and dissatisfaction on the mother's part with her role in life. And, indeed, these same relationships appeared in this present study—even though the sample used in this research came from a generally lower social class than did the Sears' sample and the methods of observation in the two studies were quite different.

These various relationships between the nature of a child's family and his level of aggressive behavior could be interpreted in at least four different ways:

1. Some analysts might contend that aggression on the child's part actually provokes certain "typical" responses from the parents. By this interpretation, the child's innate aggressive behavior evokes rejecting attitudes, punitiveness, and inconsistency from the parents; the behavior itself is regarded as creating new conditions within the family. While it seems highly probable that the child's behavior reciprocally affects parental attitudes towards him, it would be stretching this interpretation unduly to argue that the child's behavior also causes such diverse phenomena as conflict between the parents, lack of supervision, parental deviance, and low esteem on the parents' part for each other.

2. Some might argue that the parents' behavior and the child's aggression are produced by common genetic factors and that the apparent environmental relationships are illusory. Within the confines of this study, it is impossible to evaluate this opinion directly. In the absence of definitive genetic evidence, however, it seems most reasonable to view this interpretation as a rather remote possibility.

3. Some social scientists, particularly sociologists, might well contend that both the parents' and the boys' behavior result from similar vectors in the social environment. These analysts would place special emphasis upon the similar experiences undergone by the parents' and the boy in their relations with the "outside" world: the school, the occupational environment, the neighborhood or the ethnic culture. Since there was no independent relation between the child's level of aggression and the family ethnic group or social class, this explanation does not appear to do justice to the findings.

4. Although the previous interpretations cannot be dismissed, it seems most reasonable to assume that the familial environment is an independent variable affecting the child's behavior. The evidence presented in this study (and the facts accumulated by previous work) suggest that aggression in childhood is a form of behavior developed in response to specific environmental conditions; conditions created by man and thus, potentially changeable by man. Clearly, aggression is a universal capacity of human nature, a capacity which is first expressed in the unfocused rage of infants. But the development of this trait—whether it is transformed into a pervasively destructive syndrome of behavior or whether it goes fallow—seems to lie well within the realm of human culture, as this culture is mediated through early familial experiences.

REFERENCES

Bandura, A., & Walters, R. *Adolescent aggression*. New York: Ronald, 1959.

Glueck, S., & Glueck, E. *Unraveling juvenile delinquency*. New York: Commonwealth Fund, 1950.

McCord, W., McCord, J., & Gudeman, J. *Origins of alcoholism*. Stanford: Stanford Univer. Press, 1960.

McCord, W., McCord, J., & Zola, I. *Origins of crime*. New York: Columbia Univer. Press, 1959.

Powers, E., & Witmer, H. *An experiment in the prevention of delinquency*. New York: Columbia Univer. Press, 1950.

Sears, R., Maccoby, E., & Levin, H. *Patterns of child rearing*. Evanston, Ill.: Row, Peterson, 1957.

Weiss, W., & Fine, B. The effect of induced aggressiveness on opinion change. *J. abnorm. soc. Psychol.*, 1956, **52**, 109–114.

18. THE RELATION BETWEEN SEVERAL PARENT

MEASURES AND THE CHILD'S EARLY

ADJUSTMENT TO SCHOOL

GENE R. MEDINNUS

The present paper reports data dealing with first grade readiness and adjustment in first grade. The purpose of this study was to explore the relationship between parental attitudes toward a number of aspects of child rearing, as assessed through questionnaires administered to both parents and through interviews with the mother, and the child's general adjustment in Grade 1.

METHOD

Subjects

The subjects in the investigation were a group of first graders and their parents. Two groups of children were identified through the teacher's rating of their adjustment in first grade on a five-point scale, with 5 representing good adjustment, 3 typical of the adjustment of the "average" child, and 1 denoting poor adjustment. The rating was made on the basis of and following the teacher's rating of the children on a 52-item First Grade Adjustment Scale. Those 10 children receiving ratings of 4 and 5 were treated as one group; the other group was comprised of those 9 with ratings of 1 and 2. The mean IQ of the children was 111.6 according to the Stanford-Binet (Form L) intelligence tests administered by the investigator. The socioeconomic status of the families was approximately evenly divided between the upper-lower and lower-middle classes according to Warner's Index of Status Characteristics (Warner, Meeker, and Eells, 1949). At the beginning of the study the mean ages of the mothers and fathers were 32.1 and 34.1 years, respectively, and the corresponding mean years of education were 12.0 and 12.2.

Scales

The two instruments employed to assess parental attitudes and behavior will be described first. Data from these two measures were obtained during the year prior to the child's entrance into first grade.

Reprinted from the *Journal of Educational Psychology,* 1961, **52,** 153–156, with permission of the author and the American Psychological Association.

The parents were asked to complete a form of the Parent Attitude Research Instrument (PARI) developed at the National Institute for Mental Health. The development of the scale, its uses and reliability coefficients have been described in some detail by Schaefer and Bell (1955, 1958). Briefly, the scale is a Likert-type questionnaire consisting of a number of subscales each concerned with various aspects of family life, child rearing attitudes, and relationships. The particular forms of the scale employed consisted of 29 subscales for the mothers and 25 for the fathers. The responses to the items were scored either 4, 3, 2, or 1, depending upon whether the response was "Strongly agree," "Somewhat agree," "Somewhat disagree," or "Strongly disagree," respectively. The questionnaires were left with the parents following an evening home visit by the investigator. They were returned as they were completed.

The Fels Parent Behavior Rating Scales originally were designed in an attempt to identify areas of the home environment which might be expected to bear some causal relation to the development of the child's personality (Baldwin, Kalhorn, and Breese, 1949; Champney, 1941). Lorr and Jenkins (1953) further analyzed the intercorrelations of the Fels scales presented by Roff (1949) in an attempt to determine second-order factors of a broad character which would be useful for conceptualizing the parent-child relationship. Three factors emerged; for convenience in the present discussion these will be labeled as follows: (*a*) Dependence vs. Independence Encouraging, (*b*) Democratic vs. Authoritarian, (*c*) Degree of organization in the home. Those five scales having the highest loadings on each of these three factors were employed in the present study. The ratings were made by the investigator on the basis of home visits and interviews with the mothers. Interrater reliabilty was established through previous ratings of 10 homes by the investigator and a graduate assistant. The mean reliability of these ratings for the 15 scales was .80. A list of the 15 rating scales is provided in Table 1.

For the purpose of assessing the subjects' adjustment to the first grade situation, a First Grade Adjustment Scale was developed (Medinnus, in press). Briefly, the following procedure was employed in the construction of the scale. Twenty-five first grade teachers were interviewed concerning factors related to a child's adjustment in Grade 1. The teachers were asked to mention specific traits, abilities, and items of behavior which, in their opinions, characterize or describe good adjustment and poor adjustment in the first grade. The characteristics listed for good and poor adjustment were examined for parallel items which seemed to define opposite ends of a single continuum. Those items for which there was at least a minimum level of consensus were placed on a five-point scale, with 3 representing the midpoint or rating of the "average" child, and 1 and 5 describing poor and good adjustment, respectively. The 52 items were grouped into five major areas: Physical Status, Social Behavior, Emotional Behavior, Intellectual Abilities and Behavior, and Adjustment to Classroom Membership and Requirements. Interrater reliability coefficients for the five sections and for the full scale clustered about .75.

Table 1   *Ratings of Homes of Two Adjustment Groups*

Fels scales	Well Adjusted		Poorly Adjusted		
	M [a]	σ	M	σ	p
A. Dependence vs. Independence					
Encouraging					
4.1 General babying	51.3	7.91	42.8	7.81	.05
1.91 Child centeredness of home	55.3	7.85	42.1	6.28	.01
7.1 Solicitousness for welfare	51.0	7.82	45.1	11.69	ns
4.2 General protectiveness	52.7	6.42	40.9	8.48	.01
2.12 Intensity of contact with mother	50.6	8.93	49.0	10.99	ns
B. Autocratic vs. Democratic					
3.15 Nondemocracy of policy	46.4	8.14	52.6	12.87	ns
3.22 Coerciveness of suggestion	47.6	6.92	48.7	12.42	ns
3.14 Nonjustification of policy	44.8	6.22	56.3	10.07	.01
3.11 Restrictiveness of regulations	47.9	8.31	47.3	18.91	ns
8.2 Emotionality toward child	47.5	8.06	53.2	12.93	ns
C. Organization and Effectiveness of Control					
3.12 Readiness of enforcement	48.8	8.15	50.1	13.37	ns
3.13 Severity of actual penalties	47.2	6.57	52.8	12.97	ns
3.3 Accelerational attempt	55.7	7.86	40.7	5.48	.001
1.7 Coordination of household	49.0	7.90	45.4	10.73	ns
1.2 Activeness of home	47.6	8.18	54.9	11.78	ns

[a] The raw score ratings were converted to McCall Ts.

RESULTS

Those PARI scales which differentiated significantly between the parents of the two groups of children will be mentioned first. The fathers and mothers were compared separately since the subscales and the items were not identical for the two forms. The following scales differentiated between the mothers of the well- and poorly adjusted first graders at the .05 level or beyond: Approval of Activity, Irritability, Dependency of Mother, and Fear of Harming Baby. Mothers of the well adjusted children showed more of the attributes measured by the first three scales than did the mothers of the poorly adjusted children; the reverse was true for the fourth scale mentioned. No scales reached this significance level for the fathers.

The results for the Fels scales are given in Table 1.

DISCUSSION

If there is any validity to the premise that the child's behavior and personality are in part causally determined by parental attitudes one would expect wide differences between the attitudes of parents of well- verses poorly adjusted first grade children. That such was not revealed in the present analysis is apparent from the fact that only four scales differentiated between the two groups of mothers and none of the scales reached the significance level for the fathers. One possible interpretation of this finding emphasizes the lack of validity in the parent attitude scale employed. Another interpretation assumes that there is actually no relation between parental attitude and the child's general adjustment in the school situation. The findings with regard to the Fels scales seem to furnish evidence to discount this interpretation.

It is apparent from Table 1 that while only 5 of the 15 Fels scales differentiated between the home environments of the two groups of children, 3 of the 5 were included in the Dependence vs. Independence Encouraging factor. In addition, the parents of the well adjusted group were rated higher on the Solicitousness variable but the difference was not statistically significant. It should be noted also that in each case the homes of the well adjusted children were rated higher in the dependence-encouraging direction. While this would seem to run counter to the notion of the need for independent behavior in the school setting, the findings obtained here concerning the three scales, General babying, Child centeredness of the home, and Protectiveness, are in accord with the results of other investigations (Baldwin et al., 1949; Bandura and Walters, 1959). In their interpretation of the parent behavior ratings, the Fels researchers identified an "indulgence" pattern consisting of three variables, Babying, Protectiveness, and Solicitousness. High ratings on these variables were interpreted as indicating either one of two processes in the home: "(a) the mother is warmly doting and protective of the child; or (b) she is anxious and restrictive lest the child endanger himself or discommode her" (Baldwin et al., 1949, p. 8). On the basis of the relationship of these three variables to other rating scales, these investigators concluded that "there is a definite tendency for those parents who are rated high on indulgence to be warm, emotional, and unable or unwilling to give the child either emotional or physical freedom" (p. 8).

While two possibilities were described to explain high ratings on the indulgence variables, the burden of the present discussion is to argue that, in the present study at least, the higher ratings of the homes of the well adjusted first graders on these variables indicate acceptance of the child while the lower ratings of the homes of the poorly adjusted children point to rejection of the child. Great concern with encouraging independence may actually reflect parental rejection of the child. Parental declarations that the child must learn to "stand on his own two feet" and "fight his own battles" may be attempts to justify nonnurturant and nonsupporting behavior growing out of feelings of rejection.

This interpretation is similar to that of Bandura and Walters (1959) who found that the parents of aggressive boys tended to discourage dependency behavior in their sons and that parental rejection was related to nonnurturant parental behavior. The authors state: "Indeed, parental rejection seems to involve a pervasive form of punishment of the child's attempts to gain emotional support from his parents" (p. 68).

SUMMARY

The present paper presented data concerning the relationship between various parental attitudes and behavior and the child's adjustment in first grade.

A comparison was made of the parent attitude scores and Fels home ratings of two groups of children, 10 well adjusted first graders and 9 poorly adjusted first graders.

The following results emerged from the study:

1. Four of the 29 PARI subscales differentiated significantly between the mothers of the groups. None of the scales reached the .05 level for the fathers.

2. Five of the 15 Fels scales differentiated between the home environments of the two groups of children. Three of the 5 scales were included in the Dependence vs. Independence Encouraging factor.

The results were interpreted as indicating that the lower ratings of the homes of the poorly adjusted children on the several dependence-encouraging variables reflected parental rejection which was a causal factor in the children's poor adjustment to the demands of the first grade situation.

REFERENCES

Baldwin, A. L., Kalhorn, Joan, & Breese, Fay H. The appraisal of parent behavior. *Psychol. Monogr.*, 1949, **63**, 4 (Whole No. 229).

Bandura, A., & Walters, R. H. *Adolescent aggression*. New York: Ronald, 1959.

Champney, H. The measurement of parent behavior. *Child Develpm.*, 1941, **12**, 131–166.

Lorr, M., & Jenkins, R. L. Three factors in parent behavior. *J. consult. Psychol.*, 1953, **17**, 306–308.

Medinnus, G. R. The development of a first grade adjustment scale. *J. exp. Educ.*, in press.

Roff, M. A factorial study of the Fels Parent Behavior Scales. *Child Develpm.*, 1949, **20**, 29–45.

Schaefer, E. S., & Bell, R. Q. Parental Attitude Research Instrument (PARI): Normative data. Unpublished manuscript, National Institutes of Health, 1955.

Schaefer, E. S., & Bell, R. Q. Development of a Parental Attitude Research Instrument. *Child Develpm.*, 1958, **29**, 339–361.

Warner, W. L., Meeker, Marchia, & Eells, K. *Social class in America*. Chicago: Science Research Associates, 1949.

19. EFFECT OF CHILDREARING PRACTICES ON DEVELOPMENT OF DIFFERENTIAL COGNITIVE ABILITIES

ELIZABETH BING

Individual differences in cognitive development have come to be considered the result of interactions between a child's life experiences and the set of genes with which he has been endowed. Relations have been found between cognitive abilities and perceptual and cognitive style on one side and personality traits on the other side, and some investigators have made efforts to identify antecedent conditions in the home which might be responsible for differences in children's personality as well as cognitive development. Thus "democratic homes" (1, 2), "maternal acceleration" (18), and a "warm, positive family atmosphere" (17) have been reported to increase the rate of growth of children's intelligence, especially verbal ability. Results of investigations of the effect of institutionalization and prolonged hospitalization of infants, summarized by McCarthy (15, pp. 584–585), uniformly indicate retardation in language development. On the other hand, there has been suggestive evidence that certain conditions favor disproportionately the development of verbal ability and possibly impede the development of nonverbal skills, like numerical and spatial ability. Suggested as antecedents for such differential development in favor of verbal ability were "growth restricting" childrearing practices (24), such as parental overlimitation and excessive control, "maternal overprotection" (14), "emphasis on verbal accomplishment" (13), and a "demanding discipline with emphasis on academic achievement" (11). Similarly, overanxious discipline (11) and tense parent-child relationships (10) were postulated to be responsible for low nonverbal, especially spatial, ability in children.

While the consistently found superiority of boys over girls in spatial ability may be considered innate (5, 6, 8, 9), there has been suggestive evidence that this may be the result of differences in roles assigned to males and females in our culture (4, 7, 19, 22).

Most of these studies, while yielding intriguing leads, failed to measure children's verbal and nonverbal abilities with relatively "pure" tests. Also, these studies investigated primarily parents' present-day childrearing behavior

Reprinted from *Child Development*, 1963, **34**, 631–648, with permission of the author and the Society for Research in Child Development.

205

and did not attempt to investigate the very early mother-child relationships. Furthermore, the sole measure of parents' behavior used was the interview of the parent.

In the present study, specifically designed tests were used to measure children's verbal and nonverbal abilities, such as spatial and numerical, as well as their total IQ in order to identify groups of children with discrepant abilities. An effort was made to investigate not only present, but also early childrearing practices as far as they may be assumed to be antecedents to differential cognitive development in children. And, finally, the mother's actual mode of interaction with the child was observed in a fairly structured situation.

From the theoretical considerations and available research findings, it was assumed that childrearing practices which stimulate, reward, and encourage verbal or nonverbal abilities should increase either one of these abilities and that fostering dependency should favor verbal ability while at the same time depressing nonverbal ability, whereas fostering independence should have the opposite effect. While not consistent over all age groups, some studies indicate female superiority in verbal and male superiority in numerical ability (12). It was therefore thought worthwhile to test the hypothesis that emphasis on sex-typing should reinforce verbality as a sex-appropriate trait in girls and spatial and numerical ability in boys.

An interview and questionnaire were designed to obtain information on the variables which were assumed to be more strongly represented in high verbal or in high nonverbal groups, and the following predictions were made:

A. *Verbal ability* should be associated with (positive association unless otherwise indicated)
   1. Verbal stimulation and interest shown by mother
      a. especially during early childhood: amount of playtime mother had with infant, verbal stimulation of infant, mother's verbal responsiveness to child's questions, taking child on outings, amount of early reading to child, tutoring before school, interest shown in child's good speech habits, importance attached to early accomplishments.
      b. during school age years: number of story books, use of encyclopedia and "word games" played by family.
   2. Verbal freedom: permissiveness for verbal aggression, punishment for verbal aggression (negative association) and for poor speech (negative association), participation in meal conversation, permissiveness to listen to, or participate in adult conversation, permissiveness for discussion of "adult" topics, democratic family discussion.
   3. Emphasis on academic achievement: rewarding good and criticizing poor academic achievement, level of schooling desired for child, amount of present tutoring.
   4. Emphasis on sociability: rewarding sociability, providing opportunity for sociability, teaching manners and discouraging sociability (negative association).

5. Emphasis on sex-typing and parent's own verbal interest: for girls, mother's emphasis on girl's femininity and sex-appropriate behavior, and father being stricter than mother as a sign of adherence to appropriate sex-role behavior in family's pattern of living; for both sexes, like-sex parent's time spent reading.
B. *Nonverbal ability* should be associated with
   1. Nonverbal stimulation and freedom of exploration.
      a. Opportunity for object experimentation: number of toys at pre-school age, extent to which tools, gadgets, and objects are available to child for experimentation.
      b. Freedom to explore the environment: permissiveness for early exploration and object experimentation, lack of restrictions indoors and outdoors, and strictness of time schedules (negatively associated).
   2. Emphasis on sex-typing and parent's own nonverbal interest: for boys, mother's emphasis on boy's masculinity and boy's sex-appropriate behavior; for both sexes, parent's time spent together with child in arts, crafts, hobbies, and do-it-yourself activities.
C. Verbal ability should be positively associated with mother's dependency-fostering behavior and nonverbal ability with behavior fostering independence.
   1. Fostering Dependency: encouragement and lack of punishment of emotional dependency, permissiveness for instrumental dependency, protectiveness, anxiety arousal in cautiousness training, continuity of mother-child relationship and of caretaking activity.
   2. Fostering Independence: earliness of age at which mother expects independence to be achieved in different areas, pressure for responsibilities, permissiveness to spend allowance freely, permissiveness for independence, pressure for independence.

Furthermore, an observation session was designed in which the child was asked to do verbal as well as performance tasks in the presence of the mother in order to elicit from the mother a variety of behaviors which would make it possible to test the following predictions:

1. High verbal group mothers should be more active verbally than the low verbal group mothers in all categories of help-giving behavior (focusing, encouragement, approval, prompting, and answering problem for child).
2. High verbal group mothers should use more "pressure for improvement."
3. High verbal group mothers should have more "positive" interaction with child, i.e., give help more often after a request from the child.
4. High nonverbal mothers should disapprove and withhold help more often when requested by the child.
5. High verbal group mothers should ask the observer more questions.
6. On the performance tasks, high verbal group mothers should give more physical help and abstain less often from giving any help.
7. On performance tasks, high verbal group mothers should give physical help sooner.

METHODS AND PROCEDURES

Subjects

The subjects of the sample consisted of 60 mothers who had children who were in the fifth grade and had discrepant cognitive abilities. The selection was made from a total of 1214 children representing the universe of fifth grade children in the public school system of Redwood City and San Carlos, two communities in the San Francisco Bay Area. The basic discrepancy that was of interest for the purpose of the study was the comparison of high verbal children with low verbal children of similar IQ, the complementary nonverbal abilities being either spatial or numerical ability.

Verbal and nonverbal mental abilities were partly assessed on the basis of results of the Thurstone's SRA Primary Mental Abilities for ages 7 to 11 (Form AH) which was administered to all fifth grade children in their classrooms. The scores obtained by each child on the verbal, spatial, and numerical parts of this test were supplemented by scores from the Iowa Achievement Test or the California Mental Maturity Test. Cases with total PMA scores below 125, cases with visual or hearing impairment, cases from foreign language homes, and cases whose "high" ability was below the population median, and those whose "low" ability was above the population median were dropped from the sample.

With this selection procedure the following four major groups could be established: 16 high verbal boys, 16 low verbal boys, 12 high verbal girls, and 16 low verbal girls. The contrasting ability was spatial ability for one half and numerical ability for the other half of these groups with the exception of the group of the 12 high verbal girls. Eight of these were low in space and four were low in number. Cases of girls with high verbal, low number ability were surprisingly difficult to find.

Only four cases which should have been included in the final sample of 60 were lost and replaced by comparable cases. In two of these cases the experimental conditions were spoiled by the presence of the fathers, and in two cases the mothers were not available for the interview.

The groups were fairly well equated on "general intelligence," as measured by total PMA score; analysis of variance did not reveal any significant differences between means for the groups. Furthermore, differences between group averages with respect to socioeconomic status of the family and with respect to parents' education were not significant.

Measurement of Antecedent Variables

Questionnaire. The mother was asked to fill in a questionnaire which consisted of 20 groups of questions referring to factual material in relation to the mother's caretaking activity of the child, the child's first verbal and nonverbal accomplishments, kinds of toys, number of story books, and the mother's as well as her husband's interest in reading and manual activities. The mother was also asked to estimate age levels at which she thought the average child would have usually learned a variety of listed behaviors, some of these based on Winterbottom's scale (23), such as feeding himself, keeping room tidy, shopping for own clothing, crossing busy street, etc.

On the basis of a previously constructed rating scale, a total of 16 dimensions representing possible antecedent variables was rated. Some of the scales could be objectively scored according to a specified point system; in cases where the answer could be given in numerical form, the number was regarded as the score, transformed into a standard score in accordance with the total frequency distribution; for other scales, five fairly specific levels were indicated ranging from a high level of 5 to a low level of 1.

Three raters were used for the ratings. They did not know to which group the case belonged and assignments were made in such a way that each one of the three raters double rated at least 10 cases with each of the other two raters.

Interview. The interviews with the mothers were semistructured with open-ended questions similar to the type developed by Sears, Maccoby, and Levin (20) and by Bandura and Walters (3). It was attempted to cover in the interviews the child's early history as well as the present with respect to the mother's behavior regarding her relationship with the child, verbal stimulation provided by her, fostering dependency or independence in the child, verbal freedom allowed, permission for object experimentation, emphasis on sociability, academic achievement and sex-typing, and restrictiveness. The interviews lasted from 1 to 2 hours, were tape recorded, and conducted by one graduate student in psychology and the author. Neither of the two interviewers knew to which group the mother belonged.

Three graduate students in psychology and the author rated the interviews from the tape recordings according to preconstructed rating scales comprising 41 dimensions. Most of these scales were 5-point scales, specifying five different levels of behavior or attitudes. All 60 interviews were rated by various combinations of two of the four raters, and none of the raters knew to which group the case belonged.

Interaction situation. Either before or after the interview, the child was called in and the mother was asked to read some verbal problem questions to the child, and, following the completion of this task, the child was requested by the observer to perform two nonverbal tasks.

While seemingly the child's performance was the focus of attention, the situation was devised to obtain firsthand observational data on the mother's mode of interaction with the child. The situation was so constructed that the mothers could demonstrate a great variability of behavior, from no intervention at all to a high degree of helping, pressuring, or disapproving types of behavior.

For the verbal task, a comprehension type test was used. It contained five problem situations which were rather difficult for 10-year-old children to answer satisfactorily. The questions were also worded in such a way that several solutions were possible. Two of the questions required the child to give reasons to explain a fact; the reasons being manifold, it gave the mother an opportunity to prompt, encourage, or pressure the child to improve his answer. (Example: Why should children not be out in the street alone at night?)

The first of the nonverbal tasks consisted of putting together a complicated jigsaw puzzle (commercially available, Kwazy Quilt, Tryne, No. 114). The child had to fit the colored pieces together into a pattern following a model. At the same time, the mother was provided with a model which showed the placement of all pieces more clearly than the child's model did, thus putting the mother in a position where she was able to help and could do so as much as she wanted to and in whatever way she chose. The other nonverbal task was the Healy Picture Completion Test, in which the child was requested to put the block with the best fitting picture detail in a large picture with recessed spaces for the blocks. While there is always one "best" solution, there are also other adequate solutions. This situation provided the mother again with the opportunity to assist or pressure the child for improvement of his solution. The two performance tasks gave the mother an opportunity for helping the child not only with verbal means, but also with a variety of physical ways of assisting, like actually moving pieces into place or handing the appropriate piece to the child.

In order to have the interaction situations as comparable as possible, the following procedures were adhered to:

After mother and child were comfortably seated side by side at the table opposite to the observer, the following instructions were given:

"Since (child's name) happens to be in this project, we know a little bit how he is learning at school. However, we know very little about how he and children in general are learning in the home. We have here a number of fairly hard tasks. Let's suppose these are problems that (child's name) has brought home and is supposed to solve. I would like you to have (child's name) do these tasks in whatever way you think would give him a chance to do his best. Here are some questions that I would like you to read to (child's name) and later on we have some puzzles to do. Now pretend that I am not here and go ahead as you would at home."

The observer handed to the mother the question sheet which contained five problem tasks. After mother and child had finished these tasks, the observer asked the child to do a puzzle with the help of a model, and the mother was given the more clearly marked model; both were told that the mother's copy made the solution of the problem easier. After completion of the puzzle or after 10 minutes, whichever was earlier, the Healy Picture Completion Test was presented with standardized instructions. After 10 minutes or after completion of this task, the observer commended the child for his efforts and ended the session. Whenever during the procedure the mother asked the observer any question about her participation in the situation, he said: "You can enter into this as much or as little as you feel like." The whole procedure usually lasted about half an hour, and most children seemed to like the novelty of the situation.

The mother's behavior with the child during the verbal and nonverbal tasks was analyzed according to pre-established categories which were thought to represent different degrees and manners of stimulating and helping the child with his tasks. The following nine categories could be distinguished for both verbal and performance tasks: Focusing, Approval, Encouragement, Prompting, Giving answers (instead of letting child answer), Pressure for improvement, Disapproval, Withholding help, and Helping after request from child. One category covering the number of questions the mother asked the experimenter was devised as yielding a possible measure of the mother's dependency needs, or at least her need for more structure. Three additional categories were established for the nonverbal tasks, dealing with the mother's physical help-giving behavior, such as the mother's own handling of puzzle pieces, showing of her own copy to child, and the time elapsed until the mother made her first help-giving response. This resulted in a total of 22 categories.

The scoring was done by the person who conducted the interview. For five cases of the sample the alternate interviewer was also present and scored the behavior independently so that the reliability of the scoring was established on the basis of these five sample cases in addition to five pretesting cases which were double scored.

Reliabilities of Ratings

As a measure of the reliabilities of the ratings for the questionnaire and the interview, the percentage of cases with perfect agreement between two raters and the percentage of cases with 1 and with more than 1 point difference was computed for every scale. Perfect agreement of ratings ranged from 62 to 100 per cent of the cases for the questionnaire scales and from 48 to 88 per cent for the interview scales. Agreement within 1 point ranged from 89 to 100 per cent for questionnaire scales and from 87 to 100 per cent for the interview scales.

The percentage of cases showing perfect agreement between two scores for the various categories of the interaction situation ranged from 50 to 150 and agreement within 1 point ranged from 80 to 100 per cent.

Correlational Analysis and Combination of Variables

From the questionnaire, the interview, and the interaction situation, a total of 79 variables was obtained. In cases where variables were assumed to belong to the same complex of behavior, but to represent different aspects of it, the scores of these variables were combined if the variables also actually showed a correlation of at least .26 which corresponds to the .05 level of significance for our sample of 60 cases. As a result of these combinations the 16 questionnaire and 41 interview variables were reduced to a total of 34 variables and the 22 interaction categories or variables to a total of 15.

The differences between the means of all variables for the high verbal children as compared to the low verbal children and for the high verbal boys and girls as compared to the low verbal boys and girls had to be tested for significance. This was done by the t technique for testing differences between independent means for small samples. For two variables showing extreme skewed distributions, the chi square method for testing the significance of the differences between the distributions for two contrast groups was used.

RESULTS

Interview and Questionnaire

Of the 34 single and combined variables of the interview and questionnaire, 10 were found to distinguish significantly between high and low verbal groups (see Table 1).

Antecedents of Verbal Ability

1. *Verbal stimulation and interest shown by mother.* For the early childhood period, a combination of measures relating to the child's early verbal stimulation (amount of playtime mother had with infant, verbal stimulation of infant, mother's responsiveness to child's early questions, taking young child on outings, early reading to child, tutoring before school, interest shown in child's good speech habits) differentiated on a highly significant level between high verbal and low verbal groups for boys and for sexes combined as predicted, $p < .001$ in favor of more verbal stimulation during infancy occurring with high verbal than with low verbal groups. While for the girls, taken by themselves, the mean of this variable was higher for the high verbal than for the low verbal group, the difference was not large enough to be significant.

Using the number of memories that a mother was able to report on her baby's early verbal and nonverbal accomplishments as a measure of importance attached to these and as an indirect measure of attention given to the child, it was found that this variable, also, was significantly higher for high verbal groups, if boys and sexes combined were considered. However, the difference, while in the expected direction, did not reach significance for girls.

For the period after school age, the specific measures hypothesized to differentiate between HiV and LoV groups were (a) number of story books and (b) use of encyclopedia and "word-games" played by family. Only with regard to story books, the hypothesis was confirmed for boys and sexes combined.

Caution is needed in interpreting the higher number of story books in

... and Girls (N = 28) and Sexes Combined (N = 60) on All Variables Distinguishing Between These Groups

	Boys			Girls			Sexes Combined		
	High	Low	p	High	Low	p	High	Low	p
Interview and Questionnaire Variables									
Early verbal stimulation	44.1	34.4	<.001	38.9	33.6	ns	41.9	34.0	<.001
Memory for early accomplishments	19.1	14.4	>.05*	16.0	12.6	ns	17.8	13.5	.02*
Number of story books	36.3	23.9	>.05	37.0	24.2	ns	36.6	24.1	<.05
Punishment for poor speech	5.4	5.8	ns	4.7	6.1	<.05	5.1	6.0	ns
Participation in meal conversations	6.4	4.3	<.01	6.4	6.1	ns	6.4	5.2	<.05
Criticism for academic achievement	7.6	6.4	<.05	6.7	5.3	<.05	7.2	5.8	<.01
Permissiveness for object experimentation and lack of restrictions	17.6	22.2	<.05	18.5	15.9	ns	18.0	19.0	ns
Anxiety arousal in cautiousness training	4.9	3.9	>.05	4.3	3.8	ns	4.6	3.8	<.05
Father's reading time	12.0	15.6	ns	14.1	6.3	<.001	12.9	11.0	ns
Father's strictness	5.3	4.4	ns	6.1	4.6	ns	5.6	4.5	.05*
Situation Variables									
Helping on verbal and nonverbal tasks [a]	404.7	386.7	ns	438.0	388.1	<.01	419.0	387.4	<.01
Helping on nonverbal tasks [b]	157.7	142.7	<.05	166.3	143.9	<.01	161.4	143.3	<.01
Approval on nonverbal tasks	47.9	48.4	ns	56.2	47.9	<.05	51.4	48.1	ns
Focusing on verbal tasks	48.4	48.4	ns	55.0	49.3	<.01	51.3	48.8	ns
Pressure for improvement on nonverbal tasks	47.6	50.7	ns	54.8	47.2	<.05	50.5	47.8	ns
Pressure for improvement on verbal and nonverbal tasks	99.6	99.7	ns	105.2	96.1	<.05	102.0	97.9	ns
Help after request	3.0	3.3	ns	6.1	1.7	<.01	4.3	2.5	<.05
Child's bids for help	4.1	3.7	ns	6.8	2.3	<.01	5.3	3.0	<.05
Withholding help and disapproval	4.6	3.3	ns	4.4	1.9	<.05*	4.5	2.6	<.05*
Mother questions observer	2.2	1.6	ns	3.1	1.7	<.05	2.6	1.6	>.01

[a] Combination of eight categories: focusing, prompting and encouragement, approval, giving answers on both verbal and on nonverbal tasks.

[b] Combination of three categories: focusing, prompting and encouragement, and giving answers on nonverbal tasks.

Note. All tests are one-tailed unless p value is followed by an asterisk.

the HiV group as an antecedent to the child's high verbal ability. The possession of a greater number of books by age 10 may be a consequence of the child's high verbal interest and ability. It is interesting to note that Milner (17) found a greater number of story books among her high verbal 6-year olds, an age level at which being exposed to story books can be considered as an antecedent condition to a greater extent, since the child's reading ability has hardly developed.

2. *Verbal freedom.* Two of the seven scales assumed to measure different aspects of verbal freedom differentiated significantly between groups as predicted. Punishment for poor speech differentiated significantly in favor of LoV as compared to HiV girls, and amount of meal conversation distinguished HiV from LoV groups significantly for boys and for sexes combined. None of the differences on the measures dealing with permissiveness or punishment for verbal aggression, permissiveness to listen and participate in adult conversation, and freedom for democratic discussion to discuss "adult" topics was significant.

3. *Emphasis on academic achievement.* The hypothesis that verbal ability should be associated with emphasis on academic achievement was confirmed when criticism for poor academic achievement was taken as a separate measure, but not for a combination of this measure with rewarding academic achievement, level of schooling desired by parents, and amount of present tutoring. Criticism for poor academic achievement, taken by itself, discriminated significantly between HiV and LoV groups for boys, girls, and for sexes combined, the means of criticism of poor academic achievement being higher for all high verbal groups.

5. *Sex-role differentiation and parent's own verbal interest.* It was hypothesized that, for girls, verbal ability should be positively associated with mother's emphasis on the girl's adopting a feminine role and sex-appropriate behavior and with father's relative strictness and that for both sexes it would be associated with like-sex parent's amount of time spent reading. The hypothesis with respect to father's strictness was partly confirmed; significant results were obtained though not predicted for girls with respect to father's reading time. None of the other variables of this cluster distinguished significantly between groups.

While mothers of the high verbal group girls reported on the average that their husbands were stricter than themselves, this difference failed to reach significance. However, further analysis of the data indicated that, for those of the HiV girls whose low ability was space, the difference was significant at the .05 level, the stricter father being associated with the HiV girl group.

One assumption had been that the mother's perception of the father as the "Master" would enhance the masculinity of the male role and implicitly the feminine role of the girl in the family and might reveal the importance that the mother attaches to appropriate sex-typing and thereby strengthening girls' verbal ability. This was borne out with respect to the HiV-LoS girls and their contrast group.

The fact that father's reading time discriminated highly in favor of high verbal ability only for girls and not for boys was just as surprising as the fact that mother's reading time did not differentiate between any of the groups. The latter fact may be due to lower dispersion of scores of reading time for mothers. The assumption that with respect to verbal and nonverbal ability children would model themselves after the like-sex parent was not borne out. Many of the mothers' behavior patterns and attitudes that were investigated through the interview seemed to influence boys' cognitive development, but not girls'; on the other hand, of the very few behavior patterns pertaining to fathers that were evaluated, two proved to be significantly associated with girls' cognitive development. This points to the possible importance of the influence of the opposite-sex parent on the child's cognitive development. Such an influence is hard to account for in terms of our present knowledge of personality development, but merits further investigation.

Antecedents of Nonverbal Ability

1. *Nonverbal stimulation and freedom of exploration.* It was hypothesized that nonverbal ability should be associated with opportunity and freedom for exploration and object experimentation at preschool age and at present. This hypothesis was confirmed with respect to boys for a combination of the measures of permissiveness for object experimentation at preschool age, availability to child of tools, gadgets, and objects for experimentation at present, and lack of restrictions indoors and outdoors. It was not confirmed for the measures of number of toys at preschool age and strictness of time schedules.

While the number of toys that children have before school age did not seem to be a significant antecedent to nonverbal cognitive development, the freedom the children have in playing with these toys and in exploring their environment was the condition that discriminated significantly between HiV and LoV groups of boys, the greater freedom being associated with the low verbal boys who are high either in space or number.

2. *Sex-role differentiation and parent's own nonverbal interest.* It was hypothesized that nonverbal ability should be positively associated for boys with mother's emphasis on the boy's adopting a masculine role and sex-appropriate behavior and for both sexes with parents' time spent with child in arts, crafts, hobbies, and do-it-yourself activities. None of these hypotheses was confirmed.

Dependency-Independence

It was hypothesized that verbal ability was associated with mother's behavior fostering dependency and nonverbal ability with behavior fostering independence. Dependency-fostering behavior was measured by (*a*) encouragement of emotional dependency and lack of punishment for dependency; (b) permissiveness for instrumental dependency; (c) anxiety arousal in cautiousness training; (d) continuity of mother-child relationship; and (e) continuity of caretaking activity. One of these five measures, anxiety arousal in cautiousness training, differentiated between the high and low verbal group, greater anxiety arousal being associated with the HiV group for boys and sexes combined.

The assumption was thus borne out, at least for boys, that the mother who tried to impress the child more with the potential dangers of the environment would make the child more anxious, insecure, and dependent and thus less capable of dealing with cognitive tasks presumably requiring more independence, such as arithmetic and spatial relations.

Behavior fostering independence was measured by (a) earliness of age at which mothers expect the achievement of independence by child in different areas; (b) pressure for responsibilities; (c) permissiveness to spend allowance freely; and (d) a combined scale of permissiveness for independence, pressure for independence, and lack of protectiveness. None of these four measures distinguished between High verbal and Low verbal groups as predicted.

The result that some of the variables, like pressure for responsibility and pressure for independence, which were considered to belong to the cluster of variables fostering independence did not differentiate between the groups is probably due to the fact that there is no linear relation between these variables and independence. An excess of pressure for mature behavior may lead to more manifestations of dependency. Similarly, permissiveness for dependency on the part of the parent does not necessarily show a linear relation with dependency behavior in the child. It may also be useful in future studies to distinguish between "independence" in the sense of self-help and "independence" in the sense of self-determination. Conditions which foster dependency or independence are varied, subtle, and extremely difficult to measure through one standardized interview. It might very well be that the observational method proved to be more sensitive and apt to pick up differences between mothers with respect to the dependency-independence dimension.

Interaction Situation

Six of the seven hypotheses were essentially confirmed. One hypothesis was not only confirmed, but the opposite of the stated hypothesis was confirmed (see Table 1).

1. The hypothesis that high verbal mothers should be more active in all categories of help-giving behavior (focusing, encouragement, approval, prompting and answering problems for child) was confirmed, at least when these categories were combined. The differences were significant at the $< .01$ level for girls and for sexes combined. However, the differences were not

significant for boys alone. When the help-giving behavior on the nonverbal tasks alone was considered, the differences in favor of the high verbal mothers were highly significant for the same groups, in addition to a difference at the $< .05$ level for the boys. On the other hand, if one considers some of the help-giving activities on the verbal tasks alone, they did not yield significant differences. This was true for approval and for the combination of focusing and prompting and giving answers, where the differences for the means were for all groups in the predicted direction, but did not reach significance. However, with respect to helping the child focus on the verbal task as a separate variable, the mothers of HiV girls were significantly higher on this behavior category than the mothers of the LoV girls.

2. The hypothesis that high verbal group mothers should be higher in pressure for improvement was confirmed for HiV girls as compared to LoV girls. This held true for nonverbal tasks as well as for the combination of verbal and nonverbal tasks, but not for verbal tasks alone.

3. The hypothesis that high verbal group mothers should give help more often after request was confirmed for girls and sexes combined. There were no differences for any of the boys' groups. The number of times a mother helped a child after request was partly a function of the child's asking for help. It appeared that the child who had learned to expect an answer, at least intermittently, would ask more questions. The child's asking questions in the observed interaction situation may then be partly a measure of the mother's past (unobserved) behavior in interaction with the child; this category may thus reflect not so much temporary behavior specific to the experimental situation, but rather usual interaction patterns between mother and child.

Considering, then, differences in the children's behavior, the high verbal groups of girls and sexes combined asked for help significantly more often than the respective low verbal groups. No significant differences were found for boys. An analysis of these data by sex indicated that the total group of girls, on the average, did not ask their mothers for help significantly more often than the boys.

4. The hypothesis that high nonverbal mothers should disapprove and withhold help more often was not only not confirmed, but the observed differences were significant in the opposite direction. High verbal group mothers disapproved and withheld help more often. This was true for girls and sexes combined, while the difference for boys was in the same direction but failed to reach significance. On this measure of "negative" interaction, just as on "help after request," a measure of "positive" interaction, high verbal mothers scored significantly higher. It appears, therefore, that what is important seems to be the degree of interaction between mother and child rather than its content.

5. As predicted, high verbal group mothers asked the observer more questions. This was true for girls' mothers with respect to HiV as compared

to LoV groups. Again, no significant differences were found for boys' mothers. It was thought that the mother's need to ask questions about procedure would be a measure of one aspect of her dependency needs. That this measure yielded significant results for girls' mothers, but not for boys' mothers, came as a surprise, but was consistent with results for the other categories where mother's behavior was found to be significant mainly for girls' discrepancy groups.

6. The hypothesis that high verbal group mothers should give more physical help was confirmed when the chi square method of analyzing the data instead of the comparison of means was used. Twelve of the 32 LoV group mothers abstained completely from giving any physical help as compared to four of the 28 HiV group mothers ($\chi^2 = 4.19$; $df = 1$), a difference significant at the $< .05$ level for a one-tailed test.

7. The hypothesis that on performance tasks HiV mothers should give help sooner was also confirmed, when they were compared with LoV mothers for the whole sample as to whether they waited 30 seconds or less (8 HiV and 6 LoV), 30 seconds to 5 minutes (15 HiV and 12 LoV), or more than 5 minutes (5 HiV and 14 LoV) before helping physically. The difference was significant ($\chi^2 = 4.73$; $df = 2$) at the .05 level for a one-tailed test.

The pattern of behavior of the high verbal girls' mothers was thus quite different from the behavior of the low verbal group. The HiV mothers showed on the average more positive and negative interaction with the child, the child asking more often for help and getting the help part of the time. Most of the help was given without being requested by the child, and these mothers helped their children, especially on the performance tasks, in all categories of helping behavior. Their motivation might very well have been their eagerness for the child to do well on the tasks, since these were also the mothers who, on the average, pressured their children more for improvement of responses than the mothers of the high nonverbal children. While thus attempting to help their children, these mothers of high verbal children revealed themselves to be rather controlling and pressuring while the mothers of the high nonverbal group left their children more on their own and interfered less with their responses.

Comparison of Results of Interview and Interaction Situation

Comparing the results of the interview with those of the interaction situation, it appeared that the interview variables that distinguished significantly between groups did so mainly for boys, while the observation situation variables did so mainly for girls.

Several possible explanations for this discrepancy have to be considered. One is the difference in means and variability for the whole group of girls as compared to the whole group of boys. Comparing all the help-giving activities in the interaction situation, one finds that the means on these variables were consistently, though not significantly, higher for the girls than for the boys. The lower means for boys, in addition to smaller range and less variability of the help-giving variables, could partly explain the fact that the situation measures failed to distinguish between the boys' discrepant abilities groups. (An observation of a father and son interaction might have been more revealing of differences between boys' groups.) However, this explanation does not hold for the interview. The interview variables which differentiated the ability groups for boys and not for girls did not show consistent differences in means and variability.

Another possible explanation for the difference between results from interview variables and situation variables may be found in the time factor. Most interview variables refer to the child's early history, while the situation variables refer essentially to present behavior. Could one assume that it is at an early age that child training practices influence boys' cognitive development but that girls' cognitive development is differentially enhanced by parents' attitudes and behavior at a later time during childhood? This would contradict what we know about the relative stability of specific abilities (21). Yet, one cannot exclude the possibility that the significant antecedents during infancy for the development of verbal ability may not be identical for boys and girls. Kagan, also, has suggested that different agents may be responsible for the degree of development of different cognitive styles in boys and in girls (10). It may be that early verbal stimulation is more decisive for the development of verbal ability in boys. In this connection, it is interesting to note that Levy (14), who found maternal overprotection associated with high verbal ability, had almost exclusively boys in his sample.

There is one further reason that might be considered for the differential significance of the interview and situation data for boys and for girls. The validity of the interview as a measurement may be greater for boys than for girls. If it can be assumed that mothers feel more responsible about the development of their daughters than their sons (partly because of a culturally accepted feeling, "like father, like son"), then one might expect more defensiveness on the part of the mothers of the LoV girls than of LoV sons. While mothers were quite aware of their children's verbal ability, since it is reflected in reading ability and vocabulary, they were less aware of their children's spatial ability. There was therefore no reason for the mothers of the HiV-LoSpace girls defensively to enhance the role of nonverbal stimulation provided for their daughters. Yet, being often aware of their daughters' low verbal ability, some of the LoV girls' mothers may have tended to exaggerate the verbal stimulation they gave to them.

At the present time, there is not enough evidence to explain definitely the lack of more complete consistency between the results from the interview and the interaction situation.

Implication of Results

Considering all the results which indicate that the HiV groups have received more and earlier help, physical or verbal, on nonverbal tasks as well as verbal tasks, a possible question arises about interpreting the mother's behavior as an antecedent to the child's cognitive functioning. One might argue that mothers of the HiV group whose children are low in space or number have developed a pattern of helping their children more on performance tasks because their children showed more difficulties with such problems. However, one of our nonverbal tasks, the Healy Picture Completion, did not involve spatial ability. Furthermore, if the child's ability had consistently determined the mother's degree of help-giving behavior, the mothers of high verbal children would have presented verbal tasks to them without any admonishment, realizing that their children have little difficulty with verbal tasks. Nevertheless, mothers of HiV girls scored significantly higher on "focusing" their children's attention on these verbal tasks than mothers of LoV girls.

We therefore felt entitled to interpret the mother's behavior in the interaction situation as a sample of the kind of behavior which in the past was antecedent to the child's cognitive development.

The data do not support the contention that a child develops a particular ability because his parents are selectively training him in it. Rather, the high level of interaction between mother and child must produce some intervening conditions which enhance verbal more than number or spatial performance.

The essential condition for the development of verbality is probably the close relationship with an adult, and verbal ability is fostered by a high degree of interaction between mother and child. In contrast, the development of number ability requires, above all, concentration and ability to carry through a task by oneself. Similarly, spatial ability is probably developed through interaction with the physical rather than the interpersonal environment. A marked pattern of help seeking and help giving interferes with the development of an independent and self-reliant attitude, which may be the intervening condition for a high degree of development of spatial and numerical ability.

It seems therefore likely that the mother of a child in the HiV-Low nonverbal group is much more emotionally involved with her child, having given more attention and stimulation to the baby, but tending to pressure, restrict, and control the child more later than the low verbal, high nonverbal mother.

SUMMARY

It was the purpose of this study to examine the differences in mothers' childrearing practices and in their behavior with their children in relation to differences in children's cognitive development.

The subjects were 60 mothers of fifth grade children of either high or low verbal ability with similar total IQ, the compensating nonverbal ability being spatial or numerical ability.

A comparison of the high with the low verbal groups on an interview, questionnaire, and a mother-child interaction situation showed the following significant differences:

In accordance with predictions, high verbal group mothers (whose children were low in either spatial or number ability) gave their children more verbal stimulation during infancy and early childhood, remembered a greater number of their children's early accomplishments, let their children participate more in mean conversations, punished them less for poor speech, bought more story books for them, and criticized them more for poor academic achievement, used anxiety arousal more in cautiousness training, showed less permissiveness with object experimentation, had more restrictions, and perceived their husbands as stricter than themselves. Contrary to predictions, not the mother's but the father's reading time was very significantly higher for the high verbal girls' group.

With respect to the interaction session, as predicted, high verbal group mothers were found to be higher than low verbal mothers in all categories of helping behavior, in pressure for improvement, in giving help after request by child, in asking the observer more questions, in giving more physical help, and in giving such help sooner. Contrary to the prediction, high verbal mothers were also higher on withholding help and disapproval than the low verbal mothers.

The findings led to the general conclusion that discrepant verbal ability is fostered by a close relationship with a demanding and somewhat intrusive mother, while discrepant nonverbal abilities are enhanced by allowing the child a considerable degree of freedom to experiment on his own.

REFERENCES

1. Baldwin, A. L., *Behavior and development in childhood,* New York: Dryden, 1955.
2. Baldwin, A. L., Kalhorn, J., & Breese, F. H. Patterns of parent behavior, *Psychol. Monogr.,* 1945, **58,** No. 3 (Whole No. 268).
3. Bandura, A., & Walters, R. H. *Adolescent aggression,* New York: Ronald, 1959.
4. Bieri, J. Parental identification, acceptance of authority, and within sex differences in cognitive behavior. *J. abnorm. soc. Psychol.,* 1960, **60,** 76–79.
5. Bieri, J., Bradburn, W. M., & Galinsky, M. D. Sex differences in perceptual behavior. *J. Pers.,* 1958, **26,** 1–12.
6. Emmet, W. C. Evidence of a space factor at eleven and earlier. *Brit. J. Psychol.,* 1949, **2,** 3–16.
7. Gardner, R. W., Holzman, P. S., Klein, G. S., Lintːn, H. B., & Spence, D. P. Cognitive control: a study of individual consistencies in cognitive behavior. *Psychol. Issues,* 1959, **1,** No. 4.
8. Herzberg, F., & Lepkin, M. A study of sex differences on the primary mental abilities test. *Educ. psychol. Measmt,* 1954, **14,** 687–689.
9. Hobson, J. R. Sex differences in primary mental abilities. *J. educ. Res.,* 1947, **41,** 126–132.
10. Kagan, J., & Moss, H. A. The psychological significance of styles of conceptualization. Draft of paper presented at a conference on basic cognitive process in children

sponsored by the Social Science Research Council, Minneapolis, Minnesota, April 21–23, 1961.

11. Kent, M., & Davis, D. R. Discipline in the home and intellectual development. *Brit. J. med. Psychol.*, 1957, **30**, 27–34.

12. Kuckenberg, L. Effects of early father absence on subsequent development of boys. Unpublished doctoral dissertation, Harvard Univer., 1962.

13. Levinson, B. M. Cultural pressure and WAIS scatter in a traditional Jewish setting. *J. genet. Psychol.*, 1958, **93**, 277–286.

14. Levy, D. M. *Maternal overprotection.* Columbia Univer. Press, 1943.

15. McCarthy, D. Language development in children. In L. Carmichael (Ed.), *Manual of child psychology.* (2nd Ed.) New York: Wiley, 1954. Pp. 492–630.

16. Maccoby, E. E., & Rau, L. Differential cognitive abilities. Contract No. 1040, USOE manuscript in preparation, 1962.

17. Milner, E. A study of the relationships between reading readiness on grade one school children and patterns of parent-child interactions. *Child Develpm.*, 1951, **22**, 95–112.

18. Moss, H. A., & Kagan, J. Maternal influences on early IQ scores. *Psychol. Rep.*, 1958, **4**, 655–661.

19. Pettigrew, Y. F. The measurement and correlates of category width as a cognitive variable. *J. Pers.*, 1958, **26**, 532–544.

20. Sears, R. R., Maccoby, E. E., & Levin, H., *Patterns of child rearing,* Evanston, Ill.: Row, Peterson, 1957.

21. Sontag, L. W., Baker, C. T., & Nelson, V. L. Mental growth and personality development: a longitudinal study. *Monogr. Soc. Res. Child Develpm.*, 1958, **23**, No. 2 (Serial No. 68).

22. Wallach, M. A., & Caron, A. J. Attribute criteriality and sex-linked conservatism as determinants of psychological similarity. *J. abnorm. soc. Psychol.*, 1959, **59**, 43–59.

23. Winterbottom, M. R. The relation of childhood training in independence to achievement motivation. Unpublished doctoral dissertation, Univer. of Michigan, 1953.

24. Witkin, H. A. The perception of the upright. *Sci. Amer.*, 1959, **200**, 50–56.

20. CHILDREARING PRACTICES AND MORAL

DEVELOPMENT: GENERALIZATIONS FROM

EMPIRICAL RESEARCH

Martin L. Hoffman

In complex areas such as that of morality and its antecedents no single research can supply the answers to all important questions. Each study can do no more than shed light on a small facet of the problem, especially in the early stages of research when measuring instruments and experimental procedures are cumbersome and inefficient. Progress therefore requires many research efforts, along with systematic attempts to assess methods and integrate results. This paper is such an attempt. Its purpose is to pull together the research findings on parental practices and the child's moral development so as to point up tentative generalizations, gaps, and inconsistencies which can be used as guides in further research. The studies examined are those which were designed primarily to investigate parental antecedents of moral variables and which meet current methodological standards. The focus is substantive although methodological points are made where necessary in interpreting contradictory findings and suggesting directions for further research.

THEORETICAL FOUNDATIONS OF THE RESEARCH

Most of our theoretical knowledge about moral development derives from the works of Piaget and Freud. Piaget and his followers have focused on the cognitive aspects of the child's moral orientation, and their empirical investigations have centered on the child's concepts of justice, his attitudes toward rules, and toward violations of moral norms (e.g., 17, 19, 28). In these studies the child's moral perspective has been probed with great depth, and a number of valuable concepts bearing on the cognitive aspects of morality have been contributed to the field, e.g., moral realism, immanent justice, and the role of cognitive processes in moral growth. Although considerable importance is assigned to decreased adult constraint and increased interaction with peers, the main interest of these investigators is to establish

Reprinted with abridgement from *Child Development*, 1963, **34**, 295–318, with permission of the author and the Society for Research in Child Development.

developmental sequences which are more or less universal, fixed, and intrinsic to the organism, rather than to study individual differences and the antecedent role of the parent. The one exception, a study of the effects of parental restriction on the child's moral judgment (23), produced inconclusive results.

Psychoanalytic theory, on the other hand, is concerned primarily with the emotional and motivational aspects of personality structure. And although this theory too was initially intended as a universal explanation of the processes underlying the formation of conscience rather than a source of hypotheses about individual differences, it has provided the main inspiration and the over-all direction for most of the research on the role of parental practices in shaping and determining moral character.

Although Freud did not organize the theory into a coherent whole, its concepts are unveiled in scattered references throughout the literature and it may be reconstructed briefly as follows: The young child is inevitably subjected to many frustrations, some of which are due to parental control and some of which have nothing directly to do with the parent, e.g., illness and other physical discomforts. All of these frustrations contribute to the development of hostility toward the parent. The child's anxiety over counter aggression by the parent or over the anticipated loss of the parent's love leads him to repress his hostility, incorporate the parent's prohibitions, and generally model his behavior after that of the parent. Among the important parental characteristics adopted by the child is the capacity to punish himself when he violates a prohibition or is tempted to do so—turning inward, in the course of doing this, the hostility which was originally directed toward the parent. This self-punishment is experienced as guilt feelings which are dreaded because of their intensity and their resemblance to the earlier fears of punishment or abandonment by the parent. The child, therefore, tries to avoid guilt by acting always in accordance with the incorporated parental prohibitions and erecting various mechanisms of defense against the conscious awareness of impulses to act contrary to the prohibitions.

This theory is thus far unchallenged as a comprehensive account of the role of family dynamics in the moral development of the child. Although many researchers in the field disagree with some of its details, most have accepted its basic premise: that sometime in early childhood the individual begins to model his behavior after that of the parent and through this process of identification codes of conduct such as moral standards and values, which are originally externally enforced, become part of the child's own set of standards.

Because of the complexity of the theory no investigator has attempted to test it in its entirety. Instead, each study has focused on one or another of its concepts—such as identification or guilt—often modifying it somewhat in line with other theoretical approaches, e.g., reinforcement learning theory.

IDENTIFICATION

The psychoanalytic concept that has received the most attention from theorists and researchers is identification. Two general types of identification are discussed in the literature. In one—referred to as identification with the aggressor or defensive identification—the child, treated punitively by the parent but fearful of further punishment if he fights back, avoids the conflict and gains further parental approval by taking on the characteristics and point of view of the parent. Although Freud considered this type of identification to be central to the development of a conscience, especially in the male, it is now often thought of as a more or less temporary mechanism or one which leads to an aggressive, hostile outlook toward the world rather than a process which underlies the development of an inner conscience (11). The other type, referred to as developmental or anaclitic identification (7), is based on the child's anxiety over the loss of the parent's love. To get rid of this anxiety and assure himself of the parent's continued love, the child strives to become like the parent—to incorporate everything about him including his moral standards and values. This type of identification, seen by Freud as especially characteristic of females, is assumed by most present-day writers to underlie the development of an inner conscience.

Numerous attempts have been made in recent years to clarify these concepts and to place them within broader theoretical frameworks. In each case the concepts are modified somewhat in line with the author's theoretical preference, resulting in a variety of subtly different notions that have guided the empirical research on identification. With each investigator stressing one or another aspect, e.g., motivation to emulate the parent, actual similarity between parent and child, or similarity as perceived by the child, the measures used have been many and varied and there has been little overlap between those used in the different studies.

In a study of 5-year-old boys (30) the manipulation of the father doll in a structured doll play situation was used as an index of father identification and was found to relate positively to the father's warmth and affection toward the boy, as reported by the mother. Further evidence that paternal warmth contributes to the boy's identification with the father comes from a study of high school juniors and seniors (27) in which an "actual similarity" measure of identification was used—the extent to which the boys responded to personality and attitude tests the same way their fathers did. Here a positive relationship was obtained between identification and the perception of the father as warm, helpful, and kind—as revealed by the boy's completion of a number of stories dealing with family interaction, e.g., one in which an adolescent boy wants to use the family car. The results of these two studies are generally taken as support for the anaclitic view of identification. Although they demonstrate that identification relates to *receiving* parental love—rather than being *threatened with its loss,* as the anaclitic view would predict—it seems reasonable to assume that discipline by a loving father is more apt to elicit anxiety over love-withdrawal than discipline by a nonloving one.

Seemingly contradictory findings were obtained in another study, using high school senior boys as subjects (10). This study was guided by the Freudian notion that the boy, motivated by fears and anxieties related to hostility toward his father, shifts his identification from the mother to the father during the Oedipal phase of development. Identification with the father was measured in terms of the similarity between the boy's responses on a vocational interest blank and the responses he thought his father would make. In accordance with the theory, identification was found to relate positively to intensity of castration anxiety, as measured by the Blacky Test—a projective device using dogs to represent family figures. On the assumption that castration anxiety in boys signifies the fear of a physically punitive father, this finding is viewed as providing some empirical support for the notion of identification with an aggressive parent rather than with a loving one.

Thus, although the aggressive and anaclitic conceptions of identification dynamics are quite different, each has some empirical support. It is difficult to assess which receives the greater support, since the identification measures used in these studies differ widely and we do not know which are more valid. While these measures leave much to be desired (6), they all have a certain amount of face validity since they tap aspects of behavior which are manifestly close to the concept of parent identification. Thus, two deal directly with the similarity—real or perceived—between the child and his own parent. The third is less direct and makes the assumption that taking the father role projectively reflects identification with the father, and not merely with adult males in general or with an abstract conception of the paternal role. But the subjects in this study seem young enough to justify this assumption.

The other studies of the antecedents of identification generally support the view that love rather than punitiveness is the significant parent variable, but the evidence provided is limited since the identification measures used are highly indirect and therefore of questionable validity. These measures deal with personality characteristics such as sex-role typing (8, 20, 24, 25) and conscience (31) which are sometimes presumed on theoretical grounds to be consequents of parent identification and therefore adequate as measures of identification. However, they may also result from other developmental processes including identification with persons other than the same-sexed parent.

A possible explanation for the support given both the aggressive and anaclitic conceptions is that the significant antecedent of father identification is the father's *salience* in the child's experience, which can be heightened by *either* affection or punitiveness. Another possible explanation, suggested by the predominantly lower class sample in the study finding father identification related to punitiveness (10) is that identification may have different bases in different segments of the population. Identification with the aggressor may more often be the underlying process in the lower class setting with its more traditional orientation toward obedience and more frequent use of physical discipline (1, 4, 5, 15, 18). In the more psychologically oriented middle class, on the other hand, the parental pattern may be more conducive to anaclitic identification.

Knowing the antecedents of identification, however, would still leave us a long way from our goal of understanding the dynamics of conscience formation. For one thing, there is no empirical support for the implicit assumption made by some researchers that identification is total, i.e., that the child strives to emulate the parent in all respects. It is therefore theoretically possible for a highly motivated child to adopt certain valued parental characteristics like mechanical skills, social prestige, sense of humor, and power, but not others, values and moral standards included. Even assuming identification in the moral realm, the child's moral structure would still be unknown unless the particular parental standards internalized could be ascertained. Another reason for not inferring conscience from parent identification is that parents' consciences vary in strength and in content. The child who identifies with his parent is not necessarily more moral than one who identifies with a teacher, minister, or older sibling. The general problem of the relation between the process of identification and what aspect of the parent model is internalized is highlighted by the finding, reported by McCord and McCord (21), that boys whose fathers are criminals are less apt to become criminals if accepted by their fathers than if rejected by them. Apparently paternal acceptance may operate *against* identification when the parent model is opposed to the norms of the larger society.

Perhaps the precise role of parent identification in moral development would be clarified by developing measures of the child's identification with the parent's moral standards and using these in conjunction with independenet indices of what the parent's moral standards actually are. These measures might then be studied in relation to the child's identification in other areas than the moral and in relation to parental practices.

REACTIONS TO TRANSGRESSION

A more profitable approach to the role of the parent in the child's moral growth is to drop, tentatively, the assumption that identification is the intervening process and study the various manifestations of conscience more directly. The focus of our research efforts would then become the parent's role in developing a child whose motives are generally to behave in a morally acceptable way; who, when under pressure from external forces or inner desires to violate a moral standard, can generally exercise the controls necessary to resist these pressures; who, when he does submit to temptation or accidentally violates a standard, can generally be expected to recognize the wrong, be aware of his own responsibility, experience an appropriate amount of guilt or remorse, and attempt to make reparations where possible. Further, to react in all these ways not due to fear of external consequences but due to an inner moral sense.

Allinsmith distinguished between two broad types of discipline: corporal discipline, which includes spanking, whipping, slapping, and beating the child, and psychological discipline, which includes manipulation of the child by shaming, appeals to pride and guilt, and expressions of disappointment. His hypothesis that psychological discipline would contribute to guilt severity, especially around aggression, was derived from the theory that in disciplining the child psychologically the parent provides a model of self-restraint about aggression and about the manner in which to express disapproval, thus contributing to the child's tendency to inhibit and feel guilty about his own hostile tendencies. Further, in psychological discipline the punishment is not likely to be gotten over and done with, and the parent's anger is apt to smolder unexpressed and thus convey strong disapproval, thereby increasing the child's anxiety about displeasing the parent. The parent who favors corporal punishment, on the other hand, was viewed as providing a model of aggression and as condoning it implicitly, if not explicitly, and also as providing the child with a suitable target for the direct expression of aggression. Allinsmith found no relationship between the two discipline categories and the child's guilt, but in a later study (3), using a more homogeneous middle class college sample, he found that male students who recalled both parents (especially their mothers) as having used mainly psychological discipline, obtained higher guilt-over-aggression scores on a story completion measure than those whose parents used corporal punishment. The female subjects only showed a slight tendency in the same direction, but, as the authors point out, this may be due to the fact that the story-beginning used was designed for boys and had a masculine theme. Heinicke found a similar pattern with his 5-year-olds. The frequent use of praise and the infrequent use of physical punishment and isolation related to high guilt. Heinicke also found that the parent's expression of affection toward the child is positively related to the child's guilt.

Further evidence for the relation between psychological discipline and guilt severity comes from the Whiting and Child cross-cultural study (33). They found a positive relation between their cultural index of guilt and the prevalence in a culture of "love-oriented" techniques of discipline. These techniques overlap considerably with those fitting Allinsmith's "psychological" category. However, whereas Allinsmith views these techniques as providing a model of restraint, Whiting and Child's theory is that they contribute to guilt by keeping the child oriented toward the goal of affection and at the same time arousing uncertainty as to the attainment of this goal. Examples are rewarding by praise, punishing by isolation, and punishing by the withdrawal of love.

Sears, Maccoby, and Levin (31) found similar results with kindergarten children, using as a measure of conscience another aspect of the child's behavior following a transgression: whether he characteristically confesses, hides, or lies—as reported by the parent. This index related positively to the mother's reported use of love-oriented techniques and negatively to the use of object-oriented techniques (tangible rewards and incentives, physical punishment, deprivation of privileges as punishment). But the love-oriented discipline pattern was found to relate to the child's conscience only in conjunction with the frequent expression of love and affection. That is, mothers who were both warm and used love-oriented techniques produced children who tended to confess to their deviations rather than hide or deny them. The author's explanation for this finding is that the effectiveness of love withdrawal depends somewhat upon the amount of love that is being taken away. That is, the child who generally experiences a warmly affectionate relationship with his parents is more affected by the threat that this relationship will be broken than the child who has never enjoyed such parental warmth. In response to the pressure to devise habitual means of insuring the continuation of the parent's love, the child adopts as his own the parent's restrictions and ideals.

Aronfreed (4) investigated still another aspect of the child's post-transgression behavior: whether it is motivated by internal or external forces. He studied sixth grade children, using a projective story completion technique. In each story-beginning the central figure commits an act of aggression, the stories varying with respect to the person toward whom the aggression is directed and in the type of aggression expressed. The story completions were coded according to whether the central figure, without any reliance on outside forces or events, accepts responsibility for his action and actively seeks to correct the situation, for example, by making reparation or modifying his future behavior in the direction of social acceptability; or whether the events following the transgression are dominated by external concerns, mainly in the form of accidents or other unpleasant fortuitous happenings. Data on parent discipline were obtained by interviewing the mothers about how they handled aggression in the child. The discipline techniques reported were classified as "induction" techniques or "sensitization" techniques. The "induction" category is similar to Allinsmith's "psychological" one, but in his theory about the effects of this type of discipline Aronfreed focuses not so much on its relevance for the kind of behavior model presented the child, as Allinsmith does, but more directly on its capacity to arouse unpleasant feeling reactions in the child about his misbehavior, reactions which are seen as being independent of external threat. Certain induction techniques (asking the child why he behaved as he did, insisting that he correct the damage he has done, or refraining from punishment when he takes the moral initiative) are also seen as encouraging the child to accept responsibility for his actions. And others, especially the use of explanations or reasoning, are viewed as "utilizing a verbal and cognitive medium of exchange that can provide the child with his own resources for evaluating his behavior" (4, p. 226). The "sensitization" category resembles Allinsmith's "corporal" techniques but also includes attempts to control the child through direct verbal assault (yelling, shouting, bawling-out, etc.). These techniques are viewed as attempting only to extinguish or control the child's unacceptable behavior and as tending "not to be translated into a set of independent moral functions because they emphasize only the painful external consequences of the child's transgression and the importance of external threats or demands in carrying out moral actions" (4, p. 226). Aronfreed found, as he hypothesized, that the use of induction techniques is positively related to a high degree of internally motivated self-corrective action in the child stories and with the absence of punishment from external forces. Mothers who used more sensitization techniques, on the other hand, had children whose stories contained more external punishment.

Hoffman and Saltzstein (16) obtained similar results with seventh grade children. The children were asked to make moral judgments about norm violations (e.g., stealing, lying, violating a trust) committed under different conditions and to give the reasons for their judgments. Their responses were classified as expressing an internalized standard or merely the fear of detection and punishment by external authorities. The data on parental practices were obtained from the children's responses to highly structured objective items bearing on the parent's current disciplinary pattern in several types of situations, expressions of affection toward the child, and participation in child-centered activities. The results were that the more internalized boys as compared to those who were more externally oriented reported that both parents were more permissive in their discipline; that their mothers less often used techniques which openly asserted their power over the child (this category included the use of force, threat of force or deprivation, and direct commands, and therefore resembles Allinsmith's "corporal" and Aronfreed's "sensitization" categories); that their mothers more often used techniques indicating the painful consequences of the child's act for the parents; and that their mothers were more affectionate. The only significant findings for girls were that the internalized girls less often reported their mothers as threatening to have their father discipline them and more often reported their fathers as using rational appeals in their discipline. The internalized subjects of both sexes also gave more consistently severe guilt responses than the externals on a story completion measure. Thus, although the above findings are more directly relevant to the child's conscious moral orientation, they also have a bearing on his reactions to transgression.

Despite the diversity of theoretical approaches, measuring instruments, and moral content areas involved in the studies discussed in this section, their results have a common core of agreement that is encouraging. The relatively frequent use of discipline which attempts to change the child's behavior by inducing internal forces toward compliance appears to foster the development of an internalized moral orientation, especially as reflected in the child's reactions to his own transgressions. The use of coercive measures that openly confront the child with the parent's power, on the other hand, apparently contributes to a moral orientation based on the fear of authority.

Further, the studies in this group that include data on parental affection (13, 16, 31) suggest that this variable, too, contributes to internalization. Putting all of this together, we may tentatively conclude that an internalized moral orientation is fostered by an affectionate relationship between the parent and child, in combination with the use of discipline techniques which utilize this relationship by appealing to the child's personal and social motives.

RESISTANCE TO PRESSURES TO DEVIATE

Perhaps a more important index of conscience than the child's reaction to transgressing is the degree to which he behaves in accordance with his standards and avoids transgressing in the first place. The ability to resist pressures to deviate from one's standards may be a better test of their strength and integration with the personality than the experiencing of guilt after having transgressed. Pressures to deviate may be external (e.g., peer-group pressures) or internal (e.g., desires for objects which are themselves forbidden or which require prohibited action for their attainment). Some research has been done on parental antecedents of the child's response to external pressures (14, 26), but not where the pressures were opposed to the child's values and standards. The latter is an important aspect of the larger social problem of how the individual learns to resolve conflicts between inner- and other-directed pressures (29). There is need for empirical research on this problem, for example, on the antecedents of the moral strength or courage necessary to resist social pressures to deviate from one's internalized standards, and, more generally, on the antecedents of how one copes with conflict between moral norms internalized in the home and opposing pressure from peers.

Although external pressures against moral standards have been neglected in research, considerable work has been done on resistance to inner temptation. In the Allinsmith study already cited, two additional story-beginnings were included, one dealing with theft and the other with disobedience, in which the hero has not yet transgressed but is tempted to do so. The subject's resistance-to-temptation score was determined by whether or not in his story-completions the hero transgressed. One of the several parental background variables investigated, the use of explained requests rather than arbitrary demands, was found to be positively associated with the resistance-to-temptation scores obtained for both stories. In an earlier study MacKinnon (22) used a more direct behavioral index of resistance to temptation. His subjects, all college students, took a written test under conditions of no tangible reward. Cheaters were detected without their knowledge by observations through a one-way screen. Data on early parental practices were obtained from questionnaires filled out by the student. The findings showed a positive relation between physical punishment and cheating and between psychological punishment—defined as techniques which indicate that the child had fallen short of some ideal in some way or hurt the parents and therefore that they love or approve of him less—and not cheating. Although these results are broadly consistent with Allinsmith's findings, the latter's own measures of psychological and corporal discipline did not relate to resistance to temptation.

Further confusion as to the antecedents of resistance to temptation is apparent when we examine the results of the three most recent studies in this area. Two used preschool age children (9, 32) and the other, 11- to 12-year-olds (12). All three used the child's behavior in an experimental test situation as the index of his ability to resist temptation. The test consisted of placing the child in a situation in which he was tempted to violate the rules of the game in order to win a prize and then leaving him to play alone. Although the child thought no one was watching him, his reactions were observed through a one-way-screen, as in the MacKinnon study; and he was assigned scores indicating whether or not and to what degree he cheated or resisted the temptation to do so. All three studies used parent interviews consisting of a large number of structured and unstructured items, and there is considerable overlap in the items used. Despite the similarities in conceptual approach, the way in which resistance to temptation was measured, and the parent interview items used, the findings in the three studies have little in common. Each investigator found several parent variables to relate to the child's ability to resist temptation, but there was little agreement among them as to which of the many parent variables used were the ones which related significantly to the child measure. Further, in those few cases in which the parent variables relating significantly to the child's resistance to temptation were similar, the direction of the relations were as likely to be discrepant as not. Here are two examples: Burton *et al.* and Grinder each found the severity with which the child was weaned to relate positively to resistance to temptation, but Sears *et al.* found the same variable to relate negatively; and, whereas the general pattern of the Grinder and the Sears *et al.* findings was for resistance to temptation to relate to verbal rather than physical means of control, the Burton *et al.* findings tended to be in the opposite direction. Finally, none of these three studies replicated Mac-

Kinnon's findings of a positive relation between psychological discipline and not cheating, although all three had obtained psychological and physical discipline scores roughly comparable to those used by MacKinnon.

GENERALIZATIONS ABOUT PARENTAL ANTECEDENTS

Though definite conclusions can not be drawn from the work on parental antecedents of moral development done thus far, several tentative generalizations can be made which may help serve as a guide for future research in this area. The first is that the research generally supports the view that the frequent expression of warmth and affection toward the child helps promote identification with the parent, although there is some evidence that a threatening and punitive approach might in some cases also contribute to identification. Second, the use of discipline techniques which attempt to change the child's behavior by inducing internal forces toward compliance (e.g., by appealing to the child's needs for affection and self-esteem and his concern for others), especially in the context of an affectionate parent-child relationship, appears to foster the development of an internalized moral orientation at least with respect to one's reactions following the violation of a moral standard. The use of techniques that involve physical coercion or that directly assert the parent's power over the child, on the other hand, are more conducive to the development of a moral orientation based on fear of external detection and punishment. The third and most tentative generalization is that the particular kind of psychological techniques used, i.e., the particular aspect of the child's need system to which appeal is generally made, may affect the type of internalized morality that develops, e.g., whether it is oriented predominantly toward human need or conventional authority, and the degree to which it is integrated with the rest of the personality. Summarizing and stating these generalizations most broadly, we would offer the following tentative synthesis of the research findings to date: affection contributes to identification; psychological discipline which capitalizes on the affectionate relationship (and its resulting identification) fosters the development of internalized moral structures in general; and variations in type of psychological discipline may then account for the particular kind of internalized moral structure that develops.

The Role of the Father

In the studies reporting data on the discipline used by both parents, father discipline emerges as relatively unimportant in young children but as taking on increased significance with older ones. Perhaps it is only after the child has attained a relatively advanced level of cognitive maturity that the father's discipline can have important effects despite his absence most of the day from the child's immediate life space.

The influence of the father is most pronounced in the two studies using college students as subjects: in one (3), discipline by the father as well as the mother related to guilt, and, in the other (22), discipline by the father and not the mother related to resistance to temptation. In addition to highlighting the increased importance of the father with age, these findings, together with those obtained in the studies of younger children, also seem to suggest that mothers and fathers may be particularly influential with respect to different aspects of moral development. That whereas the mother may be the main socializing agent with respect to guilt, the father may play the more important role in the development of resistance to pressures to deviate from moral standards. At least this may be true for boys—perhaps, because of the importance that self-control, a masculine ideal in our culture, has for this aspect of morality. Thus, early discipline by the mother may contribute more to guilt and later discipline by the father, to the controls necessary for resisting pressures to transgress.

REFERENCES

1. Allinsmith, B. B. Expressive styles: II. Directness with which anger is expressed. In D. R. Miller and G. E. Swanson (Eds.), *Inner conflict and defense.* New York: Holt, 1960. Pp. 315–336.

2. Allinsmith, W. Moral standards: II. The learning of moral standards. In D. R. Miller and G. E. Swanson (Eds.), *Inner conflict and defense.* New York: Holt, 1960. Pp. 141–176.

3. Allinsmith, W., & Greening, T. C. Guilt over anger as predicted from parental discipline: a study of superego development. *Amer. Psychologist,* 1955, **10,** 320. (abstract)

4. Aronfreed, J. The nature, variety, and social patterning of moral responses to transgression. *J. abnorm. soc. Psychol.,* 1961, **63,** 223–241.

5. Bronfenbrenner, U. Socialization and social class through time and space. In E. E. Maccoby, T. M. Newcomb, and E. L. Hartley (Eds.), *Readings in social psychology.* New York: Holt, 1958. Pp. 400–425.

6. Bronfenbrenner, U. The study of identification through interpersonal perception. In R. Tagiuri and L. Petrullo (Eds.), *Person perception and interpersonal behavior.* Stanford, Cal.: Stanford Univer. Press, 1958. Pp. 110–130.

7. Bronfenbrenner, U. Freudian theories of identification and their derivatives. *Child Develpm.,* 1960, **31,** 15–40.

8. Bronson, W. C. Dimensions of ego and infantile identification. *J. Pers.,* 1959, **27,** 532–545.

9. Burton, R. V., Maccoby, E. E., & Allinsmith, W. Antecedents of resistance to temptation in four-year-old children. *Child Develpm.,* 1961, **32,** 689–710.

10. Cava, E. L., & Raush, H. Identification and the adolescent boy's perception of his father. *J. abnorm. soc. Psychol.,* 1952, **47,** 855–856.

11. Freud, A. *The ego and the mechanisms of defense,* New York: International Universities Press, 1946.

12. Grinder, R. E. Behavior in a temptation situation and its relation to certain aspects of socialization. Unpublished doctoral dissertation, Harvard Univer., 1960.

13. Heinicke, C. M. Some antecedents and correlates of guilt and fear in young boys. Unpublished doctoral dissertation, Harvard Univer., 1953.

14. Hoffman, M. L. Some psychodynamic factors in compulsive conformity. *J. abnorm. soc. Psychol.,* 1953, **48,** 383–393.

15. Hoffman, M. L. Power assertion by the parent and its impact on the child. *Child Develpm.*, 1960, **31**, 129–143.

16. Hoffman, M. L., & Saltzstein, H. D. Parent practices and the child's moral orientation. Paper read at Amer. Psychol. Ass., Chicago, Sept., 1960.

17. Kohlberg, L. The development of modes of moral thinking and choice in the years 10 to 16. Unpublished doctoral dissertation, Univer. of Chicago, 1958.

18. Kohn, M. L. Social class and the exercise of parental authority. *Amer. sociol. Rev.*, 1959, **24**, 352–366.

19. Lerner, E. *Constraint areas and the moral judgment of children.* Menosha, Wisconsin: Banta, 1937.

20. Levin, H., & Sears, R. R. Identification with parents as a determinant of doll play aggression. *Child Develpm.*, 1956, **27**, 135–153.

21. McCord, J., & McCord, W. The effect of parental role model on criminality. *J. soc. Issues*, 1958, **14**, 66–75.

22. MacKinnon, D. W. Violation of prohibitions. In H. W. Murray, *Exploration in personality.* New York: Oxford Univer. Press, 1938. Pp. 491–501.

23. MacRae, D., Jr. A test of Piaget's theories of moral development. *J. abnorm. soc. Psychol.*, 1954, **49**, 14–18.

24. Mussen, P., & Distler, L. Masculinity, identification, and father-son relationships. *J. abnorm. soc. Psychol.*, 1959, **59**, 350–356.

25. Mussen, P., & Distler, L. Child rearing antecedents of masculine identification in kindergarten boys. *Child Develpm.*, 1960, **31**, 89–100.

26. Mussen, P., & Kagan, J. Group conformity and perception of parents. *Child Develpm.*, 1958, **29**, 57–60.

27. Payne, D. E., & Mussen, P. H. Parent-child relations and father identification among adolescent boys. *J. abnorm. soc. Psychol.*, 1956, **52**, 358–362.

28. Piaget, J. *The moral judgment of the child.* New York: Free Press, 1948.

29. Riesman, D., Denney, R., & Glaser, M. *The lonely crowd.* New York: Doubleday Anchor, 1953.

30. Sears, P. S. Child rearing factors related to the playing of sex-typed roles. *Amer. Psychologist*, 1953, **8**, 431. (Abstract)

31. Sears, R. R., Maccoby, E. E., & Levin, H. *Patterns of child rearing.* Evanston, Ill.: Row, Peterson, 1957.

32. Sears, R. R., Rau, L., & Alpert, R. Identification and child training: the development of conscience. Paper read at Amer. Psychol. Ass., Chicago, Sept., 1960.

33. Whiting, J. W. M., & Child, I. L. *Child training and personality.* New Haven: Yale Univer. Press, 1953.

21. RELATION OF PRESCHOOL DEPENDENCY

BEHAVIOR TO FAMILY SIZE AND DENSITY

Mary F. Waldrop and Richard Q. Bell

Up to the present little attention has been paid to the effects of density and size of family on dependency behavior in children. Density is defined here as variation in intervals between siblings, short intervals denoting high density. Aspects of family structure such as ordinal position and sex of siblings have been related to child behavior in several studies (2, 10, 16, 17, 21). None of these studies have taken into consideration the specific relevance to child behavior of the gross structure of the family as reflected in number and spacing of children. This area seems important since family density itself may affect a mother's contact behavior with a child or her ability to prevent the occurrence of anxiety producing situations, regardless of her method of childrearing. For example, a mother may have a high potential for rewarding the dependency behavior of a child or for anticipating and avoiding situations overwhelming to the child, but be unable to manifest this with a particular child because of the demands placed on her by the competing needs of other children.

The intensity and retention of the rhesus infant's orientation toward and attachment to the mother or mother surrogate has been demonstrated by Harlow (6). Extrapolating to humans, we can hypothesize a need in children for contact with a mother; if this need is subjected to deprivation we would expect an increase in the child's efforts to obtain physical contact from adult supportive figures.

Recent studies have described how the lack of social availability of an adult figure enhances dependency behavior in children; therefore it would follow that the lack of social availability of a mother because of a large high-density family should result in an enhancement of dependency behavior. Rheingold (14) has shown that home infants received care 4.5 times as often as did infants in an institution. Low frequency in caretaking contacts was associated with greater response in institutionalized infants to social behavior of caretakers in another study (15).

In one study by Gewirtz, Baer, and Roth (5) a group of preschool children showed a reliably greater mean number of attention-seeking responses under the apparent low availability of the adult (seated at a distant desk

Reprinted from *Child Development*, 1964, **35**, 1187–1195, with permission of the senior author and the Society for Research in Child Development.

engaged in paper work) than did a different group under the apparent high availability of the adult (seated behind child, attending completely to him). In a comparison study they demonstrated that the mean relative frequency of behaviors for approval was increased reliably by a preceding 20-minute period of social isolation (deprivation) relative to a condition in which the same children had not been isolated (nondeprivation). To test an alternative hypothesis, Walters and Ray (22) carried out a study adding anxiety as another independent variable. They drew on the theories of Brown (3), Taylor and Spence (20), and Taylor (19) to interpret the results obtained, stating that the findings attributed to the arousal of a social drive could be explained as due to the arousal of anxiety.

We would expect children from large and dense families to have had more opportunities to be in situations of stress. Some of these anxiety arousing situations would occur when the mother was absent and thus the child would be in a position to associate anxiety or stress with absence of the mother. Nevertheless, anxiety reduction would be associated with the mother, since, even when her reappearance is delayed, she is still the usual person who allays fears and gives comfort and protection.

Anxiety has been reported by Schachter (17) to increase affiliation and susceptibility to social influence. Using female college students as subjects he found that neither size of family nor having younger siblings had any effect on an anxious subject's expression of preference for being with others rather than being alone. He did find, however, that the higher the ordinal position the less the preference for affiliation. It is difficult to relate these findings on college students to young children. An additional problem is posed by a report that different methods used in eliciting a statement of preference can reverse the results (23).

Sears, Maccoby, and Levin (18, p. 141) comment: "In a normal young child, the dependency motive appears to be a powerful one. It cannot be eliminated and it cannot be ignored. In fact, the more the child's efforts to satisfy it are frustrated, the more insistent and all-absorbing are his supplications. . . . If she begins to be less responsive to his customary ways of seeking her affection and attention, his first reaction will be to redouble his efforts. That is, he will behave 'more dependently.' "

On the basis of the studies reviewed above we would expect children from large, high-density families to show more affiliative behavior with an adult "protective figure" in a strange new situation than would children from small, low-density families. This may be true because the adult protective figure would be seen as preventing the occurrence of or reducing the anxiety generated by stressful situations. It would also be predicted on the basis of a postulated deprivation of a dependency drive due to low maternal availability. Restating the hypothesis more specifically in terms of the age and sex of a sample available to the authors of this study, we would expect that boys between the ages of two and three who come from large high-density families would seek more contact with a female teacher than would boys of the same age from small, low-density families.

METHOD

Data to test the hypothesis were obtained from a study designed to test the relation to preschool behavior of congenital characteristics in the first month as estimated from maternal retrospection. This research is tangential to the purposes of the present paper and will be described only briefly to provide a background for the reporting of the present data analysis. Children near $2\frac{1}{2}$ years of age were selected for observation at a research nursery school on the basis of a retrospective questionnaire containing 21 11-point scales, filled out by the mother, comparing the first month's behavior of her two-year-old with the first month's behavior of another sibling of the same sex. Pearson product-moment correlations were computed between the 21 items on the retrospective questionnaire. A centroid factor analysis was performed on the correlations using the University of Michigan complete centroid program. Four factors were rotated using a varimax computer program (8). All children were factor scored on the two most important factors which emerged from this questionnaire.

The first factor was referred to as an Oral factor. The scales having significant positive loadings were:

1. Rate, vigor, and steadiness of sucking.
2. Vigor of onset of sucking.
3. Vigor of reaction when interrupted.
4. Speed of reaction when interrupted.
5. Amount of looking.
6. Rate and loudness of crying when hungry.

The second factor was referred to as a Skin-Sleep factor. The scales having significant loadings were positive except where indicated:

1. Assumption of cuddling posture.
2. Amount of time spent sleeping.
3. Soothing effect of body movement.
4. Speed of return to sleep.
5. Soothing effect of body contact.
6. Vigor of reaction when interrupted (neg.).
7. Awakening to household noises (neg.).
8. Rate and loudness of crying after feeding (neg.).
9. Activity in deep sleep (neg.).

Boys were selected for the nursery school if they were extreme on both factors, extreme being defined as the upper and lower third of the frequency distributions on the factor scores for the factors. During 1959–1960 seven groups of six or seven boys attended the nursery school for a period of four weeks per group. The behavior of these 44 children was studied by direct observations. In addition, the two teachers, male and female, rated each child each day on a variety of scales.

One of the rating scales was entitled "Child initiated contact with female teacher." A rating of 11 was defined as follows: "Spends an unusually large amount of time in child initiated contact with female teacher for warmth, surface stimulation or security purposes; nuzzles, hugs, curls up in arms; signals for contact either by constantly standing within arms' reach, following closely or using direct gestures." A rating of six, the mid-point of the scale, was defined as follows: "Once or twice per day during play or almost always at rest and/or in car establishes contact." "Initiates no contact with female teacher" defined step one on the scale. The score for a child was the mean of the five to seven ratings during the one month of attendance. A correlation of .81 was obtained between the independent ratings of the two teachers on a sample of 37 children, indicating sufficient agreement for our purposes.

In addition, another rating entitled "Maternal initiation of contact with the child" was obtained by an independent observer in the home. A rating of eleven indicated that "Mother initiated body contact very frequently when child did not show a need (excluding negative contact as in punishment)." A mother who initiated very little, if any, body contact was rated one on this scale.

To test the previously mentioned hypothesis, four variables were considered pertinent measures of family size and density which would affect the time a mother would have available to give to one particular child: (*a*) total number of children in the family; (*b*) time span between this child and the next younger sibling; (*c*) time span between this child and the next older sibling; (*d*) average time span between births. Scores for these four family

Table 1 *Statistical Characteristics of Four Measures of Family Size and Density*

	Range	Mean	SD	Factor Weight
1. Number of children	2–8	3.90	1.5	−.767
2. Time span to next younger	13–30 mos	26.41	5.23	.776
3. Time span to next older	12–50 mos	27.30	9.69	.883
4. Average time between births	14–43 mos	26.54	7.79	.827

Intercorrelations	1	2	3	4
1		−.509	−.507	−.439
2			.539	.430
3				.790

variables were obtained, their means and standard deviations calculated, and their intercorrelations computed. One factor was extracted from these six intercorrelations, using Hotelling's principal components method. Table 1 summarizes these data and provides factor weights. It should be noted that the correlations of variable 4 with variables 2 and 3 are part-whole correlations and thus the contribution of 2 and 3 to the factor is somewhat overestimated.

As in the case of the factors from the retrospective questionnaires, factor scores were obtained. This was done by standardizing each score distribution and multiplying each standard score by the factor loading. Each score was multiplied by 100 and a constant was added in order to yield positive integers. For convenience the last digit may be dropped. In order to have the highest scores represent the largest, most dense families the signs of the factor weights were reversed. For example, for a child coming from a family of four children where the months to the next younger are 20, the months to the next older sibling are 26 and the average span between births is 28, the formula would be:

$$(\ 4 \ - \ \ 3.90) \ \div \ 1.5 \ \times \ (+.767) \ + \ 2.10 \ \times \ 100 \ = \ 215$$
$$(20 \ - \ 26.41) \ \div \ 5.23 \ \times \ (-.776) \ + \ 2.10 \ \times \ 100 \ = \ 305$$
$$(26 \ - \ 27.30) \ \div \ 9.69 \ \times \ (-.883) \ + \ 2.10 \ \times \ 100 \ = \ 222$$
$$(28 \ - \ 26.54) \ \div \ 7.79 \ \times \ (-.827) \ + \ 2.10 \ \times \ 100 \ = \ 194$$

Sum or Index of Family Size and Density $= \ 936$ or 94

Table 2 provides a convenient system for deriving a composite measure of family size and density. Since the differences between factor loadings were small there would be no great loss of precision in computing the index by simply combining standard scores for the four variables. Too, a multiple correlation could have been computed between the family characteristics and the measure of contact with the female teacher. This would have necessitated a second sample for purposes of cross-validation because of the tendency to shrinkage in multiple correlations. The procedure used in this study was based on an a priori selection of variables and a weighting based on their empirical relations but did not use the measure of contact behavior as one of these variables. Thus the magnitude of the relation of the index to contact behavior is not subject to shrinkage associated with use of a maximizing function.

RESULTS

In this study of 44 boys the correlation of the family size and density index with the nursery school rating "Child initiated contact with female teacher" was .53. Because this was a selected population, the correlations of the retrospective factors with this index and with "Child initiated contact with

Table 2   *Conversion Table for Family Size and Density Index*

Total Number of Children		Months to Next Younger		Months to Next Older		Average Months between Births	
Number	Weight	Number	Weight	Number	Weight	Number	Weight
11	572	10	453	10	368	10	385
10	521	11	439	11	359	11	374
9	470	12	424	12	349	12	363
8	419	13	409	13	340	13	353
7	368	14	394	14	331	14	342
6	317	15	379	15	322	15	332
5	266	16	364	16	313	16	321
4	215	17	350	17	304	17	310
3	164	18	335	18	295	18	300
2	113	19	320	19	285	19	289
1	62	20	305	20	276	20	279
		21	290	21	267	21	268
		22	276	22	258	22	258
		23	261	23	249	23	247
		24	246	24	240	24	236
		25	231	25	231	25	226
		26	216	26	222	26	215
		27	202	27	212	27	205
		28	187	28	203	28	194
		29	172	29	194	29	184
		30	157	30	185	30	173
		31	142	31	176	31	163
		32	127	32	167	32	152
		33	112	33	158	33	141
		34	98	34	149	34	131
		35	83	35	139	35	120
		36	68	36	130	36	110
		37	53	37	121	37	99
		38	38	38	112	38	89
		39	23	39	103	39	78
		40	8	40	94	40	68
		(or more)		41	85	41	57
				42	75	42	46
				43	66	43	36
				44	57	44	25
				45	48	45	15
				46	39	46	4
				47	30	(or more)	
				48	21		
				(or more)			

Weights

Number of children	———
Months to next younger	———
Months to next older	———
Average months between births	======
Sum or index score	———
($M = 83.7$ $\sigma = 27.67$)	

female teacher" were partialed out. The correlation was essentially unchanged —changing only from .53 to .52. Since this index correlated significantly with a measure of the father's education and occupation adapted from Hollingshead and Redlich (7), this too was partialed out, leaving a correlation of .46 ($p < .005$). Because the partialing out of the retrospective factors and the education-occupation level of the fathers only slightly affected the hypothesized correlation, the results are not restricted either by the selection procedures used or by the social status of the parents. A correlation of −.38 ($p < .01$) was found between the index of family size and density and the home rating of maternal initiation of contact with the child. The correlations of the individual components of this index with child initiated contact with female teachers were: family size, .51; average span between births, −.18; span to next older, −.43; span to next younger, −.38.

DISCUSSION

The results confirmed the hypothesis that preschool boys between the ages of two and three who come from homes where family size and density are high will seek more contact with a female teacher than will boys of the same age who come from homes where family size and density are low. The direction of the correlation was predicted on the basis of the expectation that family size and density would have a close relation with maternal availability, though this study was not designed to provide definitive results concerning this relation. However, this interpretation of the family size and density index as measuring maternal availability is supported by the finding of a significant negative relation between the index and a measure of maternal contact made in the home.

Certain data are available bearing on an alternative explanation. Contacts with the teacher might have been greater because of more general training in social contacts resulting from experiences with more siblings. On this basis more friendliness with peers would also be expected, but there was no significant correlation between the index of family size and density and a rating entitled "Friendliness with peers." This rating was made at the same intervals and covered the same period as the other rating. Furthermore, if this alternative explanation were correct, only family size should correlate with contact with the teacher. Actually, a correlation of .48 was obtained between the rating of contact with the teacher and the index with the family size component subtracted.

There is some indication from the authors' subsequent preliminary studies of female children that the rating of contact does not reflect the same factors in females and thus a check on this hypothesis in female samples may require different measurements of the dependent variable. Female social behavior appeared more sophisticated; less actual physical contact was involved and more intense relations of a symbolic nature were noted. However, these observations are merely conveyed as impressions at the present.

Lasko (11) rated the parents of 40 pairs of first and second children on the Fels Parent Rating Scales. Even though parents tended to protect and be more solicitous of the second child, the warmth of the first child's environment was not present. After the birth of a third sibling the mother's behavior to the second was a modified replica of her change in behavior with the first. Children displaced at three years of age were affected more than children displaced at age four.

Kent and Davis (9) found a correlation between discipline of the unconcerned type and tendency to have more older siblings. This would indicate that after a mother has had more than the average number of children she tends to become unconcerned about the younger ones. This unconcern may make her unresponsive to the dependency demands made by a preschool child, and also less likely to protect the child from anxiety-arousing situations.

This study does not provide any data on optimal periods for maximal contact with the mother. However, there are studies to indicate that if high dependency behavior continues to the later preschool years (four to six) these children are low achievers and are less popular with their peers. Crandall, Preston, and Rabson (4), using observations of 30 nursery school children made both at school and in the home, concluded that high achievers depended less on adults for help and emotional support. They also showed that direct rewarding of achievement and approval seeking were positively related to achievement. It could be concluded from this that when a mother is not available to reward achievement or approval-seeking behavior the child is apt to become less independent and spend more time in support-seeking behavior. McCandless, Belous, and Bennett (12) found peer popularity in preschool age socialization to be negatively correlated with emotional dependency on adults and correlated negatively with number of adult contacts.

Ainsworth (1), in reviewing the literature on maternal deprivation, said: "One important feature of Prugh and Harlow's [13] contribution is to correct the widespread misconception that the so-called maternal deprivation theorists concern themselves only with the effects of deprivation associated with mother-child separation, and ignore deprivation that may occur through insufficient interaction between the child and his mother at home."

REFERENCES

1. Ainsworth, M. D. The effects of maternal deprivation: a review of findings and controversy in the context of research strategy. In *Deprivation of maternal care: a reassessment of its effects*. Public Health Papers, 14, 1962, Geneva: World Health Organization.
2. Brim, O. G., Jr. Family structure and sex role learning by children: a further analysis of Helen Koch's data. *Sociometry*, 1958, **21**, 1–16.

3. Brown, J. S. Problems presented by the concept of acquired drives. In *Current theory and research in motivation: a symposium.* Lincoln: Univer. of Nebraska Press, 1953.

4. Crandall, V., Preston, A., & Rabson, A. Maternal reactions and the development of independence and achievement behavior in young children. *Child Develpm.,* 1960, **31**, 243–251.

5. Gewirtz, J. L., Baer, D. M., & Roth, C. H. A note on the similar effects of low social availability of an adult and brief social deprivation on young children's behavior. *Child Develpm.,* 1958, **29**, 149–152.

6. Harlow, H. F. Primary affectional patterns in primates. *Amer. J. Orthopsychiat.,* 1960, **30**, 676–684.

7. Hollingshead, A. B., & Redlich, F. C. *Social class and mental illness.* New York: Wiley, 1958.

8. Kaiser, H. F. The varimax criterion for analytic rotation in factor analysis. *Psychometrika,* 1958, **23**, 187–200.

9. Kent, N., & Davis, D. R. Discipline in the home and intellectual development. *Brit. J. med. Psychol.,* 1957, **30**, 27–33.

10. Koch, H. L. Influence of siblings on the personality development of younger boys. *Jb. Psychol. Psychother.,* 1958, **5**, 211–225.

11. Lasko, J. K. Parent behavior toward first and second children. *Genet. Psychol. Monogr.,* 1954, **49**, 97–137.

12. McCandless, B. R., Belous, C. B., & Bennett, H. Peer popularity and dependence on adults in pre-school age socialization. *Child Develpm.,* 1961, **32**, 511–518.

13. Prugh, D. G., & Harlow, R. G. "Masked deprivation" in infants and children. In *Deprivation of maternal care: a re-assessment of its effects.* Public Health Papers, 14, 1962, Geneva: World Health Organization.

14. Rheingold, H. L. The measurement of maternal care. *Child Develpm.,* 1960, **31**, 565–575.

15. Rheingold, H. L., & Bayley, N. Later effects of an experimental modification of mothering. *Child Develpm.,* 1959, **30**, 363–372.

16. Rosen, B. C. Family structure and achievement motivation. *Amer. sociol. Rev.,* 1961, **26**, 574–585.

17. Schachter, S. *Psychology of affiliation.* Stanford, Cal.: Stanford Univer. Press, 1959.

18. Sears, R. R., Maccoby, E. E., & Levin, H. *Patterns of child rearing.* Evanston, Ill.: Row, Peterson, 1957.

19. Taylor, J. A. Drive theory and manifest anxiety. *Psychol. Bull.,* 1956, **53**, 303–320.

20. Taylor, J. A., & Spence, K. W. Relationship of anxiety level to performance in serial learning. *J. exp. Psychol.,* 1952, **44**, 61–64.

21. Toman, W. *Family constellation.* New York: Springer Publishing Co., 1961.

22. Walters, R. H. & Ray, E. Anxiety, social isolation and reinforcer effectiveness. *J. Pers.,* 1960, **28**, 358–367.

23. Weiss, J., Wolf, A., Wiltsey, R., "Two studies regarding birth order and preference for volunteering for group, individual or isolation studies. Paper read at Amer. Psychol. Ass., Philadelphia, August, 1963.

Section IV

Children's Perception of Parents and Identification

Introduction

The studies included in the two previous sections attempted to relate various parental characteristics to certain child characteristics. It is apparent that these have met with only moderate success. One explanation for this is that, while parental report (either on a questionnaire or in an interview) is important, the child's perception of the parent and of the general family situation is of even greater psychological significance to the child. Thus, more positive family relations were reported by high-achieving high school boys as compared with low-achieving ones in the Morrow and Wilson study. In the Medinnus investigation, perceptions of parents of a group of delinquent boys were compared with those of a control group on a standardized instrument. As predicted, marked differences were found between the two groups in their perceptions of their fathers, especially with respect to the Neglecting and Rejecting scales.

Although this phenomenological approach is not without merit, some methodological problems are present. Are we justified in concluding that the poor adjustment of a group of children is due to their unfavorable perceptions of their parents? Almost equally plausible is that they view their parents unfavorably because of their poor adjustment. Also, children's reports of earlier parental attitudes and behavior are subject to the same kinds of distortion as parental report.

In a study of the relation between adjustment and perception of parents in a group of late adolescents (Medinnus, 1965), a closer relation was found between these two variables for boys than for girls. This suggests that perhaps boys are more susceptible to parental influence than are girls, and this

245

may account for the higher frequency of delinquency, stuttering, schizophrenia, and reading and behavior problems in boys. Relevant to this point are data (Bayley, 1964) showing higher correlations between ratings of maternal behavior from birth to three years and the child's intelligence for boys than for girls. Furthermore, the effects of maternal behavior on intelligence were more persistent over time for boys. Similarly, early maternal behaviors showed persistent relations with certain aspects of the boys' but not with the girls' adolescent behavior (Schaefer and Bayley, 1963).

While the concept of identification has been subject to a variety of definitions, it has been used to explain the development of conscience, sex-appropriate behavior, and other behaviors in children. The findings of several studies (Sears, 1953; Payne and Mussen, 1956) suggest that the boy's identification with his father is facilitated by a warm, affectionate relation between them.

Bandura and Huston interpret identification as a process of incidental imitative learning. The findings of their interesting experimental study confirmed the prediction that such learning is promoted by the presence of affection and nurturance in the adult-child interaction. The selection by Lynn presents an interesting formulation of sex differences in identification and sex differences in personality development in general. He postulates that males identify with a cultural stereotype of the masculine role, while females tend to identify with aspects of their own mothers' role behavior. Evidence from numerous studies is given in support of this hypothesis.

References

Bayley, Nancy. Research in child development: a longitudinal perspective. *Merrill-Palmer Quarterly,* 1965, **11,** 183–208.

Medinnus, G. R. Adolescents' self-acceptance and perceptions of their parents. *Journal of Consulting Psychology,* 1965, **29,** 150–154.

Payne, D. E., & Mussen, P. H. Parent-child relations and father identification among adolescent boys. *Journal of Abnormal and Social Psychology,* 1956, **52,** 358–362.

Schaefer, E. S., & Bayley, Nancy. Maternal behavior, child behavior and their intercorrelations from infancy through adolescence. *Monographs of the Society for Research in Child Development,* 1963, **28,** No. 3.

Sears, Pauline S. Child-rearing factors related to playing of sex-typed roles. *American Psychologist,* 1953, **8,** 431. (Abstract)

22. FAMILY RELATIONS OF BRIGHT

HIGH-ACHIEVING AND UNDER-ACHIEVING

HIGH SCHOOL BOYS

WILLIAM R. MORROW AND RORERT C. WILSON

The present article reports data on the family relations of bright high school boys making good grades as compared with bright high school boys making mediocre or poor grades.

Of numerous studies of school achievement, few have obtained data regarding family relations correlates. These few have indicated a positive association between student achievement and emotionally supportive home situations. This general finding applies to elementary school pupils (4, 9, 15, 18, 20,), high school students (13, 14), and college students (12).

More specifically, parents of high-achievers have been found to give their children more praise and approval (18), to show more interest and understanding (19), to be closer to their children (14), to make their children feel more family "belongingness" (20) and identification with parents (19). On the other hand, parents of under-achievers have been reported to be more domineering (12, 14) and overrestrictive (18) and to use more severe and frequent punishment (4, 14), which is at the same time less effectual (4). Parents of under-achievers have also been found more likely either to baby their youngsters *or* to push them excessively (9) and to present to their youngsters either low *or* extremely high (pressuring) demands for achievement (18). Finally, homes of under-achievers are reported to show more tension (12) and more parental disagreement as to standards of behavior expected of their youngsters (19).

Most of these studies have been based on qualitative data such as interviews. Many had sampling limitations such as a very small sample and questionable equation of groups. No previous study seems to have dealt with family relations correlates of school achievement among high school students of superior intelligence.

In the present research the groups compared were carefully equated, the sample was relatively homogeneous in intelligence, all subjects being of superior intelligence, and the data were obtained by structured measuring instruments.

Reprinted from *Child Development*, 1961, **32**, 501–510, with permission of the senior author and the Society for Research in Child Development.

247

Before the present study was initiated, exploratory interviews covering various topics including family relations were held with a few bright high- and under-achieving high school boys. On the basis of these interviews as well as the studies cited, it was hypothesized that the reported family relations of high-achievers, as contrasted with those of under-achievers, are characterized by: (a) more emotionally supportive home environments; and, more specifically, (b) greater family sharing in recreation, decision-making, and exchange of confidences and ideas; (c) greater mutual parent-child affection, acceptance, trust, and approval; (d) less parental domination, severity, and restrictiveness; (e) more sympathetic parental encouragement of achievement, but less overinsistence on achievement; (f) greater harmony between parents and more regularity of home routines.

It was hypothesized further that students' family relations influence their school achievement via certain mediating variables. Specifically, it was hypothesized that supportive home environments are associated with positive student attitudes toward (a) teachers, (b) school, and (c) intellectual activities, as representing the adult world of parents, and that each of these mediating attitude variables would be associated with school achievement.

METHOD

Sample

The sample included two equated groups each containing 48 high school boys of superior intelligence (120 IQ or above). The groups were equated for grade in school, socioeconomic status, and intelligence. Each group contained 19 ninth-graders, 14 tenth-graders, and 15 eleventh-graders. Each group likewise contained one upper class, 15 upper-middle class, 23 lower-middle class, and 9 lower class boys. The mean IQ of the high-achieving group was 126.0; that of the under-achievers, 125.3, the difference being nonsignificant.

The groups differed in grade-point average in academic courses (with a minimum of three academic courses for each student). The high-achievers maintained an average of 1.00 to 1.67 (1 being the best grade possible, 5 the poorest) during the school year 1955–1956. The under-achievers maintained an average of 2.75 to 5.00, 2.75 being regarded as under-achievement for students of superior intelligence.

Data Collection

Several types of information about family relations were obtained from the students through group-administered questionnaires. The students were not asked to sign their names, but birthdates and other data were used to identify questionnaires for the purpose of selecting the sample. Otherwise, anonymity was maintained and information on individuals kept confidential.

The students' family relations as seen by themselves were evaluated primarily by 16 self-report Family Relations Scales. Each scale consisted of six questions about the student's relations with his parents (or foster parents). The scales were presented in consecutive order, but without scale titles or breaks in spacing. Each student was asked to indicate to what extent each item described his own home situation, using the following four response categories:

1. Not at all   *or* Almost Never
2. A Little   *or* Sometimes
3. Considerably *or* Often
4. Very Much   *or* Very Often (or Almost Always)

The student was assigned a score on each scale by summing his scores on the six items in the scale. A score was also obtained on the total of all scales (except Harmony of Parents), conceived as an index of Over-all Family Morale.

The general form of the scales, as well as much of their content, was adapted from a questionnaire developed by Brown and his associates (10, Ch. 21). Seven scales were added; and a number of Brown's items were omitted, revised, or supplemented by additional items. Other sources of item content included instruments developed by Block (1), Itkin (11), Rickard (18), Stott, and Strodtbeck, as well as our preliminary interviews.

Following are the scale titles and a sample item for each scale:

1. *Family Sharing of Recreation.* "Do you and your family go on picnics or outings or trips together?"
2. *Family Sharing of Confidence and Ideas.* "Do your parents discuss their work and activities with you?"
3. *Family Sharing in Making Decisions.* "Do your parents let you help decide everyday family policies, rules, and ways of living?"
4. *Parental Approval.* "Does either parent ever seem to wish that you were a different sort of person?" (Negative item, scored in reverse.)
5. *Parental Affection.* "Do your parents openly show affection for you by word or action?"
6. *Parental Trust.* "How confident do your parents seem to be that you will behave properly away from home?"
7. *Parental Approval of Peer Activities.* "Do your parents object to some of your activities with your friends and acquaintances?" (Negative item.)
8. *Student Acceptance of Parental Standards.* "Do you agree with your parents' ideas about life?"
9. *Student Affection and Respect for Parents.* "Would you like to be the same kind of parent that your parents have been?"
10. *Lack of Parental Overrestrictiveness.* "Do your parents try to direct your activities?" (Negative item.)
11. *Lack of Parental Severity of Discipline.* "How often do your parents punish you?" (Negative item.)
12. *Lack of Parental Overprotection.* "Do your parents try to protect you too much against difficulties or dangers?" (Negative item.)

13. *Lack of Parental Overinsistence on Achievement.* "Are your parents always after you to work hard to become a success?" (Negative item.)

14. *Sympathetic Encouragement of Achievement.* "Do your parents inspire you to want to develop your abilities?"

15. *Regularity of Home Routine.* "Are your meals served at regular hours?"

16. *Harmony of Parents.* "Do your parents openly show affection or consideration for each other?"

The students were also asked to provide sociological data on parents' marital status, occupation, and education and on the ages and sexes of their siblings. In addition, each student was asked to respond to three checklists: (*a*) a list of activities (e.g., "music," "insects or beach life," "fish or hunt," "billiards") to be checked as to which ones his parents had taught him or developed his interest in, yielding an "intellectual," a "nonintellectual," and a total score; (*b*) a list of 11 high school goals or values (in the areas of academic achievement, athletics, social relations and status, general adjustment, morals, and religion) to be checked as to which his parents considered "most" and "least" important (three each to be checked) for him to attain; (*c*) a similar list of 11 adult goals (e.g., "be outstanding in your occupation," "live a happy life," etc.) to be checked the same way.

The questionnaire also included four open-ended questions: "What sort of person is your mother?" "What sort of person is your father?" "What do you like most about your home and family?" "What would you like to change about your home and family?"

The following measures of hypothesized mediating variables (between family relations and school achievement) were obtained: (*a*) a six-item attitude scale (with a five-point scale for each item) designed to measure Negative Attitudes to Teachers, which yielded a corrected odd-even reliability of .69; (*b*) a similar six-item attitude scale designed to measure Negative Attitudes to School, which yielded a corrected odd-even reliability of .85; (*c*) a 72-item interest-inventory scale (with dichotomous items) designed to measure Interest in Intellectual Activities (esthetic activities, social problems, natural science, and formal symbol manipulation such as mathematics and puzzles), which yielded a corrected odd-even reliability of .77.

Analysis of Data

The internal consistency reliability of each Family Relations Scale and of the Over-all Family Morale Scale was evaluated by computing an odd-even product-moment reliability coefficient. Differences between high- and under-achievers on each scale and on the Over-all scale were tested for significance by a median test.

Group differences in checklist responses were tested for significance by a median test for scale scores and by a chi square test for single items.

As for the open-ended questions, response categories potentially differentiating between the two achievement groups were determined by studying an inspection sample. These categories were cross-validated by being scored "blind" on another sample of 66 boys in each group with groups equated for grade in school, socioeconomic status, and intelligence. Differences between groups were tested for significance by chi square and median tests.

Pearson product-moment correlations were obtained between the Over-all Family Morale scale and the several measures of mediating variables concerned with attitudes toward teachers, school, and intellectual activities. These correlations were computed separately for the total sample, for high-achievers only, and for under-achievers only. In addition, differences between achievement groups on these mediating variables were tested for significance by a median test.

All tests of significance used were two-tailed.

RESULTS

Family Relations Scales

Results on the Family Relations Scales are presented in Table 1. The internal consistency reliability of the 16 six-item scales appeared to be sufficiently satisfactory for purposes of group comparison: all but three of the

Table 1 *Family Relations Scales: Median Tests* [a]

| | | Per Cent Above Median | | |
| | | Highs | Lows | |
Scale Title	r [b]	($N = 48$)	($N = 48$)	p
Family sharing of recreation	.76	69	44	.02
Family sharing of confidence and ideas	.84	63	35	.01
Family sharing in making decisions	.88	60	44	ns
Parental approval	.56	73	33	.001
Parental affection	.88	60	42	ns
Parental trust	.73	60	25	.001
Parental approval of peer activities	.94	71	42	.01
Student acceptance of parental standards	.69	52	25	.01
Student affection and respect toward parents	.91	58	44	ns
Lack of parental overrestrictiveness	.63	56	29	.01
Lack of parental severity of discipline	.70	69	42	.01
Lack of parental overprotection	.77	52	56	ns
Lack of parental overinsistence on achievement	.75	63	46	ns
Parental encouragement of achievement	.74	60	40	.05
Harmony of parents ($N = 40$)	.72	63	48	ns
Regularity of home routine	.76	52	46	ns
Over-all family morale	.97	67	33	.001

[a] Two-tailed tests.
[b] Odd-even reliability coefficient, corrected by Spearman-Brown formula.

corrected odd-even coefficients were above .70. The 90-item Over-all Family Morale Scale yielded a reliability of .97.

Nine of the 16 six-item scales differentiated between the high- and under-achieving groups in the predicted direction beyond the .05 level, seven of these nine beyond the .01 level. The Over-all Family Morale Scale differentiated beyond the .001 level.

High-achievers more often than under-achievers (*a*) described their families as typically sharing recreation, ideas, and confidences; (*b*) described their parents as approving and trusting (the areas of sharpest difference between the two groups), affectionate, encouraging (but not pressuring) with respect to achievement, and relatively nonrestrictive and nonsevere; and (*c*) described themselves as accepting their parents' standards.

An equal majority of both groups described their parents as having a relatively harmonious relationship, portrayed their homes as having a fairly regular routine, denied that they were either seriously overprotected or excessively pressured to achieve, and said they felt considerable respect and affection for their parents.

Even in the areas of greatest difference, however, there was considerable overlap between the two groups. On the Over-all Family Morale Scale nearly a third of the high-achievers scored below the median, and nearly a third of the under-achievers scored above the median.

Sociological Data

The two groups did not differ significantly in any of the sociological factors on which data was obtained. The data contradict the stereotyped notion that a mother's working outside the home inevitably leads to neglect which conduces to poor school performance (and other dire consequences). Actually 47 per cent of the high-achievers (as against 37 per cent of the under-achievers) reported that their mothers were working outside the home!

Check Lists

The two groups showed essentially no significant differences in their responses to the check lists.

Open-Ended Questions

In the inspection sample 34 potentially differentiating response categories were noted, of which 25 were grouped in five "high" combined categories and nine were grouped in three "low" combined categories. In the cross-validation only two "high" combined categories (out of eight combined categories) and four single "high" categories differentiated significantly (in the predicted direction).

Fifty-one per cent of the high-achievers as against 33 per cent of the under-achievers (*p* < .05) were scored in the combined category, "Positive references to intrafamily relationships." Two single categories in this grouping also differentiated significantly: "References to parental interest in family or student" (29 per cent to 12 per cent, $p < .01$): and "References to parents' outgoing, positive shaping of student's development" (12 per cent to 0 per cent, $p < .02$).

The combined category, "References to 'Golden Rule' virtues of parents" was scored significantly more often for high-achievers (56 per cent to 29 per cent, $p < .01$). Two single categories in this grouping also differentiated significantly: "Parents described as 'considerate' or 'thoughtful'" (17 per cent to 4 per cent, $p < .05$); and "Parents described as 'understanding'" (36 per cent to 17 per cent, $p < .02$).

These results are consistent with those on the Family Relations Scales.

Mediating Variables

The correlation between Over-all Family Morale and Negative Attitudes to Teachers was $-.67$ for the total sample, $-.46$ for high-achievers only, and $-.60$ for under-achievers only. The corresponding correlations between Family Morale and Negative Attitudes to School were $-.69$, $-.32$, and $-.65$. The correlations between Family Morale and Intellectual Interests were $.57$, $.31$, and $.49$. All of the obtained correlations are significant at the $.05$ level or better. On each of the three measures of mediating variables the two achievement groups differed at the $.001$ level in the expected direction.

These results are consistent with the hypothesis that supportive family relations foster academic achievement *via* promoting positive attitudes toward teachers, school, and intellectual activities, as symbols of the adult world of parents. However, other interpretations of the direction of causality are not excluded.

SUMMARY

The reported family relations of 48 high school boys of superior intelligence making high grades were compared with those of a group making mediocre or poor grades, equated for grade in school, socioeconomic status, and intelligence. The main measuring instrument was a set of 16 six-item questionnaire scales (with a four-point scale for each item), on which each subject was asked to describe his family relations. The students also provided sociological data, check-list data on parental goals for the student, and open-ended question data on conceptions of parents. In addition, attitude scale data were obtained on variables hypothesized to mediate the influence of family morale on student achievement.

The results supported the hypotheses that bright high-achievers' parents reportedly engage in more sharing of activities, ideas, and confidences; are more approving and trusting, affectionate, and encouraging (but not pressuring) with respect to achievement; are less restrictive and severe; and enjoy more acceptance of parental standards by their youngsters. Not supported were hypotheses that under-achievers' families show more over-protectiveness, more high-pressure for achievement, more parental disharmony, more irregularity of home routine; differences in goals for their youngsters; or differences in sociological factors such as parents' marital status, current occupation of either parent, or number and ages of siblings.

The results also supported the hypothesis that family morale fosters academic achievement among bright high school boys *via* fostering positive attitudes toward teachers and toward school and interest in intellectual activities, as mediating variables. However, other hypotheses as to the direction of causality are not ruled out.

REFERENCES

1. Block, V. L. Conflicts of adolescents with their mothers. *J. abnorm. soc. Psychol.,* 1937, **32,** 193–206.
2. Coleman, H. A. The relationship of socio-economic status to the performance of junior high school students. *J. exp. Educ.,* 1940, **9,** 61–63.
3. Collins, J. H., & Douglas, H. R. The socio-economic status of the home as a factor in success in the junior high school. *Elem. Sch. J.,* 1937, **38,** 107–113.
4. Conklin, A. M. Failures of highly intelligent pupils. *Teach. Coll. Contrib. Educ.,* 1940, No. 792.
5. Gough, H. G. The relationship of socio-economic status to personality inventory and achievement test scores. *J. educ. Psychol.,* 1946, **37,** 527–540.
6. Guilford, J. P., Christensen, P. R., Bond, N. A., Jr., & Sutton, M. A. *Technical appendices to the research bulletin. A factor-analytic study of human interests.* Beverly Hills, Calif.: Sheridan Supply Co., 1953.
7. Guilford, J. P., Christensen, P. R., Bond, N. A., Jr., & Sutton, M. A. A factor analysis study of human interests. *Psychol. Monogr.,* 1954, **68,** No. 4.
8. Harris, D. Factors affecting college grades: a review of the literature, 1930–1937. *Psychol. Bull.,* 1940, **37,** 125–161.
9. Hattwick, B. W., & Stowell, M. The relation of parental over-attentiveness to children's work habits and social adjustments in kindergarten and the first six grades of school. *J. educ. Res.,* 1936, **30,** 169–176.
10. Havighurst, R. J., & Taba, H. *Adolescent character and development.* New York: Wiley, 1949.
11. Itkin, W. Some relationships between intra-family attitudes and preparental attitudes toward children. *J. genet. Psychol.,* 1952, **80,** 221–252.
12. Jones, E. S. The probation student: what he is like and what can be done about it. *J. educ. Res.,* 1955, **49,** 93–102.
13. Kimball, B. The sentence-completion technique in a study of scholastic achievement. *J. consult. Psychol.,* 1952, **16,** 353–358.
14. Kimball, B. Case studies in educational failure during adolescence. *Amer. J. Orthopsychiat.,* 1953, **23,** 406–415.
15. Leibman, O. B. The relationship of personal and social adjustment to academic achievement in the elementary school. Unpublished doctoral dissertation, Columbia Univer., 1953.
16. Lewis, W. D. A comparative study of the personalities, interests, and home backgrounds of gifted children of superior and inferior educational achievement. *J. genet. Psychol.,* 1941, **59,** 207–218.

17. Musselman, J. W. Factors associated with the achievement of high school pupils of superior intelligence. *J. exp. Educ.*, 1942, **11,** 53–68.
18. Rickard, G. The relationship between parental behavior and children's achievement behavior. Unpublished doctoral dissertation, Harvard Univer., 1954.
19. Tibbets, J. R. The role of parent-child relationships in the achievement of high school pupils. *Dissert. Abstr.*, 1955, **15,** 232.
20. Walsh, A. *Self-concepts of bright boys with learning difficulties.* New York: Columbia Univer., 1956.

23. DELINQUENTS' PERCEPTIONS OF THEIR PARENTS

Gene R. Medinnus

A variety of explanations have been offered to account for delinquency. In general these can be divided into two groups depending upon whether they emphasize sociological or psychological factors. The latter position seems to be the dominant one today due in part perhaps to the fact that, sociologically at least, it is easier to account for the delinquency of some adolescents than it is to explain the non-delinquency of their siblings. Both are exposed to poverty, deteriorating neighborhoods, and slum conditions. The difference between them must rest in psychological factors in the home.

Evidence is accumulating that a pattern of disruption of the relationship between father and son exists in the case of delinquent and aggressive boys. In an investigation comparing attitudes toward parents of a group of delinquent boys and a group of matched controls, Andry (1960) found that the delinquents, in contrast to the controls, felt more loved by mothers than by fathers. Also, the delinquents expressed dissatisfaction with the reasonableness of parental punishment. They felt that their fathers especially were defective in use of praise. Similarly, Bandura and Walters (1959) found the relationship between father and son marked by rejection, antagonism, and hostility for a group of aggressive boys. However, few differences were apparent between the aggressive group and the controls with regard to attitudes toward their mothers. Both of the above investigations were based on interviews.

HYPOTHESES

The purpose of the present study was to compare the perceptions of a group of institutionalized delinquents with matched controls using an objective instrument. The two hypotheses tested were (1) that a significant difference exists between delinquent and non-delinquent boys in their perceptions of their parents, with the latter group holding more favorable attitudes, and (2) that greater differences exist between the two groups with regard to perception of father than perception of mother.

Reprinted from the *Journal of Consulting Psychology*, 1965, **29**, 592–593, with permission of the author and the American Psychological Association.

METHOD

Subjects

The delinquent group was composed of 30 boys who had been formally committed to a California state training school for boys. They ranged in age from 12 to 17 with a mean of 15 years. The control group drawn from a high school population, was matched with the delinquents on sex, CA, and father's occupational status. All of the Ss were white.

Procedure

The Parent-Child Relations questionnaire (PCR) developed by Roe and Sigelman (1963) was administered to the two groups of Ss. Both the mother and father forms were used. The PCR consists of 130 statements divided into 10 scales. Each statement is responded to by checking one of four choices: Very True, Perhaps True, Perhaps Untrue, and Very Untrue. For quantification purposes, weights from 4 to 1, respectively, were assigned arbitrarily to these choices so that the higher scores indicated greater agreement with the title of each scale. A list of the scales can be found in Table 1.

RESULTS AND DISCUSSION

The t test comparisons of the means of the delinquent and control groups on the PCR scales are provided in Table 1. The first hypothesis was

Table 1   *Differences Between Means of Delinquent and Control Groups on PCR Scales*

	Mother Form			Father Form		
PCR Scales	Delin-quents	Controls	t	Delin-quents	Controls	t
Protecting	33.8	35.2	.86	32.6	34.8	2.80 [b]
Symbolic-love punishment	26.9	23.5	3.01 [b]	26.1	22.0	4.55 [b]
Rejecting	31.7	25.4	3.09 [b]	34.2	25.8	6.06 [b]
Casual	36.7	34.7	.91	35.2	35.6	.29
Symbolic-love reward	26.9	28.4	1.06	24.3	26.9	2.99 [b]
Demanding	40.5	36.7	2.19 [a]	39.9	36.3	3.98 [b]
Direct-object punishment	24.0	22.8	.76	24.4	22.2	1.97
Loving	44.8	47.6	1.31	38.2	45.5	4.94 [b]
Neglecting	26.2	23.3	1.63	30.3	25.6	6.57 [b]
Direct-object reward	23.9	22.3	1.02	21.3	22.0	.71

[a] $p < .05$ [b] $p < .01$

clearly confirmed since 7 of the 10 scales differentiated significantly between the two groups on the father form and 3 of the 10 scales on the mother form reached significance. The second hypothesis concerning greater difference between the two groups in their perception of their fathers than their mothers was also confirmed.

The findings of the present investigation strongly support those of the Andry and Bandura and Walters studies in showing marked differences between delinquents and nondelinquents in their perceptions of their fathers, and in showing fewer differences between the two groups in their attitudes toward their mothers. The consistently unfavorable attitude of the present sample of delinquents toward their fathers was especially marked on the Rejecting and Neglecting scales.

Several implications of the present findings seem clear. The distrust and antagonism frequently shown by delinquents toward police and parole officers and other societal authority figures are not surprising in view of their attitudes toward their fathers. Further, treatment of male delinquents must involve the establishment of a trusting, affectionate relation between them and a male adult if the rewards and punishments employed by society are to be effective in producing conformity to the rules, regulations, and demands of society. Of great importance are psychologically trained male teachers in lower class neighborhoods where divorce and delinquency are prevalent.

REFERENCES

Andry, R. *Delinquency and parental pathology*. London: Methuen, 1960.

Bandura, A., & Walters, R. H. *Adolescent aggression*. New York: Ronald, 1959.

Roe, Anne, & Sigelman, M. A Parent-Child Relations questionnaire. *Child Development*, 1963, **34**, 355–369.

24. IDENTIFICATION AS A PROCESS OF

INCIDENTAL LEARNING

Albert Bandura and Aletha C. Huston

Although part of a child's socialization takes place through direct training, much of a child's behavior repertoire is believed to be acquired through
identification with the important adults in his life. This process, variously
described in behavior theory as "vicarious" learning (Logan, Olmsted, Rosner,
Schwartz, and Stevens, 1955), observational learning (Maccoby and Wilson,
1957; Warden, Fjeld, and Koch, 1940), and role taking (Maccoby, 1959;
Sears, Maccoby, and Levin, 1957) appears to be more a result of active
imitation by the child of attitudes and patterns of behavior that the parents
have never directly attempted to teach than of direct reward and punishment
of instrumental responses.

While elaborate developmental theories have been proposed to explain
this phenomenon, the process subsumed under the term "identification" may
be accounted for in terms of incidental learning, that is, learning that
apparently takes place in the absence of an induced set or intent to learn the
specific behaviors or activities in question (McGeoch and Irion, 1952).

During the parents' social training of a child, the range of cues employed
by a child is likely to include both those that the parents consider immediately
relevant and other cues of parental behavior which the child has had ample
opportunities to observe and to learn even though he has not been instructed
to do so. Thus, for example, when a parent punishes a child physically for
having aggressed toward peers, the intended outcome of the training is that
the child should refrain from hitting others. Concurrent with the intentional
learning, however, a certain amount of incidental learning may be expected to
occur through imitation, since the child is provided, in the form of the parent's
behavior, with an example of how to aggress toward others, and this incidental
learning may guide the child's behavior in later social interactions.

The use of incidental cues by both human and animal subjects while
performing nonimitative learning tasks is well documented by research
(Easterbrook, 1959). In addition, studies of imitation and learning of
incidental cues by Church (1957) and Wilson (1958) have demonstrated
that subjects learn certain incidental environmental cues while imitating the
discrimination behavior of a model and that the incidental learning guides the

Reprinted from the *Journal of Abnormal and Social Psychology*, 1961, **63**, 311–318,
with permission of the senior author and the American Psychological Association.

subjects' discrimination responses in the absence of the model. The purpose of the experiment reported in this paper is to demonstrate that subjects imitate not only discrimination responses but also other behaviors performed by the model.

The incidental learning paradigm was employed in the present study with an important change in procedure in order to create a situation similar to that encountered in learning through identification. Subjects performed an orienting task but, unlike most incidental learning studies, the experimenter performed the diverting task as well and the extent to which the subjects patterned their behavior after that of the experimenter-model was measured.

The main hypothesis tested is that nursery school children, while learning a two-choice discrimination problem, also learn to imitate certain of the experimenter's behaviors which are totally irrelevant to the successful performance of the orienting task.

One may expect, on the basis of theories of identification (Bronfenbrenner, 1960), that the presence of affection and nurturance in the adult-child interaction promotes incidental imitative learning, a view to which empirical studies of the correlates of strong and weak identification lend some indirect support. Boys whose fathers are highly rewarding and affectionate have been found to adopt the father-role in doll play activities (Sears, 1953), to show father-son similarity in response to items on a personality questionnaire (Payne and Mussen, 1956), and to display masculine behaviors (Mussen and Distler, 1959, 1960) to a greater extent than boys whose fathers are relatively cold and unrewarding.

One interpretation of the relationship between nurturance and identification is that affectional rewards increase the secondary reinforcing properties of the model and, thus, predispose the imitator to reproduce the behavior of the model for the satisfaction these cues provide (Mowrer, 1950). Once the parental characteristics have acquired such reward value for the child, conditional withdrawal of positive reinforcers is believed to create additional instigation for the child to perform behaviors resembling that of the parent model, i.e., if the child can reproduce the parent's rewarding behavior he can, thus, reward himself (Sears, 1957; Whiting and Child, 1953). In line with this theory of identification in terms of secondary reward, it is predicted that children who experience a warm, rewarding interaction with the experimenter-model should reproduce significantly more of the behaviors performed by the model than do children who experience a relatively distant and cold relationship.

METHOD

Subjects

The subjects were 24 boys and 24 girls enrolled in the Stanford University Nursery School. They ranged in age from 45 to 61 months, with a mean age of 53 months. The junior author played the role of the model for all 48 children, and two other female experimenters shared in the task of conducting the study.

General Procedure

Forty subjects were matched individually on the basis of sex and ratings of dependency behavior, and subdivided randomly in terms of a nurturant-nonnurturant condition yielding two experimental groups of 20 subjects each. A small control group comprising 8 subjects was also studied.

In the first phase of the experiment half the experimental and control subjects experienced two nurturant rewarding play sessions with the model while the remaining subjects experienced a cold nonnurturant relationship. For the second phase of the experiment subjects performed a diverting two-choice discrimination problem with the model who exhibited fairly explicit, although functionless, behavior during the discrimination trials, and the extent to which the subjects reproduced the model's behavior was measured. The experimental and control procedures differed only in the patterns of behavior displayed by the model.

Matching Variable

Dependency was selected as a matching variable since, on the basis of the theories of identification, dependency would be expected to facilitate imitative learning. There is some evidence, for example, that dependent subjects are strongly oriented toward gaining social rewards in the form of attention and approval (Cairns, 1959; Endsley and Hartup, 1960), and one means of obtaining these rewards is to imitate the behavior of others (Sears, Maccoby, and Levin, 1957). Moreover, such children do not have the habit of responding independently; consequently they are apt to be more dependent on, and therefore more attentive to, the cues produced by the behavior of others (Jackubczak and Walters, 1959; Kagan and Mussen, 1956).

Measures of subjects' dependency behavior were obtained through observations of their social interactions in the nursery school. The observers recorded subjects' behavior using a combined time-sampling and behavior-unit observation method. Each child was observed for 12 10-minute observation sessions distributed over a period of approximately 10 weeks; each observation session was divided into 30-second intervals, thus yielding a total of 240 behavior units.

The children were observed in a predetermined order that was varied randomly to insure that each child would be seen under approximately comparable conditions. In order to provide an estimate of reliability of the ratings, 234 observation sessions (4680 behavior units) were recorded simultaneously but independently by both observers.

The subjects' emotional dependency was assessed in terms of the frequency of behaviors that were aimed at securing a nurturant response from others. The following four specific categories of dependency behavior were scored: seeking help and assistance, seeking praise and approval, seeking physical contact, and seeking proximity and company of others.

The dependency scores were obtained by summing the observations made of these five different types of behaviors and, on the basis of these scores, the subjects were paired and assigned at random to the two experimental conditions.

Experimental Conditions

In the *nonnurturant* condition, the model brought the subject to the experimental room and after instructing the child to play with the toys that were spread on the floor, busied herself with paper work at a desk in the far corner of the room. During this period the model avoided any interaction with the child.

In contrast, during the *nurturant* sessions the model sat on the floor close to the subject. She responded readily to the child's bids for help and attention, and in other ways fostered a consistently warm, and rewarding interaction.

These experimental social interactions, which preceded the imitation learning, consisted of two 15-minute sessions separated by an interval of approximately 5 days.

Diverting Task

A two-choice discrimination problem, similar to the one employed by Miller and Dollard (1941) in experiments of matching behavior, was used as the diverting task which occupied the subjects' attention while at the same time permitting opportunities for the subjects to observe behavior performed by the model in the absence of any instructions to observe or to reproduce the responses resembling that of the model.

The apparatus consisted of two small boxes, identical in color (red sides, yellow lid) and size ($6'' \times 8'' \times 10''$). The hinged lid of each box was lined with rubber stripping so as to eliminate any auditory cues during the placement of the rewards which consisted of small multicolor pictures of animals and flowers. The boxes were placed on small chairs approximately 5 feet apart and 8 feet from the starting point.

At the end of the second social interaction session the experimenter entered the room with the test apparatus and instructed the model and the subject that they were going to play a game in which the experimenter would hide a picture sticker in one of the boxes and that the object of the game was to guess which box contained the sticker.

The model and the subject then left the room and after the experimenter placed two stickers in the designated box, they were recalled to the starting point in the experimental room and the model was asked to take the first turn. During the model's trial, the subject remained at the starting point where he could observe the model's behavior.

Although initially it was planned to follow the procedure used by Miller and Dollard (1941) in which one of two boxes was loaded with two rewards and the child made his choice immediately following the leader's trial, this procedure had to be modified when it became evident during pretesting that approximately 40% of the subjects invariably chose the opposite box from the model even though the nonimitative response was consistently unrewarded. McDavid (1959), in a recent study of imitative behavior in preschool children, encountered similar difficulties in that 44% of his subjects did not learn to imitate the leader even though the subjects were not informed as to whether the leader was or was not rewarded.

In order to overcome this stereotyped nonimitation, the experimenter placed two rewards in a single box, but following the model's trial the model and the subject left the room and were recalled almost immediately (the intratrial interval was approximately 5 seconds), thus creating the impression that the boxes were reloaded. After the subject completed his trial, the model and the subject left the room. The experimenter recorded the subject's behavior and reloaded the boxes for the second trial. The noncorrection method was used throughout. This procedure was continued until the subject met the learning criterion of four successive imitative discrimination responses, or until 30 acquisition trials had been completed. The slight modification in procedure proved to be effective as evidenced by the fact that only 9 of the 48 children failed to meet the criterion.

In order to eliminate any position habit, the right-left placements of the reward were varied from trial to trial in a fixed irregular order. This sequence was randomly determined except for the limitation that no more than two successive rewards could occur in the same position.

The number of trials to criterion was the measure of the subjects' imitation behavior on the discrimination task.

Although the establishment of imitative choice responses was, in itself, of some theoretical interest, the discrimination problem was intended primarily as an orienting or distraction task. Thus, on each discrimination trial, the model exhibited certain verbal, motor, and aggressive behaviors which were totally irrelevant to the performance of the task to which the subject's attention was directed. At the starting point, for example, the model remarked, "Here I go," and then marched slowly toward the box containing the stickers repeating, "March, march, march." On the lid of each box was a small rubber doll which the model knocked off aggressively when she reached the designated box. She then paused briefly, remarked, "Open the box," removed one sticker and pasted it on a pastoral scene that hung on the wall immediately behind the boxes. The model terminated the trial by replacing the doll on the lid of the container. The model and the subject then left the room briefly. After being recalled to the experimental room the subject took his turn, and the number of the model's behaviors reproduced by the subject was recorded.

Control Group

In addition to the two experimental groups, a control group, consisting of eight subjects, comparable to the experimental groups in terms of sex distribution, dependency ratings, and nurturant-nonnurturant experiences was studied. Since the model performed highly novel patterns of responses unlikely to occur independently of the observation of the behavior of the model, it was decided to assign most of the available subjects to the experimental groups and only a small number of subjects to the control group.

The reasons for the inclusion of a control group were twofold. On the one hand, it provided a check on whether the subjects' behavior reflected genuine imitative learning or merely the chance occurrence of behaviors high in the subjects' response hierarchies. Second, it was of interest to determine whether the subjects would adopt certain aspects of the model's behavior that involved considerable delay in reward. With the controls, therefore, the model walked to the box, choosing a highly circuitous route along the sides of the experimental room; instead of aggression toward the doll, the model lifted it gently off the container and she left the doll on the floor at the completion of a trial. While walking to the boxes the model repeated, "Walk, walk, walk."

Imitation Scores

On each trial the subjects' performances were scored in terms of the following imitation response categories: selects box chosen by the model; marches; repeats the phrases, "Here I go," "March, march," "Open box," or "Walk, walk"; aggresses toward the doll; replaces doll on box; imitates the circuitous route to the box.

Some subjects made a verbal response in the appropriate context (for example, at the starting point, on the way to the box, before raising the lid of the container) but did not repeat the model's exact words. These verbal responses were also scored and interpreted as partially imitative behavior..

In order to provide an estimate of the reliability of the experimenter's scoring the performances of 19 subjects were scored independently by two judges who alternated in observing the experimental sessions through a one-way mirror from an adjoining observation room.

RESULTS

Reliability of Observations of Dependency Behavior

The reliability of the observers' behavior ratings was estimated by means of an index of agreement based on the ratio of twice the number of agreements over the combined ratings of the two observers multiplied by 100. Since small time discrepancies, due to inevitable slight asynchronism of the observers' timing devices, were expected, a time discrepancy in rating a given behavior category greater than two 30-second intervals was interpreted as a disagreement.

The interobserver reliabilities for the dependency categories considered separately were as follows: Positive attention seeking, 84%; help seeking, 72%; seeking physical contact, 84%; and seeking proximity, 75%.

Reliability of Imitation Scores

The percentage of agreement in scoring imitative behavior in the experimental sessions is presented in Table 1. Except for *other imitative responses,* the subjects' behavior was scored with high reliability and, even in the letter response category, the scoring discrepancies arose primarily from the experimenter's lack of opportunity to observe some of the behaviors in question rather than from differences of interpretation, for example when the subject made appropriate mouth movements but emitted no sound while marching toward the containers, this partial imitation of the model's verbalizations could not be readily observed by the experimenter (who was at the starting point) but was clearly evident to the rater in the observation room.

Incidental Imitation of Model's Behavior

Since the data disclosed no significant sex differences, the imitation scores for the male and female subgroups were combined in the statistical analyses.

Ninety percent of the subjects in the experimental groups adopted the model's aggressive behavior, 45% imitated the marching, and 28% reproduced the model's verbalizations. In contrast, none of the control subjects behaved aggressively, marched or verbalized, while 75% of the controls and none of the experimental subjects imitated the circuitous route to the containers. Except for replacing the doll on the box, which was performed by most of the experimental and control subjects, there was no overlap in the imitative behavior displayed by the two groups (see Table 2).

Table 1 *Scorer Reliability of Imitative Responses*

Response Category	Percentage Agreement
Aggression	98
Marching	73
Imitative verbal behavior	80
Partially imitative verbal behavior	83
Other imitative responses	50
Replaces doll	99
Circuitous route	96

Table 2   *Amount of Imitative Behavior Displayed Subjects in the Experimental and Control Groups*

Response Category	Experimental Subjects N = 40		Control Subjects N = 8	
	Percentage Imitating	Mean Per Trial	Percentage Imitating	Mean Per Trial
Behaviors of experimental model				
Marching	45	.23	0	0
Verbal responses	28	.10	0	0
Aggression	90	.64	13	.01
Other imitative responses	18	.03	0	0
Partially imitative verbal behavior	43	.11	0	0
Replacing doll	90	.60	75	.77
Behaviors of control model				
Circuitous route	0	0	75	.58
Verbal responses	0	0	13	.10

Note. The mean number of trials for subjects in the experimental group (13.52) and in the control group (15.25) did not differ significantly.

While the control subjects replaced the doll on the box slightly more often than the subjects in the experimental group, this difference tested by means of the median test was not statistically significant ($\chi^2 = 1.49$; $df = 1$). Evidently the response of replacing things, undoubtedly overtrained by parents, is so well established that it occurs independently of the behavior of the model. Since this was clearly a nonimitative response, it was not included in the subsequent analyses.

To the extent that behavior of the sort evoked in this study may be considered an elementary prototype of identification, the results presented in Table 2 add support to the interpretation of identification as a process of incidental imitative learning.

Effects of Nurturance on Imitation

In order to make comparable the imitation scores for the subjects who varied somewhat in the number of trials to criterion, the total imitative responses in a given response category were divided by the number of trials. Since only a small number of subjects in the nonnurturant condition displayed imitative nonaggressive behavior and the distributions of scores were markedly skewed, the sign test was used to estimate the significance of differences between the two experimental groups.

The predicted facilitating effect of social rewards on imitation was essen-

Table 3 *Significance of Differences in Imitative Behavior Exhibited by Subjects in the Nurturant and Nonnurturant Experimental Conditions*

Response Category	Number of Subjects Imitating		p
	Nurturant ($N = 20$)	Nonnurturant ($N = 20$)	
Nonaggressive behaviors	15	7	.04
Marching	13	5	.05
Verbal behavior	9	2	.05
Other imitative responses	6	1	.06
Aggressive behavior	20	16	ns
Partially imitative verbal responses	12	5	.04

Note. The two groups of subjects did not differ in the mean number of trials to criterion. The means for subjects in the nurturant and nonnurturant conditions were 13.75 and 13.30, respectively.

tially confirmed (see Table 3). Subjects who experienced the rewarding interaction with the model marched and verbalized imitatively, and reproduced other responses resembling that of the model to a greater extent than did the subjects who experienced the relatively cold and distant relationship. Aggression, interestingly, was readily imitated by subjects regardless of the quality of the model-child relationship.

Imitation of Discrimination Responses

A three-way analysis of variance (McNemar, 1955, Case XVII) of the trials scores failed to show any significant effects of nurturance or sex of imitator on the imitation of discrimination responses (see Table 4), nor did the two groups or experimental subjects differ significantly in the number of trials in which they imitated the model's choice or in the number of trials to the first imitative discrimination response.

While nurturance did not seem to influence the actual choices the subjects made, it nevertheless affected their predecision behavior. A number of the children displayed considerable conflictful vacillation, often running back and forth between the boxes, prior to making their choice. In the analysis of these data, the vacillation scores were divided by the total number of trials, and the significance of the differences was estimated by means of the sign test since the distribution of scores was markedly skewed. The results of this test revealed that the subjects in the nurturant condition exhibited more conflictful behavior than subjects in the nonnurturant group ($p = .03$). This

Table 4   *Analysis of Variance of Subjects Trials Scores on the Discrimination Learning Tasks*

Source of Variance	df	Variance Estimate	F	p
Sex	1	294	4.20	.10 > p > .05
Nurturance	1	4	< 1	ns
Sex × nurturance	1	158	1.45	ns
Matched pairs	14	70		
Remainder	14	109		

Note. One subject who refused to continue the task before he reached the learning criterion and three subjects who could be run for only 20 trials had to be excluded from this analysis. The results, therefore, are based on 32 matched pairs.

finding is particularly noteworthy considering that one has to counteract a strong nonimitation bias in getting preschool children to follow a leader in a two-choice discrimination problem as evidenced by McDavid's (1959) findings as well as those of the present study (i.e., 75% of the subjects made nonimitative choices on the first trial).

Dependency and Imitation

Correlations between the ratings of dependency behavior and the measures of imitation were calculated separately for the nurturant and nonnurturant experimental subgroups, and where the correlation coefficients did not differ significantly the data were combined. The expected positive relationship between dependency and imitation was only partially supported. High dependent subjects expressed more partially imitative verbal behavior ($r_t = .60$; $p < .05$) and exhibited more predecision conflict on the discrimination task ($r = .26$; $p = .05$) than did subjects who were rated low on dependency.

Dependency and total imitation of nonaggressive responses was positively related for boys ($r_t = .31$) but negatively correlated for girls ($r_t = -.46$). These correlations, however, are not statistically significant. Nor was there any significant relationship between dependency and imitation of aggression ($r = .20$) or discrimination responses ($r = -.03$).

DISCUSSION

The results of this study generally substantiate the hypotheses that children display a good deal of social learning of an incidental imitative sort, and that nurturance is one condition facilitating such imitative learning.

The extent to which the model's behavior had come to influence and control the behavior of subjects is well illustrated by their marching, and by their choice of the circuitous route to the containers. Evidence from the pretesting and from the subjects' behavior during the early discrimination trials revealed that dashing toward the boxes was the dominant response, and that the delay produced by marching or by taking an indirect route that more than doubled the distance to the boxes was clearly incompatible with the subjects' eagerness to get to the containers. Nevertheless, many subjects dutifully followed the example set by the model.

Even more striking was the subjects' imitation of responses performed unwittingly by the model. On one trial with a control subject, for example, the model began to replace the doll on the box at the completion of the trial when suddenly, startled by the realization of the mistake, she quickly replaced the doll on the floor. Sure enough, on the next trial, the subject took the circuitous route, removed the doll gently off the box and, after disposing of the sticker, raised the doll, and then quickly replaced it on the floor reproducing the model's startled reaction as well!

The results for the influence of nurturance on imitation of verbal behavior are in accord with Mower's (1950) autism theory of word learning. Moreover, the obtained significant effect of nurturance on the production of partially imitative verbal responses indicates that nurturance not only facilitates imitation of the specific behaviors displayed by a model but also increases the probability of responses of a whole response class (for example, verbal behavior). These data are essentially in agreement with those of Milner (1951), who found that mothers of children receiving high reading readiness scores were more verbal and affectionately demonstrative in the interactions with their children than were the mothers of subjects in the low reading ability group.

That the incidental cues of the model's behavior may have taken on positive valence and were consequently reproduced by subjects for the mere satisfaction of performing them, is suggested by the fact that children in the nurturant condition not only marched to the containers but also marched in and out of the experimental room and marched about in the anteroom repeating, "March, march, march," etc., while waiting for the next trial. While certain personality patterns may be, thus, incidentally acquired, the stability and persistence of these behaviors in the absence of direct rewards by external agents remains to be studied.

A response cannot be readily imitated unless its components are within the subjects behavior repertoire. The fact that gross motor responses are usually more highly developed than verbal skills in young children may explain why subjects reproduced the model's marching ($p = .05$) and aggression ($p < .001$) to a significantly greater extent than they did her verbal behavior. Indeed several subjects imitated the motor component of speech by performing the appropriate mouth movements but emitted no sound. The greater saliency of the model's motor responses might also be a possible explanation of the obtained differences.

"Identification with the aggressor" (Freud, 1937) or "defensive identification" (Mowrer, 1950), whereby a child presumably transforms himself from object to agent of aggression by adopting the attributes of an aggressive, punitive model so as to allay anxiety, is widely accepted as an explanation of the imitative learning of aggression. The results of the present study, and those of a second experiment now in progress, suggest that the mere observation of aggressive models, regardless of the quality of the model-child relationship, is a sufficient condition for producing imitative aggression in children. A comparative study of subjects' imitation of aggressive models who are feared, who are liked and esteemed, or who are more or less neutral figures would throw some light on whether or not a more parsimonious theory than the one involved in "identification with the aggressor" can explain the modeling process.

Although the results from the present study provide evidence that nurturance promotes incidental imitative learning, the combination of nurturance followed by its withdrawal would be expected, according to the secondary reinforcement theory of imitation, to furnish stronger incentive than nurturance alone for subjects to reproduce a model's behavior. It is also possible that dependency may be essentially unrelated to imitation under conditions of consistent nurturance, but may emerge as a variable facilitating imitation under conditions where social reinforcers are temporarily withdrawn.

The experiment reported in this paper focused on immediate imitation in the presence of the model. A more crucial test of the transmission of behavior through the process of social imitation involves the generalization of imitative responses to new situations in which the model is absent. A study of this type, involving the delayed imitation of both male and female aggressive models, is currently under way.

SUMMARY

The present study was primarily designed to test the hypotheses that children would learn to imitate behavior exhibited by an experimenter-model, and that a nurturant interaction between the model and the child would enhance the secondary reward properties of the model and thus facilitate such imitative learning.

Forty-eight preschool children performed a diverting two-choice discrimination problem with a model who displayed fairly explicit, although functionless, behaviors during the trials. With the experimental subjects the model marched, emitted specific verbal responses, and aggressed toward dolls located on the discrimination boxes; with the controls the model walked to the boxes choosing a highly circuitous route and behaved in a nonaggressive fashion. Half the subjects in the experimental and control groups experienced a rewarding interaction with the model prior to the imitative learning while the remaining subjects experienced a cold and nonnurturant relationship.

The following results were obtained:

1. The experimental and the control subjects not only reproduced behaviors resembling that of their model but also, except for one response category, did not overlap in the types of imitative responses they displayed.

2. The predicted facilitating effect of social rewards on imitation was also confirmed, the only exception being for aggression, which was readily imitated by the subjects regardless of the quality of the model-child relationship.

3. Although nurturance was not found to influence the rate of imitative discrimination learning, subjects in the nurturant condition exhibited significantly more predecision conflict behavior than did subjects in the nonnurturant group.

REFERENCES

Brofenbrenner, U. Freudian theories of identification and their derivatives. *Child Develpm.*, 1960, **31**, 15–40.

Cairns, R. B. The influence of dependency-anxiety on the effectiveness of social reinforcers. Unpublished doctoral dissertation, Stanford University, 1959.

Church, R. M. Transmission of learned behavior between rats. *J. abnorm. soc. Psychol.*, 1957, **54**, 163–165.

Easterbrook, J. A. The effect of emotion on cue utilization and the organization of behavior. *Psychol. Rev.*, 1959, **66**, 183–201.

Endsley, R. C., & Hartup, W. W. Dependency and performance by preschool children on a socially reinforced task. *Amer. Psychologist*, 1960, **15**, 399. (Abstract)

Freud, Anna. *The ego and the mechanisms of defence.* London: Hogarth, 1937.

Jackubczak, L. F., & Walters, R. H. Suggestibility as dependency behavior. *J. abnorm. soc. Psychol.*, 1959, **59**, 102–107.

Kagan, J., & Mussen, P. H. Dependency themes on the TAT and group conformity. *J. consult. Psychol.*, 1956, **20**, 29–32.

Logan, F., Olmsted, D. L., Rosner, B. S. Schwartz, R. D., & Stevens, C. M. *Behavior theory and social science.* New Haven: Yale Univer. Press, 1955.

Maccoby, Eleanor E. Role-taking in childhood and its consequences for social learning. *Child Develpm.*, 1959, **30**, 239–252.

Maccoby, Eleanor E., & Wilson, W. C. Identification and observational learning from films. *J. abnorm. soc. Psychol.*, 1957, **55**, 76–87.

McDavid, J. W. Imitative behavior in preschool children. *Psychol. Monogr.*, 1959, **73**, 16 (Whole No. 486).

McGeoch, J. A., & Irion, A. L. *The psychology of human learning.* New York: Longmans, Green, 1952.

McNemar, Q. *Psychological statistics.* New York: Wiley, 1955.

Miller, N. E., & Dollard, J. *Social learning and imitation.* New Haven: Yale Univer. Press, 1941.

Milner, Esther. A study of the relationship between reading readiness and patterns of parent-child interaction. *Child Develpm.*, 1951, **22**, 95–112.

Mowrer, O. H. Identification: A link between learning theory and psychotherapy. In *Learning theory and personality dynamics.* New York: Ronald, 1950. Pp. 573–616.

Mussen, P., & Distler, L. M. Masculinity, identification, and father-son relationships. *J. abnorm. soc. Psychol.,* 1959, **59,** 350–356.

Mussen, P., & Distler, L. M. Child-rearing antecedents of masculine identification in kindergarten boys. *Child Develpm.,* 1960, **31,** 89–100.

Payne, D. E., & Mussen, P. H. Parent-child relationships and father identification among adolescent boys. *J. abnorm. soc. Psychol.,* 1956, **52,** 358–362.

Sears, Pauline S. Child-rearing factors related to playing of sex-typed roles. *Amer. Psychologist,* 1953, **8,** 431. (Abstract)

Sears, R. R. Identification as a form of behavioral development. In D. B. Harris (Ed.), *The concept of development.* Minneapolis: Univer. Minnesota Press, 1957. Pp. 149–161.

Sears, R. R., Maccoby, Eleanor E., & Levin, H. *Patterns of child rearing,* Evanston: Row, Peterson, 1957.

Warden, C. J., Fjeld, H. A., & Koch, A. M. Imitative behavior in cebus and rhesus monkeys. *J. genet. Psychol.,* 1940, **56,** 311–322.

Whiting, J. W. M., & Child, I. L. *Child training and personality.* New Haven: Yale Univer. Press, 1953.

Wilson, W. C. Imitation and learning of incidental cues by preschool children. *Child Develpm.,* 1958, **29,** 393–397.

25. SEX-ROLE AND PARENTAL IDENTIFICATION

David B. Lynn

It is doubtful that psychological theories have fully posed much less resolved the question of the extent of sex differences in personality development. In this connection Sarason *et al.* comment: "No one to our knowledge has denied they [such sex differences] are pervasive, and yet the problem of degree of pervasiveness has not been critically examined despite its implications for theory, methodology, and the direction of future research" (23, p. 260).

A perusal of the journals shows that many studies, which include both male and female *S*s in the sample, do not make provisions for sex differences in the hypotheses. Where sex differences are found they are, consequently, rationalized *post facto*. Moreover, often no statistical analysis of sex differences is performed, despite their importance in psychological processes.

This paper presents a theoretical formulation which postulates basic sex differences in the *nature* of sex-role and parental identification, as well as basic differences in the *process of achieving* such identification. The developmental processes described are considered neither inevitable nor universal. If they are appropriate to the U.S. culture today, they may, nevertheless, be inappropriate for many other cultures and for a significantly altered U.S. culture of the future. This formulation refers to the "typical" pattern, although recognizing that a "typical" pattern, if not a myth, is at least an exception. Research findings considered relevant to this formulation are reviewed.

Before developing this formulation, let us briefly define identification as it is used here. *Sex-role identification* refers to the internalization of the role considered appropriate to a given sex and to the unconscious reactions characteristic of that role. *Parental identification* refers to the internalization of personality characteristics of one's own parent and to unconscious reactions similar to that parent. Thus, theoretically, an individual might be well identified with the appropriate sex-role generally and yet poorly identified with his same-sex parent specifically. This differentiation also allows for the converse circumstances wherein a person is well identified with his same-sex parent specifically and yet poorly identified with the appropriate sex-role generally. In such an instance the parent with whom the individual is well identified is himself poorly identified with the appropriate sex-role. An

Reprinted from *Child Development*, 1962, **33**, 555–564, with permission of the author and the Society for Research in Child Development.

example might be a girl who is well identified with her own mother, but the mother is identified with the masculine rather than the feminine role. Such a girl, therefore, through her identification with her mother, is poorly identified with the feminine role.

In a previous paper (17) the author differentiated the concept of *sex-role identification* from *sex-role preference* and *sex-role adoption*. The present formulation is a departure from that previous paper and also shares various features in common with others (2, 3, 11, 24).

This formulation uses a hypothesis from the previous paper as a postulate from which to deduce a number of new hypotheses. Hopefully, this formulation will offer a unified theoretical framework consistent with a number of varied findings concerning sex differences.

The aspects of the previous formulation pertinent to the present one are summarized as follows:

Both male and female infants were hypothesized to learn to identify with the mother. Boys, but not girls, must shift from this initial identification with the mother to masculine identification. The girl has the same-sex parental model for identification (the mother) with her more than the boy has the same-sex model (the father) with him. Much incidental learning takes place from the girl's contact with her mother which she can apply directly in her life.

However, despite the shortage of male models, a somewhat stereotyped and conventional masculine role is nonetheless spelled out for the boys, e.g., by his mother and women teachers in the absence of his father and male teachers. In this connection a study by Sherriffs and Jarrett (28) indicated that men and women share the same stereotypes about the two sexes. Through the reinforcement of the culture's highly developed system of rewards for indications of masculinity and punishment for signs of femininity, the boy's early learned identification with the mother eventually weakens and becomes more or less replaced by the later learned identification with a culturally defined, somewhat stereotyped masculine role. *"Consequently, males tend to identify with a cultural stereotype of the masculine role, whereas females tend to identify with aspects of their own mothers' role specifically"* (17, p. 130). This hypothesis was generally supported by the research findings reviewed (9, 16).

This hypothesis is not meant to minimize the role of the father in the development of males. Studies of father-absence suggest that the presence of the father in the home is of great importance for boys (1, 18, 25). It is beyond the scope of this paper to elaborate on the role of the father, but it is our position that it has a very different place in the development of the boy's masculine-role identification than does the mother in the girl's mother identification. The father, as a model for the boy, may be thought of as analogous to a map showing the major outline but lacking most details, whereas the mother, as a model for the girl, might be thought of as a detailed map. The father, of course, serves many other functions besides that of model for the boy's masculine-role identification. He may, for example, reinforce the boy's masculine strivings and stimulate his drive to achieve masculine-role identification. Because fathers typically do spend so much time away from home and, even when home, usually do not participate in as many intimate activities with the child as does the mother (e.g., preparation for bed), it is probably true that the time spent with the father takes on much importance in the boy's identification development.

Although recognizing the contribution of the father in the identification of males and the general cultural influences in the identification of females, it nevertheless seems meaningful, for simplicity in developing this formulation, to refer to *masculine-role identification* in males as distinguished from *mother identification* in females.

It is postulated that the task of achieving these separate kinds of identification for each sex requires separate methods of learning. These separate identification tasks seem to parallel the two kinds of learning tasks differentiated by Woodworth and Schlosberg: the *problem* and the *lesson.* "With a problem to master the learner must explore the situation and find the goal before his task is fully presented. In the case of a lesson, the problem-solving phase is omitted or at least minimized, as we see when the human subject is instructed to memorize this poem or that list of nonsense syllables, to examine these pictures with a view to recognizing them later. . . ." (36, p. 529). The task of achieving mother identification for the female is considered roughly parallel to the learning *lesson,* and the task of achieving masculine-role identification for the male is considered roughly parallel to the learning *problem.*

It is assumed that finding the goal does not constitute a major problem for the girl in learning her mother identification lesson. Since the girl, unlike the boy, need not shift from the initial mother identification and since she typically has the mother with her a relatively large proportion of the time, it is postulated that the question of the object of identification (the mother) for the girl seldom arises. She learns the mother identification lesson in the context of an intimate personal relationship with the mother, partly by imitation, which as used here includes covert practice of the actions characteristic of the mother (19). She also learns the mother identification lesson through the mother's selective reinforcement of mother-similar tendencies in the girl. Hartup (12) did a relevant study concerning parental imitation in children aged 3 to 5 in which he correlated sex-role preference in the Brown It Scale (2) with the degree to which the S's doll play showed the child doll imitating the same-sex parental doll. The results suggested to Hartup that girls become feminine partly as a result of a tendency to imitate their mothers more than their fathers and that the acquisition of masculinity by boys appears to be independent of the tendency to imitate the father more than the mother.

Similarly, abstracting principles defining mother identification is not considered a concern for the girls. Any bit of behavior on the mother's part may be of potential importance in learning the mother identification lesson, and therefore the girl need not abstract principles defining the feminine role. It is not principles defining the feminine role that the girl need learn, but rather an identification with her specific mother.

It is assumed, on the other hand, that finding the goal *does* constitute a major problem for the boy in solving the masculine-role identification problem. There is evidence to indicate that between two-thirds and three-fourths of children by the age of 3 are able to make the basic distinction between sexes (6, 7, 26). When the boy begins to be aware that he does not belong in the same sex-category as the mother, he must then find the proper sex-role identification goal. Hartley says, of the identification problem that faces the boy, ". . . the desired behavior is rarely defined positively as something the child *should* do, but rather negatively as something he should *not* do or be—anything, that is, that the parent or other people regard as 'sissy.' Thus, very early in life the boy must either stumble on the right path or bear repeated punishment without warning when he accidentally enters into the wrong ones" (11, p. 458). From these largely negative admonishings, often made by women and often without the benefit of the presence of a male model during most of his waking hours, the boy must learn to set the masculine role as his goal. He must also restructure the admonishings, often negatively made and given in many contexts, in order to abstract the principles defining the masculine role.

One of the basic steps in this formulation can now be taken. It is assumed that, in learning the appropriate identification, each sex is thereby acquiring separate methods of learning which are subsequently applied to learning tasks generally. The little girl acquires a learning method which primarily involves: (*a*) a personal relationship and (*b*) imitation rather than restructuring the field and abstracting principles. On the other hand, the little boy acquires a different learning method which primarily involves: (*a*) defining the goal; (*b*) restructuring the field; and (*c*) abstracting principles.

HYPOTHESES

The following hypotheses are considered to follow from the above formulation:

1. It is in the context of a close personal relationship with the mother that the little girl learns the mother identification lesson. She is reinforced by appropriate rewards for signs that she is learning this lesson. Since the little girl is rewarded in the context of the personal relationship with her mother, maintaining the rewarding relationship with her mother should acquire strong secondary-drive characteristics. By generalization, the need for affiliation in other situations should also have strong secondary-drive characteristics for the girl.

The boy, relative to the girl, has little opportunity to receive rewards for modeling an adult male in a close personal relationship. He receives his rewards for learning the appropriate principles of masculine-role identification as they are abstracted from many contexts. Therefore, the need for affiliation in general should not acquire as much strength as a secondary drive for males as for females. *Consequently, females will tend to demonstrate greater need for affiliation than males.*

2. In learning to identify with the mother, any bit of behavior on the mother's part might be of potential importance in the girl's perception of her. The mother identification lesson does not require that the girl deviate from the given, but rather that she learn the lesson as presented.

For the boys, solving the problem of masculine-role identification must be accomplished without adequate exposure to adult male models. It must be solved by using the admonishings, such as "don't be a sissy," which, occurring in many contexts, serve as guides in defining the masculine role. To solve the masculine-role identification problem the boy must restructure the field. Therefore, the masculine learning method *does* include restructuring the field as a learning principle. *Consequently, females tend to be more dependent than males on the external context of a perceptual situation and hesitate to deviate from the given.*

3. In the process of solving the masculine-role identification problem, the male acquires a method of learning which should be applicable in solving other problems. On the other hand, the feminine learning method, emerging from the process of learning the mother identification lesson, is not well geared to problem-solving. *Consequently, males tend to surpass females in problem-solving skills.*

4. The masculine learning method is postulated to include abstracting principles, whereas the feminine one is not. The tendency to abstract principles should generalize to other problems in addition to the problem of achieving masculine-role identification. It should, for example, generalize to the acquisition of moral standards. If one is very responsive to the moral standards of others, it is relatively unnecessary to internalize standards. If one, on the other hand, tends to learn moral standards by abstracting moral principles rather than being highly responsive to the standards of others, then one *does* need to internalize one's standards. If one is to stick by one's principles, they had better be internalized. It is postulated that males more than females will tend to learn moral standards by abstracting moral principles. *Consequently, males tend to be more concerned with internalized moral standards than females.*

5. Conversely, the feminine learning method indicates that one learns by imitation through a relationship whereas the masculine learning method does not. The little girl, it was assumed, tends to learn the lesson as given, without restructuring. Such a learning method should generalize to the

acquisition of standards. *Consequently, females tend to be more receptive to the standards of others than males.*

RELEVANT FINDINGS

Let us now see how consistently these hypotheses correspond to previous findings and whether this formulation helps clarify and unify the data.

Hypothesis 1, predicting that females will demonstrate greater need for affiliation than males, is supported by a study by Edwards (4) which showed that women have significantly higher means than men on affiliation on the Edwards Personal Preference Schedule (EPPS).

McClelland, Atkinson, Clark, and Lowell (20) found that college women did not show an increase in achievement motive scores as a result of the arousal instruction, based on reference to leadership and intelligence, effective for male college students. Women did obtain higher scores, however, when the dimension of "achievement" was social acceptability.

Lansky, Crandall, Kagan, and Baker (15), in a study of children aged 13 to 18, used the French Insight Test (5) to measure affiliation. The French test, as used in this study, consisted of 20 items describing a characteristic behavior of a boy (girl), e.g., "Tom never joins clubs or social groups." For each item the S answers these three questions: (a) what is the boy (girl) like? (b) what does he (she) want to have or do? and (c) what are the results of his (her) behavior apt to be? Girls were significantly higher than boys on preoccupation with *affiliation,* which was scored when the goal is to be liked or accepted by others or to be part of a group.

When Harris (10) repeated Symonds' 1935 studies (30, 31) of having adolescents rank interests, he found that girls persist in their greater interest in social relations than boys. When Winkler (34) analyzed the replies of children aged 7 to 16, he found that girls seemed more interested than boys in social relationships, especially face-to-face contacts. The girl's early preoccupation with affiliation was noted by Goodenough (8) who found that nursery school girls drew more pictures of persons and mentioned persons more often than boys.

Thus, these data are consistent with hypothesis 1 that females will demonstrate greater need for affiliation than males.

Evidence concerning hypothesis 2, predicting that females tend to be more dependent than males on the external context of a perceptual situation and will hesitate to deviate from the given, is furnished by Witkin, Lewis, Hertzman, Machover, Meissner, and Wapner (35). They found that female Ss were more readily influenced by misleading cues than were male Ss and thus were higher in "perceptual-field dependence."

Additional evidence concerning this hypothesis is found in a study by Wallach and Caron (33) with sixth-grade school children. These children were given a concept attainment session in which to establish criteria concerning geometric forms with certain characteristics. A test session followed in which the Ss judged whether figures of varying deviation from the standard were similar to it. It was found that girls tolerated less deviation than males by every index, thus agreeing with the hypothesis that females more than males hesitate to "move away" from the given. Both studies are in agreement with hypothesis 2.

Studies reported by Sweeney (29) are relevant to hypothesis 3 that males generally surpass females in problem-solving skills. Most of the studies reported by Sweeney support this hypothesis. Moreover, he reported experiments of his own which demonstrate that men solve certain classes of problems with greater facility than do women, even when differences in intellectual aptitude, special knowledge or training, and special abilities are controlled. Sweeney obtained scores on the College Board Scholastic Aptitude test for 130 men and 139 women to whom McNemar (21) had given four tests of logical reasoning: False Premises, Essential Operations, Syllogisms, and Problem Solving. Significant differences favoring the men were found on all four of these tests for 100 pairs who had been matched in verbal aptitude scores. For 90 pairs matched in mathematical aptitude and 69 pairs matched both in verbal and mathematical aptitude, a difference was obtained only for Problem Solving, a test which essentially involves arithmetic reasoning. In Sweeney's most elaborate experiment, large samples of men and women were given a wide variety of problems. Significant sex differences were obtained for groups matched in general intelligence, spatial ability, mechanical comprehension, mathematics achievement, or the amount of training in mathematics. In general, the results confirmed the hypothesis that sex differences favoring men will occur in problems which involve difficulties in restructuring, but not in similar problems which involve no such difficulties.

Milton's study (22) with college students is pertinent to hypothesis 3 concerning sex differences in problem-solving skills. In this study the Terman-Miles M-F test (32) was the primary index of sex-role typing, although other M-F questionnaires were also employed. Two types of problem-solving skill, restructuring and straightforward solution, were employed, half requiring numerical solutions and half nonnumerical. In general, the results indicate that there is a positive relation between the degree of masculine sex-role typing and problem-solving skill both across sexes and within a sex. When this relation is accounted for, the difference between men and women in problem-solving performance is diminished.

Thus, these studies are consistent with hypothesis 3 that males generally surpass females in problem-solving skills. Moreover, Milton's study also suggests that these differences are accounted for in the typical sex-role development of each sex.

Hypothesis 4, suggesting that males tend to be more concerned with internalized moral standards than females, is consistent with findings in the previously mentioned study of children aged 13 to 18 by Lansky, Crandall, Kagan, and Baker (15). The Ss were given a story completion test which was designed to elicit responses regarding severity of moral standards and defenses against guilt following transgression of such standards. *Severity of moral standards* was rated for the degree to which the hero (heroine) punished himself, consciously or unconsciously, for his actions. The boys scored higher than girls on this variable. This finding is considered to support hypothesis 4 in that the *severity of moral standards* was scored when the hero (heroine) punished himself, thus implying that the standards are internalized.

Data from two national sample interview studies of adolescents, reported by Douvan (3), have relevance here. In answer to two questions to detect self-awareness, boys showed greater concern with establishing satisfactory internal standards and personal control than girls.

Findings in Douvan's studies are also in agreement with hypothesis 5 that females will be more receptive to the standards of others than males. Douvan found that girls are more likely to show an unquestioned acceptance of parental regulation. Koch (13, 14), along with Sheehy (27), found girls to be more obedient and amenable to social controls than boys. Thus, these studies seem consistent with hypothesis 5.

In general, the hypotheses that were generated by the theoretical formulation seem consistent with the data. Thus, by postulating that separate learning methods for the two sexes are derived in the process of acquiring appropriate identification, one can formulate hypotheses which are consistent with very diverse findings ranging from the males' superior problem-solving skill to the females' greater need for affiliation. It is not assumed that this formulation, in and of itself, adequately accounts for these diverse findings even though it is generally consistent with them. It is beyond the scope of this paper to attempt to integrate motivation into the formulation, or the psychological implications of anatomical and physiological differences, or adequately to place the role of the father in the development of identification in each sex. These steps, and others, would be necessary adequately to account for these findings. However, it is felt that a formulation along the lines presented here may prove to have a place in more elaborate theories of identification development and may prove helpful in making more sensitive hypotheses concerning psychological sex differences.

SUMMARY

The purpose of this paper is to present a theoretical formulation which postulates basic sex differences in the *nature* of sex-role and parental identification, as well as basic differences in the *process of achieving* such identification. There was a differentiation made between *sex-role identification* and *parental identification*.

The theoretical formulation in this paper used a hypothesis from a previous one (17) as a postulate from which to derive a number of new hypotheses. That hypothesis suggested that males tend to identify with a cultural stereotype of the masculine role, whereas females tend to identify with aspects of their own mothers' role specifically. For simplicity this paper refers to *masculine-role identification* in males as distinguished from *mother identification* in females.

This formulation adopted the distinction made by Woodworth and Schlosberg (36) between two kinds of learning tasks, viz., the problem and the lesson. This distinction was used in describing the separate task assigned each sex in learning the appropriate identification. It was further assumed that, in learning the appropriate identification, each sex acquires separate methods of learning which are subsequently applied to learning tasks generally. In learning the mother identification lesson, the little girl acquires a learning method which primarily involves: (*a*) a personal relationship and (*b*) imitation rather than restructuring the field and abstracting principles. In solving the masculine-role identification problem, the boy acquires a learning method which primarily involves: (*a*) finding the goal; (*b*) restructuring the field; and (*c*) abstracting principles.

By assuming that these learning methods are applicable to learning tasks generally, the following hypotheses were derived:

1. Females will demonstrate greater need for affiliation than males.

2. Females are more dependent than males on the external context of a perceptual situation and will hesitate to deviate from the given.

3. Males generally surpass females in problem-solving skills.

4. Males tend to be more concerned with internalized moral standards than females.

5. Females tend to be more receptive to the standards of others than males.

These hypotheses were in general agreement with the research findings which were reviewed.

REFERENCES

1. Bach, G. R. Father-fantasies and father-typing in father-separated children. *Child Develpm.*, 1946, **17**, 63–80.
2. Brown, D. G. Sex-role preference in young children. *Psychol. Monogr.*, 1956, **70**, No. 14 (Whole No. 421).
3. Douvan, E. Independence and identity in adolescence. *Children*, 1957, **4**, 186–190.
4. Edwards, A. L. *Edwards Personal Preference Schedule.* Psychological Corp., 1959.
5. French, E. G. Development of a measure of complex motivation. In J. W. Atkinson (Ed.), *Motives in fantasy, action, and society: a method of assessment and study.* Princeton: Van Nostrand, 1958. Pp. 242–248.
6. Gesell, A., *et al. The first five years of life.* New York: Harper, 1940.

7. Gesell, A., Ilg, F. L., et al. *Infant and child in the culture of today.* New York: Harper, 1943.

8. Goodenough, E. W. Interest in persons as an aspect of sex differences in the early years. *Genet. Psychol. Monogr.,* 1957, **55,** 287–323.

9. Gray, S. W., & Klaus, R. The assessment of parental identification. *Genet. Psychol. Monogr.,* 1956, **54,** 87–109.

10. Harris, D. B. Sex differences in the life problems and interests of adolescents, 1935 and 1957. *Child Develpm.,* 1959, **30,** 453–459.

11. Hartley, R. E. Sex-role pressures and the socialization of the male child. *Psychol. Rep.,* 1959, **5,** 457–468.

12. Hartup, W. W. Some correlates of parental imitation in young children. *Child Develpm.,* 1962, **33,** 85–96.

13. Koch, H. L. Some personality correlates of sex, sibling position, and sex of sibling among five- and six-year old children. *Genet. Psychol. Monogr.,* 1955, **52,** 3–51.

14. Koch, H. L. The relation of certain family constellation characteristics and attitudes of children toward adults. *Child Develpm.,* 1955, **26,** 13–40.

15. Lansky, L. M., Crandall, V. J., Kagan, J., & Baker, C. T. Sex differences in aggression and its correlates in middle-class adolescents. *Child Develpm.,* 1961, **32,** 45–58.

16. Lazowick, L. M. On the nature of identification. *J. abnorm. soc. Psychol.,* 1955, **51,** 175–183.

17. Lynn, D. B. A note on sex differences in the development of masculine and feminine identification. *Psychol. Rev.,* 1959, **66,** 126–135.

18. Lynn, D. B., & Sawrey, W. L. The effects of father-absence on Norwegian boys and girls. *J. abnorm. soc. Psychol.,* 1959, **59,** 258–261.

19. Maccoby, E. E. Role-taking in childhood and its consequences for social learning. *Child Develpm.,* 1959, **30,** 239–252.

20. McClelland, D. C., Atkinson, J. W., Clark, R. A., & Lowell, E. L. *The achievement motive.* New York: Appleton-Century-Crofts, 1953.

21. McNemar, O. W. Word association, methods of deduction and induction, and reactions to set in good and poor reasoners. *Stanford Univer. Depart. of Psychol., Tech. Rep.* 1954, No. 2.

22. Milton, G. A. The effects of sex-role identification upon problem-solving skill. *J. abnorm. soc. Psychol.,* 1957, **55,** 208–212.

23. Sarason, S. B., Davidson, K. S., Lighthall, F. F., Waite, R. R., & Ruebush, B. K. *Anxiety in elementary school children.* New York: Wiley, 1960.

24. Sears, R. R., Maccoby, E. E., & Levin, H. *Patterns of child rearing.* Evanston: Row, Peterson, 1957.

25. Sears, R. R., Pintler, M. H., & Sears, P. S. Effect of father separation on pre-school children's doll play aggression. *Child Develpm.,* 1946, **17,** 219–243.

26. Seward, G. H. *Sex and the social order.* New York: McGraw-Hill, 1946.

27. Sheehy, L. M. *A study of preadolescents by means of a personality inventory.* Catholic Univer. of America, 1938.

28. Sherriffs, A. C., & Jarrett, R. F. Sex differences in attitudes about sex differences. *J. Psychol.,* 1953, **35,** 161–168.

29. Sweeney, E. J. Sex differences in problem solving. *Stanford Univer. Depart. of Psychol., Tech. Rep.* 1953, No. 1.

30. Symonds, P. M. Life interests and problems of adolescents. *Sch. Rev.,* 1936, **44,** 506–518.

31. Symonds, P. M. Sex differences in the life problems and interests of adolescents. *Sch. & Soc.,* 1936, **43,** 751–752.

32. Terman, L. M., & Miles, C. C. *Sex and personality.* New York: McGraw-Hill, 1936.

33. Wallach, M. A., & Caron, A. J. Attribute criteriality and sex-linked conservatism as determinants of psychological similarity. *J. abnorm. soc. Psychol.*, 1959, **59**, 43–50.

34. Winkler, J. B. Age trends and sex differences in the wishes, identifications, activities and fears of children. *Child Develpm.*, 1949, **20**, 191–200.

35. Witkin, H. A., Lewis, H. B., Hertzman, M., Machover, K., Meissner, P. B., & Wapner, S. *Personality through perception.* New York: Harper, 1954.

36. Woodworth, R. S., & Schlosberg, H. *Experimental psychology.* New York: Holt, 1954.

Section V
Social Class

Introduction

Differences among children related to their social class backgrounds were examined intensively in the early days of child development research. Social class of subjects was (and still is) required information in any research report. Intelligence, language development, delinquency, physical health, and parental behavior are variables which have been found to be social-class linked. Although the general interest in social class differences has waned, much attention continues to be focused on these differences in the area of parent-child relations.

The ease with which the social class variable can be assessed probably accounted in part for its wide use. Although a number of factors (area of residence, education of father, type of house) have been used to determine social class membership, father's occupation alone is a fairly accurate index. The fact that there were marked differences among social classes in the 1920's and 1930's in this country led to the success with which this variable differentiated among children on a number of dimensions.

In a careful summary of the parent-child literature, Bronfenbrenner (1958) has shown that differences among social classes in child-rearing attitudes and practices have diminished in the past twenty years. The blurring of social class distinctions can be attributed to many factors: rise in economic conditions, higher general educational levels attained, and smaller income differences between white and blue collar workers.

The selections included in this section deal with several aspects of parent-child relations. Kohn (Selection No. 26) attributes the differences among social classes in child-rearing practices to differences in values held. These in turn are explained by conditions of life of the various social classes. The three remaining studies help to explain differences in behavior and level of functioning between children of the lower and the middle social class. Based on controlled observations, Walters, Connor, and Zunich (Selection No. 27) found marked differences between lower- and middle-class mothers, especially with regard to sheer amount of contact between mother and child. The general area of coerciveness and restrictiveness was differentiated between middle- and lower-class mothers in the Waters and Crandall study (Selection No. 28). As compared with lower-class boys, Rosen (Selection No. 29) found that boys from the middle class perceived their fathers as more competent, emotionally secure, accepting, and interested in their child's performance. In line with our discussion of identification and children's perception of parents in Section IV, Rosen's findings suggest stronger identification among middle-class than lower-class boys. Theoretically, this should lead to stronger conscience development.

The greater restrictiveness of the lower-class mother should be frustration-producing and lead to hostility and aggression. Also, since there is some evidence that democracy in the home and amount of parent-child contact encourage creativity and intellectual functioning, autocratic attitudes and restrictiveness of the lower-class home may help to account for class differences in intelligence and achievement.

References

Bronfenbrenner, U. Socialization and social class through time and space. In Eleanor E. Maccoby, T. M. Newcomb, & E. L. Hartley (Ed.), *Readings in social psychology.* New York: Holt, 1958. Pp. 400–425.

26. SOCIAL CLASS AND PARENT-CHILD

RELATIONSHIPS: AN INTERPRETATION

Melvin L. Kohn

This essay is an attempt to interpret, from a sociological perspective, the effects of social class upon parent-child relationships. Many past discussions of the problem seem somehow to lack this perspective, even though the problem is one of profound importance for sociology. Because most investigators have approached the problem from an interest in psychodynamics, rather than social structure, they have largely limited their attention to a few specific techniques used by mothers in the rearing of infants and very young children. They have discovered, *inter alia,* that social class has a decided bearing on which techniques parents use. But, since they have come at the problem from this perspective, their interest in social class has not gone beyond its effects for this very limited aspect of parent-child relationships.

The present analysis conceives the problem of social class and parent-child relationships as an instance of the more general problem of the effects of social structure upon behavior. It starts with the assumption that social class has proved to be so useful a concept because it refers to more than simply educational level, or occupation, or any of the large number of correlated variables. It is so useful because it captures the reality that the intricate interplay of all these variables creates different basic conditions of life at different levels of the social order. Members of different social classes, by virtue of enjoying (or suffering) different conditions of life, come to see the world differently—to develop different conceptions of social reality, different aspirations and hopes and fears, different conceptions of the desirable.

The last is particularly important for present purposes, for from people's conceptions of the desirable—and particularly from their conceptions of what characteristics are desirable in children—one can discern their objectives in child-rearing. Thus, conceptions of the desirable—that is, values—become the key concept for this analysis, the bridge between position in the larger social structure and the behavior of the individual. The intent of the analysis is to trace the effects of social class position on parental values and the effects of values on behavior.

Since this approach differs from analyses focused on social class differences in the use of particular child-rearing techniques, it will be necessary to

Reprinted with abridgement from the *American Journal of Sociology,* 1963, **68**, 471–480, with permission of the author and the University of Chicago Press.

re-examine earlier formulations from the present perspective. Then three questions will be discussed, bringing into consideration the limited available data that are relevant: What differences are there in the values held by parents of different social classes? What is there about the conditions of life distinctive of these classes that might explain the differences in their values? What consequences do these differences in values have for parents' relationships with their children?

SOCIAL CLASS

Social classes will be defined as aggregates of individuals who occupy broadly similar positions in the scale of prestige. In dealing with the research literature, we shall treat occupational position (or occupational position as weighted somewhat by education) as a serviceable index of social class for urban American society. And we shall adopt the model of social stratification implicit in most research, that of four relatively discrete classes: a "lower class" of unskilled manual workers, a "working class" of manual workers in semiskilled and skilled occupations, a "middle class" of white-collar workers and professionals, and an "elite," differentiated from the middle class not so much in terms of occupation as of wealth and lineage.

Almost all the empirical evidence, including that from our own research, stems from broad comparisons of the middle and working class. Thus we shall have little to say about the extremes of the class distribution. Furthermore, we shall have to act as if the middle and working classes were each homogeneous. They are not, even in terms of status considerations alone. There is evidence, for example, that within each broad social class, variations in parents' values quite regularly parallel gradations of social status. Moreover, the classes are heterogeneous with respect to other factors that affect parents' values, such as religion and ethnicity. But even when all such considerations are taken into account, the empirical evidence clearly shows that being on one side or the other of the line that divides manual from nonmanual workers has profound consequences for how one rears one's children.

STABILITY AND CHANGE

Any analysis of the effects of social class upon parent-child relationships should start with Urie Bronfenbrenner's analytic review of the studies that had been conducted in this country during the twenty-five years up to 1958. From the seemingly contradictory findings of a number of studies, Bronfenbrenner discerned not choas but orderly change: there have been changes in the child-training techniques employed by middle-class parents in the past quarter-century; similar changes have been taking place in the working class, but working-class parents have consistently lagged behind by a few years; thus, while middle-class parents of twenty-five years ago were more "restrictive" than were working-class parents, today the middle-class parents are more "permissive"; and the gap between the classes seems to be narrowing.

It must be noted that these conclusions are limited by the questions Bronfenbrenner's predecessors asked in their research. The studies deal largely with a few particular techniques of child-rearing, especially those involved in caring for infants and very young children, and say very little about parents' over-all relationships with their children, particularly as the children grow older. There is clear evidence that the past quarter-century has seen change, even faddism, with respect to the use of breast-feeding or bottle-feeding, scheduling or not scheduling, spanking or isolating. But when we generalize from these specifics to talk of a change from "restrictive" to "permissive" practices—or, worse yet, of a change from "restrictive" to "permissive" parent-child relationships—we impute to them a far greater importance than they probably have, either to parents or to children.

There is no evidence that recent faddism in child-training techniques is symptomatic of profound changes in the relations of parents to children in either social class. In fact, as Bronfenbrenner notes, what little evidence we do have points in the opposite direction: the over-all quality of parent-child relationships does not seem to have changed substantially in either class. In all probability, parents have changed techniques in service of much the same values, and the changes have been quite specific. These changes must be explained, but the enduring characteristics are probably even more important.

Why the changes? Bronfenbrenner's interpretation is ingenuously simple. He notes that the changes in techniques employed by middle-class parents have closely paralleled those advocated by presumed experts, and he concludes that middle-class parents have changed their practices *because* they are responsive to changes in what the experts tell them is right and proper. Working-class parents, being less educated and thus less directly responsive to the media of communication, followed behind only later.

Bronfenbrenner is almost undoubtedly right in asserting that middle-class parents have followed the drift of presumably expert opinion. But why have they done so? It is not sufficient to assume that the explanation lies in their greater degree of education. This might explain why middle-class parents are substantially more likely than are working-class parents to *read* books and articles on child-rearing, as we know they do. But they need not *follow* the experts' advice. We know from various studies of the mass media that people generally search for confirmation of their existing beliefs and practices and tend to ignore what contradicts them.

From all the evidence at our disposal, it looks as if middle-class parents not only read what the experts have to say but also search out a wide variety of other sources of information and advice: they are far more likely than are working-class parents to discuss child-rearing with friends and neighbors, to consult physicians on these matters, to attend Parent-Teacher Association meetings, to discuss the child's behavior with his teacher. Middle-class parents seem to regard child-rearing as more problematic than do working-class parents. This can hardly be a matter of education alone. It must be rooted more deeply in the conditions of life of the two social classes.

Everything about working-class parents' lives—their comparative lack of education, the nature of their jobs, their greater attachment to the extended family—conduces to their retaining familiar methods. Furthermore, even should they be receptive to change, they are less likely than are middle-class parents to find the experts' writings appropriate to their wants, for the experts predicate their advice on middle-class values. Everything about middle-class parents' lives, on the other hand, conduces to their looking for new methods to achieve their goals. They look to the experts, to other sources of relevant information, and to each other not for new values but for more serviceable techniques. And within the limits of our present scanty knowledge about means-ends relationships in child-rearing, the experts have provided practical and useful advice. It is not that educated parents slavishly follow the experts but that the experts have provided what the parents have sought.

To look at the question this way is to put it in a quite different perspective: the focus becomes not specific techniques nor changes in the use of specific techniques but parental values.

VALUES OF MIDDLE- AND WORKING-CLASS PARENTS

Of the entire range of values one might examine, it seems particularly strategic to focus on parents' conceptions of what characteristics would be most desirable for boys or girls the age of their own children. From this one can hope to discern the parents' goals in rearing their children. It must be assumed, however, that a parent will choose one characteristic as more desirable than another only if he considers it to be both important, in the sense that failure to develop this characteristic would affect the child adversely, and problematic, in the sense that it is neither to be taken for granted that the child will develop that characteristic nor impossible for him to do so. In interpreting parents' value choices, we must keep in mind that their choices reflect not simply their goals but the goals whose achievement they regard as problematic.

Few studies, even in recent years, have directly investigated the relationship of social class to parental values. Fortunately, however, the results of these few are in essential agreement. The earliest study was Evelyn Millis Duvall's pioneering inquiry of 1946. Duvall characterized working-class (and lower middle-class) parental values as "traditional"—they want their children to be neat and clean, to obey and respect adults, to please adults. In contrast to this emphasis on how the child comports himself, middle-class parental values are more "developmental"—they want their children to be eager to learn, to love and confide in the parents, to be happy, to share and co-operate, to be healthy and well.

Duvall's traditional-developmental dichotomy does not describe the difference between middle- and working-class parental values quite exactly, but it does point to the essence of the difference: working-class parents want the child to conform to externally imposed standards, while middle-class parents are far more attentive to his internal dynamics.

The few relevant findings of subsequent studies are entirely consistent with this basic point, especially in the repeated indications that working-class parents put far greater stress on obedience to parental commands than do middle-class parents. Our own research (Kohn, 1959), conducted in 1956–57, provides the evidence most directly comparable to Duvall's. We, too, found that working-class parents value obedience, neatness, and cleanliness more highly than do middle-class parents, and that middle-class parents in turn value curiosity, happiness, consideration, and—most importantly—self-control more highly than do working-class parents. We further found that there are characteristic clusters of value choice in the two social classes: working-class parental values center on conformity to external proscriptions, middle-class parental values on *self*-direction. To working-class parents, it is the overt act that matters: the child should not transgress externally imposed rules; to middle-class parents, it is the child's motives and feelings that matter: the child should govern himself.

In fairness, it should be noted that middle- and working-class parents share many core values. Both, for example, value honesty very highly—although, characteristically, "honesty" has rather different connotations in the two social classes, implying "trustworthiness" for the working-class and "truthfulness" for the middle-class. The common theme, of course, is that parents of both social classes value a decent respect for the rights of others; middle- and working-class values are but variations on this common theme. The reason for emphasizing the variations rather than the common theme is that they seem to have far-ranging consequences for parents' relationships with their children and thus ought to be taken seriously.

It would be good if there were more evidence about parental values—data from other studies, in other locales, and especially, data derived from more than one mode of inquiry. But, what evidence we do have is consistent, so that there is at least some basis for believing it is reliable. Furthermore, there is evidence that the value choices made by parents in these inquiries are not simply a reflection of their assessments of their own children's deficiencies or excellences. Thus, we may take the findings of these studies as providing a limited, but probably valid, picture of the parents' generalized conceptions of what behavior would be desirable in their preadolescent children.

EXPLAINING CLASS DIFFERENCES IN PARENTAL VALUES

That middle-class parents are more likely to espouse some values, and working-class parents other values, must be a function of differences in their conditions of life. In the present state of our knowledge, it is difficult to disentangle the interacting variables with a sufficient degree of exactness to ascertain which conditions of life are crucial to the differences in values. Nevertheless, it is necessary to examine the principal components of class differences in life conditions to see what each may contribute.

The logical place to begin is with occupational differences, for these are certainly pre-eminently important, not only in defining social classes in urban, industrialized society, but also in determining much else about people's life conditions. There are at least three respects in which middle-class occupations typically differ from working-class occupations, above and beyond their obvious status-linked differences in security, stability of income, and general social prestige. One is that middle-class occupations deal more with the manipulation of interpersonal relations, ideas, and symbols, while working-class occupations deal more with the manipulation of things. The second is that middle-class occupations are more subject to self-direction, while working-class occupations are more subject to standardization and direct supervision. The third is that getting ahead in middle-class occupations is more dependent upon one's own actions, while in working-class occupations it is more dependent upon collective action, particularly in unionized industries. From these differences, one can sketch differences in the characteristics that make for getting along, and getting ahead, in middle- and working-class occupations. Middle-class occupations require a greater degree of self-direction; working-class occupations, in larger measure, require that one follow explicit rules set down by someone in authority.

Obviously, these differences parallel the differences we have found between the two social classes in the characteristics valued by parents for children. At minimum, one can conclude that there is a congruence between occupational requirements and parental values. It is, moreover, a reasonable supposition, although not a necessary conclusion, that middle- and working-class parents value different characteristics in children *because* of these differences in their occupational circumstances. This supposition does not necessarily assume that parents consciously train their children to meet future occupational requirements; it may simply be that their own occupational experiences have significantly affected parents' conceptions of what is desirable behavior, on or off the job, for adults or for children.

These differences in occupational circumstances are probably basic to the differences we have found between middle- and working-class parental values, but taken alone they do not sufficiently explain them. Parents need not accord pre-eminent importance to occupational requirements in their judgments of what is most desirable. For a sufficient explanation of class differences in values, it is necessary to recognize that other differences in middle- and working-class conditions of life reinforce the differences in occupational circumstances at every turn.

Educational differences, for example, above and beyond their importance as determinants of occupation, probably contribute independently to the differences in middle- and working-class parental values. At minimum, middle-class parents' greater attention to the child's internal dynamics is facilitated by their learned ability to deal with the subjective and the ideational. Furthermore, differences in levels and stability of income undoubtedly contribute to class differences in parental values. That middle-class parents still have somewhat higher levels of income, and much greater stability of income, makes them able to take for granted the respectability that is still problematic for working-class parents. They can afford to concentrate, instead, on motives and feelings—which, in the circumstances of their lives, are more important.

These considerations suggest that the differences between middle- and working-class parental values are probably a function of the entire complex of differences in life conditions characteristic of the two social classes. Consider, for example, the working-class situation. With the end of mass immigration, there has emerged a stable working class, largely derived from the manpower of rural areas, uninterested in mobility into the middle class, but very much interested in security, respectability, and the enjoyment of a decent standard of living. This working class has come to enjoy a standard of living formerly reserved for the middle class, but has not chosen a middle-class style of life. In effect, the working class has striven for, and partially achieved, an American dream distinctly different from the dream of success and achievement. In an affluent society, it is possible for the worker to be the traditionalist—politically, economically, and, most relevant here, in his values for his children. Working-class parents want their children to conform to external authority because the parents themselves are willing to accord respect to authority, in return for security and respectability. Their conservatism in child-rearing is part of a more general conservatism and traditionalism.

Middle-class parental values are a product of a quite different set of conditions. Much of what the working class values, they can take for granted. Instead, they can—and must—instil in their children a degree of self-direction that would be less appropriate to the conditions of life of the working class. Certainly, there is substantial truth in the characterization of the middle-class way of life as one of great conformity. What must be noted here, however, is that *relative to* the working class, middle-class conditions of life require a more substantial degree of independence of action. Furthermore, the higher levels of education enjoyed by the middle class make possible a degree of internal scrutiny difficult to achieve without the skills in dealing with the abstract that college training sometimes provides. Finally, the economic security of most middle-class occupations, the level of income they provide, the status they confer, allow one to focus his attention on the subjective and the ideational. Middle-class conditions of life both allow and demand a greater degree of self-direction than do those of the working class.

CONSEQUENCES OF CLASS DIFFERENCES IN PARENTS' VALUES

What consequences do the differences between middle- and working-class parents' values have for the ways they raise their children?

Much of the research on techniques of infant- and child-training is of little relevance here. For example, with regard to parents' preferred techniques for disciplining children, a question of major interest to many investigators, Bronfenbrenner summarizes past studies as follows: "In matters of discipline, working-class parents are consistently more likely to employ physical punishment, while middle-class families rely more on reasoning, isolation, appeals to guilt, and other methods involving the threat of loss of love" (p. 424). This, if still true, is consistent with middle-class parents' greater attentiveness to the child's internal dynamics, working-class parents' greater concern about the overt act. For present purposes, however, the crucial question is not *which* disciplinary method parents prefer, but when and why they use one or another method of discipline.

The most directly relevant available data are on the conditions under which middle- and working-class parents use physical punishment. Working-class parents are apt to resort to physical punishment when the direct and immediate consequences of their children's disobedient acts are most extreme, and to refrain from punishing when this might provoke an even greater disturbance (Kohn, 1959). Thus, they will punish a child for wild play when the furniture is damaged or the noise level becomes intolerable, but ignore the same actions when the direct and immediate consequences are not so extreme. Middle-class parents, on the other hand, seem to punish or refrain from punishing on the basis of their interpretation of the child's intent in acting as he does. Thus, they will punish a furious outburst when the context is such that they interpret it to be a loss of self-control, but will ignore an equally extreme outburst when the context is such that they interpret it to be merely an emotional release.

It is understandable that working-class parents react to the consequences rather than to the intent of their children's actions: the important thing is that the child not transgress externally imposed rules. Correspondingly, if middle-class parents are instead concerned about the child's motives and feelings, they can and must look beyond the overt act to why the child acts as he does. It would seem that middle- and working-class values direct parents to see their children's misbehavior in quite different ways, so that misbehavior which prompts middle-class parents to action does not seem as important to working-class parents, and vice versa. Obviously, parents' values are not the only things that enter into their use of physical punishment. But unless one assumes a complete lack of goal-directedness in parental behavior, he would have to grant that parents' values direct their attention to some facets of their own and their children's behavior, and divert it from other facets.

The consequences of class differences in parental values extend far beyond differences in disciplinary practices. From a knowledge of their values for their children, one would expect middle-class parents to feel a greater obligation to be *supportive* of the children, if only because of their sensitivity to the children's internal dynamics. Working-class values, with their emphasis upon conformity to external rules, should lead to greater emphasis upon the parents' obligation to impose constraints. And this, according to Bronfenbrenner, is precisely what has been shown in those few studies that have concerned themselves with the over-all relationship of parents to child: "Over the entire twenty-five-year period studied, parent-child relationships in the middle-class are consistently reported as more acceptant and equalitarian, while those in the working-class are oriented toward maintaining order and obedience" (p. 425).

This conclusion is based primarily on studies of *mother*-child relationships in middle- and working-class families (see Kohn and Carroll, 1960). Class differences in parental values have further ramifications for the father's role. Mothers in each class would have their husbands play a role facilitative of the child's development of the characteristics valued in that class: Middle-class mothers want their husbands to be supportive of the children (especially of sons), with their responsibility for imposing constraints being of decidedly secondary importance; working-class mothers look to their husbands to be considerably more directive—support is accorded far less importance and constraint far more. Most middle-class fathers agree with their wives and play a role close to what their wives would have them play. Many working-class fathers, on the other hand, do not. It is not that they see the constraining role as less important than do their wives, but that many of them see no reason why they should have to shoulder the responsibility. From their point of view, the important thing is that the child be taught what limits he must not transgress. It does not much matter who does the teaching, and since mother has primary responsibility for child care, the job should be hers.

The net consequence is a quite different division of parental responsibilities in the two social classes. In middle-class families, mother's and father's roles usually are not sharply differentiated. What differentiation exists is largely a matter of each parent taking special responsibility for being supportive of children of the parent's own sex. In working-class families, mother's and father's roles are more sharply differentiated, with mother almost always being the more supportive parent. In some working-class families, mother specializes in support, father in constraint; in others, perhaps in most, mother raises the children, father provides the wherewithal.

Thus, the differences in middle- and working-class parents' values have wide ramifications for their relationships with their children and with each other. Of course, many class differences in parent-child relationships are not directly attributable to differences in values; undoubtedly the very differences in their conditions of life that make for differences in parental values reinforce, at every juncture, parents' characteristic ways of relating to their children. But one could not account for these consistent differences in parent-child relationships in the two social classes without reference to the differences in parents' avowed values.

CONCLUSION

This paper serves to show how complex and demanding are the problems of interpreting the effects of social structure on behavior. Our inquiries habitually stop at the point of demonstrating that social position correlates with something, when we should want to pursue the question, "Why?" What are the processes by which position in social structure molds behavior? The present analysis has dealt with this question in one specific form: Why does social class matter for parents' relationships with their children? There is every reason to believe that the problems encountered in trying to deal with that question would recur in any analysis of the effects of social structure on behavior.

In this analysis, the concept of "values" has been used as the principal bridge from social position to behavior. The analysis has endeavored to show that middle-class parental values differ from those of working-class parents; that these differences are rooted in basic differences between middle- and working-class conditions of life; and that the differences between middle- and working-class parental values have important consequences for their relationships with their children. The interpretive model, in essence, is: social class—conditions of life—values—behavior.

The specifics of the present characterization of parental values may prove to be inexact; the discussion of the ways in which social class position affects values is undoubtedly partial; and the tracing of the consequences of differences in values for differences in parent-child relationships is certainly tentative and incomplete. I trust, however, that the perspective will prove to be valid and that this formulation will stimulate other investigators to deal more directly with the processes whereby social structure affects behavior.

REFERENCES

Bronfenbrenner, U. Socialization and social class through time and space. In Eleanor E. Maccoby, T. M. Newcomb, & E. L. Hartley (Eds.), *Readings in social psychology.* New York: Holt, 1958. Pp. 400–425.

Duvall, Evelyn M. Conceptions of parenthood. *Amer. J. Sociol.,* 1946, **52,** 193–203.

Kohn, M. L. Social class and parental values. *Amer. J. Sociol.,* 1959, **64,** 337–351.

Kohn, M. L. Social class and the exercise of parental authority. *Amer. sociol. Rev.,* 1959, **24,** 352–366.

Kohn, M. L., & Carroll, Eleanor E. Social class and the allocation of parental responsibilities. *Sociometry,* 1960, **23,** 372–392.

27. INTERACTION OF MOTHERS AND CHILDREN FROM LOWER-CLASS FAMILIES

JAMES WALTERS, RUTH CONNOR, AND MICHAEL ZUNICH

The present report describes an experimental study of the facilitory and inhibitory behaviors that lower-class mothers use in the guidance of their children. It was designed to parallel closely Merrill's initial classical study (4) of parent-child relationships in which she sought to determine in what ways mothers would modify their interaction with their children when they were led to infer that their children were not performing satisfactorily in terms of their potentialities.

Merrill observed middle- and upper-class mothers with their children in an unstructured laboratory setting. It was the mother's behavior that was observed and rated, but the mothers were led to believe that it was their children who were being observed. After an initial observation period, Merrill arranged for a second appointment explaining that an additional play session was necessary in order to sample more completely the child's activity. Prior to the second observation, the mothers were divided into experimental and control groups, and each of the mothers in the experimental group was led to believe that the experimenter was disappointed in her child's constructiveness, imagination, and maturity. The experimenter expressed the hope to each mother in the experimental group that on the second trial, when the situation was more familiar, the child's performance would reflect greater achievement. Mothers in the control group were not given information concerning the level of performance of their children, but were told that the procedure was exactly that of the previous session. In each half-hour session, the mother's behavior was recorded every 5 seconds in terms of 22 categories. Merrill found that the change in the behavior of the mothers in the experimental group was characterized by increased domination of the child's actions expressed in arbitrary directing of and interference with the child's activities.

The present study was undertaken to discover whether the same general pattern of response would appear among lower-class subjects in order to determine whether Merrill's conclusions might be generalized to include lower-class mothers concerning what Martin and Stendler have called "sensitivity of the modern mother to advice and criticism of the expert" (3, p.

Reprinted from *Child Development*, 1964, **35**, 433–440, with permission of the senior author and the Society for Research in Child Development.

346). Also, data were obtained concerning the frequency of selected behaviors which the mothers exhibited in an initial session—before the group was divided into experimental and control groups—in order to provide a basis for formulating hypotheses concerning the nature of differences among social classes in terms of parent-child interaction.

PROCEDURE

Forty lower-class mothers together with one of their children served as subjects in the present study. The mothers were white, American born, 20 to 30 years of age, and full-time homemakers with two or more children. One half of the subjects were observed with a male child and one half with a female child. Information concerning source of income, education, and occupation of the father was obtained through interview with the mother. The McGuire-White Index of Social Status (short form) (2) was utilized as a measure of socioeconomic class.

None of the husbands of the subjects of the study had graduated from high school and all received their income from hourly wages. Among the occupations represented were truck driver, service station worker, furniture mover, mechanic, painter, printer, carpenter, plumber, construction worker, welder, electrician's helper, and mill worker. Thus, the subjects were of the upper-lower and middle-lower classes.

Children were selected from Sunday Schools of Protestant churches. The ministers, in cooperation with the Sunday School teachers, were asked to identify lower-class families who, according to their knowledge, met the established criteria. The ministers made some errors in the judgments of the social status of the subjects, but only those were included in the study who clearly fell within the lower class as determined by the McGuire-White Index.

The observations were conducted in the Child Study Laboratory in the School of Home Economics at the Florida State University where there are facilities for observation through a one-way mirror. Each mother was observed with her $3\frac{1}{2}$- to 5-year-old child. The behavior of the mother with the child was recorded under 17 categories every 5 seconds for 30-minute periods. The categories were: *being uncooperative, contacting, criticizing, directing, giving permission, giving praise or affection, helping, interfering, interfering by structurizing, lending cooperation, observing attentively, playing interactively, reassuring, remaining out of contact, restricting, structurizing, teaching.* Detailed descriptions of these categories have been presented by Zunich (7, 8). These categories differ slightly from Merrill's original categories. Refinement of the categories was based upon Merrill's findings, her later work published under her married name, Bishop (1), and the work of Moustakas, Sigel, and Schalock (5) at the Merrill-Palmer Institute.

Prior to the collection of the data, reliability was measured by calculating percentages of agreement between two observers recording simultaneously at 5-second intervals for 30-minute periods. When the observers achieved a competency reflected by agreement of 80 per cent or higher between independent observations in at least five consecutive sessions, the collection of data for the project began. Percentages of agreement ranged from 83 to 100 per cent for 13 of the 17 categories. During the pre-data collection sessions with lower-class mothers, behaviors classified under the categories, *being uncooperative, criticizing, giving praise and affection,* and *reassuring,* did not appear. In preliminary sessions, however, when one of the investigators was observed in interaction with his preschool-aged daughter, the observers were able to identify and record these behaviors reliably. As it became apparent that these behaviors might rarely be evidenced in the lower-class group in the laboratory setting, it was decided to progress to the data collection stage.

RESULTS AND DISCUSSION

In summarizing her results, Merrill writes: "The control-group mothers evidenced consistent trends in behavior from first to second session. The experimental group showed a significant increase at the second session in *directing, interfering, criticizing,* and *structurizing-a-change-in-activity* types of behavior" (4, p. 49). This change has been interpreted, as was mentioned earlier, as reflecting "sensitivity of the modern mother to advice and criticism of the expert."

Results of the present study may be summarized as follows:

1. As will be noted in Table 1, no significant differences were observed between experimental and control groups at the initial session based upon a test analysis of the significance of the differences of mean scores. From the initial to the second session, there was only one significant difference in the control group, i.e., the control *S*s evidenced more *helping* behavior at the second than at the initial session.

2. As might be expected from Merrill's findings, there was a significant increase among the lower-class experimental subjects from the initial to the second session in *contacting, directing,* and *structurizing* responses. A significant decrease was observed in behavior rated as *remaining out of contact.* Thus, it appears that the facilitory and inhibitory patterns of the mothers to have their children perform well were influenced in the lower-class group, as in the middle- and upper-class group, by their desire to make their children appear "adequate" in the presence of a child development expert.

3. The frequency of the mother's responses appeared to be independent of the sex of the child with whom she was observed. However, mothers observed with daughters evidenced significantly more *contacting* and *structurizing* behavior, while the mothers with sons evidenced more *restricting* behavior. Each of the differences observed was significant at the .05 level.

In intrepreting these results, it is well to keep in mind the ages of the

Table 1 *Significance of Differences between Mean Scores Obtained by Experimental and Control Subjects at Initial and Final Sessions*

| | Observation I | | Observation II | |
| | Experimental Group | Control Group | Experimental Group | Control Group |
Categories				
Contacting	58.7	61.1	145.7	65.1 [c]
Directing	2.8	4.3	17.4	4.9 [c]
Helping	1.0	.7	1.5	1.2 [a]
Lending cooperation	1.0	.8	1.4	.5
Observing attentively	76.4	65.4	114.1	57.1 [b]
Remaining out of contact	211.6	219.3	63.1	224.0 [c]
Restricting	1.3	1.3	1.8	1.3
Structurizing	3.2	3.5	9.3	3.8 [b]
Teaching	3.0	3.4	4.1	1.7 [b]

[a] From the initial to the second session there was only one significant difference (.05 level) in the control group. The control Ss evidenced more *helping* behavior at the second than at the initial session.

[b] Significant at the .05 level.

[c] Significant at the .01 level.

Note. The infrequency of the following behaviors made statistical comparisons between experimental and control subjects unwarranted: being uncooperative, criticizing, giving permission, giving praise or affection, interfering, interfering by structurizing, playing interactively, and reassuring.

children. It was not anticipated that many of the differences in parent-child interaction commonly observed at later age levels would appear at the preschool level. However, the fact that mothers observed with daughters evidenced significantly more *contacting* responses than mothers observed with sons suggests that differences in mother-son and mother-daughter interaction typical of the elementary-school years were evident to some extent among the group studied.

4. In terms of the average number of 5-second intervals devoted to each category of behavior at the first play session, Merrill's middle and upper-class mothers spent, on the average, only 178 intervals as a silent onlooker or in activity which was rated as independent at the adult level, whereas the lower-class mother spent, on the average, 286 intervals in such activities. Thus, it is clear that there was much more interaction observed among Merrill's middle- and upper-class mothers with their children than among the lower-class mothers and their children.

5. A comparison of the data collected by Merrill in her initial session with that obtained in the initial session with the lower-class mothers, in terms of time spent in various activities presented in Table 2, revealed that Merrill's middle- and upper-class mothers evidenced nearly four times more

Table 2   *Mean Scores on Behavior Categories in Five Studies of Observed Mother-Child Interaction*

Behavior Categories	Present Study [a] $N = 40$	Merrill [a] $N = 30$	Bishop $N = 34$	Schalock $N = 20$	Zunich [b] $N = 40$
Being uncooperative	.1	1.9	—	.3	.2
Contacting	59.9	—	—	—	160.5
Criticizing	.1	—	3.9	.1	.3
Directing	3.5	13.0	13.7	18.0	23.0
Giving permission	.1	—	—	3.7	.8
Giving praise or affection	—	—	3.1	2.5	1.1
Helping	.9	7.1	4.8	8.1	2.1
Interfering	.2	—	—	.2	.9
Interfering by structurizing	.3	—	—	.2	2.3
Lending cooperation	.9	—	—	10.3	4.3
Observing attentively	70.9	—	—	114.1	117.2
Playing interactively	.2	41.6	11.0	—	5.1
Reassuring	—	—	—	.4	1.0
Remaining out of contact	215.4	—	—	10.7	32.1
Restricting	1.3	—	—	.3	.8
Structurizing	3.4	16.2	14.8	23.5	3.3
Teaching	3.2	11.9	21.4	52.7	5.3

[a] Averages of scores of experimental and control subjects in initial session.
[b] Calculated from frequency scores presented by Zunich (7).
Note. Mean scores were not available for some categories in one or more studies.

directing behavior, nearly nine times more *helping* behavior, nearly five times more *structurizing* behavior, and over three times more *teaching* behavior than the lower-class mothers. The ratio of time units spent playing interactively with their children between the two groups was nearly 250 to 1, the lower-class mothers playing interactively with their children very little.

The evidence of differences existing between lower-class and middle-class mothers is given further support by comparing the mean scores of the lower-class group with the mean scores presented in Table 2 of the middle-class groups studied by Bishop (1), Schalock (6), and Zunich (7). In all of these studies a rating of behavior was recorded every 5 seconds for a half-hour period.

Comparisons of all behavior categories are not possible except with Zunich's data because of differences in categories used by the different investigators. For example, Bishop omitted the category *contacting* and used *remaining out of contact* as an inverse measure of contacting responses. A few similar findings are evidenced when those of the present study are compared with those of Schalock's study. Both investigations had a high mean score for the category *observing attentively*. Low mean scores were obtained in the following categories: being *uncooperative, criticizing, interfering,* and *interfering by structurizing.*

Several differences may be noted between the present study and the other studies. The mean scores in the other studies are somewhat higher than in the present study for *directing, helping, structurizing,* and *teaching.* In both the Merrill and Bishop studies utilizing middle-class subjects, mean scores were higher for the category, *playing interactively,* than in the present study.

Of special significance, however, are the data reported by Zunich (7) on middle-class mothers because the categories used in his analysis are identical with those used in the present study of lower-class mothers. Zunich's middle-class mothers as compared to the lower-class mothers evidenced significantly more responses classified as *contacting, directing, helping, interfering by structurizing, lending cooperation, observing attentively, playing interactively,* and *teaching.* Yet the fact that statistical significance between the two groups was found does not indicate fully the dramatic nature of the differences. Over 6400 *contacting* responses were observed in Zunich's middle-class group while less than 2400 *contacting* responses were observed in the lower-class group. Over six times as many *directing* responses and twice as many *helping* responses were used by the middle-class mothers as compared to the lower-class mothers in guiding their children. Behavior classified as *interfering by structurizing* was over eight times as frequent among the middle-class group, and behavior classified as *lending cooperation* was nearly five times more frequent among the middle-class group. Behavior rated as *playing interactively* was nearly 30 times greater in the middle-class group.

In view of Schalock's study (6) of interactive behavior of mother-child pairs in the laboratory and in the home which indicates that the behavior of mothers in a laboratory setting is not, in many respects, comparable to their behavior at home, the inference to which the above findings lead should be accepted with caution. The familiarity of Merrill's mothers with a university child development laboratory situation presumably would have been greater than that of our lower-class mothers, since all of Merrill's subjects and none of the lower-class subjects had children enrolled in a nursery school laboratory. This factor may have been responsible, in part, for the greater "freedom of response" of the middle- and upper-class mothers.

It is difficult to relate the present results to many of the published findings concerning social class differences in parent-child relationships because, with only few exceptions, investigations of parent-child relationships have relied on information gained from interviews and questionnaires rather than upon direct observation. The results of Zunich's analysis of the relation between maternal behavior and attitudes concerning the guidance of children, for example, are rather disappointing in that his data indicate that considerable inconsistency exists between what parents report to be their attitudes concerning the guidance of children and their behavior when observed in interaction with their children.

From the data reviewed herein based on studies utilizing direct observation, however, the hypothesis appears warranted that very real differences exist in patterns of mother-child interaction among social classes which are understood only in the most general terms. In one sense, the data obtained cross-validate Merrill's conclusions concerning the sensitivity of mothers to criticism of experts, yet patterns of mother-child interaction between social classes appear very different. If any conclusion is warranted from the studies which have employed direct observation, it is that the middle-class child in contrast to the lower-class child lives in a parent-dominated world.

REFERENCES

1. Bishop, B. M. Mother-child interaction and the social behavior of children. *Psychol. Monogr.*, 1951, **65**, No. 11.
2. McGuire, C., & White, G. D. The measurement of social status. Unpublished research paper in human development No. 3 (Rev.), Univer. of Texas, 1955.
3. Martin, W. E., & Stendler, C. B. (Eds.), *Readings in child development*. New York: Harcourt, Brace, 1954.
4. Merrill, B. A measurement of mother-child interaction. *J. abnorm. soc. Psychol.*, 1946, **41**, 37–49.
5. Moustakas, C. E., Sigel, I. E., & Schalock, H. D. An objective method for the measurement and analysis of child-adult interaction. *Child Develpm.*, 1956, **26**, 109–134.
6. Schalock, H. D. Observation of mother-child interaction in the laboratory and in the home. Unpublished doctoral dissertation, Univer. of Nebraska, 1956.
7. Zunich, M. Study of relationships between child rearing attitudes and maternal behavior. *J. exp. Educ.*, 1961, **30**, 231–241.
8. Zunich, M. Relationship between maternal behavior and attitudes toward children. *J. genet. Psychol.*, 1962, **100**, 155–165.

28. SOCIAL CLASS AND OBSERVED MATERNAL

BEHAVIOR FROM 1940 TO 1960

ELINOR WATERS AND VAUGHN J. CRANDALL

Almost all theories of personality stress the importance of a child's nuclear family in his social learning experiences and personality development. Early personality theories, however, primarily discussed parent-child relations and children's personality development as though the child and his family lived in a social and cultural vacuum. Some of the more recent research addressed to this general question, in contrast, has attempted to assess directly various cultural and social factors influencing childrearing practices and child development. During the last 15 years, for example, numerous articles have appeared in sociological and psychological journals assessing relations between social class membership of American families and their childrearing attitudes and behaviors. Results of these studies, however, have often been contradictory or equivocal. For example, while the oft-quoted Chicago study of Davis and Havighurst (10) found that middle class mothers were more restrictive than lower class mothers, several recent investigations including the Harvard Project (21) and two California studies (3, 25) have reported the opposite to be true. Still a third conclusion was reached by Littman's study of an Oregon sample of mothers (17) which found that social class status was essentially unrelated to a variety of child socialization practices. Several reasons have been suggested for the discrepancies among these studies and other similar investigations. These include the fact that data were gathered at different periods of time and in various parts of the country, that the studies often employed samples differing in their socioeconomic composition, that different assessment methods were used, and that analogous findings have sometimes been interpreted differently by investigators with varying points of view.

The current study had two general aims. The first was similar to the previously mentioned research, i.e., to assess the influence of socioeconomic status on maternal childrearing practices. The second was concerned with evaluating changes in maternal behaviors and socialization techniques during the last 20 years to ascertain if consistent trends are evident and, if so, whether these patterns parallel changing currents in recommended childrearing procedures.

Reprinted from *Child Development*, 1964, **35**, 1021–1032, with permission of the senior author and the Society for Research in Child Development.

Changes in the types of advice given by "experts" to American parents over the years have been reported by Stendler (23) and by Wolfenstein (26), and possible concomitant changes in childrearing practices have been discussed in two excellent summaries by Bronfenbrenner (4, 5). In the 1930's, rigid schedules of caretaking, discipline, and training were strongly espoused, probably as the result of Watsonian behaviorism. This was followed by a pendulum swing during the 1940's and early 1950's to a "permissive era" influenced by psychoanalytic dicta. By the early 1960's, a shift back toward a middle ground was evident and parents were enjoined to establish the limits of acceptable behavior for their children.

Regrettably, maternal behavior data as far back as the early 1930's were not available for the present study. The earliest information which could be used had been obtained around 1940 when the transition from the rigid to the permissive era had already begun. The years around 1950 were chosen to represent the height of permissiveness, and the 1960 period was selected because it provided more recent data on the relation of social class and childrearing practices than any yet reported. The inclusion of data from 1950 to 1960 also provided an opportunity to see if any evidences of the presumed "retreat" from permissiveness in maternal behavior during the past decade would manifest themselves.

METHOD

Sample

All *S*s were mothers of families enrolled in the Fels Research Institute's longitudinal study of human development. From its inception in the early 1930's, this research project has studied social, psychological, and physical factors influencing normal children's growth and development from birth to maturity (16). An integral part of this longitudinal assessment has been the Institute's home visit program. From 1937 until the present time, specially trained home visitors have made semiannual visits to the homes of all families with preschool age children participating in the Fels study. During these visits, the home visitors have observed *in situ* mother-child interactions and have rated mothers' behaviors using the Fels Parent Behavior Rating Scales (1, 2, 6).

In conducting the present study, it was decided that all data must be based on direct observation of overt maternal behaviors rather than mothers' self reports. In this respect, it might be noted that most current information on social class differences in American childrearing practices comes from research based on mothers' verbal—and often retrospective—reports rather than their actual behaviors. The credibility of the findings of such studies rests on two basic assumptions: first, that mothers' contemporary reports of their behaviors with their children are free from distortion, defensive or otherwise; and, second, that retrospective reports are essentially uninfluenced by selective memory. A substantial body of general psychological knowledge, e.g., recent research on the social desirability factor in subjective reports (7, 12, 19, 24), suggests that uncritical acceptance of these assumptions may be unwarranted. Moreover, one recent study has reported that mothers' subjective evaluations of their maternal behaviors may reflect their actual actions in certain areas, but bear little or no relation to their childrearing practices in other areas (9).

The decision to use only data based on observed maternal behaviors in the current investigation limited the study to mothers who had nursery-school-age children at the time they were observed. Children of elementary school age and older are not characteristically in their homes in interaction with their mothers for reasonably long periods except during the dinner and evening hours, when home visit observations are impractical.

In order to assess changes in childrearing practices over three different time periods it was, of course, mandatory that the three subsamples of mothers representing these time periods should not differ in their socioeconomic composition.

Finally, within each of the three subsamples, it was thought desirable to include approximately equivalent numbers of mothers of 3-, 4-, and 5-year-old children, as well as an equal proportion of mothers of boys and girls.

On the basis of the preceding criteria, all available home visit data of the Fels Research Institute obtained during the last 25 years were evaluated before the study was begun. From this preliminary perusal, 107 mothers were selected who met all of the three criteria. A 1940 group was made up of 40 mothers who were observed by Fels home visitors in interaction with their nursery-school-age children between 1939 and 1941; a 1950 subsample consisted of 32 mothers on whom similar observations and ratings had been made between 1948 and 1952; and a final group, designated the 1960 subsample, contained 35 mothers on whom maternal behavior data had been obtained between 1959 and 1961. All mothers in this final sample were white, and resided in communities within a 30-mile radius of the Fels Institute in southwestern Ohio. The three subsamples did not differ significantly in their socioeconomic distributions as measured by the Hollingshead Index of Social Position discussed below.

Assessment of Socioeconomic Status

The socioeconomic status (SES) of the families of the study was determined by Hollingshead's Two Factor Index of Social Position, an index based on the type of occupation and amount of education of the head of the family (13). Scores ranged from 11 for families with the highest social status to 77 for families having the lowest socioeconomic position. These raw scores can be divided into five groups using cutting points suggested by Hollingshead. When this was done with the present sample of 107 families, 10.3 per cent fell in class I (scores 11 to 17), 17.8 per cent in class II (scores 18 to

27), 36.5 per cent in class III (scores 28 to 43), 30.8 per cent in class IV (scores 44 to 60), and 4.7 per cent in class V (scores 61 to 77). Since Hollingshead has not specified how his categories relate to the lower, middle, and upper class distinctions usually employed in sociological research, illustrative families of the current study falling into each of the Hollingshead classifications are briefly described. Class I contained heads of households who were, for example, a dentist, an aeronautical engineer, and a college professor, all with graduate degrees. Class II included a high level—but not top management—executive with some college training and a high school principal with an M.A. degree. Class III encompassed a broad grouping including, among others, the owner of a medium sized business who had a high school education, a farmer with a college degree, and an insurance adjustor and a machine tool manufacturing supervisor, both of whom had some college training. Examples of class IV were a clerical worker with a high school education and a carpenter and a television repairman who had some formal technical training in addition to a high school education. Class V was represented by heads of households such as a construction laborer who had gone to high school for two years and a truck driver with a grade school education.

Unfortunately, the sample is not as representative of the American population as would be desirable. While the over-all sample produced a distribution of families on the SES variable that closely approximated a bell-shaped curve, this is not a typical SES distribution. In New Haven where Hollingshead's indices (13, 14) were developed and in other parts of the country where SES has been evaluated by other means, the distribution of families has consistently been skewed with the preponderance of families falling toward the lower class end of the scale. Thus, the current sample is "top-heavy" as compared with usual SES distributions and almost entirely lacking in lower-lower class families. It is important, then, to keep the characteristics of the sample and its limitations in mind when the results and discussion of this study are presented later.

Assessment of Maternal Behaviors

The Fels Institute's home visit program is unique in developmental research in that, for the last 25 years, naturally occurring mother-child interactions in home settings have been routinely assessed in a consistent fashion. Typically, the Fels home visitors have attempted to make their visits as frequent, natural, and nonprofessional-appearing as possible. In contrast to many studies of maternal behavior, these visits are not "one-shot affairs" in which the observer's or interviewer's presence in the home is a novel, and perhaps threatening, experience for many mothers. Rather, from the time each child in the Fels longitudinal study is born, a home visitor periodically and informally spends some time in the home so that the mother becomes accustomed to her presence. Also, the mother is led to believe that the major focus of each visit is on the child's development rather than on her own behavior. Finally, on no occasion are the usual observer or interviewer accoutrements (e.g., check lists, note-taking, etc.) employed during visits. The aim of these procedures is to allow the mother to become acclimated to the home visitor's presence and to encourage her to behave as naturally as possible with her child. This is not to say that a mother's behavior is totally unaffected by the presence of a home visitor; an unknown degree of protective coloration undoubtedly manifests itself. However, every conceivable effort is made to minimize this factor.

The basic maternal behavior data were the home visitor's ratings of the mothers. Here the Fels Parent Behavior Rating Scales (PBRs) were used. Each scale has a verbal definition of the variable under consideration and five or more cue-point descriptions placed on a 90-millimeter line along which a rater distributes the mothers. The PBR scales and their intra- and interrater reliabilities have been reported in detail elsewhere (1, 2, 8) and will not be duplicated here. Suffice it to say, acceptable inter- and intrarater reliabilities for the variables studied in the present investigation have been consistently reported over the years.

Not all PBR variables were investigated in this study. The full set of 30 scales was originally constructed to assess a diverse range and large variety of parental behaviors. Subsequently, and from time to time, data obtained with these scales have been submitted to various statistical techniques to determine the basic underlying dimensions represented by the scales. These analyses have included syndrome analysis (2), cluster analysis (8), and first- and second-order factor analyses (18, 20). As a result of these findings, only 10 of the original scales are currently employed in the Fels home visit program. The present study limited its analysis of maternal behaviors to nine of these variables (the tenth, "general adjustment of the home," was not a maternal behavior variable per se and was, therefore, excluded). Of the remaining nine variables, three pairs represent three broad dimensions of parent behavior, i.e., nurturant, affectionate, and coercive behaviors, which were identified in previous research (8). The additional three PBR variables do not satisfy statistical requirements for inclusion in any one of these three clusters of maternal behaviors and, for the purpose of this study, have been designated as "miscellaneous" PBR variables.

A brief description of the nine PBR variables used in this study follows. The two scales representing *nurturant maternal behaviors* were entitled Protectiveness and Babying. The Protectiveness scale contained cue points running from extreme sheltering of the child to frequently exposing him to actual or potential psychological and physical frustrations and dangers. The Babying scale was concerned with the degree to which a mother offered instrumental help to her child and ranged from behaviors of mothers who consistently helped their offspring whether they needed it or not to mothers who rarely assisted their children even in difficult situations. The two scales concerned with *affectionate maternal behaviors* pertained to overt displays of maternal affection and to the characteristic direction of criticism used by the mother. The former, Affectionateness, ranged from extremely affectionate to consistently hostile maternal behaviors. The second, Direction of Criticism, focused on whether a mother typically approved or criticized her child's everyday actions. The two PBR scales concerned with *coercive maternal behaviors* were entitled Coerciveness of Suggestions and Severity of Penalties. The first covered the degree to which a mother's suggestions to her child regarding his behaviors required mandatory or optional compliance. The other, Severity of Penalties, referred to punitive maternal behaviors and ranged from severe punishment to mild reprimand for various infractions of maternal rules and prohibitions. The final three scales—which did not represent any of the three above-mentioned dimensions of maternal behavior but are still a part of PBR assessment of maternal behaviors—were designated *miscellaneous maternal behaviors.* The first of these, Restrictiveness of Regulations, was concerned with the number of restrictions a mother characteristically imposed on her child's actions. A second miscellaneous scale was entitled Clarity of Policy and was based on home visitors' judgments of how clear or vague a mother's sanctions and proscriptions were. Finally, maternal Accelerational Attempts were observed and rated. Here, the observers evaluated the degree to which a mother attempted to foster and facilitate her child's development of independent problem solving techniques and achievement skills.

Data Analysis

Nonparametric statistical procedures were used for all data analyses of the study. Mann-Whitney U tests were applied to data requiring tests of difference, and rank difference correlations were employed as measures of association. Two-tailed tests of significance are reported throughout the Results section which follows.

RESULTS AND DISCUSSION

Social Class and Maternal Behavior

Relations between family socioeconomic status and observed maternal behaviors for the three time periods and for the total sample of mothers are presented in Table 1. Before discussing the results summarized in this table, two comments are in order. First, it will be noted that SES-maternal behavior correlations in Table 1 do not differentiate maternal actions toward boys and girls. Correlations were run separately by sex of the child, but, since neither the direction nor the significance of the associations were found to differ appreciably, they are not reported separately. Second, since Hollingshead's Index of Social Position uses a rating system in which smaller numbers represent higher socioeconomic status, correlation signs were reversed

Table 1   *Socioeconomic Status and Maternal Behaviors at Three Periods of Time and for Total Sample: Rank Difference Correlations*

PBR Variables	1940 ($N = 40$)	1950 ($N = 32$)	1960 ($N = 35$)	Total Sample ($N = 107$)
Nurturant behavior				
Babying	.12	.07	.31	.14
Protectiveness	.21	.16	.10	.16
Affectionate behavior				
Affectionateness	.17	.18	− .02	.08
Direction of criticism				
(Approval)	.38 [a]	.14	.28	.26 [a]
Coercive behavior				
Coerciveness of suggestions	− .54 [a]	− .13	− .45 [a]	− .43 [a]
Severity of penalties	− .21	− .15	− .44 [a]	− .25 [a]
Miscellaneous PBR scales				
Restrictiveness of regulations	− .55 [a]	− .37 [a]	− .39 [a]	− .43 [a]
Clarity of policy	.40 [a]	.18	.13	.26 [a]
Accelerational attempt	.63 [a]	.31	.02	.34 [a]

[a] $p < .01$.

in the present study to avoid unnecessary confusion. Relations can thus be interpreted in the usual manner, i.e., positive correlations indicate that increased social status is associated with a greater amount of the maternal behavior under consideration. Returning to Table 1, no significant correlations were found between social class and *nurturant maternal behaviors* for the total sample of mothers nor for mothers representing any of the three separate time periods studied. Neither the mothers' tendency to over- or under-help their children nor their general protectiveness was associated with family social class status.

Family social position was also found to bear little relation to *affectionate maternal behavior*. At none of the time periods studied was the amount of spontaneous affection displayed by mothers related to their social class level. Around 1940, mothers in higher status homes were more likely to approve, and less likely to disapprove, of their children's actions than were mothers of relatively low SES. However, similar associations, while in the same direction, were not significant in either 1950 or 1960, and the significance of the correlation for the total sample seems to be mainly a function of the larger N of the total group of mothers.

In contrast to the negligible relations found between SES and nurturant and affectionate behaviors, *maternal coerciveness* was more clearly associated with social position. In the sample in general, and in the 1960 subsample in particular, SES was positively correlated with noncoercive maternal child-rearing practices. The higher the family status, the less dictatorial were mothers' attempts to influence their children's behavior, and the less severe were their penalties for misbehaviors. The maternal behavior variable which was most consistently related to SES was Restrictiveness of Regulations, which is conceptually related to coerciveness although the Crandall and Preston study (8), previously referred to, indicated that it did not meet statistical requirements for inclusion in the coerciveness category used here. At all three time periods sampled, the higher the family status, the less a mother was prone to impose restrictive regulations on her offspring's behavior.

In summary, for whatever reasons, maternal coerciveness seems to be more class-linked than either maternal affection or maternal nurturance. In this respect, it is of some interest to note that a previous study evaluating the influence of personal needs of mothers on their childrearing practices (9) found that related needs *were* predictive of mothers' affectionate and nurturant behaviors toward their children, but *were not* predictive of the degree of coerciveness they characteristically employed with their children. The combined findings of that study and the present one, both based on PBR data from home visit observations, suggests a tentative generalization. To understand and predict mothers' behaviors with their children, both types of variables are helpful—social class membership and personal needs. Moreover, when one set of variables is operative, the other may be less predictive and vice versa.

The final two PBR variables, Clarity and Accelerational Attempts, were class linked in 1940 and for the total sample. Mothers of higher SES families employed more clearly formulated policies of childrearing and more often attempted to accelerate their children's achievement development than mothers of lower social status. It is interesting to note that the SES-maternal behavior relations of these variables have progressively decreased over the last 20 years.

Before comparing the results of this study with those of previous investigations, several differences should be mentioned. First, this study used maternal behavior data based entirely on assessments of overt mother-child interactions. Hopefully, the procedures employed provided a more direct and accurate assessment of actual childrearing practices than interviews. The only other study of social class and childrearing practices in which observed maternal behaviors have been evaluated is the Bayley and Schaefer investigation in which data were based partially on such observations, but also on interviews (3). Second, while analogies are drawn to variables of other investigations which are relatively similar to those used in the present study, behavioral referents are not always exactly the same. These differences will be pointed out as the variables are discussed. Third, there are also sample differences between this study and many of the others. Lower class families were not sufficiently represented in the present sample (as was true in the Bayley and Schaefer study [3]), and this sample cannot be divided into representative middle and lower class groups. With these differences in mind, let us consider the relations of the findings of this study to those reported in previous research.

Variables used in earlier research bear very little similarity to the *maternal nurturance* variables in the present study. None seems to pertain directly to the Babying PBR which focused solely on the amount of instrumental help given a child by his mother and which was found to be unrelated to SES in our research. Previous findings relevant to the maternal Protectiveness variable studied here are somewhat contradictory. Davis and Havighurst (10) have reported that lower class mothers imposed fewer restrictions on the movements of their children outside of the home than did middle class mothers. For example, lower class children were allowed to go to the movies at an earlier age and to stay out later at night than middle class children. Sears *et al.*, on the other hand, found that middle class mothers allowed their children more freedom to cross the streets or go to visit friends than lower class mothers and less frequently checked on their whereabouts (21, p. 430). While both of these findings represent protectiveness, the second maternal nurturance variable included in the present study, they both differ from the present study in that they refer to protectiveness, or lack thereof, outside of the house while the current rating assesses maternal protectiveness solely within the home and yard. As mentioned earlier, no association between maternal protectiveness in the home environment and family social position was found in the present study.

The results of at least four studies are pertinent to the *maternal affection* dimension investigated in the current research. A suggestion that a positive relation between SES and maternal affection might exist comes from a study by Duvall (11) in which she asked mothers to describe their ideal picture of a good mother. In this research, middle class mothers expressed more concern with the affectional bond between mother and child than lower class mothers, while the latter seemed to be more interested in obedience and cleanliness training. Also, Sears *et al.* found that middle class mothers reported in interviews that they had warmer relations with their preschool children than did working class mothers (21, p. 432). The lack of consistent associations between social class and maternal affection found in the present study may be a function of sample differences with the above-mentioned research. Reports of studies based on samples which were more comparable to the present one agree with those results reported here. For example, Bayley and Schaefer (3), whose distribution was very similar to the present one, report no class differences in maternal affection. And an incidental finding in a study by Kagan and Freeman on early childhood experiences and later adolescent behavior (15), which also used the Fels Institute's longitudinal sample, was that maternal affection and acceptance were essentially unrelated to mothers' education, a variable closely associated with social position. Why should the findings of Duvall and Sears differ from those of Bayley and Schaefer, Kagan and Freeman, and the present study? Two possibilities suggest themselves. First the SES samples of Duvall and Sears *et al.* were such that they could be neatly divided into middle and working class dichotomies, and they also had a larger proportion of lower class families than the other three studies. Second, the Sears and Duvall studies used mother interviews, while the data of the remaining three studies were based, at least in part, on direct observations of maternal behavior.

The negative associations found in the current study between social class position and *maternal coerciveness* are consistent with other reports of class differences in disciplinary techniques used by American families. There is agreement from a variety of source (e.g., 3, 21, 25) that lower class mothers use more forceful and punitive methods of discipline than middle class mothers. Bronfenbrenner's summary of recent research reports on middle vs. lower class disciplinary techniques is relevant. He states that middle class parents are "in the first place, more likely to overlook offenses, and when they do punish they are less likely to ridicule or inflict physical pain. Instead they reason with the youngster, isolate him, appeal to guilt, or show disappointment" (4, p. 419). Our study, despite its more restricted SES range, found the same to be true, with lower social status mothers especially prone to use coercive suggestions and severe penalties.

Changes in Maternal Behavior Over Time

Table 2 presents median maternal behavior scores for the nine PBR variables at each of the three time periods investigated. Direction of changes between the periods are also given, along with the levels of significance of the differences. Two basic trends are apparent. First, several of the maternal behavior variables exhibit curvilinear trends between 1940 and 1960 paralleling changing advice by child-care experts during this time. The so-called "permissive era" in child care literature probably reached its peak in the early 1950's. This was the period in which mothers in the present study were observed to display the most nurturance and affection toward their children. During this period these mothers also made the greatest efforts to make their policies clear to their offspring, possibly in response to advice to give children reasons for demands put upon them. By 1960, the mothers studied were more similar to the 1940 sample and displayed less babying, protectiveness, affection, and approval than the 1950 mothers.

It is interesting to note that Spock, perhaps the single most influential adviser of American parents, made changes and additions to his book on child care and training which preceded, and predicted, changes in maternal practices found in the current study. While it is impossible to determine whether Spock or other "experts" were actually instrumental in bringing about any of the changes in maternal behaviors reported here, the congruence of advice and behaviors is interesting. In this respect Spock's introduction to the 1957 revision of his book lucidly describes his conscious efforts

Table 2   *Median Ratings of Maternal Behavior at Three Time Periods and Differences between Periods*

PBR Variables	1940 (N = 40)	Direction of Differences	p	1950 (N = 32)	Direction of Differences	p	1960 (N = 35)
Nurturant behavior							
Babying	59.5	<	ns	61.5	>	.01	45.1
Protectiveness	57.5	<	ns	64.5	>	.01	50.0
Affectionate behavior							
Affectionateness	69.0	<	ns	71.5	>	.01	58.0
Direction of Criticism (approval)	53.0	<	.05	62.5	>	.01	45.0
Coercive behavior							
Coerciveness of Suggestions	58.5	>	.05	48.0	>	.05	43.7
Severity of penalties	52.0	>	ns	48.0	>	ns	44.8
Miscellaneous PBR scales							
Restrictiveness of regulations	54.5	>	ns	54.0	>	.01	42.8
Clarity of policy	58.5	<	ns	64.5	>	.01	55.0
Accelerational attempts	54.0	=	ns	54.0	>	ns	53.2

to influence American childrearing practices, first toward permissiveness and later toward a more moderate position (22).

A second trend which is evident in other maternal behaviors in the present study can be characterized by a progressive, rather than a curvilinear, change over time. This trend is primarily seen in the degree of coerciveness the mothers employed in their socialization techniques. From 1940 through 1950 to 1960 maternal coerciveness gradually decreased. During the last 20 years the mothers studied have become less prone to make coercive suggestions requiring mandatory compliance from their children, employ less restrictive regulations of their children's activities, and are less severe in the way they punish misbehaviors.

REFERENCES

1. Baldwin, A., Kalhorn, J., & Breese, F. Patterns of parent behavior. *Psychol. Monogr.*, 1945, **58**, No. 3 (Whole No. 268).
2. Baldwin, A., Kalhorn, J., & Breese, F. The appraisal of parent behavior. *Psychol. Monogr.*, 1949, **63**, No. 4 (Whole No. 299).
3. Bayley, N., & Schaefer, E. Relationships between socio-economic variables and the behavior of mothers toward young children. *J. genet. Psychol.*, 1960, **96**, 61–77.
4. Bronfenbrenner, U. Socialization and social class through time and space. In E. Maccoby, T. Newcomb, & E. Hartley (Eds.), *Readings in social psychology*. (3rd ed.), New York: Holt, 1958. Pp. 400–425.

5. Bronfenbrenner, U. The changing American child—a speculative analysis. *J. soc. Issues,* 1961, **17**, 6–18.
6. Champney, H. The measurement of parent behavior. *Child Develpm.,* 1941, **12**, 131–166.
7. Christie, R., & Lindauer, F. Personality structure. *Annu. Rev. Psychol.,* 1963, **14**, 201–207.
8. Crandall, V., & Preston, A. Patterns and levels of maternal behavior. *Child Develpm.,* 1955, **26**, 267–277.
9. Crandall, V., & Preston, A. Verbally expressed needs and overt maternal behaviors. *Child Develpm.,* 1961, **32**, 261–270.
10. Davis, A., & Havighurst, R. Social class and color differences in child rearing. *Amer. sociol. Rev.,* 1948, **11**, 698–710.
11. Duvall, E. Conceptions of parenthood. *Amer. J. Sociol.,* 1946, **52**, 193–203.
12. Edwards, A. *The social desirability variable in personality assessment and research.* New York: Dryden Press, 1957.
13. Hollingshead, A. *The two factor index of social position.* New Haven: Privately printed, 1957.
14. Hollingshead, A., & Redlich, F. *Social class and mental illness.* New York: Wiley, 1958.
15. Kagan, J., & Freeman, M. The relation of childhood intelligence, maternal behaviors, and social class to behavior during adolescence. *Child Develpm.,* 1963, **34**, 899–911.
16. Kagan, J., & Moss, H. *Birth to maturity.* New York: Wiley, 1962.
17. Littman, R., Moore, R., & Pierce-Jones, J. Social class differences in child rearing: a third community for comparison with Chicago and Newton. *Amer. scoiol. Rev.,* 1957, **22**, 694–704.
18. Lorr, M., & Jenkins, R. Three factors in parent behavior. *J. consult. Psychol.,* 1953, **17**, 306–308.
19. Marlowe, D., & Crowne, D. Social desirability and response to perceived situational demands. *J. consult. Psychol.,* 1961, **25**, 109–115.
20. Roff, M. A factorial study of the Fels Parent Behavior Scales. *Child Develpm.,* 1949, **20**, 29–45.
21. Sears, R., Maccoby, E., & Levin, H. *Patterns of child rearing.* Evanston: Row, Peterson, 1957.
22. Spock, B. *Baby and child care.* New York: Pocket Books, 1957.
23. Stendler, C. Sixty years of child training practices. *J. Pediat.,* 1950, **36**, 122–134.
24. Taylor, J. What do attitude scales measure: the problem of social desirability. *J. abnorm. soc. Psychol.,* 1961, **62**, 386–390.
25. White, M. Social class, child rearing practices and child behavior. *Amer. sociol. Rev.,* 1957, **22**, 704–712.
26. Wolfenstein, M. Trends in infant care. *Amer. J. Orthopsychiat.,* 1953, **23**, 120–130.

29. SOCIAL CLASS AND THE CHILD'S
PERCEPTION OF THE PARENT

Bernard C. Rosen

The socialization of the child in American society is markedly influenced by his parents' position in the class structure (3, 7, 8, 10, 13). Research findings over the past twenty-five years show parents in the middle classes to be more accepting and equalitarian in their relationship to the child than parents in the lower class (2, 6, 9). Middle-class parents are more tolerant of the child's needs and impulses (1); they are more likely to take into account his intent and motives when transgressions occur than lower-class parents, who tend to respond to the immediate consequences of the child's actions (5). In disciplining the child, middle-class parents more often use reasoning and appeals to guilt, and are somewhat less likely to employ physical punishment than parents in the lower class (11, 12).

The lower-class family system has been described as rigid and hierarchical, both as regards husband-wife and parent-child relationships (6). Lower-class parents are less accessible to the child, particularly the father, whose supportive role in childrearing is less emphasized by lower-class than by middle-class mothers. The lower-class mother expects her husband to be more authoritative and to play a major role in disciplining the child. The father who is accessible both as a companion and an authority figure, especially for the son, is far more often found in middle- than in lower-class families (3).

This paper examines some aspects of the way boys from middle- or lower-class families perceive their parents. Our basic questions are: (a) do boys from middle-class or lower-class families differ in their perception of the parent; and (b) are these differences such as could be expected given the distinctive patterns of affection, authority and control which research has shown characterize the several social classes. For example, does the middle-class boy perceive his parents as more accepting and supportive than do boys in the lower class, as researchers report them to be? Is the somewhat more inaccessible and less attentive role of the father in the lower class perceived as such by the child? It seemed appropriate to find the answers to these questions by asking the boys themselves.

Reprinted from *Child Development*, 1964, **35**, 1147–1153, with permission of the author and the Society for Research in Child Development.

METHOD

The data for this study were collected from 367 Ss who constituted virtually the entire universe of boys, 9 through 11 years of age, enrolled in the elementary schools of three Connecticut towns. The Ss were white, predominantly Protestants or Roman Catholic, and had a mean age of about 10 years. The respondent's social class was determined by a modified version of the Hollingshead (4) Index of Social Position, which uses the occupation and education of the main wage earner, usually the father, as the principal criteria of status. Ss were classified according to this index into one of five social classes, from the highest status group (class I) to the lowest (class V). We consider classes I, II, and III to be middle class, and classes IV and V as lower class. Classes I and II include for the most part professionals, large proprietors, executives and other managerial groups; many are college graduates, all have at least some college training. Class III is made up of small shopkeepers, salespersons, clerks, and other minor white collar workers; most are high school graduates. Persons in class IV are primarily skilled manual workers with some high school training, while class V is composed of semiskilled and unskilled workers who have never attended high school.

A structured questionnaire was administered to groups of Ss in their classrooms. This questionnaire was designed to provide information on some aspects of the boy's perception of his parents: e.g., the extent to which they emphasized self-reliance, competition and excellence; their willingness to grant him autonomy and their involvement in, and evaluation of, his performance in a variety of activities. Only the data relevant to the present problem will be presented in this paper.

The Ss were asked to respond to a number of adjectives and statements in terms of how accurately they described the parents by circling a number along a six-point continuum. Only the end points of the continuum had verbal labels. First, a series of words, listed on separate sheets for father and mother, were presented to the Ss and the question was put in this way: "Here are some words which boys have used to describe their fathers (mothers). Is your father (mother) like these words? If your father is *Not at All* like a word circle number 1. If he is *Completely* like a word circle number 6. You can circle any number from one to six. The closer you circle to number 1 the less your father is like a word; the closer you circle to number 6, the more he is like a word. Circle a number for each word." In a following section of the questionnaire, Ss were asked whether they agreed or disagreed with a number of statements, again by circling a number along a six-point continuum in which number 1 represented "strongly disagree" and number 6 "strongly agree." Instructions as to the meanings of the numbers were comparable to those used in the case of the adjectives.

RESULTS AND DISCUSSION

Pearsonian correlations were computed between 21 items of information and a first-step cluster analysis was employed to obtain clusters. Three clusters resulted from this analysis which seemed conceptually meaningful:

Parental competence. A combination of three evaluations of the parent in response to the question, "Is your father (or mother) like these words?" The words were: *smart, ambitious, successful.* The word *successful* was not used in the case of the mother. This cluster provides a measure of the boy's perception of parental drive and ability.

Parental security. A combination of assessments of the parent in terms of his similarity to three adjectives: *shy, nervous, worried.* This cluster provides a measure of the child's perception of parental self-assurance and security.

Parental acceptance and support. A combination of responses indicating the degree to which the boy believes that the following statements apply to his parents:

Father
1. My father is too busy to pay much attention to me.
2. My father shows me he is interested in how I am doing in school.
3. My father acts as though I were in the way.
4. My father is interested in almost everything I do.
5. It's hard to get my father to listen to what I have to say.

Mother
1. My mother tells me about the good things other kids do.
2. My mother shows me she's interested in how I'm doing in school.
3. My mother gives me the feeling I'm somebody special.
4. When I have something to say, my mother listens.
5. My mother doesn't say much about the good things I do, but she is always talking about the bad.

This cluster provides a measure of the boy's perception of parental interest and support.

Six cluster scores, three for the father and three for the mother, were obtained in the following manner. The distribution of responses for each of the 21 items for the entire sample was first determined. The median point on a 6-point continuum for each item within a cluster was found and the S was given a point whenever his response was above the median, and a zero weight for responses below the median. Scores for all items within a cluster were then summed. Scores above the median always indicate a relatively negative evaluation of the parent where "negative" means the relative absence of parental self-confidence, competence, and support for the boy. Thus, *the higher the cluster score, the more negative the perception of the parent.*

The mean cluster scores for the five social classes are shown in Table 1.

Table 1 *Boys' Perception of Parents in Mean Cluster Scores by Social Class*

Perception of Parent	Social Class				
	I	II	III	IV	V
Parental competence					
Father	1.2	0.8	1.1	1.6	1.9 [a]
Mother	1.4	1.3	1.6	1.7	1.8 [b]
Parental security					
Father	1.2	1.1	1.2	1.5	1.7 [c]
Mother	1.1	1.2	1.0	1.3	1.3
Parental acceptance and interest					
Father	1.6	1.1	1.8	2.4	2.7 [a]
Mother	2.2	1.5	2.2	2.3	2.4 [d]
Number of cases	(39)	(23)	(99)	(161)	(45)

[a] Differences between each middle-class stratum (I, II, or III) and each lower-class stratum (IV or V) significant at the .05 level or better.

[b] Differences between classes I and V, II and IV, II and V significant at the .05 level.

[c] Differences between classes I and V, II and V, III and V significant at the .05 level.

[d] Differences between classes II and IV, II and V significant at the .05 level.

Note. Tests of significance (t test) are between the middle and lower classes. Each middle-class stratum (classes I, II, III) was compared with each lower-class stratum (classes IV or V).

Tests of statistical significance of the differences between the middle strata and the lower strata were computed by means of the t test. Each middle stratum (classes I, II, or III) was compared with each of the lower strata (classes IV or V). The ts reported in the text are only a sample of the significant results. A report of all the significant differences obtained in comparisons between the middle and lower strata can be found in Table 1.

Parental Competence

Middle-class boys tended to evaluate their parents' ability, performance, and drive more positively than did boys in the lower class. Fathers in the middle class were more likely than lower-class fathers to be perceived as successful, ambitious, and smart by their sons. This was particularly true when the boys in class II were compared with their peers in classes IV or V: the mean score of the former was less than half the score of boys in the lower strata (classes II and IV, $t = 3.40$, $p < .001$; classes II and V, $t = 4.43$, $p < .001$). Differences between other middle and lower strata while not as great were also significant. For example, between classes I and V the $t = 2.17$, $p < .05$; classes III and IV, $t = 1.99$, $p < .05$. The differences between the social classes in the perception of the mother were much less marked. There was a greater tendency for middle-class boys to perceive their mothers as *ambitious* and *smart* than boys in the lower class, but except in the comparison between classes II and IV ($t = 2.00$, $p < .05$), and classes II and V ($t = 2.00$, $p < .05$) the differences were small and statistically nonsignificant.

Parental Security

Boys in the lower class tended to perceive their parents as less secure than boys in the middle class. Lower-class fathers were perceived as significantly more *nervous, shy,* and *worried* than fathers in the middle class: for example, classes II and V, $t = 2.11$, $p < .05$; classes I and V, $t = 1.99$, $p < .05$. The differences between the middle strata and class IV, however, were not significant. Lower-class mothers were more often perceived as *nervous, shy,* and *worried* than middle-class mothers, but in this case none of the differences were significant.

Parental Acceptance and Interest

The differences between middle- and lower-class boys in their perception of parental acceptance and support were the greatest of the three clusters. Middle-class boys were more likely than boys in the lower class to report their fathers as interested in their performance in school and elsewhere, and more responsive to their requests for attention. Tests between the middle strata and lower strata were statistically significant: for example, classes II and V, $t = 4.75$, $p < .001$; classes I and V, $t = 3.68$, $p < .001$; classes III and IV, $t = 2.59$, $p < .02$. Lower-class mothers were also perceived as less interested and supportive than mothers in the middle class, but the differences were only significant in comparisons between classes II and the lower strata: classes II and IV, $t = 2.54$, $p < .02$; classes II and V, $t = 2.12$, $p < .05$.

While there are no data to explain why class differences in the perception of the parents were consistently greater with respect to the father than the mother, a tentative interpretation can be offered. It may be that mother-son relations are typically more secure than those between father and son, so that the boy is better able to accept a higher level of control and direction from his mother than his father without it adversely affecting his perception of the parent. The relatively authoritarian, seemingly uninterested father may appear to be a threat to the boy, possibly because he views his father as a competitor and is viewed as such by the father. In this connection it should be emphasized that the data reported in this study were obtained only from boys. There is some evidence to show that social class differences in parent-daughter relations are not identical to those between parent and son. Hence, it is possible that the results found here would not necessarily hold true for girls. The reason for the persistently more positive evaluations made by boys in class II than by their peers in the other middle strata is also not clear. Perhaps it reflects some sampling peculiarity of this relatively small group. On the other hand, it may be due to genuine differences within the middle classes which are obscured when researchers treat the middle class as a homogeneous group, as is often the case.

No doubt many kinds of experiences shape the child's perception of his parents, other than the childrearing practices described in the opening paragraphs of this paper. The child in American society, moreover, is exposed to many sources of information and numerous socialization agents other than his parents (peers, teachers, the mass media of communication, to name but a few) which provide frames of reference within which the parent is evaluated. What the parent actually does may in some cases be less important so far as the child's perception is concerned than the extra-familial influences which provide interpretations of parental behavior. Nonetheless, the data show that the boy's perceptions of parental interest, support, competence, and security (particularly of the father) are congruent with researchers' reports of differences in the socialization practices employed by various social classes.

REFERENCES

1. Bayley, N., & Schaefer, E. S. Relationship between socio-economic variables and behavior of mothers toward young children. *J. gen. Psychol.*, 1960, **96**, 61–77.
2. Bronfenbrenner, U. Socialization and social class through time and space. In E. E. Maccoby, T. M. Newcomb, & E. L. Hartley (Eds.), *Readings in social psychology*, New York: Holt, 1958. Pp. 400–425.
3. Clausen, J. A., & Williams, J. Sociological correlates of child behavior. In H. W. Stevenson, J. Kagan, & C. Spiker (Eds.), *Child psychology.* 62nd Yearb., Nat. Soc. Stud. Educ., 1963 (I).
4. Hollingshead, A., & Redlich, F. C. Social stratification and psychiatric disorders. *Amer. Sociol. Rev.*, 1953, **18**, 163–169.
5. Kohn, M. Social class and the exercise of parental authority. *Amer. sociol. Rev.*, 1959, **24**, 352–366.
6. Mass, H. S. Some social class differences in the family system and group relations of pre- and early adolescents. *Child Develpm.*, 1951, **22**, 142–152.
7. Miller, D. R., & Swanson, G. E. *The changing American parent.* New York: Wiley, 1958.
8. Rosen, B. C. The achievement syndrome: a psychocultural dimension of social stratification. *Amer. sociol. Rev.*, 1956, **21**, 203–211.
9. Rosen, B. C. Race, ethnicity and the achievement syndrome. *Amer. sociol. Rev.*, 1959, **24**, 47–60.
10. Rosen, B. C. Family structure and achievement motivation. *Amer. sociol. Rev.*, 1961, **26**, 574–585.
11. Rosen, B. C. Family structure and value transmission. *Merrill-Palmer Quart.*, 1964, **10**, 59–76.
12. Sears, R. R., Maccoby, E. E., & Levin, H. *Patterns of child rearing.* Evanston: Row, Peterson, 1957.
13. Sewell, W. H. Social class and childhood personality. *Sociometry*, 1961, **24**, 340–356.

Section VI

Cultural Factors

Introduction

Frequently an examination of child training practices in other cultures sheds light on our own practices in terms of their effects on the child's personality development. Also, some perspective is gained by placing our culture in relation to others. Are we more strict or more permissive than other cultures? Do we encourage independence earlier or later than other societies? Is the relation between parent and child closer in our culture than in others?

The first selection describes the historical and philosophical background of the establishment of the communal settlements in Israel. While research concerning the effects of the rather unique arrangement of childrearing adopted in these settlements is not clear-cut, Rapaport concludes that such a system of collective upbringing is successful in producing individuals who are capable and willing to perpetuate the Kibbutz way of life.

The Kohn selection in Section V postulated that conditions of life determine social class differences in childrearing practices. Selection No. 31 suggests that differences between American and Vietnamese children seem to reflect larger cultural differences, which in turn affect the roles family members play and the relationship among them. Straus (Selection No. 32) examines four child-rearing practices—feeding, toilet training, affection, and discipline—within the framework of the total context of a Ceylonese cultural group. The oft-mentioned autocratic approach of the European parent is borne out by Rapp's study (Selection No. 33) which found more controlling child-rearing attitudes among German mothers as compared with American mothers.

30. BEHAVIOR RESEARCH IN COLLECTIVE SETTLEMENTS IN ISRAEL: THE STUDY OF KIBBUTZ EDUCATION AND ITS BEARING ON THE THEORY OF DEVELOPMENT

DAVID RAPAPORT

I

The upbringing of children in the agricultural collectives in Israel is for the social scientist what an "experiment of nature" is for the natural scientist. The surviving preliterate cultures also furnish such "experiments of nature," but their historical background, their language, and the other communication barriers which exist between them and us, set a limit on what they can teach us about the relationships between instinctual drives, ego, and environment, that is to say, about the relationship between the life of a society and the upbringing and development of children in it. On the other hand, neither the historical conditions which brought about the kibbutz and its method of upbringing nor the communication barriers interfere prohibitively with investigating it. I shall use the meager data we do have in an attempt to expose some of the theoretical questions to the answer of which we may expect a contribution from the study of kibbutz upbringing and of the forms child development takes in it.

II

The Kibbutz Movement is about 40 years old. It arose from the Zionist-Socialist youth movement of Eastern Europe, the main tenets of which were: (a) Zionist ideology; (b) socialist ideology; and (c) the principle of realization, i.e., the commitment to translate ideology into action. In keeping with the Zionist tenet, the Movement steeped itself in the history of Jewry, in its contemporary cultural, social, economic and political situation, in the contemporary conditions of Palestine, and in the reviving Hebrew language. In keeping with the Socialist tenet, the Movement adopted a socialist ideology and explored its ethical, humanistic, social, economic and political implica-

Reprinted from the *American Journal of Orthopsychiatry*, 1958, **28**, 587–597, with permission of Dr. Elvira S. Rapaport and The American Orthopsychiatric Association, Inc.

tions, striving to create within itself human relationships based on reason, justice, cooperation, and equality. In keeping with the principle of realization, the members of the Movement prepared to go to Palestine, to become people of the soil—in contrast to their East European parents who were intellectuals or merchants or artisans or laborers in industries threatened with extinction by advancing industrialization—and to create on that soil a Hebrew community based on reason, justice, equality and cooperation.

These are the roots from which the agricultural collectives of present-day Israel grew. The principal tenets, though not unmodified by experience and circumstances, remain: (*a*) dedication to the building of a Jewish national home; (*b*) agriculture as the primary economic base of existence; (*c*) a fraternal community, small enough so that face-to-face contact and familiarity permit the application of the principle "from each according to his abilities and to each according to his needs"; (*d*) communal life in which a common ideology and practice, decided by the majority, prevails, but where the individual's and minorities' needs are considered as long as these do not clash with the cohesiveness of the community; (*e*) communal life based on cooperation, equality, justice and reason, free of competition, private property, exploitation, differences in the status of men and women, and other practices founded on passion or prejudice—religious, moralistic, conventional, or simply thoughtless and unscientific. How fully these ideals have been realized, or to what extent they have become merely lip service divorced from practice, it is not our task to examine.

Thus the Kibbutz Movement arose as a rebellion against the religious, paternalistic-familial, socioeconomic and minority life of East European Jewry, much of which is well described by Zborowski and Herzog (6).

III

What is the upbringing—referred to as "collective education"—which issued from these tenets? The two main characteristics of "collective education" are: (*a*) The upbringing of the children is the economic as well as the theoretical and ideological responsibility of the community, and not of the individual parents. (*b*) The upbringing of children by parents in their home is replaced by an upbringing in communal children's houses, where members of the community, trained for this job, are the caretakers and educators.

The leaders of kibbutz education and most observers agree that the objective of "collective education" is to raise a generation which will perpetuate the collective way of life and the ideals it stands for. There is less agreement as to the forces and aims which shaped this education. The divergent views seem to reflect the multitudinous historical, cultural, socioeconomic, traditional, and ideological factors which have shaped collective education in particular and probably shape other forms of education as well.

Let us stop for a moment and consider the theoretical implications. The educational goal of any society is to perpetuate its way of life and ideals. The analysis of the specific conditions which shape a given form of education should reveal *how* and *by what* forces that educational process was shaped in order to achieve that goal. If, for instance, the social conditions in this country usually result in our children having a lot to do with "sitters," and our socioeconomic conditions usually result in our children being taught by teachers who, in relation to their training and to the prevailing wages of labor, are badly underpaid, then these socioeconomic facts are some of the factors which bring about that form of education by which our society perpetuates itself. At first this conclusion may seem arbitrary, particularly to you, many of whom must often have protested against the misuses of "sitters" and against the low wages paid to teachers. But our protests are just as much part of the procedure by which our society creates the form of education by which it perpetuates itself, as the factual conditions and their well-known refractoriness to change. The proof for such assertions should be sought, for instance, in the fact that our society has not yet collapsed, though the teacher's wages and status seem to have been relatively unchanged for several generations.

What are the factors variously assumed to be responsible for the institution of collective education?

Some of the writers mentioned consider the major factor to be the changed role of the woman in the collective. If she was to become man's equal and a worker just like him, she had to be freed from household chores. Thus the upbringing of children had to become a job, to be performed by those who could do it best or who were available.

To other writers the salient factor seemed to be the rebellion against the patriarchal authority of the East European Jewish father. The pressure of paternal authority was heavy on the Jewish youth of Eastern Europe and bred the determination that their own children should not labor under this burden. This determination seems to be shared by the European immigrant to America also, and may be one of the factors which shape the upbringing of our children too. This explanation implies that rebels against parental authority do not find it easy to take on the parents' role and therefore relegate it to experts.

Still another explanation, mindful of the rationalist ideology of the youth movement and the collectives, attributes a paramount role to the wish to prevent the individual parental predilection or pathology from determining the child's upbringing, and to rely rather on up-to-date expert knowledge. Spiro (5) indicates that this reliance on the expert and this providing *the best* for the children is a continuation of trends basic to Eastern European Jewish life: reverence for knowledge and reason, and a paramount interest in the future of the child. The kibbutz is a child-centered society in which the children's interest overrides everything except perhaps the cohesiveness of the community and the demands of the farm economy.

Other writers consider collective education a means of dispensing with the institution of the bourgeois family, which results in the patriarchal position of the father-provider, the subordinate position of the mother-housekeeper, the hypocritical morality fostered by the conventions and economics of the marriage bond, and the dependence of upbringing on the will of the parents and particularly on the oppressive authority of the patriarchal father. They stress that the narrow loyalties of the bourgeois family, and its divisive emotional life and interests, are incompatible with communal life.

The last explanation to be mentioned is perhaps the only historically and factually incorrect one: economic need demanded that women, like men, work in the field, and gave rise to this economical, communal, care of children. It is true that the collectives grew up in most adverse economic circumstances which could not help having a determining influence on their form of life and education. This economic influence, however, is mingled with and often overshadowed by the puritanical ethics and ideological intents of the youth movement from which these collectives stemmed, and thus is by no means simple and direct. Factually, it cannot be determined whether collective upbringing is the most economical form of upbringing, because we do not know the cost of upbringing which *these* people would have had to pay if they had not embarked on collective education. What would have happened if Napoleon had *not* been beaten at Waterloo is an unanswerable question. The comparison with the cost of upbringing in cooperative (not communal) settlements seems to show that collective education is the more expensive of the two.

Let us assume, with Erik Erikson (1), that in bringing up of children, every society confronts each developmental (psychosexual and ego) stage of the child, through its caretaking people and institutions, with the demands of its living conditions, traditions and attitudes, in such a way as to enable and compel the child so to solve the psychosexual and psychosocial crises brought on by development, that the solution will bring him a step closer to becoming a viable and effective member of that society. On this assumption, the factors responsible for the existing form of kibbutz upbringing appear as the mediating links between the way of life of this community and the methods it uses to shape new generations to perpetuate it. The uniqueness of collective education lies in, among other things, the fact that these mediating factors could be directly studied, and would not have to be unearthed at a distance of centuries or against the handicap of our own inclination to take our system of upbringing for granted. Such a study may pave the way toward the understanding of Western systems of education and may even begin to show us the ways in which they adjust or can be adjusted to the needs of our changing social conditions. We may even learn to accept the idea that in the upbringing which we gave our children, and in their developmental crises and pathology, we pay the price for our social-technological "achievements." We may cease to be alarmed about our upbringing, or may accept our alarm as an indispensable part of the process of adjustment of upbringing to changing social conditions.

IV

The study of kibbutz education could shed light not only on how social, historical and economic conditions shape educational institutions, but also on how these institutions of upbringing shape the development of the individual child. Our own form of bringing up children and the changes which are taking place in it give rise to many developmental forms, and some of these alarm us because they seem to be pathological. In addition, our increasing knowledge about psychopathology and psychodynamics, and public consciousness of "mental health," spotlight our children's behavior, doing away with the old privacy of development and education, and we seem to see pathology everywhere. In spite of the contributions toward the understanding of "normal," "healthy" development by Erikson (2) and others, we—and the parents—are often bewildered when we have to decide what is pathological and what is developmental. The study of collective education, in which the privacy of familial education is eliminated by factors other than insight and public consciousness, may provide some of the means for deciding whether some of our observations of "problem" behavior are merely developmental, transient though necessary consequences of our changing educational institutions, or pathological outcomes of our failing upbringing.

Let us therefore briefly review the meager information available on the institutions of collective upbringing and on the development of children in the kibbutz.

1. Collective upbringing begins when the child and the mother return from the hospital to the kibbutz. The infant spends his first year in the "infants' house," in which there may be up to 15 infants, who, under optimal conditions, are cared for by a *metapelet* and her two aids, all trained for their work. For 6 weeks the mother does not work; after that she gradually returns to her regular work, though she continues to feed the child on "worktime" until he is weaned (6 to 8 months), whether the feeding is from the breast or from the bottle. The feeding mothers are usually together at the 6 feeding times of the 4-hour schedule. For the first 6 months the infant does *not* leave the infants' house, but is visited there by the parents and siblings for an hour in the evening. After 6 months he is taken to the parents' room for the evening visits. Otherwise the care of the child is entirely entrusted to the *metapelet*.

2. In general, after the first year the children move to the "toddlers' house," where a new *metapelet* looks after a group of four to six toddlers, taking care of their needs, training in eating and toilet training. The visits with the parents now become two hours long in the evening, and include the whole Sabbath, but remain a time of play, walks, and entertainment. Between the

second and third years a nursery teacher enters the toddlers' group; like the *metapelet*, she looks after their physical needs, but is primarily concerned with their social and intellectual development.

3. At 4 years of age the children enter kindergarten, and generally move to a new house; the group is enlarged to 16–18, with a new teacher and *metapelet*. This larger group, though it will change its form of life, will stay together till it enters high school at 12. Free and supervised play, excursions to the farm, arts, group readings, visits with the parents on evenings and holidays, are the children's daily routine; and their care, discipline, and the fostering of group spirit and intellectual development are the responsibility of the *metapelet* and teacher.

4. A year or two in kindergarten is followed by a "transitional" year, i.e., preparation for grammar school, and with it an hour's work daily in taking care of their house, school, garden and a few fowl. In the grammar school, teaching is by the project method, and the children have their say in it. The relation to the teacher is informal and passing to the next grade is automatic.

5. With the twelfth year comes the high school, a male teacher and educator, and membership in the youth movement. The group is enlarged to 25 members and includes children from other kibbutzim and from cities. At this point the children begin to work 1½ to 3 hours a day on the big farm. The curriculum is more like that of a European than of an American high school. Besides the teachers, the educator and the group itself play a major role in planning and in the maintenance of discipline.

The effects of this education on development, behavior and interpersonal relations I shall discuss under three headings: the development of interpersonal relationships; the development of behavior "problems"; and the development of personal effectiveness.

1. The parents seem to play no less of a role in the young child's life than in familial-parental education. The child reacts to their absence, illness, or death *very* strongly, and if the parent (being a *metapelet*) takes care of other children, jealousy is intense; but reactions to the absence or change of the *metapelet* are often just as strong. The anticipation of the visit with the parents is great, but so is the anticipation of returning to the children's house. The disciplinary figure is the *metapelet;* the parents are, in general, permissive figures. The tension between the parents and the disciplining "parent substitutes" seems to result in problems both for the organization of education and for the children in regard to their loyalties, (though definitive data on these are not yet available.) According to Spiro's questionnaire study (4), the parent is the person from whom the child can expect praise but not blame. Blame is expected from the *metapelet* and from the group, though praise too is expected from the group and more often so than from the parents. Moreover, when the children enter high school, the attachments to the parents, the frequency of visits, and the intimacies fall off sharply.

The importance of the peer group begins early and steadily increases. In the toddler and nursery school groups, quick shifts from warm cooperation to angry clashes are common. Yet the peer group early becomes the most important "praising figure," and as the time for high school approaches, the *metaplot* and teachers yield their preeminence as the most important blaming figures to the group. The prevalent characteristics of the high school group are mutual assistance and protection of the weaker members. Identification with the group is strong and is the major source of security. Possessiveness, acquisitiveness, and striving for personal success are minimal, and the striving for excellence is motivated by social responsibility.

2. The facts concerning behavior problems are even sketchier. Various observers report:

(*a*) Relative severity of toilet training, and of the problems connected with it. This is attributed partly to the limited time available to the *metapelet*, who therefore deals with the toilet training of the children as a group and not individually. The "difficulties" are also made obvious by the fact that "picking up" children at night is out of the question for practical reasons. The relative severity of training is mitigated by the informedness about prevailing psychological views. The public obviousness of any difficulty may give an exaggerated picture of the incidence of difficulties. No strictly comparable data from other forms of upbringing are extant which could decisively show that the incidence of training difficulties and failures is greater in collective education. Yet reports of a greater incidence of such difficulties, particularly enuresis, cannot be discounted.

(*b*) The situation is similar concerning the claims as to a greater incidence of masturbation, nail-biting, thumb-sucking, and feeding difficulties.

(*c*) The reports also seem to suggest a selective neglect of the children at the toddler age, explained by the fact that the *metapelet,* occupied with the household of the toddler house, cannot provide individual care.

(*d*) High incidence of unmitigated aggression in the toddler and nursery age is also reported. Again, however, there are no reliable comparative data from other types of upbringing, and the public character of collective education, which exhibits rather than conceals these phenomena, cannot be discounted.

Critically inclined observers draw the conclusions:

(*a*) Collective education, by enforcing separation of the child from the parents, brings these phenomena about, and they should therefore be considered pathological symptoms of the separation.

(*b*) Mass upbringing, lacking individual care and affection, is responsible for these phenomena, which must therefore be considered pathological.

(*c*) The multiple parent figures and the division of the sources of affection and discipline are the sources of these phenomena, since they increase the opportunity for conflict, for clashing loyalties, and for frustration, rather than reducing them as kibbutz educators hoped—and at times claimed—they would.

However, the available facts, surveyed above, suggest that collective education involves no *separation* in the customary sense of the word. Tensions in general, divided loyalties and multiple parent figures in particular, are present in all forms of upbringing and may be indeed a necessary part of all except a "hothouse" upbringing. Yet these arguments do not definitely contradict the explanations listed, since there are no objective and exhaustive studies available either to refute or to corroborate these explanations.

All educational systems *have* their tensions. Erikson (1) points out that a society shapes the personality types which are viable in it, not only by providing outlets for tensions, but also by building character structure *to maintain and to contain certain tensions*. It is therefore possible that the behavior problems described are forms of developmental crises natural to collective upbringing, rather than pathological symptoms. To what extent these behavior problems are one or the other can be decided only by systematic study of the kibbutz society, of the methods of collective upbringing, and of the development and pathology of the children brought up in it as they attain adulthood. Such studies face the problem of the social relativity of pathology, one of the crucial and unsolved problems of orthopsychiatry. The increasing volume of "pathology" we seem to see in our children requires that we learn to distinguish pathological crises from the developmental crises of normal growth proper to our society and upbringing.

3. There seems to be agreement that the individuals who grow up in the kibbutz are, in general, adapted to this collective way of life: it is claimed that only 3.1 per cent of these have left it *altogether*, while the lowest percentage of members not brought up in the kibbutz who leave it is *annually* 2.9 per cent. The dissatisfactions which cause Spiro to speak of a crisis in the older generation do not, according to him, touch the younger generation which grew up in collective education.

Observers also seem to agree that the children who, as toddlers, showed such poor eating habits, so much bed-wetting, nail-biting, aggressiveness (Kardiner [3] goes so far as to report secondhand that "the law of the jungle prevails among them"), masturbation, motor restlessness, and tantrums, by the time of puberty become cooperative, self-contained, sturdy, responsible individuals. In the ranks of the commandos (Palmach) of the 1948 War of Independence, the majority of whom were recruited from kibbutzim, they acquitted themselves magnificently: the reports claim no incidence of war neuroses among them, describe them as people who readily took responsibility and initiative, and who subordinated personal interest to that of the group to the point of necessary sacrifice.

On the other hand, a tendency to cling to their group or other kibbutz groups when away from the kibbutz, in the army or in occupational training, has been variously interpreted as lack of individuality and independence. However, here again the evidence is inconclusive.

It is also reported that they lack the cultural-intellectual bent of the founding kibbutz generation and the curiosity, speculative bent, and color-fulness of the East European Jew. Some go so far as to describe them as emotionally flat and stolid. Yet the evidence of their art work, their songs and dance, and their agricultural achievements would be hard to reconcile with this sweeping generalization: a study of the actual facts is urgently needed.

The most interesting data pertain to the relationship of the sexes. Since the kibbutz ideology is opposed to all hypocrisy, collective education is coedu-cational in the full sense of the word. Boys and girls grow up in the same rooms. As toddlers and nursery school children they use the same baths and lavatories, without privacy. This lack of privacy shows a spontaneous devolu-tion; boys and girls spontaneously separate, first in the lavatories and then in the showers. Similar in portent and even more striking is the fact that this education results in exogamy: as a rule, the marriages are *not* between people who have grown up in the same group. A spontaneous "incest" taboo seems to have arisen. Last but not least, it is claimed that not a single case of homo-sexuality has been encountered amongst the young people of collective upbringing.

Let us assume for the moment that the situation with enuresis, autoerotic manifestations, aggressiveness, and impressions of neglect between the ages of one and six, is actually as the most critical reports state it; and that the situation with the young adults' adaptedness, cooperativeness, responsibility, effectiveness is actually as it is stated by the most appreciative reports. On these assumptions we would have to conclude:

(*a*) We cannot be sure whether our own upbringing, which is hidden by privacy and restraining conditions, has or does not have the same kind and amount of "behavior problems" which become manifest in collective upbring-ing which lacks such "hiding factors."

(*b*) It is possible that what we usually regard as "behavior problems" are, in certain types of upbringing, normal phenomena of a development whose outcome is a viable human being adapted to the environment from which that form of upbringing issues.

(*c*) It is likely that a society, whatever its conscious intentions, more or less inevitably produces a method of upbringing whose crises and difficulties, as well as assets, contribute to the development of human beings adapted to that society.

But these conclusions and their underlying assumptions must be verified by the comparative study of collective and familial upbringing.

V

This survey points up the burning need for systematic studies to lend solid foundations to, or to contradict, the generalizations of the reports so far published. Such systematic studies will have to include historical and factual surveys as well as investigations of attitudes and sociometric relations, as well as diagnostic and follow-up studies. Spiro (4) is so far the only one who has used some such techniques, showing an appreciation of the problems to which historical studies, interviews and direct observation alone can give no answer.

The main question to be answered by such systematic studies is: Are the behavior problems reported the natural price (i.e., attributable to developmental crises) that the education for this type of society exacts, or are they pathological symptoms indicating that collective upbringing violates human nature? The two detailed reports agree that the kibbutz is successful in raising generations who can perpetuate its way of life. If their impression be correct, before us lies an education which appears to differ in several ways from ours, which appears to pay a different price for its attempt to raise people fit to live in the society which produced it than the price we pay for our attempts to bring up children to our way of life.

Erikson has shown that the Yurok and the Sioux fostered different kinds of solutions of the common and ubiquitous developmental crises of human development than we do, and thereby raised individuals viable in their life situation and traditional framework, in which the average child brought up in our type of education might not be viable. The study of the kibbutz frame of reference, which should be so much more accessible and comprehensible to us than that of the Indians and other preliterates, may give us a better understanding of the price our education exacts. It may even give us further elaboration of the general relations Erikson infers as obtaining between (*a*) historical, institutional and economic realities of societies, (*b*) practices of upbringing, and (*c*) forms of individual development. Finally, it may show us that it is inherent in the "human condition" that all societies' education will inevitably exact, and thus all societies will pay, a price—a necessary sacrifice—in the coin of developmental crises and pathology, for their successes in adapting their successive generations to their ways of life.

The scientific problem is not whether collective education is good or bad. Even if that were the question, we would have to ask further, good or bad for whom and for what? The problem is: *What* traditional, historical, organizational, institutional and economic forces find their unnoted expression in the form of collective education, and *how* do these forms of upbringing induce behavior forms (social modalities) and behavior problems which in their genetic sequence result in individuals who perpetuate the way of life of the kibbutz?

REFERENCES

1. Erikson, E. H. *Childhood and society*. New York: Norton, 1950.
2. Erikson, E. H. Growth and crises of the "healthy personality." In C. Kluckhohn and H. Murray (Eds.), *Personality in nature, society and culture*. (2nd ed.) New York: Knopf, 1953. Pp. 185–225.

3. Kardiner, Abraham. The roads to suspicion, rage, apathy, and societal disintegration. In Iago Galdston (Ed.), *Beyond the germ theory*. New York: Health Education Council, 1954. Pp. 157–170.

4. Spiro, Melford E. Education in a communal village in Israel. *Am. J. Orthopsychiatry*, 1955, **25**, 283–292.

5. Spiro, Melford E. *Kibbutz: venture in utopia*. Cambridge, Mass.: Harvard Univer. Press, 1956.

6. Zborowski, Mark, & Herzog, Elizabeth. *Life is with people*. New York: Internat. Univer. Press, 1952.

31. FAMILY ATTITUDES AND SELF-CONCEPT IN

VIETNAMESE AND U.S. CHILDREN

Mary M. Leichty

This study is concerned with differences in self concept and in attitudes toward the family as expressed by a group of Asian children and a group of American children. The latter were living in a small town in a semirural area of Michigan. The former were living in the so-called rice bowl of Vietnam, one of the most stable and prosperous parts of the country. It has experienced a minimum of acculturation by the French and was relatively unaffected by the recent war. The economy is largely agricultural and sufficient rice is produced so that some can be exported. The Vietnamese village is hundreds of years old its families have lived there for generations with little movement of population. It is probably a community as nearly typical of the general culture as can be found in Vietnam.

GROUPS

The American sample consisted of 60 fourth- and fifth-grade children between the ages of 9½ and 11¼. The Vietnamese group was composed of 47 children in the equivalent of the fourth grade in the United States, ranging from 9 to 15 years of age. This age variation, unusual in a U.S. school, is the usual pattern in Vietnam, where school facilities are inadequate and many children are delayed several years in entering because there is no room for them. The older children in this group have not failed; failure results in withdrawal. They simply started their education later than did the younger ones. There were no significant differences in response related to age. There were 28 girls and 19 boys in the Vietnamese group and 34 girls and 26 boys in the U.S. group.

PROCEDURE

The test instrument was a sentence-completion test adapted from Sacks and Levy (1952). The 36 sentence stems were designed to tap the children's attitudes in nine areas: Father, Mother, Family, Friends, Fears,

Reprinted with abridgement from *American Journal of Orthopsychiatry*, 1963, **33**, 38–50, with permission of the author and the American Orthopsychiatric Association, Inc.

Guilt, Goals, Ambition and Future (Table 1). The sentences were translated from English into Vietnamese and given to the children on a mimeographed sheet with spaces for writing in their completions.

No specific hypotheses were formulated for the study. Responses to each sentence stem were examined and categories were chosen that appeared most clearly to differentiate the two groups of subjects. The aim of the study was to search out descriptions of these two samples. Descriptions such as the present ones could be very useful in formulating hypotheses for future cross-cultural research.

Table 1   *The Sentence Completion Test*

1. I feel that my father seldom
2. When the odds are against me
3. I always wanted to
4. To me the future looks
5. I know it is silly but I am afraid of
6. I feel that a real friend
7. Compared with most families, mine
8. My mother
9. I would do anything to forget the time I
10. If my father would only
11. I believe that I have the ability to
12. I could be perfectly happy if
13. I look forward to
14. Most of my friends don't know that I am afraid of
15. I don't like people who
16. My family treats me like
17. My mother and I
18. My greatest mistake was
19. I wish my father
20. My greatest weakness is
21. My secret ambition in life
22. Some day I
23. I wish I could lose the fear of
24. The people I like best
25. Most families I know
26. I think that most mothers
27. When I was smaller, I felt guilty about
28. I feel that my father is
29. When luck turns against me
30. What I want most out of life
31. When I am older
32. My fears sometimes force me to
33. When I'm not around, my friends
34. When I was a small child, my family
35. I like my mother but
36. The worst thing I ever did

RESULTS

When the Vietnamese responses were translated into English it was found that 4 items could not be scored. Most of the subjects had interpreted the Family Item 25, "Most families I know . . . ," to mean, "Which families do you know?" and they responded with such completions as "Hiep's family" or "those in my village." In Item 4, "To me the future looks . . . ," the Vietnamese word used for *future* was a difficult one from classical language, and the children did not understand the sentence. It was similar with Items 20 and 21. Therefore, these 4 were discarded, leaving a total of 32 sentence stems for analysis.

Father Items

Toward the father (Table 2), both U.S. and Vietnamese children showed positive feelings, but the effect of cultural experiences becomes very clear in the content of these feelings. The Vietnamese children emphasized their father's health, his working and their own education. For Item 1, 19 of the 20 children who mentioned work indicated that they felt their fathers worked hard. Of those 12 who referred to health, 10 felt their fathers were in good health. On the other hand, 9 of the 11 children who thought of their father's happiness felt he was unhappy. In completing this same sentence, only 7 of 59 U.S. children who responded utilized these three categories, work, health and happiness. Instead, they emphasized an emotional relationship: My father seldom punishes . . . gets angry . . . is mean, and the like.

The concept of the father as a person is tapped by Item 28, "I feel my father is . . . " Here, the most frequent category for both groups of children was some sort of personal attribute, positive in both cases, but with a clear qualitative difference. Twenty-three of the U.S. children used the word *nice* in describing their father. Other terms were *great guy, wonderful, sweet.* These words seem to have a different feeling tone than those used by the Vietnamese children: *serious, worthy, cares about his work.*

What the U.S. and Vietnamese children wanted from their father is shown in their responses to Items 10 and 19. The Vietnamese children had expectancies regarding education, or that their fathers be strong and work; for example, they completed the stem, "I wish that my father . . . ," with "strong to earn money for my family," "do something to have enough food and clothing for me," "would live long to take care of my family," "works to bring me up and send me to school," "send me to school, I am very happy," or "work hard, I'll help him." The U.S. children wanted from their fathers either material things or that the father do something for them. To this same stem, U.S. children gave such completions as "would play catch," "would buy me cowgirl boots." To the stem, "If my father would only . . . ," they made such responses as "buy me a horse," "get a new car," "buy me pretty presents, I would be satisfied," "let me have a BB gun."

Table 2   *Number of Michigan (M) and Vietnamese (V) Children Responding to the
Father Items*

Item 1 *I feel that my father seldom . . .*

	M	V
Work	6	20
Health, Happiness	1	23
Relationship with subject	26	2
Recreation	7	0
Miscellaneous	19	2
Total	59	47

Item 10 *If my father would only . . .*

Work	0	18
Education	0	14
Do something for subject	36	0
Emotional relationship	9	9
Miscellaneous	13	2
Total	58	43

Item 28 *I feel my father is . . .*

Work	3	12
Personal attribute	43	19
Relationship with subject	6	8
Health	2	3
Miscellaneous	5	3
Total	59	45

Item 19 *I wish my father . . .*

Work	2	14
Health	0	19
Do something for subject	24	0
Emotional relationship	3	7
Miscellaneous	28	4
Total	57	44

Mother Items

In expressing their attitudes toward the mother (Table 3), the Vietnamese children stressed work. The U.S. children stressed an emotional
relationship or some personal attribute. Items 8 and 26 indicate the attitudes
of the children toward their own mothers and toward mothers in general.
More frequently than the U.S. children, the Vietnamese expressed the idea
that mothers work hard for their families. To the stems, "My mother . . . ,"

and, "I think most mothers are . . . ," typical Vietnamese responses were "must work very hard to raise the children," "works without interruption," "works thriftily to bring me up and send me to school." In responding to these same stems, the U.S. children emphasized emotional relationships and personality attributes—"are sweet," "are mean sometimes," "are nice," "love their children."

To the stem of Item 17, "My mother and I . . . ," there was a sex difference in response between the Vietnamese boys and girls. Of the 16 children who utilized the work category, 14 were girls. They seemed to see themselves and their mothers as cooperating in working: "work very hard to

Table 3 *Number of Michigan (M) and Viet-namese (V) Children Responding to the Mother Items*

Item 8 *My mother . . .*

	M	V
Work	6	31
Personal characteristic	25	5
Relationship with subject	16	7
Miscellaneous	11	1
Total	58	44

Item 17 *My mother and I . . .*

Work	6	17
Emotional relationship	13	13
Go somewhere, do something	33	5
Miscellaneous	5	8
Total	57	43

Item 26 *Most mothers . . .*

Work	3	22
Personal characteristic	52	15
Child bearing	1	7
Miscellaneous	4	3
Total	60	47

Item 35 *I like my mother but . . .*

Subject must make return	1	23
Mother acts negatively	19	3
Subject feels negative	14	0
Miscellaneous	19	17
Total	53	43

support the family," "work hard to help my grandfather." The boys, on the other hand, stressed an emotional relationship: "My mother and I are very happy," "loves me very much." There was no sex difference in choice of category by the U.S. children. Thirteen expressed an emotional relationship with the mother, but 33 thought of their relationship with their mother as one of going somewhere or doing something together: "go down town and I go tap dance," "have fun going places," "play games," "both work in Scouts."

Item 35 was designed to elicit negative attitudes toward the mother: "I like my mother, but . . . ." The U.S. children's most frequent response was that their mothers act in some negative way. They punish, get angry and so on. The second most frequent category of response was that the child himself feels negatively: "I get mad at her," "I love my mother, but sometimes I don't." The majority of the Vietnamese children chose neither of these categories, but indicated that the child must make some return: "I love my mother but I am still young I cannot pay my debt," "I have to do something to pay the debt of gratitude a little," "I cannot do anything for my parents."

Family Items

In comparing their own families to others, in Item 7, most of the Vietnamese children made their comparisons an economic one. Twenty-four indicated that they felt their family was poorer than other families; 10 thought their families were as well off or richer than others. Most of the Michigan children indicated that their families had, to a greater degree, some positive quality: "is the best," "is happy," "is a nice one."

In describing the way their families regard them—"My family treats me like . . . ," Item 16—all but 3 of the Vietnamese expressed a positive feeling. The 3 negative responses expressed the idea that the family relationship was unhappy. The Michigan children were about equally divided in their feelings about how their families treated them. Twenty-nine indicated that their families treated them very well: "like I were a king," "like I wanted to be treated," "like I was real nice;" but 28 indicated negative or neutral reactions: "like a girl," "like a brat," "like a rat," "like a baby." Eleven said their families treated them like a baby.

The consciousness on the part of the Vietnamese child that his family has had to work hard and has labored to bring him up is clearly pointed up in the response to Item 34, "When I was a small child, my family . . . ." Most completions of this sentence fell into 3 categories, work, bringing up the child and a positive family relationship. They "worked hard in the field," or "how hard my family worked and I will pay them back." Most of the Michigan children spoke of some relationship with their families, usually a positive one. For example, "When I was a small child, my family loved me," "was kind to me," "said to me things to learn."

Friends Items

The 4 items that tapped peer relationships, examined the subjects' feelings and expectations in regard to friends. Three items dealt with what kind of people the subject likes. In responding to Item 24, "The people I like best are . . . ," both groups interpreted the sentence quite literally and responded in terms of particular people, rather than in terms of personality attributes or some other quality. However, the people the Michigan children liked best were friends, whereas the Vietnamese children indicated they liked their families best.

Item 6, "I feel a real friend . . . ," and Item 15, "I don't like people who . . . ," dealt with what were seen as the positive and negative attributes of friends. As shown in Item 6, most of the Michigan children felt that a real friend has some attribute or characteristic such as friendliness, being nice or being kind. The response of the Vietnamese children seemed to show more egocentrism, most of them utilizing some self-reference in their completions, for example, "I feel that a real friend does not say nasty things to me."

When asked to state their dislikes, Item 15, "I don't like people who . . . ," the most frequent completion in both groups was in terms of some personal characteristic: "are conceited" "are not kind," "are lazy." The children from both cultures disapproved of many of the same personal characteristics but they also seem to be learning to disapprove of divergent social attributes. For example, children in both samples disapproved of the individual who is mean or unkind. Anger, lying and cheating were also mentioned by both groups as being undesirable. On the other hand, 9 U.S. children but no Vietnamese said they did not like superior, conceited people. No Michigan child mentioned laziness as an undesirable characteristic, though this response was given by 5 Vietnamese. The second most popular category differed for the 2 groups. The Vietnamese emphasized that they did not like people who were "bad friends." The Michigan children made some self-reference, responding that they did not like people who treated them ill, giving such completions as "tease me," "laugh at me," "don't like me."

The remaining 5 areas (Fears, Guilt, Abilities, Future, and Goals) may be said to describe the subject's self-concept.

Fears Items

Inherent in a person's fears and guilt feelings are society's methods of molding the individual to fit society's needs. The Michigan children responded in a similar way to all three Items, 5, 14 and 23. (See Table 4.) They expressed an externalized fear, emphasizing animals and the dark. For example, 44 of the U.S. children utilized the objective category in Item 14; 23 said they were afraid of some animal and 11 said they were afraid of the dark. For this same Item 14, 12 of the Vietnamese also indicated some objective fear, but no Vietnamese child said he was afraid of either the dark or

Table 4   *Number of Michigan (M) and Vietnamese
(V) Children Responding to the Fears Items*

Item 5 *I know it is silly, but I am afraid of* . . .

	M	V
Parental-familial	2	13
Sociocultural	0	17
Objective	45	8
Miscellaneous	10	7
Total	57	46

Item 23 *I wish I could lose the fear of* . . .

	M	V
Failure, Inadequacy	6	23
Object, Event	44	12
Miscellaneous	6	3
Total	56	38
Realistic fear	17	21
Unrealistic fear	34	16
Other	5	1
Total	56	38

Item 14 *My friends don't know I am afraid of* . . .

	M	V
Parental-familial	1	4
Sociocultural	0	16
Objective	44	12
Miscellaneous	12	11
Total	57	43

Item 32 *My fears force me to* . . .

	M	V
Perform duty	10	24
Do something bad	21	5
Negative feelings	9	10
Other	9	4
Total	49	43

animals. Six of the 12 said they were afraid of being beaten by the teacher and 3 others said they were afraid of "cruelty," by which they may have meant physical punishment. Primarily in responding to Items 5, 14 and 23, the Vietnamese seemed to be expressing more internalized sorts of fears. They emphasized fear of personal inadequacy, failure in parental-familial relationships or some violation of sociocultural mores. They feared their parents' blame for something, or that they would make a mistake or be "stupid." School failure seems to be an important fear: "I wish I could lose the fear of marks on my exams."

Response to Item 23 was also categorized as expressing a realistic or an unrealistic fear. A realistic fear was considered to be one that might, in truth, be harmful or painful to the child, for example, fear of school or of being dis-obedient. Fear of the dark, of mice, lions, snakes were considered unrealistic. The likelihood that a Michigan child, living in a town would be injured by a lion, a spider or a poisonous snake is too remote to be considered realistic. No Vietnamese child mentioned fear of an animal in responding to this item, though poisonous snakes are relatively common in their experience.

Item 32 tells something of the effect on the child of his fears, in what way they influence his behavior. Most of the Vietnamese children indicated that their fears lead them to perform some duty, such as "work for my parents," "to go to search for snails in the pond and gather vegetables," "to work beyond my strength." Most of the Michigan children indicated that due to their fears they do something bad or undesirable: "be mean," "do bad things," "disobey my mother."

Guilt Items

In all 4 of the items tapping guilt feelings, the emphasis by the Viet-namese was on internalized guilt, some expression of personal or interpersonal inadequacy. The Michigan children's guilt was more externalized, related to some object or event. These 4 items were also categorized as to whether the guilt centered around parental-familial relationships or broader sociocultural mores. Response to Item 36 is illustrative of this categorization. Emphasis by the Michigan children was on violation of cultural mores, "The worst thing I ever did was hit Peggy," or on something that happened to the child, "I would give anything to forget the time I fell out of the car," or "first smelled ether." They seemed to emphasize some concrete, discrete incident. The 7 Vietnamese responses classified as violations of cultural mores had a far different flavor: "The worst thing I ever did was not doing things thoroughly," or "waste rice." However, more of the Vietnamese responses (18) were classified as guilt related to violation of parental-familial relationships: "The worst thing I ever did was make my parents sad," or, "disobey my parents."

Response to Item 36 also gives some indication of the depth of guilt feelings experienced by the Vietnamese children. Sixteen responses could not be categorized as either parental-familial or cultural, and were placed in a third category. Of these 16, 10 indicated a reluctance on the part of the child to confess his guilt. Samples of these responses are: "to make it good so no one blames or feels ashamed," "to get rid of it from my conscience," "make it good again." Of the 16 Michigan responses in this category, 7 indicated that the worst thing the child ever did was to have something happen to him: "being bit by a dog," "stabbed by a pitchfork."

Almost one-half the Vietnamese children gave a response to Item 9 that is very difficult to interpret. Twenty-three said they would like to forget the time "when I was young," or "when I was young my parents worked hard to bring me up." Failure in reciprocity, in fulfilling one's duty toward the parents, was also frequently expressed: "My greatest mistake was not doing anything good for my parents," "not grateful to my parents."

Abilities Items

Items 2 and 29 tell something of the way the child tries to cope with a difficult situation. The majority in both groups seemed to feel that the difficulties in any given situation are beyond their changing—the child can only accept it with some sort of negative feelings, such as "be sad" or "feel guilty." However, in responding to Item 2, 17 of the Vietnamese, as compared to 2 Michigan children, related difficulty to "luck": "When the odds are against me I am unlucky." On the other hand, 16 of the U.S. children, as compared to 3 of the Vietnamese, indicated a feeling that they might be able to do something about it themselves: "When the odds are against me I will fight," or, "I work harder to get better."

Response to Item 11 suggests that the Michigan children saw their abilities in terms of recreational goals: "I feel I have the ability to play football," or, "to sing and tap dance." The Vietnamese responses fell with equal frequency into two categories—vocational, or the ability to complete their education. Of the 23 whose responses were classified as vocational, 10 said they felt they had the ability to serve their country, 8 that they could care for their families, and 5 that they could work.

Goals Items

In thinking of their goals (Table 5), the U.S. children emphasized vocation, recreation or some material gain. The Vietnamese emphasized the attainment of some personal attribute, their family relationship or education for themselves. For example, in responding to Item 3, 35 of the U.S. children wanted something vocational or recreational: "I always wanted to go to Yellowstone," "be a nurse," or, "be a cowboy." Twenty-one of the Vietnamese children spoke of wanting an education: "I always wanted to study to be smart," or, "to go to school." A second frequent category of response for the Vietnamese was a desire for some personal attribute, most frequently to be happy.

Emphasis on material things by the U.S. children is shown by their response to Item 12. "I could be perfectly happy if . . . ." Thirty-one used the phraseology, "if I could have," or, "if I could get," for example, "cowgirl boots," "a swimming pool," "a trip to Texas." Of the 3 Vietnamese children who utilized this category of having something, 2 referred to having wealth and the other said, "I could be perfectly happy if my parents buy clothes for me to go to school." The major emphasis of the Vietnamese children was on being something or doing something. For example, "I could be perfectly happy if I finish my work," or, "if I am not wrong."

The U.S. emphasis on personal, material wants contrasts to the Viet-

Table 5   *Number of Michigan (M) and Vietnamese (V) Children Responding to the Goals Items*

Item 3   *I always wanted to . . .*

	M	V
Recreation, Vocation	35	2
Education	9	21
Personal attribute	8	17
Family relationship	1	7
Other	7	0
Total	60	47

Item 12   *I could be perfectly happy . . .*

	M	V
I am, Do something	13	30
Material, Recreational	31	3
Other	13	10
Total	57	43

Item 30   *What I want most out of life . . .*

	M	V
Have something myself	24	3
Vocational	14	0
Personal attribute	7	20
Family relationship	0	13
Other	9	8
Total	54	44

namese children's feelings of responsibility toward their parents, as brought out in response to Item 30, "What I want most out of life. . . ." Thirteen Vietnamese completions referred to family relationships: "What I want most out of life is to live to help my parents," "observe discipline," "help my young brothers and sisters," or, "do something to pay back to my parents for their work." No U.S. child referred to family relationships, whereas 24 said they wanted something material.

Future Items

These tap the child's hopes for the future (Table 6). For Item 13, most responses fell into 2 categories, either something the child desired for himself, or something he wished others to have. Twenty-one Vietnamese children hoped for something for someone else, usually something for their families: "I look forward to helping my parents," "my family healthy," or, "my parents happy."

No Michigan child's response fell into this category. Rather, they wanted something for themselves. Twenty-six indicated something material (a racoon, a new wagon, a swimming pool) or something recreational (to go somewhere,

Table 6   *Number of Michigan (M) and Vietnam-*
ese Children Responding to the Future
Items

Item 13 *I look forward to . . .*		
	M	V
Something for others	0	21
Something for subject	35	14
Personal attribute	8	7
Other	15	5
Total	58	47
Item 31 *When I am older . . .*		
Vocational	42	0
Family obligation	0	23
Do, Have something	12	0
Other	5	21
Total	59	44
Item 22 *Some day I . . .*		
Vocational	40	5
Do something, Go somewhere	16	3
Personal attribute	0	24
Other	3	10
Total	59	42

watch TV). Three looked forward to some educational goal such as college.
Of the 14 Vietnamese responses classified as something for the subject himself, all but 1 were related to education: "I look forward to rank better and
better in class, then my parents will be happy."

Regarding Items 22 and 31 there was a sharp separation between the
groups. In both items, the U.S. children emphasized vocational goals such as,
"When I am older I will be a nurse." Second in frequency they spoke of doing
or having something: "When I am older I will go to California," "have a car."
Twenty-three of the Vietnamese spoke of a feeling of obligation toward family
members: "When I am older I will pay back my debt of gratitude to my
parents," "my young brothers and sisters I must teach and advise them."

From these sentence completions emerges a fairly clear and consistent
picture of what these Vietnamese children see as their place in their society.
Work is a major aspect of the life of everyone. To these children, their family
is the core of life, and they feel they owe their parents a great deal for the
care and support they have received from them. It is parental-familial approval
that is the disciplinary guide for the growing child. Immediate personal relationships are more influential with the child than are broader sociocultural

relationships. The children's fears tend to be ones that they see as helping them to conform to the demands of society. This is done through the internalization of guilt, and the thought of having done something wrong is so exacerbating to these children that they want to forget it or do something to make amends. These Vietnamese sentence completions seem to express acceptance on the part of the child of his role in Vietnamese society. His family has given him life and has worked hard for him. For this he owes his family a debt of gratitude, which he can repay by assuming his own position of responsibility in the family structure.

The Michigan children's view of their role in society is by no means so clearly delineated. Their relationships with their parents, in fact their outlook on life, revolves about themselves. Happiness is achieved by getting or having something material, something for the child himself. The father is the agent for doing something for the child, for giving him something. The mother goes somewhere or does something with the child, participates in the child's activities. Recreation seems to be important; almost half the Michigan children spoke of their abilities as being in the recreational field. The fears and guilts of these children are externalized and expressed in terms of objective events or actions. But, parodoxically, the anxieties they expressed seemed to be unrealistic and disruptive, rather than constructive, because the children felt that instead of helping them to achieve society's aims, their fears caused them to do something they should not. Some of them are developing the feeling that they, themselves, can do something about coping with difficulties. Half the children felt that their families treat them in a negative or neutral way and, more often than the family, friends were chosen as best liked, suggesting a loosening of family ties, as well as that the factors influencing these U.S. children's behavior have a base broader than the immediate family.

These two groups of children seem to be growing up into quite different kinds of people. Because these descriptions are subjective and cannot be assumed to be typical of all Vietnamese or U.S. children, we cannot validly generalize to larger populations. Nonetheless, I would like to discuss some possible meanings of these differences.

A sex difference was noted among the Vietnamese in the way they see the mother-child relationship, but there was no difference among the U.S. children. They, both boys and girls, saw their mothers as doing something with them at their own level of activity. The Vietnamese girls saw themselves as cooperating with their mothers at their mothers' level of activity. Does this suggest an opportunity for a more adequate feminine identification for Vietnamese girls?

The fears of the Vietnamese children seem to be realistic, while those of the U.S. children are not. Perhaps this is because the Vietnamese child knows more exactly what he is supposed to be, how he can become an adequate person or, conversely, what behavior is undesirable and disapproved of. If there is a clearer sociocultural pattern for the Vietnamese child to adapt to, he may thereby be able to connect his fears to real sources rather than unrealistic ones. This could give Vietnamese children a greater sense of security.

However, the U.S. children expressed feelings of self-reliance, that they could do something to control their environment. They were also able to acknowledge negative feelings between their parents and themselves and to express criticism of their parents. Authority is not sacrosanct to them.

In the United States it is expected that at maturity, the child will, to a large extent, separate himself psychologically from his parents and assume independence in making decisions. The culture appears to be fostering this in the children through ego-development as represented by freedom to criticize authority and the child's sense that he can direct his life. But along with this there seems to be a reaching out for selfish, materialistic goals.

Vietnamese children are brought up in a predominantly Buddhist and/or ancestor-worship culture, a culture in which all final authority for the whole family rests with the father as long as he lives. In ancestor worship, this maintenance of close unity of the family is essential. Immortality is not conceived of as a life after death. The link between the past, the present and the future is maintained in the unity of the family—when the living members gather around the family altar to honor the ancestors, when they go to the altar to tell the ancestors of a marriage, or of the birth of a new generation. Child-rearing practices in this sort of culture emphasize those attributes that will maintain this family unit, a strong superego, highly internalized guilt, unquestioning acceptance of a single authority.

If such differences are developing in these children, it would be of significance beyond a simple description of two cultures. During the last quarter-century, interaction between widely divergent cultures has become of great importance to the whole world. The development of effective working relations is essential. No longer can one culture be the dominating force in a relationship. To be effective, it must, rather, be a reciprocal relationship, one based on understanding and adequate communication between the two parties. Our country has assumed the role of helping others in their development. In order to be effective in this role, to provide assistance that will in truth aid development, one needs a clear understanding of the goals and values of the society being helped. Imposing our own goals and values on a divergent culture may be a disservice both to those we are trying to aid and also to ourselves. For these reasons, it would seem essential that we make every effort to study their attitudes and value systems as an integral part of our assistance programs.

REFERENCES

Sacks, J. M., & Levy, S. The sentence completion test. In L. E. Abt & L. Bellak (Eds.), *Projective psychology*. New York: Knopf, 1952.

32. CHILDHOOD EXPERIENCE AND EMOTIONAL SECURITY IN THE CONTEXT OF SINHALESE SOCIAL ORGANIZATION

MURRAY A. STRAUS

INTRODUCTION

There is little doubt that a great part of the basic elements of personality is laid down during the socialization process. However, much of the literature on child training and personality has at least implied that the really crucial aspects of the socialization process are those which have to do with the pattern of infant discipline: feeding, elimination, mothering, and restraint. Orlansky (6) has reviewed the not inconsiderable evidence indicating the importance of post-infantile experience in the structuring of personality. He concludes ". . . that the rigidity of character structuring during the first year or two of life has been exaggerated by many authorities, and that the events of childhood and later years are of great importance in reinforcing or changing the character structure tentatively formed during infancy." More recently, Sewell (8) in commenting on the absence of relationship between infant training and the personality of the children in his sample states: "It is entirely possible that the significant and crucial matter is not the practices themselves but the whole personal-social situation in which they find their expression. . . ."

The object of the present paper is to explore the implications of the two statements cited above by means of an analysis of selected aspects of both the infant discipline and the post-infant experience of a sample of third grade children in the village of Pelpola, Raiygam Koralle. The selection has been made so as to focus on four subjects which, on the basis of current theories, should be of crucial importance for an understanding of Sinhalese personality. These are feeding, toilet training, affection, and discipline. In considering post-infantile experience, attention will be paid to certain aspects of the larger culture in which this experience takes place, on the assumption that the psychological significance of a given act may differ according to the cultural context in which it occurs.

The vast majority of the population of Ceylon are villagers and the village chosen is reasonably representative of a large block of this population.

Reprinted with slight abridgement from *Social Forces,* 1954, **33,** 152–160, with permission of the author and the University of North Carolina Press.

It has been under continuous study, both formal and informal, for a period of over three years in connection with a series of studies conducted by Bryce Ryan (7). The data reported in this paper are based on interviews with the mothers of all children who were or should have been attending the third standard in the village school. There were 48 children in this universe. There were no refusals in interviewing the mothers, but complete child training data could not be obtained for three children due to a case each of desertion, mental illness, and death.

INFANCY AND CHILDHOOD IN PELPOLA

Feeding

Of all the early experiences said to pattern the personality of an individual, feeding is usually considered of prime importance. Informal observation and the statistical data cited below leave little doubt that the feeding experience of Pelpola children, as a group, is not a traumatic one. Just over 86 percent of the children studied were fed on demand, which in Ceylon means whenever the child cries. The mean age at which weaning occurred was also late, being slightly more than two years and seven months, and the process being in most cases a gradual one. Only two mothers out of the sample said that they had any trouble in weaning the child or that the child attempted to nurse again after weaning was accomplished.

On the other hand, there were six children in the sample (14 percent) who were weaned at under six months and there were also four (9 percent) who were breast-fed until well into their fifth year. When this wide variation in age of weaning is considered in conjunction with the fact that 14 percent of the mothers took the extreme step of feeding their child according to a schedule, it is apparent that variation in feeding technic is considerable. Thus, if early feeding experiences can in fact serve to pattern certain emotional aspects of personality, this variation points to at least one of the bases for individual differences among the village population. In spite of this variability, the modal pattern is breast feeding on demand and late weaning.

Elimination

Sharing importance with feeding in the literature on child training practices and personality is elimination. Compared to the experiences of European and American children, sphincter training in Pelpola is mild indeed. However, in the light of these data, it is not strictly correct to say that "Bowel-training is practically unknown in the villages." While for the most part it is true that "there is not even a prescribed place for defecation," the overwhelming proportion (88 percent) of mothers specifically trained their children not to eliminate in the house. On the average, however, this training is very mild and is not begun until after the child's second birthday. The most frequently mentioned technic is simply to take the child out into the garden when signs of elimination are shown. Lapses are sometimes treated with a scolding and rapid achievement with praise, but the usual attitude is one of relative indifference to either event. However, the mother does examine the child's stools in order that she can treat diarrhea or constipation. Hiccoughs and belching are ignored, but if a child breaks wind in the presence of others he is ridiculed by adults. All children eventually learn to eliminate privately although they are not specifically taught to do so. The ritual of washing as opposed to the use of toilet paper is deeply ingrained. Even among the Westernized urban educated classes the use of toilet paper is to a certain extent abhorred.

The Pelpola child does seem to undergo some form of sphincter training (although extremely mild compared to that given by an American middle class family, for example) and acquires a limited repertory of anal fetishes. Nevertheless, the most important fact is not the training *per se* but the casual and indifferent atmosphere in which it occurs. In this connection, it is significant that not a single mother out of the entire sample said that she had any trouble in toilet training, in spite of the fact that 14 of the children did not learn until their fourth year. In general, there is a high degree of uniformity in the sphincter training experiences of the sample under study, and urban concepts of toilet training are practically nonexistent.

Discipline and Affection

Much recent work in the field of family sociology and child psychology has been centered on what is called a developmental approach to child rearing. This is ". . . characterized by such concepts as respect for the person (both child and adult), satisfaction in personal interaction, pride in growth and development, and a permissive, growth-promoting type of guidance as opposed to the more traditional attempts to 'make' children conform to patterns of being neat and clean, obedient and respectful, polite and socially acceptable. (3)"

While the term *permissive* is used in the description quoted, and while it is clear that permissiveness and a "developmental" attitude toward child rearing are closely related, there are nonetheless important differences. The context in which *permissive* is used shows that the concept refers primarily to what Frank (5) has called the degree of "physiological autonomy" allowed the child—in such things, for example, as feeding and elimination. That the Sinhalese child is permissively reared in this sense is clear from the description of the child training practices already presented.

A developmental approach to child rearing on the other hand refers to what might be called (paraphrasing Frank) individual, personal, or emotional autonomy. It is used primarily in the context of disciplinary training, obedience, responsibility training, and parent-child interaction. One way in which the presence or absence of a developmental attitude can be ascertained is from the response to the questions "What are the things a good mother does?" and "What are the things a good child does?" In Chicago, Duvall assigned the answers of a large sample of mothers to those two questions into two categories, developmental and traditional. According to Duvall's classification, the traditional conception of what a good child should do is expressed in such answers as "keep clean and neat," "obey and respect adults," "please adults," "respect property," "be religious," and "work well." On the other hand, the developmental concept of what a good child should do is shown in answers such as "be healthy and well," "share and cooperate with others," "be happy and contented," "love and confide in parents," "be eager to learn and show initiative," "grow as a person." Duvall reported that for the Chicago sample the proportion of developmental responses ranged from 32 to 69 percent, depending on the status level of the respondent.

In the present study Pelpola mothers were asked this question and only 5.5 percent gave an answer which can be called developmental. The single most frequently given characteristic is that the child "study well." In fact, 40 percent of all the qualities mentioned were that the child "study well." This response may merely represent a reaction to the academic role of the interviewers. On the other hand, there is abundant independent evidence that education is highly valued for its own sake and as a path to increased social status, and that status is a central value in Sinhalese culture. The importance of this value constellation is further emphasized by the fact that in this family oriented—almost family dominated—society, academic success was more frequently mentioned as a desirable quality than was the hope that the child would take care of the parents in their old age. While this latter quality was second in the frequency with which it was mentioned, it was a poor second, only 16 percent mentioning it.

An almost identical pattern of response occurred in answer to the question "What are the things a good mother does?" In contrast to Duvall's findings of from 39 to 60 percent developmental responses, the Pelpola mothers did not give any answers at all indicating a developmental conception of parenthood such as "see the child's point of view" or "make child feel secure and happy." Again the most frequently expressed trait is that a mother must see that the child "studies well." Almost 50 percent of the mothers gave this answer. Other popular answers included "make them obedient" (8 percent) and "see that they are well behaved" (6 percent) and "teach them housework" (19 percent of the answers given by the mothers of girls).

In Pelpola then, the conception of parenthood is authoritarian or traditional rather than developmental. The role of the child is a strictly subordinate one. Except for the fact that academic achievement is highly prized for the status and pecuniary rewards which it signifies, a child's first duty is to obey parental injunctions. The subordinate position of the child in Pelpola society is in accordance with the hierarchical organization which characterizes Sinhalese family and society. Subject to the qualifications inherent in the looseness of this social structure (discussed below), the father is the absolute head of the family. Below him are ranged all other family members in hierarchal order: first the wife, and then the children headed by the oldest male child. The child should not attempt to participate in adult activities. The mothers interviewed were almost unanimous in stating that a child should keep quiet when adults are around. A high premium is placed on a fertile marriage, but children are not regarded as a special and privileged group, and their inferior status is made plain to them in all dealings with adults, both at home and at school. All but two of the mothers said they insisted that the child obey without question. Children are not considered to have certain "rights" and privileges. Crimes against children are not punished with any greater severity than crimes against adults. In a rape case involving an eight year old, the offender was given a light sentence because the girl, not having attained puberty, could not (to use the local euphemism) have had her "modesty outraged," and sentences of under one year are usual in such cases. In the schools the discipline is somewhat harsh (corporal punishment is frequent) and completely arbitrary. The most common attitude of children toward their teachers is fear. Learning is by precept and rote.

On the other hand, the pattern of interpersonal relations described above, though accurate, creates a false impression through omission. In one sense, Sinhalese culture is difficult to describe. This is in part because of what can be termed the loose integration characteristic of this culture. The Sinhalese in general do not carry things to extremes. Thus, for example, it is correct (and essential for an understanding of many aspects of Sinhalese culture) to point out that women occupy a markedly inferior position in the social structure. A woman in a very real sense is the property of the husband and he acquires this property by contract with the woman's parents. At home, the husband and male children are served first, and the wife usually eats in the kitchen. When a visitor comes to the house, he will seldom see the women of the household as they remain inside and do not come out on the verandah when strange male guests are entertained. Thus many objective criteria leave little doubt about the subordinate status of women.

Yet to think that the status and role of Sinhalese women are comparable to that of Muslim women or even of Hindu women is to seriously distort the facts. The situation in Ceylon differs both in respect to the restrictions imposed, and equally or more important, the extent to which these restrictions are actually enforced. For example, there is little if any restriction on Sinhalese women appearing in public. Although the status of the woman is subordinate to that of the husband and of other males, the gulf is not wide enough to prevent the wife having a fair say in family matters or engaging in equal conversation and joking and teasing her husband and male relatives. This is also true for children. Similarly when mention is made of such characteristics as suspiciousness, jealousy, and revengefulness, it is easy for those who do not know the Sinhalese to gain the impression that they are a somber, brooding people. Not only is this not the case, but rather the Sinhalese can best be described as easygoing, laughing and carefree, with hardly a thought for the future.

When it comes to child training practices, in spite of the almost unanimous insistence on unquestioning obedience which the Pelpola parents expressed, other information indicates that such obedience is not always obtained, especially in the case of boys. Only 42 percent of the boys were reported as being "very good" about obeying. Good obedience was obtained more often from the girls, 67 percent of them being reported as "very good" about obeying. If the child does not obey, the most common disciplinary measures reported are spanking or beating the child in the case of boys (61 percent reported doing so), and scolding in the case of girls (55 percent). However, if the child commits some offense other than disobedience—e.g., destroying things, lying, etc.—verbal punishment rather than corporal punishment is more often used, only 26 percent of the mothers reporting the use of beating in such cases.

The father is a more successful disciplinarian: 81 percent of the children are reported by the mother as being very good when it comes to obeying the father, and none are reported as poor. Even here, the severity of discipline undergone by a Pelpola child is not as great as might at first be supposed. For one thing, the father, whom we have seen is the only one who really commands the type of obedience expected, plays an aloof role. He is away from the house a great deal of the day, and does not attempt to supervise the day-to-day activities of the child. The mother exercises more supervision, but even in her case it is minimal by Western standards. 43 percent of the mothers are gainfully employed; most of them work mornings on the rubber estate which almost surrounds the village. Children under five are left to the care of an older sibling or grandparents, if possible; those over five are virtually unsupervised. The material possessions of the average family are limited; there are few if any breakable objects which the child must learn not to damage. As Davis and Havighurst (2) point out, this factor alone is of considerable importance because such a situation minimizes the opportunities for disobedience and parent-child conflict.

The important fact about the disciplinary training of a Pelpola child is not the rigidity of the expected behavior, but the relatively small number of situations in which this behavior is expected, and the nonconformity of the child to the expected pattern in dealing with the mother—the parent who has real responsibility for the day-to-day training of the child. The contrast between the mother's expectation of absolute and unquestioning obedience and the actual absence of such behavior is also revealed by the finding that more than half of the mothers found it necessary to offer rewards to get the child to obey. 12 percent of the mothers interviewed indicated that they offered rewards on rare occasions, 35 percent did so "sometimes," and 14 percent made a regular practice of offering rewards for obedience. A significant role is also played by the child's grandparents who tend to dote on the child and let it have its own way. More important perhaps is the practice of children running away from home to the house of a grandparent or other near-by relative. This not too rare event (12 percent of the children had done so) can be precipitated by severe punishment or chastisement.

The father's relations with the child call for special attention. Great affection is shown by the father towards *infant* children. They are stroked, petted, kissed and fondled to a degree which would be considered almost effeminate behavior on the part of an American or English father. This treatment is obvious from informal observation of practically any family group. It is also acknowledged verbally by practically all the mothers interviewed, with 91 percent saying they thought children should have lots of babying when they are small. However, as the child grows older, this is deliberately lessened and the father's contacts with the child (especially female children) are chiefly in regard to discipline. Both parents, but especially the father, become more and more aloof and the child is no longer fondled and kissed. Village opinion is almost unanimous that to do so would be considered shameful and degrading; it would spoil the child and make him lose respect for the parents.

The permissive pattern of the Pelpola child's early experiences and the rigid and uncompromising obedience to parental authority which is demanded of the child present an interesting study in contrasts. It may be that the rigid parental expectations are an example of a culture trait which is not functionally integrated into the framework of rural Sinhalese society. However, closer analysis suggests that the very unlikelihood of complying with this expectation is itself a phenomenon of considerable importance in explaining certain aspects of this culture, and especially certain facets of Sinhalese personality. The traits referred to can be conveniently described by the use of a concept developed by Embree (4) in his study of the Thai. Embree describes Thailand as "a loosely structured social system," by which is meant "a culture in which considerable variation of individual behavior is sanctioned." By contrast, closely woven social structures—such as Japan—are those which emphasize close adherence to the behavioral norms of the culture. Low Country Sinhalese social structure does not appear to be as loosely structured as Embree's description of Thailand indicates for that society, but there is evidence to indicate that it falls well to that end of the continuum.

It is not meant to imply that the loose structuring of Sinhalese society can be traced to the discrepancy between the emotional tone imparted by childhood experiences, and the culturally approved patterns of parent-child interaction. Other and possibly more powerful factors are present—for example, Buddhism. Not only is the generalized idea of tolerance central to the Buddhist way of life, but in addition the virtual impossibility of pure *Hinayana* Buddhism as a mass religion must be considered.

Other evidence for the loose structuring of Sinhalese society is plentiful. For example, with the possible exception of the word "determined" the following quotation from Embree (4) applies equally well to Low Country Ceylon: "The longer one resides in Thailand the more one is struck by the almost determined lack of regularity, discipline, and regimentation in Thai life. In contrast to Japan, Thailand lacks neatness and discipline; in contrast to Americans, the Thai lack respect for administrative regularity and they have no industrial time sense." In business the Sinhalese are good bargainers but poor managers and administrators. They cannot stick to a rule. Sometimes the motivation is the status of the individual for whom exception is made; sometimes it is because of family pressure or other influence; sometimes it is bribery; and sometimes it is a paternalistic attitude towards those lower in status. The main point, however, is that whatever the immediate precipitating motivation there is no aversion in this culture to making exceptions. Both in business and in government, rules, regulations, fees, requirements, etc., can be easily circumvented and no stigma is attached to either party (except possibly in certain cases of flagrant bribery clearly against the public interest). Limitations of space prevent a more extensive listing of the evidence in favor of the loose structure theory, except to say that of the 19 items of evidence which Embree uses to illustrate his thesis at least 18 are also applicable to the Sinhalese.

In the contrast between the culturally determined ideal of parent-child relations and the actual non-observance of such behavior is found the earliest manifestation of the loose structuring of Sinhalese society. It is possible that this childhood experience establishes a pattern of behavior instrumental in molding other aspects of Sinhalese culture. The validity of such a causal sequence is open to considerable question. However, it seems clear that, unrealistic as they are, the cultural norms concerning parent-child relations are not an example of an unintegrated culture trait. The contrast between the ideal and the actual is a pervasive phenomenon in the loosely woven pattern of Sinhalese culture, of which the relations of parent and child are but one example. As in Thailand "The permissiveness of individual behavioral variation in the culture does not mean that the society is poorly integrated. On the contrary, the loose integration is a functional one, allowing not only variation in individual behavior but also in national behavior. It has a survival value . . . that is, a loosely integrated structure such as the Thai can adjust to external cultural influences with less drastic over-all changes than a more rigid structure such as the Japanese or Vietnamese."

CHILDHOOD EXPERIENCE AND EMOTIONAL SECURITY

There is little doubt that the Pelpola child enjoys a high degree of physiological autonomy. The type of feeding and toilet training which he undergoes are as permissive as any found in the now extensive literature on comparative child training practices. This permissiveness and the considerable affection displayed by both parents toward infant children are generally considered to provide a psychologically healthy environment, especially in that they lay the foundations for adult personality marked by confidence, security, and an absence of anxiety and tensions. In contrast to this expectation, one of the outstanding characteristics of the Sinhalese personality appears to be marked feelings of insecurity.

This then is a culture in which the infant care technics are those that lead to the expectation of an adult personality marked by confidence, security, and an absence of anxiety and tensions, but in which the modal adult is more likely to be characterized by opposite traits. Assuming the character forming efficacy of infantile disciplines to be as described in the current literature, it is necessary to turn to post-infantile experiences for an explanation of Sinhalese personality. Two aspects of the childhood experience of the Sinhalese which have been described in the paper appear to be of importance in this connection. The first is the loose structuring of Sinhalese society in general and specifically the discrepancy between the rigid verbal expectation of children's behavior and the actual weak disciplinary control and loose supervision of children. The second is the withdrawal of overt signs of parental affection after about age four or five.

As mentioned in the previous section, Sinhalese children are given a great deal of affection and attention in infancy. But after the toddling stage the picture changes abruptly. The frequency of such overt signs of affection drops rapidly and is almost completely absent by the time children reach the age of this sample (nine to ten years). The reluctance of the parents, especially the father, to show affection overtly is not matched by a similar feeling on the part of the children. Almost 73 percent of the mothers said that child likes to be cuddled "a great deal" and an additional 20 percent "some," leaving only 7 percent of the children who like to be cuddled only a little or never. The following extract from the author's field notes illustrates several important aspects of Sinhalese child-parent interpersonal relations in one brief incident:

Yesterday A.B.R.'s daughter (Chandra, aged seven) wanted to go to her grandmother's house, but her mother would not let her go. She cried for a while, and then stopped.

About half an hour later her brother (Chandrawansa, aged eight or nine) said he was hungry and he was given a biscuit. He was still hungry so two more biscuits were given to him. He wanted more but there were no more so he started crying and stamped his feet. After two or three minutes of the child's crying, his father sent to the *boutique* for some bread which he and his sister ate. He then appeared happy. A few minutes later both children went with their grandfather to his house.

Throughout this incident the father remained aloof. All the interaction was between the mother and the children. The father's part was only in the decision to send to the *boutique* for bread. Also, of the four afternoons which I have spent with this family, I can only remember one occasion in which the boy approached his father in an affectionate manner. But he made many such approaches to the mother. His sister on the other hand made two to four such approaches each afternoon. The father's reaction was merely to turn and look at the child, i.e., he did not discourage the children or reproach them for this, but he gave no response in return. The children's response then is bound to be extinguished in time. The daughter probably made more advances because she is younger and extinction was not yet as complete. Even the mother was not overly warm. She merely put her arm around the child for an instant or patted it.

Such a withdrawal of overt signs of parental affection would in many societies signify parental rejection. At first glance it may seem as though the traumatic effect of the relatively sudden withdrawal of parental affection can by itself provide an explanation for the characteristic insecurity of the Sinhalese. In this connection, comparison of the Sinhalese with the Tamil-speaking Hindu population of Ceylon's Northern Province is illuminating. If parental withdrawal were sufficient, then the Tamils should show insecurity to an even more marked degree than the Sinhalese since parental aloofness, especially in the case of the father, is probably even more severe in their case and follows an equally indulgent infancy. The element which is missing in Tamil culture is the loose structure which characterizes Sinhalese society. The Tamil child grows up in a society in which the pattern of interpersonal relations is fixed and from which few deviations occur. His place in the great family system, in the Hindu religion, and in other aspects of the society is well defined, and the rights, duties, and obligations which it implies are not open to question. The Tamil family (to use Burgess and Locke's concept) is an institution, not a companionate group. It is bound together by ties of blood and reciprocal duties and obligations which are ". . . external, formal, and authoritarian . . . [and not by] such interpersonal relations as the mutual affection, the sympathetic understanding, and the comradeship of its members" (1, p. vii). Apparently in such a social system overt signs of mutual affection, sympathy and comradeship are not absolutely essential for the development of a secure and self-confident personality. But when, as in the case of the Sinhalese, withdrawal of overt signs of parental affection occurs in the context of a society in which (though sharing the same basic family structure) the pattern of rights, duties, and obligations is always open to question and exception—i.e., in a loosely structured society—then the absence of parental affection and emotional support in childhood leads to the development of feelings of rejection and insecurity.

This conclusion can be generalized by stating that selected aspects of infant training, post-infant training, and social organization have been examined. None of these factors by itself appears to be sufficient to explain the insecurity of the Sinhalese personality. But the *combination* of this particular pattern of child rearing and this particular mode of social organization is probably of major importance. This conclusion has of course not been validated in the present preliminary analysis, and research designed to test it by more rigorous techniques is now in progress. However, we may tentatively conclude that the evidence presented in this paper adds to the growing list of cultures in which post-infantile experiences probably have a major influence on personality development and in which broad cultural patterns (in this case "loose structure") seem to be essential for an explanation of group character.

REFERENCES

1. Burgess, E. W., & Locke, H. J. *The family*. New York: American Book Company, 1945.
2. Davis, A., & Havighurst, R. J. *Father of the man*. Boston: Houghton Mifflin, 1947.
3. Duvall, Evelyn M. Conceptions of parenthood. *Amer. J. Sociol.*, 1946, **52**, 193–203.
4. Embree, J. F. Thailand—A loosely structured social system. *Amer. Anthropol.*, 1950, **52**, 181–193.
5. Frank, L. K. Cultural control and physiological autonomy. In C. Kluckhohn & H. A. Murray (Eds.), *Personality in nature, society and culture*. New York: Knopf, 1949.
6. Orlansky, H. Infant care and personality. *Psychol. Bull.*, 1949, **46**, 1–48.
7. Ryan, B. Socio-cultural regions of Ceylon. *Rural Sociology*, 1950, **15**, 3–19.
8. Sewell, W. H. Infant training and the personality of the child. *Amer. J. Sociol.*, 1952, **59**, 150–159.

33. CHILDREARING ATTITUDES OF MOTHERS IN GERMANY AND THE UNITED STATES

Don W. Rapp

Information concerning the relationship between childrearing attitudes in Germany and the United States has been, until recently, obtained largely from nonempirical data. Lewin (7), as an expert observer, expressed the view that German children are expected to exhibit unquestioning obedience, while children in the U.S. are urged to be more independent. Klineberg (5), however, has remained cautious in commiting himself to statements regarding the German family's insistence on obedience. He used the phrase "allegedly characteristic" in reference to the reported widespread emphasis on obedience in the German culture. Supporting Lewin's views with direct cross-national investigations, Anderson (1), McGranahan (8), and Schaffner (10) used German and U.S. youth and young adults in detecting national differences with respect to a more highly developed authority structure in the German culture.

Cohn and Carash (2), using the California F Test, found a German sample of working men more "authoritarian" than a similar U.S. sample. The German sample had a higher authoritarian score on the F Test than any national sample hitherto reported. Kates and Diab (4) obtained a positive, although nonsignificant correlation, between the F Test and childrearing attitudes; i.e., the more authoritarian the more controlling the attitudes concerning children.

The present study sought to investigate directly whether the childrearing attitudes of German and U.S. mothers were empirically distinguishable.

METHOD

Subjects

German subjects were mothers from the Länder of Baden in southwest Germany, who responded to a German translation of the University of Southern California Parent Attitude Survey (11), PAS, and an attached personal information sheet. The sample was obtained through a Protestant

Reprinted with abridgement from *Child Development*, 1961, **32**, 669–678, with permission of the author and the Society for Research in Child Development.
360

kindergarten organization. The investigator met with the 30 kindergarten teachers who served as liaison persons for the study. Distribution of 200 PASs was begun in May 1958, and in the same year 183 or 91.5 per cent were returned to the investigator in the U.S.

The PASs in the U.S. were distributed in 1960 to 28 Florida preschools in the same general manner as in the German sample. Of the 537 PASs distributed, 283 or 52.7 per cent were returned. The difference in the percentage of survey return between the German and U.S. samples was thought in part to be a function of the unifying organization to which the entire group of German teachers belonged. The U.S. teachers involved in this study lacked any common organizational ties.

The "kindergarten" in Germany includes a wider age range than the U.S. kindergarten; therefore the U.S. sample was drawn from mothers of kindergarten and nursery school children.

All subjects in both final samples were Caucasian, Protestant, and from intact homes. They reported parents, husbands, and themselves to be citizens of their respective countries, had at least one child in preschool, and completed PASs omitting no more than three items. Weights for omitted items were interpolated from the mean of the subscale to which they belonged.

The Index of Social Status (9), ISS, used in this study was originally based on U.S. research. Lefkowitz (6), testing its appropriateness for use with a European sample, found a correlation of $r = .82$ ($p < .01$) between expert local (Vienna, Austria) social class judgment and ISS categorical placement. The ISS determines the social status of a family by rating the occupation, source of income, and educational attainment of the "status parent." In this study information concerning the father was used. The ISS divides the social class continuum into five categories, two lower and two middle levels and one upper level. Subjects in the present study who fell into the ISS upper ($N = 4$) and upper-middle ($N = 41$) class categories were combined and designated as the "upper" class subsample with an N of 45. The subjects who fell into the ISS lower middle class category were designated as the "middle" class subsample of 41 subjects, and the subjects who fell into the upper-lower ($N = 30$) and lower-lower ($N = 8$). ISS class categories were combined into a "lower" class subsample of 38 subjects. The terms upper, middle, and lower as used in this study are relative terms and should be thought of in reference to their make-up. Social class breakdown, in ISS categories, was identical in both national samples. The upper, middle, and lower class subsamples, when considered separately, are designated as class samples; combined they are called complete samples.

The German and U.S. samples were equated by individually matching the U.S. surveys with the German surveys. Of the 124 German-U.S. pairs, 86 were matched exactly for social class, age of mother in five-year intervals, and number of children in the family. The remaining 38 pairs were matched for social class, and as closely as possible on the other two categories, neither of which was found significantly different. The mean age of the German sample was 32.96, SD 5.58; for the U.S. sample, 32.80, SD 5.78. The mean number of children per mother for the German sample was 2.3, SD 1.23; for the U.S. sample, 2.5, SD 1.33.

The education of the mothers was not controlled in the equating of the two samples. In both German and U.S. samples 48 mothers reported two or more years of college; 59 U.S. and 19 German mothers reported themselves to be at least high school graduates or the equivalent; and 17 U.S. and 43 German mothers completed 11 years of school or less. Fourteen of the German mothers failed to report their educational attainment. The χ^2 of 31.1 summarizes the educational differences between the two samples.

Instrument

Shoben's Parent Attitude Survey was utilized in German and English forms. In Shoben's original research (11), the 85-item survey discriminated between mothers of problem children and mothers of nonproblem children. A low score has been interpreted as indicating a more optimum attitude concerning child guidance; a high score indicates the reverse. Three main subscales are present in the PAS: Dominant, Possessive, and Ignoring. The Dogmatism score (3) was derived from the actual number of extreme responses, i.e., strongly agree and strongly disagree.

The PAS was translated by four bilingual Germans. The investigator was present with three of the four at the time of translation. Questions were answered concerning the particular American colloquialisms which frequent the PAS. These four translations were then used by a fifth translator to bring together the final German form.

RESULTS

The complete samples were cross-nationally compared on the five scores obtained: PAS total score, Dominant, Possessive, and Ignoring subscale scores, and the Dogmatism score. All five tests were found significant beyond the .001 level with the U.S. sample demonstrating the smaller scores or the less controlling attitudes. Figure 1 presents graphically the wide differences found between the total score distributions of the two complete samples. The median test (12) χ^2 value was 80, significant well beyond the .001 level. This large difference is reflected in the statement: only 4 per cent of the U.S. mothers had total scores above the median of the complete German sample. Other values on the complete sample cross-national tests were: Dominant subscale ($\chi^2 = 62.02$), Possessive ($\chi^2 = 76.94$), Ignoring ($\chi^2 = 12.75$), and Dogmatism ($\chi^2 = 19.76$). Considering the great disparity between the German and U.S. samples on all five scores tested, it can be said that the two samples were most probably drawn from attitudinal populations with different medians.

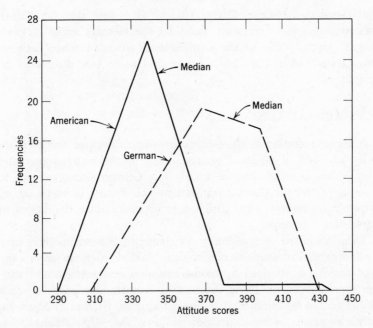

Figure 1. Distributions of total PAS scores from the complete German and United States samples. The median test χ^2 value was 80 ($p < .001$).

German and U.S. comparisons of like social classes—i.e., German upper-class to U.S. upper-class, etc.—were made using the Mann-Whitney U test (12). Corrections were made for ties. All of the three U.S. social classes were found to possess smaller PAS median scores, indicative of less controlling childrearing attitudes, than their German social class counterparts. Thirteen or 87 per cent of the 15 comparisons reached significance, one at $p < .05$ and 12 at $p < .01$. The two tests not reaching significance were the cross-national upper class comparison in the Ignoring subscale and the middle class Dogmatism comparison. They were, however, in the expected direction ($p < .10$, $p < .17$, respectively). The findings leave only a minimum of doubt that comparable German and U.S. class samples were independent samples drawn from separate populations.

Intranational class comparisons were computed between upper and middle, middle and lower, and upper and lower class samples on all five scores obtained. Twenty-seven of the 30 class comparisons indicated the following pattern: upper class scores smaller than middle and lower class scores, and middle class scores smaller than lower class scores. Ten or 33 per cent of the 30 intranational tests were found significant, four at $p < .05$ and six at $p < .01$. Significance was generally reached between upper and lower class samples in both national samples and between the German middle and lower class samples. Upper and middle class samples in both national samples responded quite similarly. Thus, it is evident that the U.S. social classes exhibited less variability than did the German social classes. The reason is primarily due to the significant differences reached between the German lower and middle classes as opposed to no U.S. differences in this relationship.

DISCUSSION AND CONCLUSIONS

A major limitation in all research crossing a language barrier is the insecurity of identical bilingual understanding of the material presented. A second limitation should also be noted. The German situation made it impossible to pretest the German translation. The manner in which the survey was translated, however, was designed to overcome these limitations to the greatest degree possible.

The PAS in the original study discriminated between mothers of problem children and mothers of nonproblem children. German scores approximated the scores obtained by mothers of problem children, and the U.S. scores approximated the scores obtained by mothers of nonproblem children. This should not be interpreted as indicating that German children have a greater chance of becoming problem children than U.S. children. In this respect the uniqueness of culture does not allow judgmental interpretation.

The German mothers reported significantly less education than the U.S. mothers. The matching inaccuracy stems from the fact that the ISS determines social class by using criteria based on the husband. The relationship indicated here is an interesting one. The educational level of the U.S. mothers in this sample was similar to that of their husbands, while the educational level of the German mothers was much less than their husbands. Relevant to the present findings, it has been found (11, 13, 14) that the more education a person has the less controlling their childrearing attitudes. It would then seem possible that part of the large score difference found in the present study could possibly be attributed to the difference in educational level of the two national samples. Analysis of this possibility was conducted as follows: The total scores of the U.S. lower class (least education of the U.S. sample) were compared with total scores of the German upper class (most education in the German sample). Differences were still found, indicating the U.S. lower class had significantly smaller scores or less controlling attitudes than the German upper class.

The three U.S. social classes exhibited less variability than did the German social classes. These data are interpreted as a reflection of cultural influences. Specifically, greater social class uniformity in the U.S. sample is seen, at least in part, as the result of the American governmental system advocating equality and the public educational system which promotes contact between social classes. Greater German social class disunity is seen partly as a result of the very recent dictatorial militaristic form of government and a more authoritarian class determining educational system. This finding is in support of McGranahan's (8) statements indicating that German-U.S. differences in attitudes are not peculiar to political attitudes, but spread throughout a wide variety of attitudinal areas into even the simplest types of social relationships.

The present study U.S. total and Dominant subscale scores appear higher than the other mean scores of previous studies, with the exception of that for Shoben's problem mother sample. The question arises, "Within the last few years are the mothers in the United States becoming more dominant and controlling over their children?" If this is evidence of a general shift to a more controlling childrearing attitude, it is one that coincides with the coming of the sputnik era with its re-emphasis on the three R's and accompanying public re-evaluation of educational techniques and curricula.

SUMMARY

The purpose of this investigation was to determine the measurability and relationship between German and U.S. childrearing attitudes. Parent Attitude Surveys from 124 Florida mothers were individually matched with translated surveys completed by 124 German mothers from Baden in southwest Germany. Matching was near perfect on three categories, social class, age, and number of children in the family.

Significant differences were found between the German and U.S. complete samples on all five scores obtained. The U.S. mothers demonstrated scores indicating less controlling attitudes than the German mothers. These differences were maintained in 13 of the 15 cross-national comparable class comparisons. The analysis within social class showed similar relationships in both samples. Upper and middle class scores were very much the same within each national sample; however, the lower classes demonstrated the most controlling and authoritarian attitudes within their respective cultures. Social classes in the U.S. were found attitudinally less variable than those in Germany with respect to childrearing attitudes.

REFERENCES

1. Anderson, H. H., Anderson, G. L., Cohen, I. H., & Nutt, F. D. Image of the teacher by adolescent children in four countries: Germany, England, Mexico, United States. *J. soc. Psychol.*, 1959, **50**, 47–55.

2. Cohen, T. S., & Carsch, H. Administration of the F scale to a sample of Germans. *J. abnorm. soc. Psychol.*, 1954, **49**, 471.

3. Freeman, R. W., & Grayson, H. M. Maternal attitudes in schizophrenia. *J. abnorm. soc. Psychol.*, 1955, **50**, 45–52.

4. Kates, S. L., & Diab, L. M. Authoritarian ideology and attitudes on parent-child relationships. *J. abnorm. soc. Psychol.*, 1955, **51**, 13–16.

5. Klineberg, O. Cultural factors in personality adjustment of children. *Amer. J. Orthopsychiat.*, 1953, **23**, 465–471.

6. Lefkowitz, M. Authoritarianism in adolescents: a cross-national study. Unpublished doctoral dissertation, Univer. of Texas, 1956.
7. Lewin, K. *Resolving social conflicts*. Harper, 1948.
8. McGranahan, D. V. A comparison of social attitudes among American and German youth. *J. abnorm. soc. Psychol.*, 1946, **41**, 245–257.
9. McGuire, C., & White, G. D. The measurement of social status. Research paper in human development, No. 3 (Rev.). Univer. of Texas, Austin, 1955.
10. Schaffner, B. *Fatherland: a study of authoritarianism in the German family*. New York: Columbia Univer. Press, 1948.
11. Shoben, E. J., Jr. The assessment of parental attitudes in relation to child adjustment. *Genet. Psychol. Monogr.*, 1949, **39**, 101–148.
12. Siegel, S. *Non-parametric statistics for the behavioral sciences*. New York: McGraw-Hill, 1956.
13. Walters, J., & Fisher, C. Changes in the attitudes of young women toward child guidance over a two-year period. *J. educ. Res.*, 1958, **52**, 115–118.
14. Zuckerman, M., Barrett, B. H., & Bragiel, R. M. The parental attitudes of parents of child guidance cases. *Child Develpm.*, 1960, **31**, 401–417.

INDEX OF NAMES